CANADIAN NATI... CINEMA

Through close textual readings, Gittings' valuable study examines the ways in which Canadian films reflect and refract social forces of their times and address contemporary issues of representation and nation.

Blaine Allan, *Queen's University*

Gittings' book presents a fresh and uncompromising angle on Canadian cultural history while it traces the social implications of its stories on film. What emerges is a close and sympathetic analysis which focuses on the difficulties facing a national industry dominated by its powerful neighbour, the politics of representation internal to a multi-ethnic and multi-racial society, and the positive effects of strategic investment in local stories as well as the indigenisation of international genres.

Graeme Turner, *University of Queensland*

Canadian National Cinema explores the idea of the nation across Canada's film history, from early treatments of colonization and white settlement such as *The Wheatfields of Canada* to more recent films such as *The Grey Fox, The Adjuster, Nô, Le confessionnal* and *Map of the Human Heart*.

Through case studies of key films – both well-known and neglected – Christopher Gittings uncovers the tensions in Canadian cinema between white Anglo and Native representations, and between Francophone and Anglo-Canadian narratives. Engaging with questions of inclusion and exclusion, race and representation, gender and sexuality, he shows how access to the production of cinematic images has determined who is represented, and how.

Following the changing images of the 'founding nations' from early ethnographic films such as *Saving the Sagas* to documentary and feature films by contemporary First Nation film-makers, *Canadian National Cinema* traces Canadian cinema's continuing reinvention of the nation.

Christopher E. Gittings is Associate Professor in the Department of English at the University of Alberta. He is the editor of *Imperialism and Gender: Constructions of Masculinity* (1996).

WITHDRAWN

NATIONAL CINEMAS SERIES
Series Editor: Susan Hayward

AUSTRALIAN NATIONAL CINEMA
Tom O'Regan

BRITISH NATIONAL CINEMA
Sarah Street

FRENCH NATIONAL CINEMA
Susan Hayward

GERMAN NATIONAL CINEMA
Sabine Hake

ITALIAN NATIONAL CINEMA 1896–1996
Pierre Sorlin

NORDIC NATIONAL CINEMAS
Tytti Soila, Astrid Söderbergh Widding and Gunnar Iversen

Forthcoming titles:

CHINESE NATIONAL CINEMA
Yingjin Zhang

SOUTH AFRICAN NATIONAL CINEMA
Jacqueline Maingard

SPANISH NATIONAL CINEMA
Nuria Triana-Toribio

CANADIAN NATIONAL CINEMA

Ideology, difference and representation

Christopher E. Gittings

London and New York

First published 2002 by Routledge
11 New Fetter Lane, London EC4P 4EE

Simultaneously published in the USA and Canada
by Routledge
29 West 35th Street, New York, NY 10001

Routledge is an imprint of the Taylor & Francis Group

© 2002 Christopher E. Gittings

Typeset in Galliard by RefineCatch Limited, Bungay, Suffolk
Printed and bound in Great Britain by
Biddles Ltd, Guildford and King's Lynn

All rights reserved. No part of this book may be reprinted or
reproduced or utilized in any form or by any electronic,
mechanical, or other means, now known or hereafter
invented, including photocopying and recording, or in any
information storage or retrieval system, without permission in
writing from the publishers.

British Library Cataloguing in Publication Data
A catalogue record for this book is available from the British Library

Library of Congress Cataloging in Publication Data
Gittings, Christopher E.
Canadian national cinema / Christopher E. Gittings.
p. cm. — (National cinemas series)
Includes bibliographical references (p.) and index.
(alk. paper)
1. Motion pictures—Canada—History. 2. Motion picture
industry—Canada—History. I. Title. II. Series.
PN1993.5.C2 G54 2001
791.43′0971—dc21 2001048304

ISBN 0–415–14281–4 (hbk)
ISBN 0–415–14282–2 (pbk)

CONTENTS

ILLUSTRATIONS

Plates

Figures

ACKNOWLEDGEMENTS

I began researching this book while working in a Department of American and Canadian Studies at the University of Birmingham, England and completed the researching and writing processes while teaching in an English Department at the University of Alberta. I owe a debt of gratitude to both institutions for facilitating teaching directly related to Canadian national cinemas. The responses of colleagues and students at Birmingham and Alberta helped to shape my thinking about intersections of cinema and nation in the Canadian context. Especially helpful were early conversations I had at Birmingham with Susan Hayward and Barbara Rasmussen. I am grateful for the teaching release time provided by the University of Alberta's *Support for the Advancement of Scholarship and Research Fund*, and for SSHRCC funds awarded by the university's Research Grants Office. I am very appreciative of the generosity and encouragement of a number of colleagues at different stages in the preparation of this book, notably Blaine Allan and Lynda Jessup who shared some of their research with me. I also benefited from conversations with Alberta colleagues Bill Beard, Mark Betz, Aniko Bodroghkozy, Cecily Devereux, Sourayan Mookerjea and Cheryl Suzack.

Many thanks to Bill O'Farrell of the National Archives whose extensive knowledge of the Archives' film holdings proved invaluable. At the Toronto Film Reference Library, I would like to thank Eve Goldin for all of her help in retrieving the stills that appear in the book. The sleuthing skills of Theresa Daniels at the University of Alberta's English Department were instrumental in tracking down various production companies and distributors on the long road to clearing copyright for the reproduction of stills. Eric Spoeth at the University of Alberta provided generous support in producing the digitized video images that illustrate parts of the book's argument.

John Greyson and Mieko Ouchi both gave generously of their time in interviews that gave me greater insight to their work.

At Routledge I would like to thank Alistair Daniel and Juliane Tschinkel for their able guidance during the editing process.

Thanks to family and friends in Ontario and Alberta whose support during the writing of this book has been sustaining. Julie Burnett's comments on the manuscript and her unwavering love and support during the writing process helped me to keep perspective and bring the project to completion.

INTRODUCTION

Canadian national cinemas – ideology, difference and representation

> As the culture produces its texts, it prefers certain meanings, thematic structures and formal strategies. Within these preferred forms and meanings we find the ideology of the culture: the way it makes sense of itself and infers meaning onto its institutions and practices.
>
> Graeme Turner (1986, 2)

> The concept of a national cinema is always implicated in a dialectic of nation and anti-nation.
>
> Philip Rosen (1996, 391)

> The master is made to recognize that His Culture is not as homogeneous, not as monolithic as He once believed it to be; He discovers, often with much reluctance, that He is just an other among others.
>
> Trinh T. Minh-ha

Reflecting the thinking of the critics cited above and my own research into Canadian cinematic production, the title of my Introduction marks the fractured, shifting, discontinuous and variegated field of Canadian cinemas. The contested ground of the national – who belongs to the nation and who is excluded from that belonging as belonging is constructed through the Indian Act, immigration legislation, the franchise, citizenship, biculturalism and multiculturalism – has determined who has access to the production of cinematic images, and accordingly who is represented, and how. The purpose of this book is to track and interrogate the signification of nation across a range of Canadian cinemas, from early white invader-settler films depicting colonization or nation-building, through to ethnographic cinemas, documentary, experimental and feature films produced by Canada's so-called 'founding nations' and including First Nations cinemas and multicultural fields of vision. Following Turner, this book unveils the shifting ways in which Canadian cultures make sense of, and locate themselves in an imagined Canadian community.

Inevitably, questions of inclusion and exclusion – canon formation – confront the author of a book on national cinema. While this book certainly is not a 'greatest hits' survey of Canadian cinema, it has no delusions about or pretensions to the encyclopaedic. In his engagement of the thorny problematic of a canon of Canadian films, film historian Peter Morris suggests that questions of canon and normative evaluation are of particular relevance to Canadian cinema: 'the number of works under discussion is relatively small and, in consequence, the significance of what is included in the canon and what is excluded, and on what terms is of greater moment' (Morris 1994, 29). I take the canon of Canadian film here to be the sometimes narrowly prescribed lists of films that critics and institutions have overdetermined as the films that matter, the key texts of a Canadian national cinema. For example, the nine Canadian films that appeared (along with one French film) on stamps introduced by Canada Post to commemorate the centenary of cinema in Canada in 1996: *Back to God's Country* (David M. Hartford 1919); *Hen Hop!* (Norman McLaren 1942); *Pour la suite du monde* (Pierre Perrault 1963); *Goin' Down the Road* (Don Shebib 1970); *Mon oncle Antoine* (Claude Jutra 1971); *The Apprenticeship of Duddy Kravitz* (Ted Kotcheff 1974); *Les ordres* (Michel Brault 1974); *Les bons débarras* (Francis Mankiewicz 1980); *The Grey Fox* (Philip Borsos 1982). These films were selected, in the case of the first three to represent pioneering efforts before 1964, and in the case of the last six, through surveys of rankings made by the Toronto International Film Festival Group in 1983 and 1994. The limited edition stamps were sold with a booklet containing a list of what it called 'Canada's Ten Best' culled from the surveys of the Toronto International Film Festival Group: *Mon oncle Antoine*; *Jésus de Montréal* (Denys Arcand 1988); *Goin' Down the Road*; *Le déclin de l'empire américain* (Denys Arcand 1986); *Les bons débarras*; *Les ordres*; *The Apprenticeship of Duddy Kravitz*; *The Grey Fox*; *I've Heard the Mermaids Singing* (Patricia Rozema 1987); *The Adjuster* (Atom Egoyan 1991).

The establishing of a canon is not necessarily a 'bad thing'; in Canada, a country where feature film production has really become viable only in the last thirty years, the delineation of a canon was proof-positive that we had a national cinema. The Toronto International Film Festival's construction of 'Canada's Ten Best' lists provided an essential marker around which debate about a representative body of Canadian cinema could begin. Piers Handling, who as Director of the Toronto International Film Festival was involved in the polling of critics, academics and industry people that forged the Ten Best lists of 1984 and 1993, is fully aware of the 'limitations' and 'contradictions' of canon construction (1994, 22). Writing in 1994, he articulates the utilitarian goals of canon-construction in the context of Festival programming and promotion of a 1984 Canadian cinema retrospective that motivated the creation of the Ten Best lists: 'As programmers, we needed to break the material down into bite-size pieces . . . as promoters we needed a simple marketing tool to pull what we thought were reluctant audiences into the cinemas' (Handling 1994, 22). Handling makes his comments in an introductory article to the top-ten lists of the ninety-six individuals solicited for the 1994 poll. As Handling notes, the publication of these 250-plus titles in the film magazine *Take One* provides a sense of the range of materials considered to be important, canon-worthy films, a field reduced to ten by the exigencies of developing a publicly recognizable body of Canadian film. Present in a few of these ninety-six individual lists is the *umheimlich* of Rosen's anti-nation: for example, *Masala* (Srinivas Krishna 1992) appears in the top-ten lists of Hussain Amarshi, Kass Banning, Brenda Longfellow, David McIntosh and Thomas Waugh, while *The Making of Monsters* (John Greyson 1991) and *Kanehsatake: 270 Years of Resistance* (Alanis Obomsawin 1993) are listed by Cameron Bailey and Longfellow. Extending its reach and depth beyond mere lists, David Clandfield's invaluable introductory survey of Canadian cinemas – *Canadian Film* (1986) – with its emphasis on postwar documentaries and feature films gestures towards a bicultural canon, as do anthologies such as Seth Feldman's *Take Two* (1986) and Piers Handling's and Pierre Véroneau's *Self Portrait: Essays on the Canadian and Quebec Cinemas* (1980). Another institutional mechanism of canon-production can be located in the selection, restoration and exhibition of films considered 'classics' or 'masterworks' of Canadian cinemas. The Toronto International Film Festival Group's Film Circuit partnered with the National Film Board of Canada to restore, re-release and exhibit *Mon oncle Antoine* in 1988.[1] Working with the National Archives, the Audio-Visual Preservation Trust and the private sector, Film Circuit has developed an annual programme of restoring and re-releasing Canadian classics. For example, Don Shebib's *Goin' Down the Road* was re-released in 1999. Similarly, AV Preservation Trust has launched a Masterworks Programme for the preservation of 'classic' Canadian titles. Selected by jury, the Masterworks 2001 films are *The Loon's Necklace* (Crawley Films 1949), *The Grey Fox* and *La vrai nature de Bernadette* (Gilles Carles 1972).[2]

Although *Canadian National Cinema* contains canonical texts that will be familiar to many, it also works to make the canon strange, in the first instance by addressing the cinema we might not know we have, or might have forgotten we have. The groundbreaking work of Morris's *Embattled Shadows* (1978) is not exploited as much as it could be in our syllabuses and research. Morris's exhaustive history of Canadian film between 1895 and 1935 provides us with co-ordinates through which we can access our early film history in the archive; it provides us with opportunities for placing early signifying practices under critical analysis. To this end I have included extended close readings of *The Wheatfields of Canada* (1908), *An Unselfish Love* (1910) and other films about white colonization that produce Anglo-Celtic whiteness as a universal signifier for belonging to the nation. Early ethnographic films such as *Nation Building in Saskatchewan* (Richard Bird 1921), *Saving the Sagas* (Marius Barbeau 1928), *Secrets of Chinatown* (Fred Newmeyer 1935) and *Of Japanese Descent* (O. C. Burritt 1945) belie the unassimilable ethnic and racial differences held at the limit of a national cinema, its anti-national component. The dialectic of nation and anti-nation that Rosen associates with any claim to a national cinema emerges in a juxtaposition of these two groups of films. The inclusion of such films also demonstrates 'how the synthesizing operation fundamental to naming a cinema as national is always potentially disturbed' (Rosen 1996, 389). Making the canon strange is another way of coming at Turner's suggestion that newer nations are always 'being caught in the act' of nation formation, 'embarrassed in the process of construction' (1994, 123). In this book I hope to catch Canadian cinema in the act of construction, to apprehend its sometimes-embarrassing aesthetic and ideological acts of self-production. *Saving the Sagas*, an ethnographic film complicit in circulating a white colonial desire for the disappearance of the Aboriginal Other, is essential to an understanding of how 'film served as an instrument of colonial domination, not just because of the ways colonialist cinema legitimated domination but also because of its value for ethnographic objectification of subjected peoples in Western "scientific" films' (Rosen 1996, 395). Similarly, the ethnographic fiction feature *Secrets of Chinatown* illuminates a construction of white nation predicated on the objectification and oppression of Chinese. In these films we can see how, as Fredric Jameson argues, 'the aesthetic act is itself ideological' (1986, 79). For Jameson 'the production of aesthetic or narrative form is to be seen as an ideological act in its own right, with the function of inventing imaginary or formal "solutions" to unresolvable social contradictions'. In both *Saving the Sagas* and *Secrets of Chinatown*, we witness the dominant white culture's desire for the removal of Aboriginal and Asian subjects from the terrain of an imagined white nation. One of the invader-settler cultures created by European imperialism, or what Turner refers to as settler/postcolonial societies, Canada, not unlike Australia, 'faces enormous challenges in articulating a common identity against competing forms of ethnicity and against a history of occupation and dispossession of the original inhabitants' (Turner 1994, 123). As Turner observes, 'the more we become aware of these internal differences and ambiguities, the more problematic becomes any simple affirmation of collective identity' (123). After the failure of what Balibar would call a regime of fictive ethnicity – Canada represented as a white Anglo-Celtic cultural formation or Québec represented as a *pur laine* Québécois cultural formation – the white phallocentric, heterosexual canon, much like the white phallocentric, heterosexual nation, is interrupted. This interruption by Others to the nation, or, after Rosen, the anti-nation, those who had formerly been held at the limit of national cinema – First Nations, peoples of colour, women and gays and lesbians – is recognized by the book as the second opportunity for making the canon strange. Here I follow the lead of critics in the 1980s and 1990s such as Kass Banning, Peter Harcourt, Richard Fung, Cameron Bailey and Helen Lee in engaging questions of race and representation in contemporary Canadian cinemas, and the work begun in the 1970s by Kay Armatage, Brenda Longfellow, Janine Marchessault and many others in engaging Canadian women's cinema. Tom Waugh's queering of the canon and Jean Bruce's work on lesbian subjectivities are opening new spaces in critical discourse on sexuality in Canadian cinemas, something I explore in Chapter 7.

Through various configurations of canon then, the nation of national cinemas troubles our ability, as Susan Hayward argues, to 'make a distinction between

4

what nations really are and what they are masquerading as' (Hayward 2000, 95). Hayward writes: 'nations are still power-related concrete practices even though they disguise themselves as abstract historicised subject-objects' (95). In the interests of unveiling the masquerades of Canadian nation, *Canadian National Cinema* emphasizes a close textual analysis that I locate in the cultural, historical, economic, political and social contexts of a film's production. In this way I hope to approach what Hayward describes as an ideal way of writing a national cinema by delving 'deep into the pathologies of nationalist discourses' and exposing 'the symbolic practices of these forms of enunciation' (101). Such sustained textual analysis necessarily limits the number of films included in this study. Hayward's suggestion that the ideal framing of national cinemas 'is one which perceives cinema as a practice that should not conceal structures of power and knowledge but which should function as a *mise-en-scène* of scattered and dissembling identities as well as fractured subjectivities and fragmented hegemonies' (101) also speaks to my selection of films. Films have been chosen on the basis of their diachronic representativeness of national(ist) poses and their deconstruction of those poses. Although not a history of Canadian film, *Canadian National Cinema* is organized around key historical moments shaping Canadian cinemas.

Chapter 1 looks at the cinema of white invasion-settlement, film as a colonizing discourse, whilst Chapter 2 asks questions about whiteness and who is ethnographiable in Canadian cinemas. Chapter 3 grounds the previous chapters, and contextualizes the next four chapters in the political economy of cinematic production in Canada. The evolution of the state's funding of, and intervention in, Canadian film production is delineated in the context of British and American hegemony, an economic dependency on the British and American industries that undermined the development of a Canadian feature film industry. Additionally, I deal with the development of programmes encouraging a diversified screen, such as the NFB's Studio D and New Initiatives in Film, and the proliferation of co-productions.

Locating Anglophone and Francophone cinemas in a subordinate position to a US industrial Other, Hollywood, Chapter 4 examines the external cultural colonialism Québec and Anglo-Canadian cinemas see themselves subjected to, and the internal cultural colonialism some Francophone film-makers see emanating from Anglo-Canada. Differences between Canada's two 'founding nations' and their cinemas prompted Québec critic Gilles Marsolais to write of a Canadian cinema composed of two divergent cinemas, 'Canadian' and Québécois (quoted in Leach 1984, 100). There are, however, dynamic moments of intersection and imbrication where a comparative context is essential for any consideration of what Bhabha has called the 'impossible unity' of nation, for any substantive engagement with the impossible unity of a Canadian national cinema (Bhabha 1990, 1). This chapter locates those moments in 1960s meditations on nationalism by Michel Brault and Claude Jutra from Québec and Joyce Wieland from Anglophone Canada (Ontario), and in representations of Anglophone and Francophone 'nations' in genre texts (melodrama, road film, western) and in films representing the crisis around the Front de Libération du Québec in 1970. The central point of analysis for the genre section of this chapter is the process of indigenizing Hollywood genres.

Chapter 5 is broken into two parts, one entitled 'Whiting Out the Indigene', which critiques white representations of Native culture, and another, 'Returning the Gaze: Aboriginal Filmmakers and Decolonization', in which the strategies Native film-makers use to decolonize the screen for representations of their own cultures are considered. The resistant and re-inscriptive practices of film-makers of colour are located in the conflicted policies and practices of biculturalism and multiculturalism in Chapter 6, whilst Chapter 7 reads women's cinema as counter-cinema and explores, after Lee Edelman, the de-scriptive practices of gay and lesbian film-makers.

With no major monograph on Canadian national cinemas covering texts ranging from 1908 to 1998 currently available on the market, this book, no doubt, is imperfect; it cannot possibly perform all of the valid works its readers might desire. In this sense, it, not unlike Canadian cinemas, bears the burden of representation. However, desires that remain unfulfilled here may be realized in the many books that need to be written in the ongoing and contested receptions of Canadian cinemas to help shape our understandings of the nation and its cinematic production of self.

1

IMMIGRATION AND EMPIRE-BUILDING

Film as a colonizing discourse

Canada has long been subject to various formations of the colonizing gaze. Here Canada is a problematic signifier. Is its signified the territory north of the forty-ninth parallel? The people – indigenous, white invader-settlers,[1] multi-cultural immigrants? The state? The nation, or in Benedict Anderson's phrase, the 'imagined community'? All of these very different but interrelated signifieds have been organized under the signifier Canada. In the present context Canada will be read as all of the cultural co-ordinates used to narrate the nation. As these co-ordinates are often variant and in competition with each other, the nation or idea of Canada is necessarily indeterminate. While the recognition of this indeterminacy, this failure of the nation to signify in a totalizing manner, is a central tenet of this project, the films considered in this chapter were created by those with an investment in a monolithic, homogeneous representation of Canada that would exclude or marginalize the ambvialent differences of 'nationness' that concern Homi Bhabha in his introduction to *Nation and Narration*:

> the *heimlich* pleasures of the hearth, the *unheimlich* terror of the space or race of the Other; the comfort of social belonging, the hidden injuries of class; the customs of taste, the powers of political affiliation; the sense of social order, the sensibility of sexuality; the blindness of bureaucracy, the strait insight of institutions; the quality of justice, the common sense of injustice; the *langue* of the law and the *parole* of the people.
>
> (Bhabha 1990, 2)

These film-makers then, are apprehending and shooting the nation through a colonizing gaze, a hegemonic and controlling way of looking at the world that is, as E. Ann Kaplan explains, 'determined by history, tradition, power hierarchies, politics, economics. Mythic or imaginary ideas about nation' and 'national identity' as well as race, gender and sexuality (Kaplan 1997, 4). This looking is structured by the white, male, heterosexual, British and Canadian colonial subjectivity of film-makers who represent Canadian landscape as a commodified resource to be exploited in the project of empire-building, and who see the indigenous peoples as entertaining spectacles, exotica, that must be traversed, denigrated, manipulated to further the ends of empire.[2] In short the lens of the cameraman views the land, its indigenous and invader-settler populations as materials to be narrated. This narration or representation of Canada determines through the codes of language and image who belongs to the nation and who does not. Jean-François Lyotard is well aware of the power of such narratives when he argues that 'Narrative is authority itself. It authorizes an infrangible we, outside of which there is only they' (Lyotard 1992, 32). The infrangible we authorized by these films is a white, Anglo-Protestant or Anglo-Saxon, male camera eye that projects itself as the normative 'we' of the imagined community Canada.

IMMIGRATION FILMS – ATTRACTING THE RIGHT/ WHITE KIND OF INVADER-SETTLERS

Among the very first cinematic images of Canada produced in 1896 by American and European firms were 'interest' shots of such physical features as Niagara Falls and the Rockies (Morris 1978, 29). These films were popular with both foreign and domestic audiences and helped to create a space in the market for what are widely regarded as the first Canadian-produced films of the country, photographed by James S. Freer. A white invader-settler from Bristol who arrived in Manitoba in 1888, Freer recorded positive experiences of immigrant life in Canada, and, with an accompanying lecture and the financial backing of the Canadian Pacific Railway Company, toured these films in Britain in 1898 under the title *Ten Years in Manitoba*. These films, which include *Harnessing the Virgin Prairie*, constitute a gendered and colonizing narrative in which the territory of the Dominion of Canada is represented as a fertile and passive terrain awaiting the cultivation or domination of the male British settler.[3] As Peter Morris comments, the tour was a great success and revealed the power of the motion picture as an 'emigration agent' (Morris 1978, 30). Both the CPR and Canadian government realized the potential of film to act as an agent for the settlement of the West. Many more films were produced to create a desire for emigration to Canada, but a very specific emigration revolving around the matter of whiteness and the furthering of the British Empire. At this time Canadian nation-building occurred within the British Empire, and was tantamount to empire-building. After all, Canada was known, in the imperial rhetoric of the day as the 'Britain of the North' (quoted in Berger 1966, 4).

What Richard Dyer refers to as the 'matter of whiteness', the construction of white as a normative category existing outside of race, suffuses the images and narratives of these films (Dyer 1997, 1). In the dominant imperial ideology of the time, white is a normative category against which all other races are judged and found lacking. French imperialist Jules Harmand spoke in 1910 of a 'hierarchy' of superior 'races and civilizations' constituted by whites that legitimized the conquest of non-white native peoples (quoted in Said 1993, 17). In Canada where between 1896 and 1914 three million immigrants arrived – 800,000 of them from the non-Anglo-Saxon world – Angus McLaren notes a similar white supremacist hierarchy of race that was deeply entrenched in thinking around immigration: 'British and Americans were viewed as the most desirable, next northern and western Europeans, after them the central and eastern Europeans (including the Jews), and last of all the Asians and blacks' (McLaren 1990, 47). Ironically, the Chinese and Sikh labour imported into British Columbia by the railway companies to complete the master code of Canadian nation, the national railway, is considered other to that nation. In the interests of creating a racially, culturally homogeneous, unitary idea of nation, images of a white Anglo-Saxon or Anglo-Protestant Canada are circulated at home, and more importantly in Britain, to solicit an immigration that might reflect this fictive ethnicity of the nation projected on to the movie screen and the national psyche. For, as Etienne Balibar argues in his theorizing of fictive ethnicity and its role in the construction of nation, 'No nation possesses an ethnic base naturally' (Balibar 1991, 96). The denigration or exclusion of a dominant group's other in social or cultural formations helps to create what Balibar describes as a 'fictive ethnicity', that is the ethnicity of the fabricated 'community instituted by the nation-state': in the Canadian context, white Anglo-Protestant or Anglo-Saxon invader-settler culture (Balibar 1991, 96).

Early immigration films such as *Wonders of Canada* (1906) produced by the English Charles Urban Trading Co. depict the process of commodifying Canada's resources. Shots of harvesting grain cut to shots of logging, which in turn give way to the harvesting of salmon at Steveston, BC. The shots of white men harnessing the resources of the land are interrupted by a Native powwow and a shot of a First Nations chief smoking a pipe in a canoe. The jump cut from a white nation-building that revolves around a harvesting of the environment to images of First Nations cultural practice creates a narrative rupture in which the ideology driving the narrative becomes visible. Juxtaposing shots brings about a collision that produces meaning; the various shots in this short film comment on each other. Although the cuts between the white invader-settler sequences are not match cuts, they do not call attention to themselves or disrupt the narrative in the way that the jump cut from white invader-settler activity to First Nations cultural practice does. The white invader-settler images illustrate the white man's industry and domination over a series of natural resources. The jump cut sets these 'progressive' activities apart from those of the Other, Indigenous peoples who are represented as indigent. Given the previous frames of film which represent the white man's successful and productive conquest of the natural world, the First Nations, figured here as non-producers, serve as a further index of the white man's domination of his environment. First Nations are indeed figured as part of that environment whites have attained mastery over. Through the technology of cinema, First Nations are commodified, 'produced' for a domestic and international market. The chain of signification initiated by the harvesting sequences of devastated forests, and geometric fields of wheat, works to deny First Nations subjectivity, structuring them as part of a disappearing wilderness. *Wonders of Canada*, an immigration recruitment film exhibited in Britain, and in Germany under the title *daas Mutterherz Joye*, establishes a racial hierarchy for the potential white immigrant spectator to identify with: whites control and benefit from the land that they have displaced First Nations from.[4] The spectator is always-already structured as white and male. If we accept that ideology is in part the 'discourse that invests a nation or society with meaning' (Hayward 1996, 181), and that 'ideology constitutes false ideas which legitimate a dominant political power' (Žižek 1994, 3), this film narrativizes the 'fact' of Canada as a white nation of male producers and fixes the Aboriginal other as an inert figure of another time on the margins of that nation. This false image of First Nations as a non-productive part of the landscape is deployed to legitimize the theft of their territories by the white nation. First Nations did work the land successfully, so successfully that on the prairies large-scale Aboriginal agricultural projects which threatened the profits of white invader-settler farmers were undermined by the white nation through the imposition of a system of 'peasant' or subsistence farming (Carter 1991).

The Wheatfields of Canada (1908), made by the English company Warwick, is another immigration film constructing a racial economy of the nation through a representation of the processes of production in Western Canada. The establishing shot shows a horse pulling a plough with white men walking behind holding the reins. This shot then cuts to an intertitle reading 'Ploughing By Steam Power – 250 Miles of Furrow Per Day', which in turn cuts to a shot of a steam-driven plough in action. As in *Wonders of Canada*, the image of a wilderness disappearing under the domination of white technology signifies progress. Subsequent shots and intertitles narrate the cycle of production: threshing, transportation to markets and the transformation of the grain into a finished product, bread. Composed of seven white children sitting in a wheatfield eating bread, the final shot of the finished product is the site of an intersection of racial, cultural and political economies of nation. A preceding intertitle interprets this image for the spectator, emphasizing the allegorical level of the film: 'The Realization of Canada's Ambition'. This film is an allegory for the production of the nation. 'Canada's Ambition' – white nation-building – is fed by the development of a vibrant economy, in this context the contribution of wheat production to a GNP, which in turn feeds the white settlers the bread necessary to sustain the settlement and nation-building process. The children's location in the field of production frames them, like the finished product they are consuming, the bread, as the produced of the national narrative, the product of a racial economics of nation underscored by the presence of an infant held in the arms of one of the children. The infant, a sign of white settler reproduction, supports Dyer's contention that heterosexuality is an essential dimension to whiteness, race and imperialism: 'If race is always about bodies, it is also about the reproduction of those bodies through heterosexuality' (Dyer 1997, 25). Heteronormativity and reproduction of white settlers are dominant motifs in films of immigration during this period.

Clan Donald: A British Farm Colony (1925), an immigration film sponsored by the Canadian Pacific Railway Company's Department of Colonization and Development, continues the 'actuality' reportage of real immigrants established by Freer, and developed by films such as *Wonders of Canada* and *The Wheatfields of Canada*. The film narrates the development of a Scottish colony at Vermillion, Alberta, by the Catholic church and contains ideological content similar to earlier films of this genre, such as the white myth of a landscape emptied of First Nations people, a landscape waiting for the enterprise of whiteness to transform it into fields of production. The second intertitle of the film interprets a shot of rolling, empty farm land: 'The land as it was taken over – virgin as when the buffalo ranged it and the Indian pitched his teepee there.' The intertitle and the accompanying image invoke the myth of the vanishing Aboriginal, suggesting that, similarly to the disappearing buffalo, First Nations people are doomed to extinction. This mythology, although useful to a national narrative of settlement that is dependent on the disappearance of Native peoples, is riven with contradictions: for one, First Nations had not vanished; they had been contained by the reservation system. Although the intertitle acknowledges that the land was 'taken over', it elides the government's role in removing First Nations from this fertile land to containment outside of the white nation, through the agency of the Department of Indian Affairs and the CPR's Department of Colonization and Development. It becomes very clear in this narration that the authorizing narratorial 'infrangible we' of this national narrative does not include Aboriginal peoples. The first order of this film is to dispose of First Nations to clear a space for the incoming immigrants who constitute the film's subject. Following the intertitle, the panning shot of empty land comes to rest on mounted white men surveying the terrain. Only after the colonizing discourse of the film erases First Nations from the landscape does the narrative backtrack to Britain and a sequence of shots representing the journey of the Scottish immigrants across the ocean and across the Dominion to Alberta. The film recalls *The Wheatfields of Canada* in a chain of signification linking the heterosexual reproduction of white settlers to the commodities they produce through their mastery of the land. A sequence of shots shows boy and girl settlers, men and women settlers walking towards the camera with horses. The camera then cuts to a married couple; this shot cuts to the mother and her child. The shot of the mother, the (re)producer of the white settler, cuts to an intertitle reading 'No time is lost in getting down to work', the work of (re)producing the nation, and transforming the land into commodity. This intertitle comments on the preceding shot of mother and child and introduces a sequence of images of production ranging from wheat and dairy production to cattle ranching.

MELODRAMA AND THE IDEOLOGICAL CINEMA
OF WHITE INVASION AND SETTLEMENT

The melodrama, a popular literary and stage genre in the nineteenth century, was soon translated into the new medium of cinema, where it proved equally successful. The CPR's Department of Colonization and Development encoded its message of white immigrant recruitment in a series of melodramas produced by the Edison Company to encourage American immigration to Western Canada. The head of the CPR's Department of Colonization, J. S. Dennis, thought this approach of inserting ideologically charged narratives of invasion and settlement into light mass entertainments to be the 'very highest class of advertising' (quoted in Morris 1978, 42). A 1910 article on the Edison films articulates the problematic of instructing an audience that wants to be entertained:

> the great mass of public want to be amused and entertained, not instructed, and if they are to be instructed, and if they are to be educated it must be in a subtle, delicate manner, absorbed, as it were, unconsciously, through the interest that the story itself creates in the minds of the audience. What does Johnny the conductor from East Harlem care about the mining industry in Southern British Columbia, or the ranching of Alberta? Not a rap. Not a jot, nor a tittle.
>
> But if the class of story that appeals to Johnny and his girl runs prominently through mining, or lumbering, or fishing, or ranching films, they will unconsciously swallow the knowledge.
>
> (quoted in Eamon 1995, 27)

This strategy is, according to Slavoj Žižek, the ideological move *par excellence* (Žižek 1994, 10). Whereas a spectator might be more conscious of the work of ideology in the 'actuality' films discussed above, the CPR-sponsored melodramas provide the illusion of stepping out of ideology; after all they are mere entertainments. This understanding of ideology reflects an Enlightenment tradition summarized by Žižek's critique of theories of ideology.

> Ideology is a systematically distorted communication: a text in which, under the influence of unavowed social interests (of domination, etc.), a gap separates its 'official,' public meaning from its actual intention – that is to say, in which we are dealing with an unreflected tension between the explicitly enunciated content of the text and its pragmatic presuppositions.
>
> (Žižek 1994, 10)

The 'unavowed social interests' of *Wonders of Canada*, *Wheatfields of Canada* and *Clan Donald: A British Farm Colony* – the white invasion and domination of the environment and First Nations – can be located in the narrative ruptures of these films. However, as discourse analysis has taught us, ideology also exists outside of this paradigm; 'the concrete intersubjective space of symbolic communication is always structured by various (unconscious) textual devices that cannot be reduced to secondary rhetoric' (Žižek 1994, 10). Even when the makers of these films are not systematically distorting their communication, they are always-already in ideology, in these cases the hegemonic and hierarchical ideology of imperial whiteness in North America. This is, as Žižek explains it, 'how the very gesture of stepping out of ideology pulls us back into it'. In this section the ideological work of whitening the West on screen through the genre of melodrama will be considered with reference to *An Unselfish Love* (1910), one of the films from the Edison series, a Canadian-produced feature, *Back to God's Country* (David M. Hartford 1919) and *Drylanders* (Don Haldane 1963), an NFB feature that recreates white settlement as part of an education package for Canadian students.

An Unselfish Love

An Unselfish Love (1910), one of two extant melodramas from the CPR's Edison series of thirteen one-reel films, revolves around a male heterosexual desire for woman that is twinned with male desire for the Canadian West, figured here as prosperity. In *An Unselfish Love* John, an American, is rejected as a suitor by the father of his girlfriend Mabel because, as the intertitle explains, John lacks wealth. Seeking greater prosperity and stability to attain the hand of Mabel, John 'decides to purchase a farm in Western Canada [Strathmore, Alberta] having heard of the wonderful opportunities of the country'.[5] This first sequence establishes the film's melodramatic status immediately with a family conflict provoked by the tyrannical capitalist patriarch's economic vision of Mabel as his commodity to sell on the marriage market. Melodrama, a large and unwieldy generic category with roots in Greek tragedy, the bourgeois sentimental novel, Italian opera and the Victorian stage, often focuses on family conflict (Gledhill 1985, 73). Susan Hayward's entry for melodrama notes that in melodrama the family becomes the site of patriarchy and capitalism and therefore reproduces them (1996, 200). We can see this reproduction at work in the sequence from *An Unselfish Love*. Christine Gledhill observes that the family melodrama 'is frequently defined as the dramatic mode for a historic project, namely the centrality of the bourgeois family to the ascendancy and continued dominance of that class' (1985, 74). John learns that only a successful member of the bourgeoisie can purchase Mabel's hand from her father. John therefore must secure property: he becomes the bourgeois patriarch ascendant.[6] The specific historic project represented in this film is the invasion and settlement of the prairies by whites; however, the narrative elides the colonizing project's displacement of Aboriginal peoples in Alberta by pre-emptively absenting them from the terrain of settlement. Here, the imbrications of capitalism, imperialism and the bourgeois family in establishing dominance over Canada's First Nations become visible in the narrative's very rendering of First Nations as invisible. As Žižek writes, 'the very logic of legitimizing the relation of domination must remain concealed if it is to be effective' (Žižek 1994, 8). In the imperial ideology of the day, the land is empty and waiting for white enterprise to develop it.

Driven by his desire to possess Mabel, John works on possessing the land, making it his own. The first images of John cultivating his newly acquired property with a large team of horses are followed by an intertitle reading 'The beginning of a fortune'. In the American East, John is not in control of his situation; in the Canadian West he is the master of his domain. As time goes by, John's financial success is communicated to the viewer through a shot of him cultivating with a steam-powered tractor. 'John prospers. The advanced type of farming in Western Canada', reads the accompanying intertitle. While John has been busy developing his property and building a home so that he can begin his own family with Mabel, Mabel's father has also been hard at work. He intercepts Mabel's and John's letters to each other and plants a false news story in an American newspaper indicating that John is doing well and has married an Alberta girl. Subsequently, Mabel accepts the overtures of a wealthy suitor selected by her father and a wedding invitation is sent to John in Alberta.

Although the twinned male desire for land and woman is represented principally by John's procurement of property so that he can attain Mabel, she is not the only woman in the film. A scene in the Strathmore post office depicts several single women who 'make eyes' at John when he comes to pick up his mail. The film solicits desire for the Canadian West from the white heterosexual male spectator through the spectacle of single white women who compete with each other for the white male invader-settler's affections. One of the women at the post office is relentless in her pursuit of John; however, when she learns of his situation with Mabel she travels east to tell her that John still loves her and is still single. The noble Alberta woman convinces Mabel to leave her father's home, and abandon her forthcoming marriage so that she can travel to Strathmore where she is reunited with John. This twist in the plot figures the Canadian West as an escape for women from tyrannical patriarchy; however, in these images of liberation and reunion, the narrative works to conceal the fact that Mabel has escaped from one patriarchal capitalist system to another. In Alberta she will contribute to the reproduction of patriarchy and capitalism through the family she will have with John. The gendered power differentials of the American East have not really shifted substantively in the Canadian West. Teresa de Lauretis's account of narrative as an Oedipal structure fed by a male desire to know, a desiring that simultaneously takes woman as its object, and displaces her from the story in favour of the male quest, is useful to an understanding of narrative desire and the gendered power differentials of this film (1984, 108–12). De Lauretis writes of the Sphinx in Oedipal narrative: 'She only served to test Oedipus and qualify him as a hero. Having fulfilled her narrative function (the function of the Donor in Propp's terms), her question is now subsumed in his; her power, his' (112). Mabel is the Donor of *An Unselfish Love*: she fulfils her narrative function as the object that initiates the quest of the hero, John. Her story is subsumed by John's narrative of successful colonization on the Canadian prairies. Her re-entry into John's narrative at the end of the film serves to qualify him as the hero; she becomes the sign of his success over the social terrain of the American East and the physical landscape of the Canadian West; she is the reward for his labour.

Traditionally melodramatic plots revolve around the powerless, and their victimization by a corrupt social system as this is represented through family relationships (Elsaesser 1974, 514–15). *An Unselfish Love* represents the powerless as Mabel and John, the corrupt and victimizing social system as the patriarchal capitalism of Mabel's father. This spectre of white powerlessness elides the empowerment of whites through the colonization that is at the centre of the film's narrative. John becomes empowered through his complicity with the Department of Indian Affairs and the CPR to disempower First Nations, to extinguish Aboriginal title to the land through the white patriarchal capitalist enterprise of settlement. The narrative represses Mabel's and John's roles as representatives of the 'corrupt social system' of the Canadian government and the CPR. This is indeed the type of narrative that authorizes an 'infrangible we, outside of which there is only they': the white 'we' of the settler nation and the other 'they' of the First Nations structured as uninfrangible by this national, raced narrative (Lyotard 1992, 32). The resonance of *An Unselfish Love* as a national narrative is clear in its roles as a CPR representation of and tool for nation-building, and in the American reception of it and the others in the CPR's Edison series. 'All the local colour is there, all the territorial idiosyncrasies of the Dominion are there. It is all, in fact, Canada on the moving picture screen', writes a New York reviewer (quoted in Morris 1978, 42).[7]

Drylanders

Covering the years 1907 to 1938, *Drylanders* (1963) follows the plight of the Greers, a Montreal family who take part in the colonization of Saskatchewan. In the discourse of the film colonization is repressed, is re-written as homesteading or settlement. Although produced in 1962 and released in 1963, the melodramatic narrative of *Drylanders* is driven by a white imperial ideology that shares much with the dominant ideology of *An Unselfish Love* and earlier immigration films that erase First Nations from the terrain of settlement by representing the land as empty except for the enterprising figure of the white settler, thereby eliding the racist politics of colonization that propel 'homesteading' or nation-building at the expense of Aboriginal cultures. Harvey Dawes, the failed American settler encountered by the Greers in the first sequence of the film, provides the narrative's only trace of the Aboriginal other when he tells Dan that Saskatchewan is 'no country for a white man', a statement the Greer narrative works to overturn. The establishing shot of *Drylanders* is a panning long shot across empty prairie landscape, a panning shot that does not rest until it alights upon a wagon carrying the Greers. At this point a cut is made from the long shot of the wagon to a medium shot of the front of the wagon revealing Dan Greer with the reins in his hand and his woman Eliza Greer at his side. This image then cuts to a close-up of the heterosexual couple, which in turn cuts to a subjective camera shot of the oxen pulling the wagon from the perspective of a passenger. The camera then cuts to the feet of the oxen and pans back across the wheels of the wagon and up to a little boy and his dog riding on the back of the wagon. These opening or establishing shots provide a *mise-en-abîme* or mirror text for the entire film and announce it as a melodrama. The white heterosexual couple and their family on the 'empty' prairie signify the reproduction of the white patriarchal social order from the East, the reproduction of white settlers. The wagon contains the provisions and tools with which they will reproduce that social order in the transformation of 'barren' prairie into fields of production through cultivation.

The presence of the enterprising family also signals to the viewer the film's generic identity as family melodrama, as does the voice-over of Eliza Greer that asks 'What were we doing here, a clerk and his wife in their city clothes?' Eliza's voice-over inflects the film with the domesticity that characterizes melodramas (Hayward 1996, 203), and emphasizes the domestication of the 'wilderness' that constitutes the colonizing project. As in *An Unselfish Love*, the homestead in *Drylanders* is a palimpsestic location that serves as the site of colonization, of domesticity and family, the melodramatic space where patriarchy and capitalism are reproduced. Similar to John in *An Unselfish Love*, Dan Greer hopes to join the developing class of landholding bourgeoisie by homesteading in Saskatchewan. As he tells Eliza, who did not want to travel West, 'this is a chance to be something more than a second grade clerk'. Here we can see melodrama again performing the work of a historic project, representing the 'centrality of the bourgeois family to the ascendancy and continued dominance of that class' through colonization (Gledhill 1985, 74). In this melodrama the protagonists, the Greer family, are not represented as powerless in relation to the corrupt social order of Elsaesser's melodramatic paradigm; they are powerless in relation to the harsh and unforgiving land that they farm. The ascendancy of the Greers is marked by the family's battle to turn a profit from the land, upgrade their homestead and increase their property holdings.

Despite his industry, Dan's first crop of wheat is destroyed by hail. The first Greer family home is a sod hut, a structure that fails to reproduce the social order of the East and is unfit for members of the bourgeoisie. Director Don Haldane communicates the bourgeois desires of the Greers, and the failure of the sod hut to realize these desires through *mise-en-scène*. Haldane introduces a fragile vase, an *objet d'art* iconic of bourgeois consumer culture, into the poorly lit and rustic interior of the hut. When Dan removes the vase from its packing case, Eliza reacts strongly, taking it away from him and returning it to its case. She tells him that the vase is the only 'beautiful thing' that they have brought with them, and that it will remain in its case until they live in a 'decent' house. This scene establishes a relationship between Eliza's desire for the bourgeois lifestyle – as it is represented in the vase and a 'decent' home – and the agricultural enterprise Dan has taken on to provide these things. A series of shots of the vase in different scenes positions it as a sign of the couple's bourgeois class aspirations and an index of the Greers' attainment of those aspirations. Following a party at the neighbouring MacPherson farm, a successful bourgeois enterprise, Eliza places the vase in the window of the sod hut.

After a shot of the vase and Dan looking at the *objet d'art*, there is an exchange of looks between Eliza and Dan, acknowledging its presence. Following this exchange of looks Eliza comments on how nice Mrs MacPherson is, and Dan agrees, saying 'yes, they are very good neighbours'. The MacPhersons have attained the bourgeois class status sought by the Greers; their crops have given them the capital to build a 'decent' home that reproduces the social order of the East. They provide the Greers with a model for bourgeois success on the prairies. The presence of the vase in the window signifies the Greers' movement toward bourgeoisie status for the viewer and serves as a reminder to the Greers in their times of struggle that they, like the MacPhersons, have the ability to become successful agricultural capitalists. When the Greers run out of food during the long winter, Dan ventures to the MacPhersons to obtain nourishment for his family. On his return journey he becomes lost in a blizzard, and is nearly consumed by the snow-covered landscape. As Dan lies semi-conscious at Eliza's feet recovering from his journey, Eliza's voice-over comments on the family's progress in Saskatchewan: 'How much could a man stand? This country was killing him, how could it ever be our home? All the old thoughts came back to me that night in my panic. And yet, soon they were gone again. Spring had come and a new life began for us. It was the turning point.'

During the voice-over narration the camera moves from Eliza and Dan to a medium shot of the vase in front of the winter window scene which dissolves into a shot of the vase against a spring window scene. The completion of the dissolve from winter to spring is synchronous with Eliza's voice-over utterance of 'It was the turning point'. This dissolve shot initiates a series of dissolve shots representing the 'turning point', the ascendancy of the Greers over a number of years through agricultural production, and is narrated by Eliza's continuing voice-over. Shots of horse-powered wheat production give way to shots of steam-driven tractors and mechanized threshers. The narrative draws a significant relationship between the Greers' attainment of their bourgeois desires and their mastery over the land in Haldane's combining of Eliza's voice-over with an image of grain that dissolves into a shot of Dan and his sons standing in front of a car with a large two-storey barn in the background: 'Dan had been right. Within seven years we had become prosperous [dissolve from grain to image of Dan and boys in front of car], even a car. So much better than being a clerk in the city.' The sequence of dissolve shots recalls the heteronormativity of settlement and reproduction of white settlers that served as dominant tropes in early twentieth-century cinema of immigration and colonization. Similarly to *Wheatfields of Canada*, *Drylanders* correlates grain production with the reproduction of white settlers. Eliza's voice-over 'There seemed to be no end to God's bounty' accompanies a shot of Greer grain on its way to market and precedes a sequence of dissolve shots linking commodity production to the reproduction of white settlers. The voice-over works to frame the entire sequence of shots as gifts bestowed by God, suggesting that white colonization is divinely authorized. During Eliza's voice-over narration of the birth of her first grandson, a shot of a grain elevator dissolves into a shot of Daniel Junior's baptism. The baptism shot is accompanied by the following Eliza voice-over: 'There was a bright future for him for our farm was getting bigger, we were buying more land.' As Eliza narrates the growth of the Greer family and their assets, the shot of the baptism dissolves into a pan shot of a wheat field. As in the 'finished product' scene of *The Wheatfields of Canada*, this scene in *Drylanders* constitutes an allegory for the production of white nation.

The production of wheat nourishes the family or nation producing more white settlers, thereby facilitating the accumulation of more land and the transformation of that land into capital through agriculture; this is the construction of white Canadian nation and an excellent illustration of the Hegelian concept of '*individualization through secondary identification*' that Žižek sees at the heart of the individual's identification with the nation-state (Žižek 1997, 41):

> In this shift from primary to secondary identification, primary identifications undergo a kind of transubstantiation: they start to function as the form of appearance of the universal secondary identification – say, precisely by being a good member of my family, I thereby contribute to the proper functioning of my Nation-State.

Žižek argues that these formations of individual and national identity are reactions to the world market. Thus the 'universal form of the Nation-State', in this case the nascent formation of the Canadian nation-state present here in early twentieth-century manifestation of Canada as a Dominion of Britain,

> is rather a precarious, temporary balance between the relationship between a particular ethnic Thing (patriotism, *pro patria mori*, and so forth) and the (potentially) universal function of the market. On the one hand, it 'sublates' organic local forms of identification into universal 'patriotic' identification; on the other hand, it posits itself as a kind of pseudo-natural boundary of the market economy, delimiting 'internal' from 'external' commerce – economic activity is thus 'sublimated', raised to the level of the ethnic Thing, legitimated as a patriotic contribution to the nation's greatness.
>
> (Žižek 1997, 42–3)

In *Drylanders* the National Film Board of Canada links the particular ethnic Thing of white Anglo-Protestant invader-settler agricultural production to a patriotic contribution to the nation's greatness.

The land transformed into white Canadian nation, however, does not always yield easily to the enterprise of the white settler; in the melodrama of *Drylanders* the treacherous land stands in for the corrupt social order that challenges the powerless in traditional family melodrama (Elsaesser 1974, 514–15). Despite the industry of the Greers, they are powerless against the Drought of 1929, and the subsequent 'dust bowl' soil erosion of the 1930s, which reduce them to a subsistence existence. Eliza tells the viewer that Dan felt 'beaten' and 'betrayed' by the prairie. Dan's death of a heart attack, brought on in part by the despair over the failure of his farm, does not signal the failure of white nation-building, but indicates the sacrifices necessary for the project of colonization and the cyclical nature of colonialism. The moment of Dan's death is marked by a sequence of flashback shots, the first of which dissolves from Dan's lifeless face to the family wagon arriving at their plot of land, to the MacPhersons' party, to Colin's wedding, to a shot of agricultural success which finally dissolves back to Dan's face in death. This sequence of dissolve shots rehearses the settlement process for the viewer and is followed by a shot of rain on Dan's grave and Eliza's final voice-over, 'Dan why can't you be here now? We're starting again.' Dan's death is represented as a sacrifice nourishing the land and perpetuating colonization which is 'starting again'. This ending contradicts the statement made by the failed invader-settler, Harvey Dawes, at the beginning of the film and avers that the Western Canadian prairie is not only fit for white men but is their domain. Ideologically, the representation of the Greers as powerless conceals the system of colonialism which lends white invader-settlers the power to dispossess First Nations.

The reproduction of patriarchy characteristic of melodrama visible in the masculinist narrative of settlement articulated above is, paradoxically, most palpable in the director's use of female first-person voice-over narrative. Although Eliza is empowered to speak, she speaks Dan's story; her story is subsumed in his. He puts his discourse inside her, and she produces boy children to further Dan's Greer narrative. Fragments of her story, visible in her initial response to homesteading or colonization – 'I hate it' – disappear following 'the turning point' sequence initiated by the dissolve shots of the vase. Eliza, similar to Mabel and de Lauretis's account of the Sphinx in Oedipal narrative, fulfils the narrative function of qualifying the male protagonist as a hero. Dissimilar to Mabel and the Sphinx, Eliza is a speaking subject for the entire narrative of *Drylanders*; however, her speaking undermines her subjectivity as it displaces her from the story to privilege the male quest. She is present only so that she may speak past her husband's death, and in her intradiegetic flashback sequences may bear witness to Dan as a tragic hero, a noble man who sacrificed himself for his family and colonization so that the white nation might be perpetuated.

Drylanders and ideology

Produced for the National Film Board of Canada (NFB) for distribution in cinemas and schools, *Drylanders* recuperates, unproblematically, the racist and patriarchal construction of a white Canadian nation for the descendants of white invader-settlers; its terms of reference and address are white.[8] The NFB is in Louis Althusser's terms an ideological state apparatus (ISA); it is a site where the state's material practice of ideology is located. Althusser argues that economic systems work to reproduce their own conditions of production. This process is dependent upon reproducing people as subjects predisposed to participate in a specific mode of production, a practice Althusser calls interpellation.[9] Although the NFB later becomes a site of struggle for contested imaginings of Canadian nation where films such as *Kanehsatake: 270 Years of Resistance* (1993) interrogate and challenge hegemonic constructions of nation, it is an ISA originally designed to represent the nation and its conditions of production to Canadians and the world. Through an historically hegemonic representation the NFB works to *reproduce* the nation as subjects who form a community of belonging to a specific imagining of Canadian nation. Historically, ISAs such as the NFB, the education system, the church and family structure or interpellate subjects as white heterosexual members of the national community. In Althusser's language, the ruling ideology of *Drylanders* 'hails' or 'recruits' spectators in the cinema and spectator-students in the classroom[10] as white invader-settler citizens engaged in the struggle of agricultural production (Althusser 1971, 162–5); the film reproduces the 1907 dominant invader-settler ideology of white nation in an educational, pedagogical context that omits state oppression of contested First Nations, an oppression the propagation of the white nation continues to be dependent upon. Under the heading 'Suggested Uses' the NFB's *Teacher's Guide* to *Drylanders* states that the film and its education package will 'increase student understanding and appreciation of settlement problems in the Canadian West after 1896'. However, that understanding is limited to the settlement problems of white farmers, and does not attempt to negotiate the problems of those dispossessed by settlement. The NFB *Annual Report* 1962–3 (5) is even more sweeping and anglocentric in its claims for the film:

> In fact, it may be said that the venture of the Greer family summarizes the entire epic of modern Western Canada – the courage of the pioneers, the difficulties encountered in settling on new land, the good crops and the prosperous period of 1910–1930, then the depression of the 30's, the severe drought that occurred at the same time, and the changes each of these events imposed on the family.

The NFB's construction of the white Anglo-Protestant invader-settler family as a summary of modern Western Canada erases the horrors of residential schools, sexual abuse and systemic racism that were 'in fact' a major component of the 'epic' of modern Western Canada that no amount of ideologically motivated 'summarizing' can remove. This summary of nation-building also excises the Eastern European and French-Canadian contributions to nation-building, placing both of these groups outside of the nation.

Back to God's Country

Back to God's Country (David M. Hartford 1919) shares with *Drylanders* what Elsaesser argues is melodrama's penchant for tailoring 'ideological conflicts into emotionally charged family situations' (Elsaesser 1974, 516). In *Back to God's Country* the ideological conflict between a white patriarchal Canadian colonial nationalism and racialized, ethnicized and gendered others is filtered through the emotionally charged family situations of Dolores LeBeau.

Long before the singing mounties of *Rose Marie* (United States: 1928, Lucien Hubbard; 1936, W. S. Van Dyke; 1954, Mervyn LeRoy), and the murdering and cocaine-snorting mountie of David Lynch's *Twin Peaks* (United States, 1990) imaged Canada for Americans and Canadians, the American writer James Oliver Curwood (1878–1927) was busy imagining highly masculinized adventure stories about Canada and Canadians. So popular was Curwood, and so colonial in its vision of self was the Canadian government, that it hired the American Curwood to write about the Canadian North (Berton 1975, 27). Many of Curwood's narratives were adapted for the screen, and three starred the Canadian actress, independent producer-director and screenwriter Nell Shipman. The best known of these films is the silent *Back to God's Country* released in 1919 and based on Curwood's short story 'Wapi the Walrus'.

Set in Canada's far North, *Back to God's Country* relates a tale of white male cruelty, racism and sexism. The film opens with the humiliation and murder of a Chinese man by a French Canadian during the Gold Rush of the nineteenth century. Forty dog generations later, Wapi, the descendant of the slain 'Chinaman's' dog, has been turned into a vicious killer by the mistreatment of white men. The main action of the film, however, involves male desire for the beautiful young Dolores LeBeau, played by Nell Shipman. In the film's nude scene – one of the first for a North American picture – the villain Rydal spies on Nell as she bathes with her animals. He spends the rest of the film eliminating Dolores's male 'protectors', her father and husband, and attempting to rape her. Wapi the killer is transformed into a hero by Dolores's kindness, and rescues her from the clutches of the evil Rydal during the film's climactic chase scene shot on a frozen Lesser Slave Lake.[11]

One of Canada's earliest and most successful extant features, *Back to God's Country* offers a disturbing yet fascinating cultural construction of Canadian nation as a white homosocial entity that does violence to racial and sexual otherness.[12] Previous criticism privileges the history of the film's production and its important and innovative contributions to the animal picture genre.[13] I will consider the film's production of nation in the context of screenwriter Nell

Shipman's resistance to Curwood's American vision of Canada, and read the film through the frames of sex, gender, race, ethnicity and melodrama.

Back to God's Country is an American and Canadian co-production backed by Curwood and Nell's husband Ernest Shipman. Initially, Curwood rejected Nell's adaptation of his story, claiming it was 'Rotten! Not my Story! Crazy Bunk!' (Shipman 1987, 70). Nell's scenario gave herself and the 'human drama' more screen time than Curwood's animal characters (Shipman 1987, 71). Although they had enjoyed commercial success together in other projects such as *God's Country and the Woman* (1915), Nell's and Curwood's artistic visions clashed on *Back to God's Country*. Nell's autobiography speaks her alterity to Curwood by contrasting their responses to the environment. She describes herself as a Canadian woman in harmony with nature, and opposed to hunting, while citing Curwood's self-publicity as a big outdoor game hunter who poses for photographs with his foot on the head of a slain grizzly (Shipman 1987, 71). In this scenario the Canadian identifies with the hunted, the American with the hunter. Nell's distaste for Curwood is provoked not only by his rejection of her script and his penchant for playing the macho hunter but also, very possibly, by his fetishistic desire for her hair, and his confusion of his star and screenwriter with his fictional character Dolores LeBeau. Nell relates how Curwood tackles her by the hair when they are alone in her cabin on the location set of *Back to God's Country*: 'He said things about my glorious brown hair, literally quotes from paragraphs of hirsute description in his own volumes. He said he but wanted to touch my hair, to remember its shining ripples' (Shipman 1987, 73). Under Curwood's gaze Nell is transformed from autonomous subject to object; she becomes the other, acted-upon girl from Curwood's fictional Canada: 'God's Country'. Although Nell states that Curwood's intentions were not sexual, this autobiographical episode echoes the voyeuristic nude scene that Curwood rewrites with her, and that she will play as Dolores:

> The Girl did not simply look at the man who would rape her as she came naked from a forest pool. She trembled. Her fluttering hands clothed her heaving bosom, tears, like spilled opals, coursed her pale cheeks and her hair, her bountiful, glorious hair, glistened wet from her swim with her pet bear and flowed about her alabaster shoulders like a protective mantle.
>
> (Shipman 1987, 72)

The white Anglo-Protestant male is the term of identity in this film, he is the measure, the standard for identification between audience and screen, spectator and nation.[14] His is the controlling, objectifying gaze that reads woman's sexual difference as lack, and interprets ethnic and racial difference as inferiority, another type of lack, a lack of 'human', read 'white' qualities. As Tzvetan Todorov argues in his discussion of alterity and race, 'the first, spontaneous reaction with regard to the stranger is to imagine him as inferior, since he is different from us: this is not even a man, or if he is one, an inferior barbarian' (1984, 76). Canada in *Back to God's Country* is constructed as an Anglo-Protestant, white, homosocial nation haunted by its others, in this case the white woman, the Inuit woman and the Chinese man. The camera denies these others subject formation; they remain spectacles looked at through a white male camera eye, subalterns subjected to humiliation, abuse and, in the case of the 'Chinaman', death. In this cinematic Canada difference is represented as something to be eradicated.

The first frames of the film indicate the racist nature of the Canadian North. Shan Tung is led into the Great 'White' North by what the intertitle describes as the 'lure of gold'. The Asian other is marked by avarice. He and his dog Tao take shelter from the elements in a saloon frequented by white Canadians. We are not told what lured these whites to the North but doubtless profit is involved; avarice knows no racial boundaries. After Shan enters the saloon and removes his parka hood revealing his racial difference, a cut is made to a reaction shot of white women's 'unheimlich terror of the space or race of the Other' (Bhabha 1991, 2). When Shan warns the women at the bar of his dog's fierceness, a French-Canadian bully cuts off his queue (Figures 1.1–1.5). The bully then mocks Chinese difference through a devaluing mimicry, sporting the queue himself before killing Shan (Figure 1.6). Reaction shots of the white patrons in the saloon indicate that they read the violation and humiliation of the Asian as entertainment (Figures 1.2, 1.3, 1.6, 1.7). The act of removing the queue may be read as both an insult to Shan's dignity (Figures 1.8–1.9) and an assimilationist practice: the queue is a sign of Shan's alterity, a challenge to the white male measure of identity as subject, and as such is eliminated along with its bearer, Shan (1.10–1.11). The French-Canadian character himself, however, is a caricature.[15] He is the mad, drunken French trapper, another form of difference reduced to spectacle and ridicule by Curwood's pen and the camera's Anglo-Protestant perspective. Curwood was not alone in his construction of cartoon-like, drunken, and violent French villains. Best-selling Anglo-Protestant Canadian author Ralph Connor created Le Noir in *The Man from Glengarry*, a novel adapted for the silent screen in 1922. The addressee of *Back to God's Country*, the spectator posed by the discursive organization of the film is a white Anglo-Protestant male who will identify with, feel empowered by the denigration of his others. This is not to suggest that the ideal spectator addressed by a film is equivalent to what Stephen Heath calls the 'spectating individual, the individual in the act of spectatorship' who Heath suggests is 'always an individual subject' (1992, 93–4).

The denigration or exclusion of a dominant group's other in social or cultural formations helps to create Balibar's 'fictive ethnicity' that is the ethnicity of the fabricated 'community instituted by the nation-state': in the Canadian context, white invader-settler culture (Balibar 1991, 96). There are two empowered white Anglo-Protestant male subjects in the film who signify two modes of nation-building, which (for the contemporary setting of the film, 1919) constitutes empire-building, and the displacement and exploitation of the embryonic nation's Indigenous peoples. Both are signs of the fabricated national community

Figures 1.1–8 Back to God's Country (1919)

Figures 1.9–11 Back to God's Country
(1919)

under construction in the film, and both share a colonizing desire that is twinned with their sexual desire for Dolores. Peter Burke, Dolores's husband, is an agent of the Canadian government's colonization of the North; he meets Dolores while cataloguing the natural life of the territory for the Department of the Interior. Rydal, the voyeur and Dolores's would-be rapist, is also involved in colonization, albeit the ugly unofficial underbelly of the process, which involves exploiting the labours of his Métis sidekick and, along with his partner Blake, re-visioning Inuit women as western-style prostitutes. We also know that Rydal and Blake are involved in some kind of trade arrangement with the Inuit. The film's narrative, however, confuses Rydal's villainous activities with signs of official patriarchal authority. He appears to Dolores in the stolen uniform of the mountie, Ottawa's Anglo-Protestant agent of order, settlement and nation, and as the captain of a ship that takes Dolores and her husband north into Inuit territory. Peter Morris reads these two incidents as diegetic signs of resistance to male authority figures (1987a, 219). One of the fundamental problems the film poses for the critic is whether or not the narrative posits a resistance to the male authority, racism, and misogyny it depicts. I will argue that, although the film invites a transgressive reading of itself as a discursive structure offering resistance to the dominant white male Anglo-Protestant power structure, it simultaneously withdraws this invitation, and re-inscribes the dominant.

We can see this offer and withdrawal of resistance to racism in the episode involving Shan. The intertitle tells us that Shan's racially motivated murder occurred 'before the long arm of the law reached into the savagery of the wilderness'. The film appears to be criticizing the cruelty and savagery of the white man whose whips and clubs transform Wapi, the descendant of Shan's dog, into a killer. However, the contemporary and racist 1919 voice of the intertitle reduces Shan to a racial stereotype: an avaricious 'yellowman' lured to his death by visions of gold. And, although the white Anglo-Protestant male characters are representative types in a melodrama, their ethnicity is naturalized.

Not only is formation of nation racialized, it is also gendered as exclusively male. George Mosse argues that 'nationalism legitimized the dominance of men over women', and *Back to God's Country* despite its transgressive appearances perpetuates this paradigm (Mosse 1985, 91). The film's constructions of race and gender work together to reduce the colonized female Inuit other who stands in the path of nation-building to a whore. The gaze of the male characters in the shipboard revelry scene denies Blake's Inuit 'guests' a subject position, reducing them to sexual objects who exist to service the white male colonizer. In this scene, what Laura Mulvey would term 'the woman displayed' (1989b, 19) functions on two levels: 'as erotic object for characters within the screen story, and as erotic object for the spectator within the auditorium' (19). There is, however, a moment of transgression in this scenario when an Inuit woman acts out: she rebuffs the advances of a lascivious sailor (Figure 1.12). This transgression is contained by the film's narrative in the exchange of Fels Naptha soap for sex, about which the woman appears to be delighted (Figures 1.13–1.17). Within the narrative structure of the film the Aboriginal woman's racial and sexual difference marks her as an ignorant and dirty whore who will sell herself for soap, a commodity she mistakes for a food product and attempts to eat. Again, in *Back to God's Country* the homosocial Anglo-Protestant white male nation is haunted by an other who must be subjugated to secure settlement and nation-building. The exchange of soap, a mass-produced Western commodity, for penetration of the female body is an economic transaction that can be read metonymically as the exchange of Western commodities for resource-rich Inuit territories. Soap itself is a sign for the civilizing discourse of Western imperialism, a commodity that would 'improve' the lives of the 'inferior' indigenes within the narrow and racist parameters of white colonial cosmology.[16] Nell Shipman's character Dolores is also re-visioned as a whore under the male gaze. In the scene immediately following the soap-for-sex transaction, Rydal forces her on to a bed and plies her with drink. All of the women in the film are displayed as erotic spectacles that are acted upon by men. Film studies has produced a great deal of work on woman as an objectified commodity of the cinematic apparatus, work that is especially helpful in reading the positions of Nell Shipman, and her screen character Dolores. Stephen Heath suggests that fiction film has excluded women as makers, and envisioned them for the most part as spectators or the 'produced of the image' (1992, 85–6). This line of thinking is problematic in the context of Nell Shipman's work; Nell is both the produced of the image, Dolores, and, in part, a producer of that image. Through her involvement with the production process as

26

a screenwriter and her input into the direction of some scenes, Nell is a maker, but a maker complicit in constructing woman as passive erotic object on display.[17] When Nell is on screen as Dolores she is surrounded by men and subjected to controlling male looks; no other women share the screen with her save for the Inuit in the brothel scene on the ship. Mulvey's conceptualization of visual pleasure in cinema argues that 'mainstream film coded the erotic into the language of the dominant patriarchal order', and that one of the erotic pleasures of this type of cinema is scopophilia, a type of voyeurism spectators engage in by projecting their repressed desire on to the performer (Mulvey 1989b, 16–17).[18] The narrative of *Back to God's Country* is structured around male voyeurism, male desire and the procurement of woman, as wife, rape victim and prostitute. This structure reflects the staging of desire with woman at the centre of a cinematic apparatus that Jacqueline Rose argues is supported by 'a whole circulation of money, fantasy and exhibition' (Rose 1986, 223). The nude scene in *Back to God's Country* was exploited in the film's advertising campaign, which included a nude drawing of Dolores and the slogan 'Is the Nude Rude?'[19]

When Nell first appears on screen as Dolores she is subject to the law of the father. Shortly after Peter enters the scene, Dolores is instructed by the father to leave the two men alone to talk. She disappears into the domestic space of the home. Father decides what is appropriate behaviour for her and Peter, and at one point directs her line of vision to take in the figure of her suitor. The evening scene with the three characters is indicative of Dolores's subordinate position in the narrative: the two men sit on stools and talk, literally over Dolores's head from her seated position at their feet where she lights her father's pipe and continually lowers her gaze to the floor. The father, played by an actor who appears to be the same age as Dolores, continually fondles his daughter, marking her as his possession and creating a disturbing incestuous sexual tension. Peter accompanies the object of his desire to the threshold of her bedchamber, giving the audience a vision of the chaste French-Canadian girl in the privacy of her shrine-like bedroom, and of course it is this virginal quality that creates male desire in the film.

After the departure of Peter, and away from the protective embrace of her father, Dolores bathes naked with her animals under the voyeuristic gaze of Rydal (Figures 1.18–1.19). Rydal and his Métis partner exchange lascivious glances as Rydal moves closer to the hidden pool to get a better look at Dolores's body (1.20). Rydal acts as an agent for the camera's and spectator's voyeuristic looking at Dolores. After Rydal and his companion walk out of the shot, the camera returns to focus on Dolores's nude body, her lack, structuring the spectator as male, and denying Dolores a subject position. This cinematic voyeurism constitutes active scopophilia, or what Stephen Heath refers to as 'seeing from the male organ' (1992, 50).[20] Heath argues that 'what the voyeur seeks, poses, is not the phallus of the body of the other but its absence as the definition of the mastering presence, the security of his position . . . the desire is for the Other to be spectacle not subject' (79).

Figures 1.12–17 Back to God's Country
(1919)

Figures 1.18–24 Back to God's Country
(1919)

29

In this respect Rydal shares with his creator Curwood a desire to see woman as spectacle not subject; remember, Curwood re-visions Nell Shipman as the fetish-ized screen spectacle Dolores when they meet on location. Dolores returns home to be left alone with Rydal, who she discovers is now a guest of her father. Rydal displaces the father, forcing Dolores to light his pipe, a task she previously per-formed for her father. In this scene, however, the lighting of the phallic pipe (Figure 1.21) is prefaced by an intertitle linking the act to the ignition of Rydal's desire: 'Rydal's smouldering desire leaps into flame' (1.22). Immediately follow-ing the firing of the pipe, Rydal tackles Dolores and attempts to rape her (Figures 1.23–1.24). Once again, the camera cuts to a voyeuristic agent, the Peeping-Tom-Métis sidekick through whom 'the spectator looks from the comfort of the dark onto the illuminated scene of the bodies moving on the screen' (Heath 1992, 82).

The film does, however, attempt to reverse the gaze of male voyeurism. After the murder of her father by Rydal, Dolores marries Peter and moves to Ottawa. One day, when she finds that Peter has locked his office door to her, she kneels down and spies on him through the keyhole. Dolores becomes an agent for the camera's and the spectator's gaze; we perceive Peter through the keyhole reading and writing official government correspondence.[21] This scene is not tantamount to a reversal of the male gaze; her look does not objectify man sexually, and she does not receive pleasure from looking. Conversely, this scene emphasizes Dolores's subordinate position. She is locked out of the patriarchal world of official discourse, she can only watch covertly as the pen that is withheld from her is wielded by her husband. Whereas Rydal's spying grants him power over Dolores, Dolores's voyeurism illustrates her lack of power.

Rydal's displacement of the father becomes clear on board ship, where he tells Dolores to forget the murder of her father: 'I am the law here [he declares]. I am Captain Rydal, the master of this ship.' Her husband disabled by Rydal, Dolores is imprisoned in the homosocial world of the ship, and subject to the constant threat of rape from her master Rydal. A corrupt version of the law of the father, Rydal monitors Dolores's activities, and marks her as his possession, informing her after a visit to Blake that she is becoming too intimate with his trading part-ner. Rydal constructs an alternative family in which he is Dolores's father and would-be lover, a melodramatic structure where patriarchy and capitalism are reproduced. In this family capitalist activity is dependent upon the subjugation and exploitation of woman as a sexual commodity that Rydal sells to merchant seamen.

However, the film's narrative structure does offer some signs of resistance to this imaging of woman as erotic spectacle. Dolores is forced into the subject position of independent actor, but only in exceptional circumstances. High in the Northern frontier of Canadian territory, her male protectors eliminated by Rydal, Dolores becomes self-reliant and acts on her own initiative to save herself and her incapacitated husband from their tormentor. In a voyeuristic scene which does empower her, Dolores spies on Rydal and Blake and gains access to knowledge of Blake's plan to deliver her to Rydal and do away with Peter. Appropriating the phallic tool of male power, Dolores threatens Blake with a handgun, forcing him to 'play square' or 'die'; when he resists she shoots him. Prior to this point in the film only men wield firearms: the murdered mountie, Rydal, the Métis, the father and Peter. Even after she is within the security of the fort, Dolores keeps a sidearm strapped to her waist. While, as Peter Morris has suggested, Dolores is an active protagonist who transgresses the period's conventional heroines of melodrama (Morris 1987a, 219), the narrative structure of the film contains any transgression of patriarchal social codes. Ultimately, any resistance to a visioning of Canada as white Anglo-Protestant and male is eradicated by the discursive structure of the film. Although Dolores rescues her husband, a male dog rescues her. Once Dolores's husband has recovered she is placed back in the same domestic scene she inhabited at the beginning of the film; as Kay Armatage concludes, Dolores, in the end, is 'firmly in the grip of the patriarchal domestic imperative' (1991, 44). The film suggests that when women are without men they are subject to rape. In the colonizing and settling of wild territory the challenges others present to white male Anglo-Protestant authority must be pacified, therefore the Asian is murdered, the Inuit woman is transformed into a sex slave, the wild dog is tamed and the independent gun-wielding white woman is re-domesticated to produce more white settlers, thereby perpetuating the fictive whiteness of Canada. The last sequence of the film, prefaced by intertitles reading 'The Old Dream' 'COME TRUE', juxtaposes shots of various animals at liberty in the wilderness to the interior of Dolores's and Peter's cabin where we find Dolores sewing and Peter writing his reports. Before fading to black, the film's closing shot shows Wapi at rest with Dolores's baby on the floor of the cabin. The film's opening image of a Chinese man and his dog is displaced by the white family and their dog. These shots are constitutive of the colonizing allegory for a heteronormative production of the white nation found in *Wheatfields of Canada* and *Drylanders*. The old dream come true is white Canadian nation-building. Anne McClintock suggests that this figuring of the nation through the 'iconography of familial and domestic space' is not uncommon nor is it surprising given the derivation of the term nation from '*natio*: to be born' (1995, 357).

Heath's discussion of sexual difference in *Touch of Evil* (Orson Welles 1958) is applied instructively to *Back to God's Country*. Dolores 'is an object of male spectacle and exchange but also resistance to be eliminated' (Heath 1992, 88). Dolores is dangerous not only because she looks back into the male gaze but also because her French-Canadian ethnicity haunts the homosocial Anglo-Protestant construction of nation generated by the film, a difference that is contained by her marriage to Peter Burke.

Although Dolores is the hero of the narrative – she defends herself and her husband against the villainous Rydal – she is, simultaneously, the object of a male desire to know, Rydal's and Burke's colonizing male quests, that ultimately displace her from the realm of active subject to passive object. Rydal's twin desires to know are manifest in his commercial, criminal mapping and exploitation of the region and its resources, and his sexual attacks on Dolores. These activities re-vision the land and woman as passive spaces for male gratification. Burke's twin desires to know the country and Dolores are manifest in his mapping of the flora and fauna of the nation for the Department of the Interior, and his mapping of Dolores as wife, an inert womb for the reproduction of white invader-settlers. These activities re-vision woman and the land as passive spaces for building of empire or nation.

Back to God's Country certainly possesses all of the pejorative characteristics that Peter Brooks suggests the popular imagination associates with the melodrama:

> the indulgence of strong emotionalism; moral polarization and schema-tization; extreme states of being, situations, actions; overt villainy; persecution of the good and the final reward of virtue; inflated and extravagant expression; dark plottings, suspense, breathtaking peripety.
>
> (Brooks 1976, 11)

Back to God's Country, *An Unselfish Love* and *Drylanders*, however, also exemplify why academics such as Brooks and Gledhill have argued for and pur-sued a re-examination of melodrama as a genre and a critical term. The politics of race, gender, sexuality and colonialism present in these melodramas lend import-ant insights into formations of national identifications, permitting the tracing of a cinematic genealogy of the racist and sexist foundations of Canadian nation.

2

WHO IS ETHNOGRAPHIABLE?

Fatimah Tobing Rony uses Claude Lévi-Strauss's bipolar paradigm of ethno-graphiable or historifiable cultural anthropology to define ethnographic cinema in her book *The Third Eye: Race, Cinema and Ethnographic Spectacle* (1996, 6–7). The historifiable is the 'non-raced', white, western and urbanized audience (8) that constitutes the spectators who view the spectacle of the other, raced, non-western, non-urbanized, ethnographiable subjects in ethnographic films. Clearly, who is ethnographized is dependent on who is doing the looking. For Rony the term ethnographic cinema describes 'the broad and variegated field of cinema which situates indigenous peoples in a displaced temporal realm' (8). Those represented in the ethnographic film are meant to be seen as 'exotic, as people who until only too recently were categorized as Savage and Primitive, of an earlier evolutionary stage in the overall history of humankind: people without a history, without writing, without civilization, without technology, without archives' (7). In this chapter I would like to rework Rony's definition to con-ceptualize a variegated field of ethnographic cinema in Canada that, while recog-nizing the unique colonized position of First Nations, includes not only white Anglo-Saxon representations of indigenous peoples but also such representations of Canadians of Eastern European and Asian descent. Canadian films such as *Nation Building in Saskatchewan* (Richard Bird 1921), *Saving the Sagas* (Marius Barbeau 1928), *Secrets of Chinatown* (Fred Newmeyer 1935) and *Of Japanese Descent* (O. C. Burritt 1945) constitute cinematic ethnographies that, in Rony's words, attempt to encapsulate a culture in one volume (1996, 7), creating intersections between 'anthropology, popular culture, and the constructions of nation and empire' (9). Before examining the discourse on the Other that is ethnographic spectacle, it is necessary to investigate more closely the problematic fiction of the 'non-raced' homogeneous white invader-settler society's represen-tation of itself as a national community. By placing white first, I do not mean to privilege whiteness as a marker of Canadian nation, but rather to denaturalize it so that we can understand white representations of otherness.

WHITE ETHNOGRAPHIES: 'SOME WHITE PEOPLE ARE WHITER THAN OTHERS'

Hot Ice

Produced by the Canadian Government Motion Picture Bureau in 1939 and released in 1940, *Hot Ice: The Anatomy of Hockey. Canada's National Game* (Irving Jacoby) elides the spectrum of whiteness that is marked in the earlier *Nation Building in Saskatchewan* (Richard Bird 1921). As Dyer suggests, and as the othered representation of Ukrainian-Canadians in *Nation Building in Saskatchewan* substantiates, there is a fluidity in whiteness that 'determines who is to be included and excluded from the category' and also discriminates 'among those deemed to be within it' (1997, 51). Whiteness is most certainly *the* visual trope for belonging to Canadian nation in films such as *Wonders of Canada*, *The Wheatfields of Canada* and *Back to God's Country* just as it is in *Hot Ice*.

A forerunner of the National Film Board of Canada, which absorbed it in 1941, the Canadian Government Motion Picture Bureau was an ideological state apparatus (ISA) that produced citizen subjects through an organization of their collective enjoyment, manifest here in the Bureau's documentary representation of the *national* game of hockey.[1] Using Lacanian psychoanalysis to understand the relationships of phantasy to formations of nationalism, Žižek explains that allegiance to a 'particular national Cause' or, after Freud, 'materialized enjoyment' is essential in the production of the citizen: 'the national Cause is ultimately the way subjects of a given nation organize their collective enjoyment through national myths. What is at stake in ethnic tensions is always the possession of the national Thing: the "other" wants to steal our enjoyment' (1991, 165). Hockey, narrated in the voice-over of *Hot Ice* as 'a beautiful thing' and 'a national folk dance', is Canada's national Thing, in the Lacanian sense 'a traumatic, real object fixing our desire', something that is simultaneously inaccessible to and purloined by the other (165). *Hot Ice* represents white male possession and domination of hockey and represses the raced other's enjoyment of this national Thing, although the historical record indicates that Blacks in Canada were participating in organized hockey as early as 1899.[2] However, Canadian public archives, late twentieth-century popular culture and scholarship mark the return of the repressed: photographs held in the Glenbow archives document Canadians of Chinese descent playing hockey during this period.[3] Anne Wheeler's 1995 made-for-television film *The War Between Us* shows the interned Japanese other of the Canadian nation-state enjoying the national game, whilst Srinivas Krishna's *Masala* (1992) depicts the Hindu deity Krishna playing goal for the Toronto Maple Leafs. John Greyson's *Making of Monsters* demythologizes hockey as a site for the social construction of a a misogynistic, racially intolerant and homophobic national masculinity. The scholarship of Richard Gruneau and David Whitson demands a rigorous critique of hockey as a national myth that is socially and culturally produced, whilst Gamal Abdel Shehid reads hockey

Plate 1 'Canadians of Chinese descent played hockey during this period'. Credit: Glenbow Archives, Calgary, Canada NA2799–2

through race, marking the erasure of blackness from the terrain of the national and contributing to the recovery of an African-Canadian hockey history (Gruneau and Whitson 1993, 26; Shehid 2000).

The establishing shots of *Hot Ice* invite the cinema spectator to identify with the idealized white community of hockey arena spectators, whose collective enjoyment is organized through a hockey game between the Toronto Maple Leafs and the New York Rangers. Hockey, with one notable exception I will discuss later, fixes the desire of all who enter the frame. The first shot shows men and women lining up at the arena box office to purchase their tickets while the male voice-over speaks in the first-person plural of the national collectivity, declaring hockey an international Thing, commodified for export – 'We've given the world a game' – but then goes on to retrieve it as a national Thing in a series of different shots. Narrating a cut from the box office shot to a shot of people dining in a restaurant the voice-over announces: 'Hockey talk flavours Canadian meals.' Jacoby, the director, then cuts to two little boys speaking in the street who are narrated as 'Canada's experts' on hockey who possess the 'inside dope'. The next shot of a busy telephone operator relaying the score of the game to her colleagues initiates a sequence of shots illustrating hockey's power as a unifying mythology, an all-inclusive nodal point of identification that appears to transcend the barriers of gender and class. A sign for unifying the nation through telecommunications, the shot of the operator is punctuated by voice-over commentary – 'What's the score? Canada wants to know' – that personifies the nation as a unitary entity whose desiring gaze is fixed on the object of hockey. The proceeding shots are composed of men discussing hockey on a streetcar, uniformed military men dining and relaxing while listening to the game on the radio, and finally a sailor alone in his hammock, supposedly listening to the same game that has galvanized the rest of the national subjects represented in the film's narrative to this point. The voice-over then informs the viewer that 'whenever Canadians get together hockey is news, good news, good enough to bring us from the fireside, crowds of us gay, hopeful, good-natured crowds'. In the film's narrative, hockey is a device that not only elides racial and ethnic alterities, it is also pressed into service as a vehicle through which socioeconomic differences are transcended; homogeneity is constructed through the national Thing. Within the diegetic world of the film no one is excluded from the 'national folk dance': 'precious tickets' are 'put aside months in advance so no one will be left out on the big night, not the prosperous broker, nor the mining men and their women, not the old timers, nor the guy giving his gal a break'. There are, however, no faces of colour on screen. This is not an oversight: short of whitening a Black subject, 1930s Canadian racism prohibited African-Canadians from participating in the National Hockey League. Herb Carnegie, a top-ranked Junior B player, was barred from playing with the Toronto Maple Leafs on the grounds of race, the founder of the team Conn Smythe commenting, 'I'd take him tomorrow if somebody could turn him white' (quoted in Ferguson 2000, 8).

Although some women are depicted as consumers of hockey, most, like the gal given a break by her guy, participate in the national folk dance through the agency of men. Obviously, times have changed, and women actively participate in the national game as is evidenced by the Canadian Women's Hockey team's 1998 Olympic gold medal win; however, some women also played the game in 1939, a fact the film both represents and conceals. In a sequence which cuts away from the hockey game in Toronto to a series of shots illustrating how hockey socializes white boys on recreational rinks all over the country, white girls playing hockey in front of a school are present for brief seconds of screen time, but not referenced by voice-over narration. Much more screen time is given over to a comic stereotype of a woman whose vanity and frivolity prohibit her from sharing in the enjoyment of watching the national Thing, much less playing it. The reaction shots of individuals in the crowd observing the NHL game are comprised, for the most part, of white men displaying their passion for the sport. Although there are some shots of women caught up in the excitement, more screen time is devoted to a woman who is bored by the proceedings. Unlike the other women who clearly enjoy the sport, this woman is given the film's only character voice-over to express her response to the game: 'Why did I let Joe bring me here? And on my birthday too, I could have gone to bed.' After cutting away from this woman and back to the game we revisit her to find her staring in a compact mirror and applying makeup while the voice-over narrates her thoughts: 'Why there's the Martins, I'll bet I'm a sight.' Hockey in this film is clearly the preserve of white men. While white women may watch this masculinized and bodily performance of nation they remain Other to it. Similar to racial and ethnic minorities, women are distanced from a raced white and male gendered national Thing.

Hot Ice is structured around the production of white heterosexual masculinity as it is figured in the fetishized athletic body of the hockey player. Early on we move from shots of the crowd purchasing tickets to a dressing-room sequence foregrounding the power and violence of the white male body. Shots of a shirtless player receiving a back rub, and another bare-chested player being taped up, are narrated by a voice-over telling us these bodies are 'catered to by experts' and that 'even the toughest of them must be patched up now and then'. The narrative is at pains to represent hockey as a training ground for young men: 'some day they'll be back in Canadian life as teachers, and businessmen, journalists and farmers. What they learn in the hockey rink they'll bring back to our national life.' More recently, John Greyson's *Making of Monsters* (1990) demythologizes hockey as a site where a misogynistic, racially intolerant and homophobic national masculinity is taught and learned. In visual and auditory tropes reminiscent of the imaging of white male settler production from *Wonders of Canada* and *Wheatfields of Canada*, *Hot Ice* offers a naturalizing representation of the male hockey player as an agricultural commodity springing from the nation's fields: 'They're regular fellows these idols, ordinary human beings . . . with millions of other lads they've come right out of the heart of Canada . . . They're the winter crops of these snow-covered fields. They were born and raised on the river banks.' During this voice-over a cut is made from a medium shot of the uniformed Toronto Maple Leafs filing past the camera to shots of frozen rivers and snow-covered fields. This series of shots forms a transition to a sequence illustrating the production of the male hockey player through playing and drilling on backyard rinks or frozen lakes and rivers across the country. This sequence is cross-cut with shots of boys constructing a male hockey-player figure from snow. The voice-over and preceding shots establish important components of hockey training such as skating. The camera cuts to a shot of a groin made of snow attached to two snow legs that have been packed into skates, while a voice-over informs us 'That's how a hockey player is made – from the ankles up.' This sequence moves from skating through to stick-handling and game strategies, until we have a concluding shot of a fully formed, life-size, snow-white hockey player. This hockey snowman is a gendered allegory for the nation, a signifier for the racial purity of North that has become entwined with the mythology of hockey as a national Thing in Canada. As Daniel Francis has suggested, hockey is a corollary for the northern myth of Canada, a nationalist myth steeped in narratives of Canada's membership to the 'Aryan' family of northern European Nations (1997, 167).[4] *Hot Ice* ends with shots of the cheering white crowd transfixed by the national Thing, and a voice-over proclaiming of hockey 'it's ours, it's us'. If, as Richard Gruneau and David Whitson argue, hockey is 'one of the country's most significant collective representations – a story that Canadians tell themselves about what it means to be Canadian', then *Hot Ice* is telling its audience that full membership in the national community is dependent on one's gender, race and sexuality (Gruneau and Whitson 1993, 13).

Nation Building in Saskatchewan: The Ukrainians

Richard Dyer's observation that 'some white people are whiter than others' (1997, 51) is substantiated for Canadians in two films produced by the Saskatchewan Department of Education and directed by Dick Bird, *Nation Building in Saskatchewan: The Ukrainians* and *The Education of the New Canadian* (1921). The representation of the Caucasian Ukrainians in these two films contrasts sharply with the representation of the Anglo-Saxon Caucasians (or Caucasians who are assimilated into the Anglo-Saxon dominant) of *Hot Ice*. Whereas the white subjects of *Hot Ice* comprise a folk dance performance of the national, the subjects of Bird's films are posited as problematic irruptions of ethnicity in the white terrain of the Canadian nation to be 'solved' through assimilation. This process is accomplished through a displacement of Ukrainian ethnicity by the production of, after Balibar, the fictive ethnicity of the Anglo-Canadian nation. The nation-building represented in both of Bird's films is a bipartite process: the physical work of nation-building performed by the Ukrainians in their transformation of the prairie into fields of agricultural production, and the assimilating cultural work of nation-building performed by the ideological state apparatuses of Saskatchewan's Scouting movement, schools, university and the film narratives themselves, all of which work to translate the Ukrainians into Canadians. This translation constitutes the process Balibar describes as integral to the production of a national people when he argues: 'A social formation only reproduces itself as a nation to the extent that, through a network of apparatuses and daily practices, the individual is instituted as *homo nationalis* from cradle to grave' (1991, 90). Nation-building is enunciated as a discourse on the Other in the establishing shot of *The Education of the New Canadian*: a line drawing in which Ukrainian immigrants, in the dress of their homeland, are directed towards a horizon of light by a uniformed, authoritarian male figure. The accompanying intertitle describes the discourse on the Other as a process of Canadianization: 'The Department of Education, Regina, Saskatchewan, has produced this picture for the purpose of showing what Saskatchewan is doing for Canadianization in the West. If we are to build up a strong and unified Canadian people in this great Dominion we must solve the problem of racial assimilation.' This formulation of the Ukrainians as a problem to be solved is a hallmark of what Bill Nichols calls the expository documentary where 'a text addresses the viewer directly, with titles or voices that advance an argument about the historical world' (Nichols 1991, 34–8). The argument being made here delineates the necessity of assimilation for the construction of a unified national field. *Nation Building in Saskatchewan* immediately establishes a power differential between the 85,000 'new' Canadians from Galicia[5] and southern Russia and what it constructs as 'legitimate' Canadians (white, Anglo-Celtic/Anglo-Saxon settlers) through its terms of address which are enunciated through the third-person plural 'they' to represent the Ukrainians, and the collective first-person plural possessive 'our' to mark the 'whiter' national collectivity excluding them: '*They* are thrifty, hard-working farmers and have brought under cultivation thousands of acres of *our* fertile prairie land' (italics added). While this disenfranchising intertitle provides a fairly positive endorsement of the Ukrainians as 'hardworking', the narrative that follows articulates Ukrainian difference found in first-generation immigrants as something to be eradicated in their children. An intertitle interpreting a pan shot of Ukrainian women in traditional headscarves constructs these bearers of Ukrainian difference for the viewer as figures of fun: 'Canadian millinery has no attraction for the older women.' The viewer is invited to laugh at these women because of their difference, and applaud the younger men and women in the next shot who eschew traditional garb for North American dress thanks to their enrolment in city schools: 'But the younger men and women – many of them Canadian-born – present a different picture. Students of the P. Mohyla Ukrainian Institute, Saskatoon, all are attending the city schools.' This movement from the Othered parents to educated or assimilated (yet, within the logic of the film narrative still Othered) children signals the evolutionary rhetoric through which the film will organize its argument; assimilation as a corollary for progress. The film then introduces a docudrama sequence that tells the story of John W—, from cradle of Ukrainian Otherness to successful assimilated 'product of Saskatchewan schools'.

My analysis focuses on the ideology of these images, how they constitute cinema as a social practice ordering the social terrain of the nation by working the 'problem' of assimilation through various ISAs. After all, images, as Nichols reminds us, 'help constitute the ideologies that determine our own subjectivity; images make incarnate those alternative subjectivities and patterns of social relation that provide our cultural ideal or utopian visions' (1991, 9). The alternative subjectivity of white Anglo-Canadian and the utopian vision of a homogeneous Dominion provided by Bird's docudrama sequence anticipate the Griersonian documentary aesthetic of creative factuality emphasizing interpretation to interpellate good citizens. John Grierson maintained that the documentary's 'use of the living article' provided 'an opportunity to perform creative work' (Grierson 1966, 147). This creative treatment belies the 'truth claims' of such films and renders objectivity a *constructed* perspective subject to the propagandist political and social desires of an elite, as Grierson demonstrates in an essay on the relationship between films and community: '[Film] really can bring the outside world alive to the growing citizen. It really can extend his experience. It really can serve an interpretative function. Working as it does from the living fact, it can, if it is mastered and organized, provide this necessary umbilical to the community outside' (1966, 194). In the case of *Nation Building in Saskatchewan* the 'interpretative function' masters and organizes Ukrainian-Canadian subjects around assimilating codes of progress towards becoming Anglo-Canadian subjects, thereby naturalizing an ethnographic hierarchy of whiteness. Bird's film positions the settlers from the Ukraine as primitive, 'of an earlier evolutionary stage' if 'not in the overall history of humankind', then most certainly in the overall history of white British settlers (Rony 1996, 7).

Although the docudrama narrative of John W— is the film's major device articulating progress, it is prefaced by other signs of development. The second intertitle describes the entire film narrative as 'A story of perseverance, pluck and progress of one of the many races that are playing a leading part in building up our new Canadian Nation'. The first evidence the film offers of this evolutionary development is the Ukrainian settler's movement from the whitewashed mud walls of one-storey European-style dwellings to two-storey 'modern Canadian homes' made from wood. Similarly, the school system's successful evacuation of visual codes of Ukrainian difference from the students' wardrobe creates a context for the transformation of John W—.

The first intertitle of the docudrama sequence simultaneously marks John W—'s ethnicity, and his potential to transcend that alterity: 'Here begins the life story of little John W—, Born in Western Canada, of Ruthenian parentage, he showed early ambition by winning first prize at a baby show.' The accompanying shot is composed of John's mother in a headscarf, the film narrative's sign of unassimilable ethnicity, holding her baby up to the camera. Within the narrative's discourse of evolutionary development, John's early success in the baby show adumbrates his scholastic achievements, achievements that signify his assimilation. The second and last image we see of John's mother and her headscarf is when she hands her six-year-old child over to the school system. At the moment of the unassimilable mother's disappearance from the narrative, John's ethnic

40

difference is no longer visible to the viewer; however, its ghost is present, coded by the process of interpellation acted out in the remainder of the sequence. The Wolf Cubs who, according to the intertitle, teach John to ' "howl" with the best of them' aid the efforts of the school system, in the rhetoric of the film, to Canadianize John. An accompanying image of John in the uniform of the Wolf Cubs shot against the ground of a Wolf Cubs banner places him at visual remove from his Ruthenian heritage. Eventually, John develops into a Scout. A shot of an adolescent John standing at attention in a Scout uniform is introduced by an intertitle describing him as 'a trained Boy Scout'. Scouting, characterized by an intertitle as 'the greatest "get together" movement in the world', was an imperial mechanism of citizenship deployed in this context to recruit John and other boys of Ukrainian descent as Canadian subjects of the British Empire.[6] Through Cubs and Scouts, John makes identifications with masculinized signs of Imperial Canada. If we take identification to be the psychic process Diana Fuss describes as naming 'the entry of history and culture into the subject, a subject that must bear the traces of each and every encounter with the external world', then these images constitute, after Fuss, the detour through the Anglo-Canadian other that defines John W—'s self (Fuss 1995, 3).

Following John's recruitment as a Boy Scout, the film narrative cuts to another apparatus that will work to institute him as *homo nationalis* and chart the distance he has travelled from baby of Ruthenian parenthood. Interpreting a shot of John in the classroom for the viewer, the transitional intertitle reads: 'At eleven we find John in Grade Eight. The spelling lesson. "That's easy" he remarks when the word "hieroglyphics" came.' John's proficiency in the national language marks an important stage in his Canadianization. For Balibar 'schooling is the principal institution which produces ethnicity as linguistic community', it provides the 'mother tongue' that becomes 'the metaphor for the love fellow nationals feel for one another' (1991, 98). By 'mother tongue' Balibar means not the language of one's real mother but the collective memory of the linguistic community 'which perpetuates itself at the cost of an individual forgetting of origins' (99). The language of John's real mother, of his origins, is forgotten, repressed; as a second-generation immigrant John can, in Balibar's terms, 'inhabit' the national language and 'through it the nation itself' (99). Once the English language is acquired, however, the nation will also 'inhabit' John, for, as Balibar reminds us, 'every interpellation is of the order of discourse' (98). English is the language of instruction for John's citizenship training, the language through which he will gain an understanding of Canadian history, politics and law. The discourse on the Other that is John's 'evolutionary' journey away from his Ukrainian origins ultimately results in his graduation with a BA from the University of Saskatchewan. Within the narrative trajectory of the film John's graduation from university is a graduation into full Canadian citizenship; graduation marks his successful assimilation: 'He is now ready to begin his life work as a Canadian citizen – a product of our Saskatchewan schools.' Here, 'our' refers to an infrangible national collectivity that excludes the ethnic Other except as the product of its disciplining educational discourse. John W— and others like him constitute the produced of a pedagogical nationalism; through the case of John W—, we see how a social formation reproduces itself as a nation not only through the apparatus of the school system but also through the technology of the cinematic apparatus.

The film's final shot of John in which, similar to the shots of him as a Wolf Cub and Scout, he bears the visual code of his assimilation – in this instance the BA hood – is followed by an intertitle hailing members of the audience as ethnicized, but assimilable subjects. 'Boys and Girls! Remember this story of John. What he did *you* can do.' Bird's film doesn't just represent the process of assimilation; it is itself part of an ideological apparatus that interpellates Canadianized subjects. Boys and girls of Ukrainian descent are asked to make an identification with the exemplary John and the academic success that symbolizes his full development into a Canadian. The film's mode of address, however, also works to recruit Anglo-Canadian citizens to support a school system that will ensure the reproduction and continued hegemony of Anglo-Canadian nation. This becomes clear in the intertitle immediately following the one hailing boys and girls: 'But to give all these boys and girls a chance to grow into loyal Canadian citizens we must have good schools. Here is Slawa school near Hafford, Sask.' At this point the focus of the film shifts to the social actors entrusted with the responsibility for the process of pedagogical Canadianization at Slawa school, the teacher who is also a Scout master and his wife, a nurse. The ideological work of the teacher and his wife is signified in a flashback to the First World War that represents them as defenders of civilization. An intertitle preceding the flashback re-enactment shot of the man in military uniform and his wife in the uniform of a nurse outside a tent reads: 'And this is the teacher and his wife. During the Great War they played their part in the defence of civilization.' Following this shot of the couple in battle gear, the next intertitle locates their present: 'Now they are helping Canada in time of peace.' The film narrative's juxtaposition of their past and present activities constructs pedagogical Canadianization as a war in which the Eastern European Other represents a threat to undo British-Canadian civilization. This 'threat' was constructed by Canadian authorities during the war when Ukrainians were, in the words of Myrna Kostash, 'disenfranchised' and 'redefined' as Austro-Hungarians and Germans, many of whom were interned as enemy aliens, a sad foreshadowing of what would happen to Canadians of Japanese descent during the Second World War (1977, 340). The teacher is represented as nurturing the minds of boys and girls, teaching them 'our' ways, while his wife 'renders assistance' providing Ukrainians with Canadian agency to health. Bird offers the couple as exemplary role models on which both Canadians of Ukrainian descent and Anglo-Canadians can model. For Ukrainian Canadians, they embody what the film constructs as the Anglo-Canadian cultural values of health and allegiance to the nation; for Anglo-Canadians they represent the self-sacrifice and duty necessary to assimilate the Ukrainian Other. According to Bird's intertitle, the boys of the community, having heard that the teacher was a

Scoutmaster before the war, want to become Scouts. The Saskatoon Rotary Club, an idealized sign of the self-sacrifice and duty assimilation requires of Anglo-Canadians, provides uniforms to facilitate the interpellation of the boys. This information, related in intertitles, initiates another sequence underlining the importance of Scouting in the nation-building of the film's title and articulating how receptive and thankful are the subjects of assimilation. In one shot two uniformed Scouts stand on either side of a sign thanking the Saskatoon Rotary Club for its largesse; they salute the camera. A medium pan shot of smiling Wolf Cubs observed by their Ukrainian mothers in headscarves is interpreted by an intertitle reading: 'The little fellows joined the Wolf Cubs and their parents called at the school to see them perform.' The Cubs are performing their Canadian subjectivity, performances which, according to intertitle and image, give them great pleasure. An intertitle asking 'Are they happy? Wouldn't you be?' cuts immediately to a close-up shot of two Cubs smiling and laughing for the camera. The pleasure displayed is structured by the intertitles and the positioning of the image in the trajectory of the film narrative to signify as pleasure derived from membership in a national community. In this assemblage of shots we have yet another example of the film's organizing rhetoric: assimilation as a corollary for progress. The unassimilable and static parent – as marked by headscarves and traditional dress – looks out from the background of the shot (from disappearing Ukrainian past to Canadian present) to witness the assimilation of her child, while the gaze of the spectator looks in to the foreground of the shot to see the pleasure the two Cubs take in their development of Canadian cultural practices. The cut away from the background 'Ukrainian' parents to the close-up of their 'Canadian' offspring emphasizes the 'evolution' produced by the film narrative and the ISAs of the school, and Scouting: the development from unassimilable first-generation immigrant to assimilable second-generation immigrant. In the composition of these shots pleasure is concomitant with the erasure of cultural difference. Moreover, the spectator is structured to derive visual pleasure from the revelation of this 'solution' to the 'problem' of ethnic difference posited at the film's outset.

Through Scouting and schooling the boys are taught the codes of Anglo-Canadian masculinity; they are imbued with what Immanuel Wallerstein calls a sense of 'pastness', the pastness of British empire and its demands for sacrifice and loyalty that provide a present context in which Canadian nation can be forged. Wallerstein suggests that 'pastness is a mode by which persons are persuaded to act in the present in ways they might not otherwise act . . . Pastness is a central element in the socialization of individuals, in the maintenance of group solidarity, in the establishment of or challenge to social legitimation' (1991, 78). Here Anglo-Canadian pastness works to displace or repress Ukrainian pastness. The composition of the shot places Ukrainian pastness, as it is represented in the traditionally dressed adults in the background, at a remove from the present, as it is represented in the foreground shot of the boys who constitute a disciplining cinematic sign inscribing and maintaining Anglo-Canadian group solidarity. The next series of shots continues this play on ideal 'British' signifiers such as the Scout and the Union Jack on to which, in the context of the film's Canadian nation-building, love for and respect of Canada are transferred to project Bird's narrative of nationalizing ideology.[7] The ideological work of Scouting and schooling overlap in shots of a school field day at Hafford where at the close of the day we see 'happy little children saluting the flag', a Union Jack that is lowered by a uniformed Scout. From these images of the nation as a social formation constructed around ideal signifiers such as the flag of the British Empire, which itself stands in for the ideal signifiers of common language and pastness, we cut away to the film's closing shot of Saskatchewan's provincial legislature, a crucible of citizenship formation, and a structure that will play a future role in building what the film narrative refers to in the second intertitle as the 'new Canadian nation'. This last image underlines the film's anticipation of Griersonian documentary cinema's education film, which Grierson thought should be used to prepare children for citizenship (1946, 194).

Although the film hails girls and boys of Ukrainian descent as Canadian subjects, it does not interpellate them as national subjects in the same ways. In the narrative of the film, boys become the embodiment of the nation and are located at the centre of its narrative, while girls are peripheralized as handmaidens to a masculinized Canada. As we have seen in Chapter 1 and in *Hot Ice*, representations of nation are dependent on unequal constructions of gender.[8] The Ukrainian mothers of Bird's film watch passively as their sons perform Canadian nation. Although much screen time is devoted to boys learning the active adventurer ethos of Scouting from the teacher or Scout master, there is comparatively little footage of his wife instructing the girls in domestic skills such as sewing. The disparity of these images renders the film's message clear; reduced screen time is a measure of what the film deems to be woman's secondary importance in the nation-building project: the construction of the domestic sphere that will sustain the film's primary figure of nation-building, the man.

Bird's film then is not a scientific document referring back to concrete reality, but a construction of a historical reality that is distorted by the phallocentric and anglocentric position of its director. Is the film racist and sexist in its assumptions? Yes. The purpose of this analysis, however, is not to indict Bird as sexist and racist but to denaturalize what Bird's socialization process has led him to believe is natural. We must remember that the occasion of our early twenty-first-century re-reading of this early twentieth-century material is framed by our knowledge of immigration history, contemporary race and gender relations and multiculturalism, whilst the production of the film is framed in the context of a patriarchal society, mass immigration, the eugenics movement and an irrational fear of ethnic and racial difference. Seven years after this film was produced, the Supreme Court of Canada ruled that women did not constitute 'persons' in the same way that men were persons and therefore declared women unfit to hold public office.[9] Sexism and racism were wired into Canadian institutional practices at this time. Fear of class, racial and ethnic differences made the 'science' of selective breeding or eugenics a popular theory and practice for many otherwise progressive people, such as the Canadian socialist Tommy Douglas, founder of the Co-operative Commonwealth Federation of Canada.[10] In Britain negative eugenics was deployed to limit the procreation of the working classes, while in Canada it was thought of as an antidote to the fear that the nation would, in the words of Ontario Public Health physician Helen MacMurchy, 'be swamped by waves of degenerate immigrants' (quoted in McLaren 1990, 46). In his framing of non-Anglo-Saxon immigration as a problem to be solved, Dick Bird is, unfortunately, in line with the majority of his contemporaries. Ignorance of the raced or ethnicized Other produced reports such as W. G. Smith's *A Study in Canadian Immigration* (1920) which, as Angus McLaren notes, called for 'the training of a new generation of "soldiers" who would wage a "battle" for the assimilation of new Canadians' (McLaren 1990, 61). While I am not aware of any evidence that Bird read Smith's report, the director's visualization of Smith's metaphor for assimilation as a war to be fought certainly suggests the cultural resonance that assimilation as warfare had for Canadians in the early 1920s. Assimilation is also presented as a solution to the problem of non-Anglo-Saxon immigration in James S. Woodsworth's influential 1909 study *Strangers at Our Gates or Coming Canadians*. In a chapter on assimilation Woodsworth recognizes the primary importance of 'our National Schools' in absorbing difference, and deplores the existence of Separate, or Catholic Schools, institutions that might deviate in the production of a fictive Anglo-Saxon, Protestant ethnicity (Woodsworth 1909, 234). Woodsworth's study divides the immigrants into national, ethnic and racial groups, providing essentialist stereotypes of each. For example, Ukrainians or Ruthenians as Woodsworth's collaborator Arthur Ford calls them, are described as 'illiterate', 'ignorant' (111) and 'animalized'; 'from centuries of poverty and oppression', however, Ford observes, the Ruthenian is 'eager to become Canadianized' (112).[11] Although it may be difficult to discern from an early twenty-first-century perspective, Woodsworth was a progressive, the first leader of Canada's socialist CCF party.

In documents such as Smith's report, Woodsworth's book and Bird's film, we see the enactment and failure of a nation-building predicated on assimilation. For immigrants such as Bird's John W— are, as I stated earlier, not just inhabited by the nation, they inhabit that nation. The Ukrainian language of John W—'s mother might be displaced by the national 'mother tongue' of Canadian English, but it is not erased; traces of that origin for ever remain in John and in Canada's terrain of the national. The identifications John W— makes with Cubs, Scouts and Canadian nation are not stable ones, they are, as Fuss suggests in her discussion of identifications, 'always shifting, reversing, multiplying, contravening one another, to disappear and reappear years later' (1995, 2). Ukrainian culture did not disappear from the Canadian cultural landscape; conversely it has become a marker of Canadian identity.[12] In its attempted incorporation of the Other, the nation forever alters itself. Anglo-Canadian nation, manifest here in its agents, the teacher, the Scout master and the film-maker, takes a detour through the

Ukrainian Other, as does the spectator of Bird's film, thereby for ever linking the Canadian nation-building of the film's title to the negotiation of Otherness. As much as Bird's film is about erasing Otherness, it is forced to register the historical reality of Ukrainian difference even as it represents the phantasy of rendering it invisible.

Saving the Sagas: salvage ethnography

White Anglo-Canadian nation-building's conflicted practices of erasing and registering Otherness manifest themselves differently when it comes to negotiating the alterity of the colonized Indigenous subject. Similarly to *Nation Building in Saskatchewan*, *Saving the Sagas* (1928), a film chronicling the ethnographic recording of Nisga'a First Nations culture by National Museum of Canada ethnologist Marius Barbeau and musicologist Ernest MacMillan, posits alterity to the Anglo white nation as a problem to be solved. However, the solution offered by the latter film is more complicated than the assimilation posed by Bird's film. Whereas the white ethnicized immigrant Ukrainian subjects of *Nation Building in Saskatchewan* are provided with an opportunity to 'pass' (through assimilation) as subjects of the white Anglo-Canadian nation, indigenous Aboriginal subjects, racialized by the white imperial gaze as 'Indian', cannot, in a racially based vision of the nation, be extended this 'opportunity'. The white Anglo-Canadian nation-building project of colonization is predicated on the disappearance or destruction of the indigenous First Nations whose claims to the territories purloined by the white nation threaten to interrupt the narrative legitimacy of Canadian nation. This is not to suggest that aggressive assimilation was not practised by Canadian governing bodies against First Nations peoples: it was, in the Gradual Civilization Act of 1857, the Indian Act of 1876 and the Indian Act of 1951. These acts, however, as Christopher Bracken (1997, 184–5) and John L. Tobias (1983, 40–5) argue, are contradictory: they attempt to legislate both the protection and, through education and eventual enfranchisement, the absorption of Native cultures. This schizophrenic tendency is encapsulated in the work of Deputy Superintendent-General of Indian Affairs Duncan Campbell Scott. As Lynda Jessup notes, Scott, who co-edited a volume of Nisga'a songs with Barbeau and MacMillan, also advocated pursuing policies of assimilation until 'there is not a single Indian in Canada that has not been absorbed into the body politic' (quoted in Jessup 1999, 57).

Historically, assimilation of Indigenous peoples in Canada and elsewhere has proved to communicate a contradictory, doubled message from the Imperial Subject: 'be like me, don't be like me' (Fuss 1995, 146). In her discussion of Frantz Fanon and the psychoanalysis of colonization, Fuss argues that the Imperial Subject's hegemonic claim on alterity as its own, its injunction to the colonial Other to approximate its likeness, but not to displace it, 'imposes upon all others, as a condition of their subjugation, an injunction to *mime* alterity', not to realize it (146). For if the Imperial Subject is to remain as such, it cannot be inhabited by the colonial subject. Through this logic 'the colonized are constrained to impersonate the image the colonizer offers them of themselves; they are commanded to imitate the colonizer's version of their essential difference' (146). Imperial Subjects such as the producers of *Saving the Sagas*, and their agents, Marius Barbeau and Ernest MacMillan, preserve their own positions of power by selecting out disciplining representations of First Nations as a prehistoric, vanishing, doomed race. This ideology of the vanishing race is a characteristic of salvage ethnography, where Rony argues the 'already posited as dead' 'vanishing' Native is '"redeemed" through taxidermic reconstruction' on film (1996, 195–6). Historically, First Nations peoples have been translated into idealized signifiers for a white national pastness, noble savages who peer out from museum displays, the paintings of Paul Kane and Emily Carr and ethnographic films as reminders of a cultural past that is constructed as the cultural inheritance of the white Anglo-Canadian nation.[13] As Daniel Francis writes, 'having first of all destroyed many aspects of Native culture, White society now turned around and admired its own recreations of what it had destroyed' (1992, 36). *Saving the Sagas*, with its racist intertitles penned by Barbeau, does exactly this. Ironically, the myth of white Anglo-Canadian nation was dependent upon the Aboriginal Other, for, as Jan Nederveen Pieterse argues, 'Otherness is the boundary of normality. As such images of otherness exercise a disciplinary function, as mirrors of difference, as markers and warning signals. The savage is indispensable in establishing a civilization's place in the universe' (1991, 201). We must remember that the otherness of the 'savage' is, as Bill Nichols suggests, 'fabricated' (Nichols 1991, 204). Nichols argues, after Sartre, that 'the figure of the Other represents that which cannot be acknowledged or admitted within the culture that engenders it' (204); a hierarchical economy manages the circulation of the Other as a means of establishing the unity, security and independence of the dominant group (202).

Saving the Sagas, sponsored by the CPR and produced by Associated Screen News Limited (a company in which the CPR was a major stockholder) with the co-operation of the National Museum of Canada, circulates in such a hierarchical economy as a tool of white Anglo-Canadian nation-building that exploits the image of First Nations as a sign of the 'doomed savage' to secure and legitimize the white nation's hold over the colonized territory of the Other, by documenting the erasure or death of that Other. The first intertitle of the film simultaneously sounds the death knell of West Coast First Nations and the preservation of that 'dying' culture by the white nation: 'A screen recording of the vanishing culture, the rites and songs and dances of the Indians of the Canadian Pacific Coast north of Vancouver.' The colonizing gaze of this film, the white looking that determines the image of the colonized Aboriginal, is established by the first figures who enter the frame, Marius Barbeau and Ernest MacMillan aboard a boat with a camera mounted on its deck (Figure 2.1). The accompanying intertitle emphasizes the white technology that will facilitate the white nation's mastery over First Nations culture: 'Marius Barbeau of the National

Museum and Mr. Ernest MacMillan of the Toronto Conservatory of Music set out with camera and phonograph.' Here First Nations are subordinate to the controlling gaze of the Canadian nation, a gaze that constitutes a marker of a colonialism that, as Fuss argues, 'works, in part, by policing the boundaries of cultural intelligibility, legislating and regulating which identities attain full cultural signification and which do not' (1995, 143). The cinematic apparatus of the white nation delimits the cultural signification of First Nations identities as a dead or dying primitive race in relation to the technologically and morally superior – in the racist cosmology of Canadian imperialism – white Imperial Subject. Following the shots of Barbeau, MacMillan and the technology of representation, we are provided with yet another sign of what the film articulates is white technology's victory over Nisga'a culture. A shot of a Nisga'a man in Western dress, wearing a radio headset and tuning in a station is interpreted as: 'The ways of the white man – and radio jazz – are sweeping away the old color of Indian life of British Columbia.' The proceeding series of shots moves from this contemporary image of the Nisga'a and their imminent absorption by white technology to the artefacts of the 'vanished' culture, performances of 'old rites', potlatch dances, the recording of songs by Barbeau and MacMillan, and newly converted Christian Nisga'a performing their Christianity for the camera. This narrative trajectory suggests, as Lynda Jessup's essay argues, that the film narrative's protagonists, Barbeau and MacMillan, and with them the spectator, are moving not just upstsream but 'backward in time', away from civilization, back to nature, and then back to civilization at the end of the film (1999, 59–60). *Saving the Sagas*, cut from the now lost National Museum of Canada film *Nass River Indians* (1927), structures the visual pleasure of the viewer around the cultural death of the Nisga'a and, alternatively, their failure to assimilate as this is demonstrated by their mimicry of whiteness.[14]

Having established the power differentials at play in the imperial looking at the colonized that comprises *Saving the Sagas*, I would like to turn my attention to an analysis of visual pleasure and entertainment in the film. As Rony contends, imperialist and nationalist propaganda films, such as *Saving the Sagas*, are part of an ethnographic cinema that acts as 'an instrument of surveillance as well as entertainment, linked like the written ethnographies of cultural anthropology to a discourse of power, knowledge and pleasure' (1996, 10). Laura Mulvey's concept of a gendered visual pleasure also involves a discourse of power, knowledge and pleasure, and may be usefully adapted to read the raced and gendered visual pleasure derived from the controlling gaze through which the Imperial Subject apprehends the colonized Nisga'a in *Saving the Sagas*. Mulvey's theory of the exchange of looks onscreen and offscreen in Hollywood cinema assumes a phallocentric, white, middle-class male spectatorial gaze and works from the premise that, as an 'advanced representation system, the cinema poses questions about the ways the unconscious (formed by the dominant order) structures ways of seeing and pleasure in looking' (1989b, 15). For her 'the paradox of phallocentrism in all its manifestations is that it depends on the image of the castrated

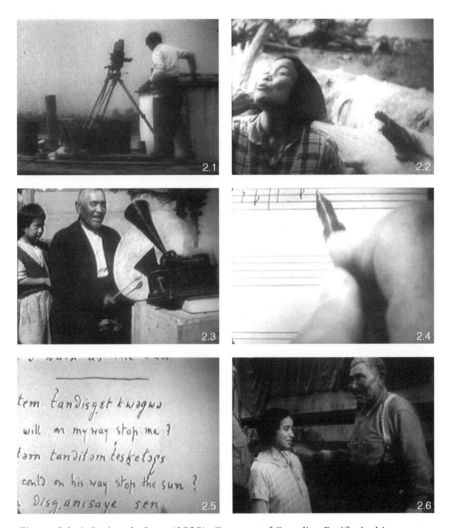

Figures 2.1–6 Saving the Sagas (1928). Courtesy of Canadian Pacific Archives

women [*sic*] to give order and meaning to its world'; woman's lack 'produces the phallus as a symbolic presence' (1989b, 14). In the case of ethnographic cinema, the constructed lack of the Other, the Other's perceived lack of 'civilization', as this eurocentric concept is marked by history, technology and Christianity, produces white phallocentrism as symbolic presence. The paradox of white phallocentric Anglo-Canadian nation-building in all its manifestations is that it depends not only on the castrated woman but also on the raced Other to give order and meaning to its world. Recalling Nederveen Pieterse, the idea of the colonized subject as 'savage' is essential to the white nation's construction of itself as civilized, as superior. Visual pleasure in the ethnographic film of imperial nation-alism then depends on the production of images that maintain this illusion.

Continuing with our adaptation of Mulvey to read a visual pleasure derived from race as spectacle in *Saving the Sagas*, let us consider her contention that 'in a world ordered by sexual imbalance, pleasure in looking has been split between active/male and passive/female. The determining male gaze projects its fantasy onto the female figure, which is styled accordingly' (1989b, 19). If I, temporar-ily, substitute white for male and Aboriginal for female, we have a paradigm for reading a world that is ordered not only by sexual imbalance but also by a racial imbalance where pleasure in looking has been split between the active white looking of the always-already male Imperial Subject and the passive, looked at, colonial Aboriginal. I qualified my substitution as a temporary one, as it is my intention not to evacuate Mulvey's paradigm of its gender politics but to insert race into that paradigm. In our reading of subjectivities in *Saving the Sagas*, we will return shortly to the sexual imbalance in looking relations. Firstly, however, I want to examine how the determining white male gaze projects its fantasy on to the Aboriginal Other, which is styled accordingly in *Saving the Sagas*. The Imperial Subject's fantasy of First Nations culture as a non-living entity con-signed to the ancient world is manifest in a series of shots depicting signs of Nisga'a culture in a terrain devoid of the Nisga'a themselves, who, the image and accompanying intertitles suggest, have disappeared. Prefacing an extreme long shot of a totem pole, a contextual intertitle reads: 'Up a river, back from the sea. Our explorers come upon the site of Angeda – an ancient town of the wolf tribe.' More extreme long shots of the totem pole are followed by an intertitle intro-ducing long shots of a memorial totem to a Wolf Chief: 'Here deep in the tangled growth, is the totem monument of a Wolf Chief.' This intertitle is followed by various long shots of sections of the pole and a long shot which pans from the top of the pole to the base before cutting to a medium shot showing the base carv-ing, and a man pulling brush away from it. This fetishistic looking at the totem pole betrays a visual pleasure derived from a doubled desire: the death or disap-pearance of the Other, and the white nations' fantasy of inheriting the Other's territory and idealized cultural signifiers. The film narrative represents the totem pole as a marker of an individual Native death; however, the tangled growth obscuring it spells a larger cultural death; the artefacts appear to be abandoned, there appears to be no one around to appreciate and preserve this culture but the white man. In the 1920s the totem pole, like other signifying systems of Abo-riginal peoples, was appropriated by the white nation as part of its heritage. As Daniel Francis comments, 'White British Columbians, and Canadians generally, decided that [totem poles] were an important national treasure, a visible link with the country's first peoples and a part of its heritage which had to be pre-served' (1997, 184–5). This conflicting white desire for the disappearance or preservation of First Nations culture is also evident in official government policy on totem poles, which banned the erection of new poles on the one hand but wished to preserve old ones.[15] Although subsequent intertitles and images provide evidence that Native cultural practices, such as the art of the totem carver, in the words of one intertitle, 'survive', the combination of images and text immediately following the film's recognition of cultural survival pronounce, again, the imminent death of the Nisga'a. A shot of a Chief in ceremonial robes, chanting and dancing beside a totem pole, is introduced as 'The Eagle Chief holds to the old rites' and interpreted for the viewer by the next intertitle: 'He is chanting his glories on the site for his grave – the way to be sure about one's funeral sermon.' Again, the active looking of the white male Imperial Subject – Barbeau and company, as well as the white male spectator posed by the discursive organization of the film – fixes the passive Aboriginal Other in a position of extinction, chanting the glories of a lost culture on its grave.

The proceeding sequence of women performing potlatch dances facilitates a reading of both the sexual and racial imbalance structuring visual pleasure in the film. The Nisga'a women are doubly colonized by the white and male gaze of *Saving the Sagas*, firstly as Aboriginal and secondly as women: the white phallo-centric gaze of the camera denies these people a subject position, reducing them to a racial and sexual epithet, the squaw. An intertitle introducing a long shot of three women dancing reads: 'The Eagle squaws still know the measures of the old potlatch dances.' The squaw is a fantasy stereotype projected on to the sexed and raced body of the Aboriginal woman by the white male gaze in the service of pleasure. A figure non-Natives constructed, and associated with drinking and prostitution, the squaw was, in the words of Daniel Francis, a stereotype for First Nations woman as a 'sexual convenience', a 'sexual commodity'; in the white symbolic order squaw signified a 'debased and immoral' Aboriginal femininity (Francis 1997, 121–2). The long shot of three women dancing is followed by an intertitle decoding the dance as a pantomime of 'singing the baby to sleep' and a medium shot of one of the women dancing. However, this image of Aboriginal mothering is quickly dispatched by the next intertitle interpreting a subsequent medium shot of a woman dancing and gesturing toward her fluttering lips: 'And if we understand Indian – and we do – this little beauty is signaling for a kiss – or maybe a drink' (Figure 2.2). Here the cultural signification of First Nations woman is delimited by a white phallocentric technology of representation that, after Fuss, commands the colonized 'to imitate the colonizer's version of their essential difference' for the pleasure and entertainment of the white male Anglo-Canadian spectator (1995, 146). Richard Dyer's conceptualization of entertain-ment suggests that 'it works with the desires that circulate in a given society at a given time, neither wholly constructing those desires nor merely reflecting desires produced elsewhere; it plays a major role in the social construction of happiness' (1992, 7). The happiness of the white nation at this time came, in part, from taking what Dyer would term 'vicious pleasures' at the expense of the Aboriginal Other (1992, ix). Not dissimilar to the racist joke, the entertainment elements of ethnographic documentaries, such as *Saving the Sagas*, project a fantasy of racial superiority and control over the Other.

These 'vicious pleasures' continue in the sequence documenting Barbeau's and

MacMillan's recording and translation of Nisga'a songs, which an intertitle states are 'fading away with the advance of the white man'. This intertitle enunciates the imperial corollary at the heart of the film: the advance of the white man is dependent upon the 'fading away' of the First Nations. This intertitle cuts to a medium shot of Barbeau and MacMillan sitting at a table transcribing music and words as a Nisga'a man, identified by Jessup as Frank Bolton (Figure 2.3), performs, and Barbeau's field assistant William Beynon translates (Jessup 1999, 64). The film narrative then cuts away from this image to an extreme close-up of Western musical notation being inscribed by a white hand (Figure 2.4). From this image we cut back to a medium shot of Beynon speaking as Barbeau writes, and then cut away again to an extreme close-up of a text comprising a parallel translation of Nisga'a words into English, the national language of the white nation (Figure 2.5). These images document the fixing of a dynamic oral Native tradition into a static Western written formation; they document the 'preservation' of a First Nations culture that elides the real agenda of the white nation: the death of a living culture indicated in the racist jocularity of the intertitle interpreting the transcription process for the viewer: 'The cannery cans the salmon, the camera cans the dances and now the phonograph cans the songs – everything canned but the Indians!'[16] Medium shots of Nisga'a singing into a wax cyliner recorder immediately follow the intertitle. The intertitle provides entertainment and humour for the white viewer by punning on the verb *can* and its preservative connotations – canned food stuffs, canned music – but also resonates with the word's slang connotations of 'to put an end to'. The fantasy of the 'Indians' being canned – made extinct – is projected on to the Nisga'a in the film by the cinematic apparatus to provide visual pleasure for the white spectator. Translation is a multivalent process in this film; not only are the songs and music of the Nisga'a translated into the signifying systems of the hegemonic Anglo-Canadian Nation; the cinematic apparatus translates the Nisga'a themselves into images which will be used by the colonizer to signify their death. The device of white 'preservation' – translation – is the technology that realizes the white fantasy of placing the Aboriginal Other under erasure; translation is an assimilative practice of imperialism.[17]

Colonial assimilation's doubled command 'be like me, don't be like me' haunts *Saving the Sagas* in the visual pleasure derived from the narrative's enactment of both assimilation and its failure as this is marked in representations of Nisga'a miming or approximating, but not realizing, whiteness. Shots of Nisga'a playing the traditional game of Lahal are reduced by an intertitle to a failed attempt to mime the colonizer: 'It's just the Indian version of the white man's old shell game.' The next intertitle and accompanying shot of Nisga'a men at a meeting of the Church Army, dressed in suits and holding Bibles, seems designed as a counterpoint both to the white-constructed 'gambling' of Lahal, and earlier images of 'pagan' rituals: 'But the Church Army now spreads salvation along the Coast.' Once again, the 'preservation' or salvaging of First Nations peoples is dependent upon the destruction of their culture, in this instance their spiritual belief systems. Pleasure, for the white viewer, is concomitant with erasure in this representation of, in the evolutionary discourse of the ethnographic film, a move from a 'pagan' culture to a civilized Christian state, as this is signified visually in the western suits worn by the men and the Bibles they hold in their hands. In the context of the film, however, these men – although converts to Christianity – still signify as 'Indian' Others for the white nation. Similarly, the sequence, immediately following, concerning the 'converted' 'pagan' Chief and the moral dilemma he finds himself in as a Christian with three wives, produces visual pleasure for the white viewer through a representation of the Other's failure to attain what the film narrative contends is the moral superiority of whiteness. The intertitle introducing this sequence enunciates the conflicted and contradictory logic of the white nation's vision of assimilation: 'When converted the last pagan chief had three wives – at least two too many for one Christian – at one time.' The Chief becomes a figure of fun for the white viewer who is invited to laugh at his failure to pass for white as this is represented in the irruption of his 'pagan polygamy'. Through a dramatic re-enactment of the Chief puzzling 'devoutly' over the polygamy 'problem' the film attempts to solve what it has posited as the problem of the Chief's 'Indian' alterity by representing his Christian decision. A shot of three seated women is prefaced by an intertitle, reading: 'Between these three squaws he had to make a Christian decision.' The film's final intertitle and image, however, mark the Chief indelibly as unassimilable 'Indian' by projecting a white male fantasy of the Aboriginal Other's primitive sexuality and sexual potency – the colonizer's version of the colonized's essential difference – on to the Chief and his chosen partner. An intertitle reading, 'he quit them *all* and took this young Hutsini beauty', is followed by a medium shot of the Chief, a man who looks to be somewhere in his mid-fifties, and his young bride, who looks to be in her mid- to late-teens (Figure 2.6).

Saving the Sagas is another example of the new white Anglo-Canadian nation working through what it constructs as the 'problem' of assimilation via an ISA, in this case the National Museum of Canada for which the original film *Nass River Indians* was produced, to be shown in conjunction with the 1927 show 'The Exhibition of Canadian West Coast Art, Native and Modern'.[18] The CPR, a corporation which historically acted as an ISA through its Department of Colonization and Development, sponsored the film. The National Museum and the CPR hail citizen subjects as white men, and discipline the colonized as aliens to the nation, the disappeared or disappearing. The CPR is a major technology of colonization that displaced First Nations and shipped immigrants – the white nation – into Western territories, and its collaboration with the National Museum, the repository of imperialism's plunders, to produce *Saving the Sagas* enacts the 'canning' of the 'Indians' alluded to in the film's intertitle. Barbeau, the National Museum and the CPR turn their collective commodifying gaze on the Nisga'a, reducing them to an entertaining white spectacle of Aboriginality that was exploited to popularize the activities of the Museum and increase the tourist traffic on the CPR's western routes while, simultaneously, documenting the assimilation of First Nations.[19]

Despite the ravages of disease brought about by contact, containment on reserves, the Indian Act's prohibition of Native cultural practices and residential school systems which forcibly removed children from their families to be immersed in white ways, the white nation's fantasy of First Nations extinction played out in *Saving the Sagas* never became a reality, and Canada continues to negotiate its position with First Nations. This negotiation of contested nations within nation ranges from the peaceful, constitutional legislation of self-government for the Inuit territory of Nunavut to the violent, armed conflict between Mohawk warriors and the Canadian Army at Oka, powerfully and poignantly documented in Alanis Obomsawin's *Kanehsatake: 270 Years of Resistance* (1993). Not dissimilar to the practice of assimilation directed towards Ukrainians in Dick Bird's *Nation Building in Saskatchewan* which marks a Ukrainianization of Anglo Canada, the assimilation directed towards First Nations in *Saving the Sagas* represents the Aboriginalization of white Anglo-Canadian nation. The detour through the Aboriginal Other taken by Barbeau, the National Museum of Canada and the CPR, the appropriation of Native culture as the white nation's inheritance, for ever associates Canada with Aboriginality. As Christopher Bracken concludes in his critique of the relationship between West Coast First Nations and white Canadian nation:

> The white nation – or to be precise, the nation that desires to be white – frames its sense of itself, its self-consciousness, by repeating over and over to itself that it is about to swallow and mourn an aboriginal other who has died. When the instant of death arrives, and even though that instant is endlessly deferred, the nation will be able to give itself a distinctive white Canadian subjectivity, but thanks to the irony that grounds it, the nation cannot realize its aim of folding others into itself because the limit that holds it apart from them is also what gives it a feeling for itself, the consciousness of its own nationhood.
>
> (1997, 231)

Secrets of Chinatown: the monstrous ethnographic

The white nation's inability to fold others into itself – as it is that distance from those others that maintains the fantasy of Canada as the white nation – characterizes its relationship to the Asian Other. A version of the policy of containment (reservations) marking Canada's negotiation of First Nations difference presents itself in the distance or limit established by the legislative and cultural construction of Chinatown in British Columbia. Restrictive custom prohibited Chinese in Vancouver from purchasing property outside the limits of Chinatown.[20] This legislation based on race was fuelled by an ongoing white cultural construction of Chinatown as a site of criminality, filth, disease and 'heathen' religious practices, a space that should be contained to protect white society.[21] Kay J. Anderson's research into this area tracks white turn-of-the-century and early twentieth-century representations of Chinese as 'heathen' (1994, 236–7) 'almond-eyed law breakers' who traffic in gambling, women and opium (1994, 238–9), and live in unsanitary conditions which threaten the health of the white community (1994, 232–3). An excerpt from the 1902 *Report of the Royal Commission on Chinese and Japanese Immigration* lays down the co-ordinates for the white racist fantasy of the Chinese as a monstrous Other:

> They come from southern China . . . with customs, habits and modes of life fixed and unalterable, resulting from an ancient and effete civiliza-tion. They form, on their arrival, a community within a community, separate and apart, a foreign substance within but not of our body pol-itic, with no love of our laws or institutions; a people that cannot assimi-late and become an integral part of our race and nation. With their habits of overcrowding, and an utter disregard for all sanitary laws, they are a continual menace to health. From a moral and social point of view, living as they do without home life, schools or churches, and so nearly approaching a servile class, their effect upon the rest of the community is bad . . . Upon this point there was entire unanimity.
>
> (quoted in Anderson 1994, 223)

This prejudicial imagining of the Chinese in Canada as an unassimilable, unhealthy menace, a problem to be solved by the white nation through a com-mission of inquiry, resonates in popular culture texts of the period such as Guy Morton's 1927 novel *The Black Robe* and the film adaptation of the book, *Secrets of Chinatown* (1935). The plot of *Secrets of Chinatown* is driven by the threat of miscegenation; Chinese male desire for the Anglo-white woman, Zenobia, is contested by an Anglo-white male desire for her. Zenobia, a blonde white woman living in Vancouver's Chinatown under the spell of the Chinese gangster and cult leader Black Robe, is at the centre of a mysterious trade in souls and narcotics represented as threatening to the city's white population.[22] The film's narrative constitutes a white male expedition into Chinatown to ascertain a knowledge of the Chinese. The secrets of the film's title – the Chinese hold on a white woman, Chinese 'heathen' worship and the drug trade – are posited as problems that will be solved, made knowable, through what is framed by the racist value system of the film narrative as a white technology of empiricism, the detective work of Donegal Dawn and Robert Rande that stands in opposition to the Taoism of the 'mysterious' Orient. This knowledge of the Other is gained, in part, by Dawn's and Rande's ability to pass for the Other. Ultimately, their pass-ing for Chinese and their powers of deduction grant them knowledge of, and therefore power over, the Other. This process reaches its climax when the Black Robe – the film's monstrous Other that stands in for all Chinese – is unmasked as the police operative Chan Tow Ling and subsequently commits suicide.

Hitherto this poorly made B-film produced by Victoria's Commonwealth Productions has gained only cursory scholarly attention as one of the many mediocre 'quota quickie' films made in Canada in the 1930s under the quota restrictions imposed by the British Cinematograph Films Act of 1927.[23] Under this regulatory legislation, designed to bolster and protect a British film industry from Hollywood, 7.5 per cent (with gradual increases to a maximum of 20 per cent) of all films screened in the UK had to be of British origin. Films qualified for entry into the UK market if they were produced in the British Empire and if 75 per cent of salaries was paid to British subjects (Morris 1978, 180). Seeing an opportunity to profit from Canada's membership in the empire, expatriate Canadian Kenneth Bishop returned from Hollywood to establish Commonwealth Productions and Central Films in Victoria for the sole purpose of producing 'quota quickies'.[24] Unfortunately, Bishop's knowledge of the British quota law was minimal. His hiring of Hollywood director Fred Newmeyer, and other Americans in the cast and crew meant that less than 75 per cent of salaries was paid to British subjects, and the film did not qualify for entry into the British market under the quota legislation. Subsequently, Commonwealth lost its American distribution deal for the film, and went into receivership (Morris 1978, 191). Northern Films completed the picture, which premiered at the Empire Theatre in Victoria on 8 March 1934, and eventually released it in the United States where it was distributed for four years until Northern Films went out of business (Browne 1979, 259). The film was exhibited in Vancouver and returned after the premiere to Victoria, where it ran for three days at the Columbia Theatre (259). Panned as a 'bottom-of-the-barrel programmer which itself should have been kept a secret' (Nash and Ross 1987, 2812) and seen by a very few people, *Secrets of Chinatown* was not a critically or financially successful film. Peter Morris contends that 'it was little more than a routine adventure film' (1978, 191). Morris's assessment, based on aesthetics and genre, is, of course, accurate; *Secrets of Chinatown* is an undeniably 'bad' film. I will argue, however, in an analysis based on the representation of race relations, that *Secrets of Chinatown* is much more than a routine adventure film: it is an important cultural document of white Canada's production of a filmic imagined community based on race. Morris's brief but very useful history of the film's production does not engage the film's virulent racism, nor does it record contemporary responses to that racism. The picture's demonization of Chinese was not lost on the producers, who, in an attempt to placate the Chinese community, renamed it *The Black Robe* when it played in Vancouver and Victoria (Browne 1979, 259). The Chinese Consul in Vancouver was also very much aware of the film's pejorative representation of Chinese when he requested that the film be withdrawn from circulation due to its racial slurs (259). Although, as Colin Browne reports, the film was seized by the British Columbia Provincial Police, and a shot of a Chinese man with a knife in his back was excised from the print projected in British Columbia, no other material 'which might be considered offensive to the Chinese community was discovered or eliminated by the censor' (259). The Consul's complaints about the film's representation of Chinatowns as 'the repositories of dark, sinister secrets' went unheeded by white authorities (259), probably owing to the cultural currency these white myths of the Chinese had in a white community that, as Anderson argues, invented Chinatown and its sinister secrets.

Anderson's critique of the 'twin ideas of *Chinese* and *Chinatown*, of race and place' maintains that Chinatown is a white European idea, that, like the category of race, has been 'an idea with remarkable social force and material effect – one that for more than a century has shaped and justified the practices of powerful institutions toward it and toward people of Chinese origin' (1994, 225). The social and material effect of Chinese and Chinatown as racialized categories of people and place is registered in *Secrets of Chinatown*, a signifying system predicated on the tropes of what Edward Said calls Orientalism. For Said Orientalism is 'a style of thought based upon an ontological and epistemological distinction made between "the Orient" and (most of the time) "the Occident" (Said 1979, 2). Orientalism is premised on the concept of exteriority, 'that is, on the fact that the Orientalist, poet, or scholar', or, in this case, film-maker, 'makes the Orient speak, describes the Orient, renders its mysteries plain for and to the West' (21). To illustrate exteriority, Said cites the dramatic immediacy of representation in Aeschylus's *The Persians*; however, his comments on this drama of antiquity prove instructive to an understanding of exteriority and Orientalism in *Secrets of Chinatown*: 'The dramatic immediacy of representation in *The Persians* obscures the fact that the audience is watching a highly artificial enactment of what a non-Oriental has made into a symbol for the whole Orient' (21). Newmeyer, the director, and Morton, the screenwriter, of *Secrets of Chinatown* are non-Orientals who make the Chinese community of Vancouver speak, who render the imagined secrets of an imagined Orient legible for and to the white viewer, while simultaneously exploiting the cinematic apparatus to obscure the artifice of this process. As Said's exteriority is at pains to make clear, the 'cultural discourse and exchange within a culture' that we see in cultural texts such as *Secrets of Chinatown* does not circulate ' "truth" but representations' (21). In *Secrets of Chinatown* these representations work concomitantly to naturalize the presence of white invader-settler culture in Canada while denaturalizing and denigrating as 'foreign' the presence of Chinese, a group that contributed the massive labour required to construct the white nation's master narrative of nation-building, the Canadian Pacific Railway. Although not a colonized people in the strictest understanding of the term, the Chinese in Canada constituted a people whose colonial construction as a diasporic and inexpensive labour pool servicing a British white invader-settler colony was determined by the racially hierarchized British colonization of China. This subjected them to the discursive practices of white Anglo-Canadian colonialism deployed to discipline a subaltern, colonized people.[25] Chineseness in *Secrets of Chinatown* is structured by the colonizing phallocentric white gaze of the Canadian nation, a gaze legislating the full cultural signification of patriarchal whiteness and delimiting the signification of Chinese to an ethnographic spectacle of miscegenation and homicidal primitivism as this is enunciated in Black Robe and his followers.

Unlike the previous ethnographic films we have looked at, *Secrets of Chinatown* is not a documentary but a feature fiction film of the commercial cinema. As such, I will argue that it falls under the category of teratology or the study of monstrosity that Rony has designated as the form taken by the Ethnographic in spectacular commercial cinema (1996, 160). As Rony writes, the Ethnographic, in the present context the Chinese Other, 'is seen as monstrous because he or she is human and yet radically different' (161). For the white nation, the Chinese register as human, yet their pigmentation and religious and cultural practices are perceived as radically Other. A film such as *Secrets of Chinatown* owes a large debt to the earlier American Fu Manchu films that constructed Chinese as monstrous embodiments of crime and evil.[26] In *Secrets of Chinatown* the ethnographic becomes monstrous at what Rony terms 'the very moment of visual appropriation', that is the very moment that Morton and Newmeyer attempt to make the Orient signify through their screen representation of Chinese (161). In the film's first scene Dr Lem Yet Sen, a Chinese man who has been 'waging a bitter war against the drug trade', is murdered in a Chinese restaurant after finding a medallion in his rice bearing the sign of Lao Tse. All of the film's murders and disappearances are preceded or followed by the appearance of this medallion, a representation of Chinese religious practice founded by Lao Tse, Taoism, that the film distorts into a blood-thirsty devil worship. Donegal Dawn refers to Lao Tse as 'the father of a strange devil worship'. Sen, the only non-monstrous Chinese in the film, is destroyed by what a series of shots and reverse shots constructs as a mysterious conspiracy of Chinatown and the 'heathen' religion of Lao Tse. The narrative cuts between medium shots of Sen to individual medium shots of three Chinese men who are in darkness and partially hidden, one by a door, another by a coat rack and the third just a disembodied head in a fedora passing by a dark window (Figures 2.7–2.9). As Sen gets up to leave, a cut is made to a medium shot of a hand throwing a knife, followed by a cut back to Sen clutching his back and crumpling in a heap on the floor. The composition of the shots obscures the full image of the conspirators in shadow and behind set and props, signifying the unknowable and murderous secrets of Chinatown that the film narrative will 'illuminate'. The Black Robe himself and his followers are cloaked, not surprisingly, in black robes, their heads and faces obscured by black hoods and veils. Through shot composition, lighting, costuming and the action of the plot the film's visual appropriation of Chinese constructs it as a monstrous unknowable category; Newmeyer and Morton translate the Chinese of Vancouver into the yellow peril of white racist mythology.[27] When sending Detective Doverscourt to investigate the murder of Dr Lem Yet Sen, the Police Commissioner cautions, 'you're going to bump into something unhealthy, something that won't stop at murder if necessary'. This dehumanized 'something' uttered by the commissioner stands in for the Chinese of Vancouver, who are represented at one point as an entity devouring, or consuming, whiteness. Following shots of Doverscourt being attacked by two Chinese men, a cut is made to the Commissioner, who says of Doverscourt's disappearance, '[It's] as if the earth had swallowed him up.' Unlike *Nation Building in Saskatchewan* or *Saving the Sagas* where Ukrainian or First Nations identities constitute signs placed under erasure by an white Anglo camera eye, *Secrets of Chinatown* represents whiteness as a sign placed under erasure by the Oriental gaze of Chinatown, thus rationalizing the film's penetration and interrogation of a Chinatown it produces as a teratological space. Although a fiction feature, *Secrets of Chinatown* played on very real attitudes of the white nation towards people of Chinese origin in Canada. Canadian Secretary of State Chapleau constructed Chinatown as 'an ulcer lodged like a piece of wood in the tissues of the human body, which unless treated must cause disease in the places around it and ultimately the whole body' (quoted in Anderson 1994, 230). This construction is very much alive in *Secrets of Chinatown* and in 1930s Canada. The monstrous Black Robe threatens to spread the disease of Chinatown – murder, devil worship, drug addiction and miscegenation – to white Vancouver in a cinematic fantasy of a racist imagination that white viewers in Victoria needed to be reminded was only fictional. According to Colin Browne's research on the film, Harry Hastings (also known as Harry Hewitson), the white actor who plays Black Robe/Chan Tow Ling prefaced each Victoria screening of the film with a reminder that it was purely fictional (1979, 259).

This threat, depicted in *Secrets of Chinatown*, of Chinatown spreading beyond its legislated borders into white physical and cultural space forms part of Rony's definition of the monstrous Ethnographic. For Rony the monster is both physically and cognitively threatening: 'its existence threatens cultural boundaries' (1996, 161). Not only does the Black Robe, the film's index for Chinese in Canada, consume the bodies and souls of white people, he also transgresses cultural boundaries through the opium trade and the threat of miscegenation invoked by his relationship with the white Zenobia. The Chinese restaurant in which we are first introduced to the white opium dealers Brandhma and the sea captain, and the Chinese curio shop in which we meet Zenobia (cross-dressed as Chinese), represent Chinese public spaces as portals facilitating incursions into or infections of white cultural space. When exposed to the 'black arts' of Chinatown, white cognitive abilities in the film narrative become clouded, they become subordinate to those of the Chinese Other. Brandhma, who has decided to co-operate with the police, is kidnapped and seduced by opium and the Black Robe's 'devil worship' to act as an agent of the Chinese Ethnographic monster in a scene set in a dungeon at Black Robe's Vancouver headquarters, the Temple of Lao Tse. A dishevelled Brandhma is pacing in his cell when he hears one of Black Robe's followers call him by a Hindu name and he walks to the door to hear a disembodied voice, in a very bad white approximation of a Chinese accent, say, 'Tonight you will win the favour of Lao Tse. You will do as you were commanded.' When he replies affirmatively, a disk is slid aside in the upper part of the door to reveal a hole through which a hand is thrust offering Brandhma a knife with a cigar full of opium tied to it (Figure 2.10). After grabbing the knife and

Figures 2.7–13 Secrets of Chinatown
(1935)

ingesting the opium, Brandhma, dressed in the hooded and veiled uniform of Black Robe's followers attempts to murder Robert Rande, who has come into the temple to rescue Zenobia. The film's contribution to the cultural construction of Chinese as abject, dehumanized, hidden, manipulators of whiteness against itself is enunciated in the iconography of this scene: the Chinese are represented metonymically in the death-dealing and drug-dealing hand of Chinatown that reaches across cultural boundaries to destroy whiteness. Despite the fact that opium was introduced to China by the British in the 1840s as part of the empire's campaign of colonization, in the white Western imagination it becomes an essentialist marker of Chinese identity.

What the film narrative and many white Canadians of the period viewed as the ultimate transgression of cultural boundaries, miscegenation – sexual relations between the monstrous male Other and the white woman – is also predicated, in *Secrets of Chinatown*, on the idea of a cognitive violence perpetrated by the Chinese through drugs and religion. The film narrative structures the presence of the white woman in Chinatown as unnatural: she is under a spell induced by opium and the Black Robe's 'devil worship', which only a white man, Robert Rande, can break. Zenobia's presence in the Chinese curio shop, dressed in a Mandarin-style jacket, coupled with her refusal to speak with him bewilders her would-be suitor Rande, who asks, 'But why, I don't understand, you're a white girl, what are you doing in a place like this?' (Figure 2.11). At this point Zenobia is unable to answer or look at Rande; he is displaced by the monstrous Ethnographic. As Rande speaks with Zenobia, a Chinese man appears at the window of the curio shop outside of Rande's range of vision, distracting her. A series of shots, however, provides the audience with the answer to Rande's question. A cut away from the medium shot of Rande, Zenobia and the Chinese man in the window to a medium close-up of the man in the window is followed by a cut to Zenobia and then back to the man to indicate subjective camera from her perspective. The subjective camera shot of the Chinese man then dissolves into a medium close-up shot of the hooded and veiled Black Robe (Figure 2.12) disciplining Zenobia not to interact with Rande. When Rande turns to see what has interrupted Zenobia's field of vision, she takes this opportunity to disappear into the curtains behind the counter. Rande's attempt to extend his looking behind the counter, furtively seeking the disappeared white woman, is met with a flying knife, the film's phallic sign for Chinese masculinity, that cuts across his line of vision before plunging into the wooden counter top within inches of his face (Figure 2.13). The white phallocentric symbolic order is disturbed. The white man is threatened with a symbolic castration by the Other, while the white woman is stolen out from under the white male gaze and transformed into the fetish object of the male Chinese gaze. As we learn later in the narrative, Zenobia is now the Eye of Lao Tse, the earthly vessel through which the desires of Lao Tse's 'devil worship' are channelled to his male followers and as such is unavailable to white men. Thus, the film narrative assuages white male fears that a white woman might choose to live in Chinatown with a Chinese man; she is in Chinatown with a Chinese man because, in the words of Rande, 'she is sick'. Zenobia's refusal to abandon the Chinese criminal for the white hero is rationalized for the audience and Rande when she tells him: 'I am not a woman, my soul is gone.' The film narrative tells its audience that only a cognitively impaired white non-woman would live in Chinatown. Detective Donegal Dawn's response to Rande's news that he has met a girl in Chinatown is simultaneously one of sarcastic distaste and racist humour: 'Well, that's a blessing. What is she, a blonde or a brunette?' Rande's response, 'yes', indicating the girl's whiteness, confounds Dawn: 'Oh, my dear fellow, you're not well.'

This fictional representation of white male Canadian anxieties around threats of miscegenation reflects the very real anxieties felt by whites in Vancouver towards mixed race relationships between Chinese men and white women. This is a very old fear perpetuated by the racist attitudes of such Canadian luminaries as the country's first Prime Minister, Sir John A. Macdonald, who, while he was content to exploit Chinese labour for the railway, did so only under the premise that the Chinese would never be permitted to settle in Canada permanently (Anderson 1991, 55). Macdonald's fear of permanent Chinese settlement is a very specific one, the spectre of miscegenation creating a degenerate 'mongrel race' on Canada's Pacific coast (quoted in Anderson 1991). No doubt Macdonald was basing his opinion on the nineteenth-century 'science' of race. Nineteenth-century theories of race such as the monogenetic argument figuring the white male as the pure origin of man and all other races as evidence of deterioration, or the polygenetic argument positing that different races were in fact different species, had a cultural resonance, not only for Sir John but also for the white nation in early twentieth-century British Columbia and for the writer and director of *Secrets of Chinatown*.[28] The White Canada Association, formed in 1929, followed a similarly anti-Chinese position, working to 'prevent further Oriental penetration in British Columbia, and [to] reduce the present menace to our national life' (quoted in Anderson 1991, 158). The white patriarchy's fear of miscegenation, and its attendant undermining of a white nation, is made very clear in infantilizing legislation designed to 'protect' the white woman from what it constructed as the monstrous Ethnographic, the lascivious Chinese man. The Factory, Shop and Office Building Act of 1914 prohibited the employment of white women by Chinese men in any 'factory, restaurant or laundry'. Similarly, the 1919 Women and Girls Protection Act outlawed white women's employment on Oriental restaurant premises.[29] This statute was enforced only sporadically until 1935 when Chief Constable Foster invoked it on 'moral grounds' against three Chinese restaurants. Foster rationalized his action in racist claims that young, inexperienced white waitresses were 'induced . . . to prostitute themselves with Chinese' and that the majority of Vancouver's known prostitutes had initiated their careers of vice through early association with Chinese cafés (Anderson 1991, 160).

The cinematic representation of miscegenation represents the relationship between Zenobia and the Chinese as horrific; the story of a white woman held against her will, the idol of a cult of devil-worshipping, opium-addicted Chinese dressed in black robes and veils bears more than a passing resemblance to the horror genre. Rony's conceptualization of the monstrous Ethnographic forges a relationship between the expedition film and the horror film, arguing that 'the archetypal narrative of many forms of ethnographic cinema, especially the expedition film, mirrors that of the horror film' (Rony 1996, 163). Like most films, *Secrets of Chinatown* is not generically pure: it is a detective crime drama shot through with elements of both the horror and expedition film. The intersection of the Hollywood horror film and the expeditionary ethnographic film can be located in narrative process. Stephen Neale's articulation of narrative process in the horror film as 'marked by a search for that specialized form of knowledge which will enable human characters to comprehend and control that which simultaneously embodies and causes its [*sic*] "trouble"', recalls the narrative process of the Barbeau expedition in *Saving the Sagas* where the white 'human' nation gains a knowledge of the decline of the 'primitive' First Nations, thereby solving the 'trouble' indigenous Others pose to the formation of a white Canadian nation (Neale 1980, 22). White patriarchal fears of displacement by the Oriental Other structure the horror created around miscegenation in *Secrets of Chinatown*, and initiate the expedition that is mounted by the police department to gain a specialized knowledge of, and destroy, the Chinese Other, thereby preempting miscegenation and restoring the white phallocentric symbolic order of Canadian nation.

The horror and detective genres collide on the site of the Black Robe's horrific crime: the Chinese 'monster's' theft of the white woman; the white womb upon which the (re)production of the white nation is dependent is stolen by the Other. As I have argued in the previous chapter, the role of the white woman in early twentieth-century Canadian nationalism is, for the most part, limited to the reproduction of the white male settler, in the rhetoric of hegemonic whiteness, the universal signifier for humanity.[30] To return to Žižek's Lacanian conceptualization of fantasy's relation to formations of nationalism, the white woman, in *Secrets of Chinatown*, stands in for materialized enjoyment, she becomes the national *thing* around which white men organize their collective enjoyment. In Žižek's terms, Zenobia is a traumatic, real object fixing the desire of a white male collectivity, she is something that is simultaneously inaccessible to, yet taken by the Other. 'What is at stake in ethnic tensions is always the possession of the national Thing: the "other" wants to steal our enjoyment' (1992, 165). The nationalist fantasy of the Other's theft of white male Canadian enjoyment in *Secrets of Chinatown* suggests a competitive, triangulated relay of looks (white men (Dawn, Rand, spectator) – Zenobia – Chinese men) that can be elucidated in a close reading of the expeditionary detective work taken on by Rande and Dawn as agents of the police department.

The narrativization of the detective expedition revolves around a racial and sexual imbalance in looking relations producing visual pleasure. The film's establishing shots are designed to disorientate the white male spectator's viewing experience, obstructing and deferring visual pleasure. The *faux*-Chinese music of the soundtrack during the title sequence, the pan shot of Chinatown's buildings covered with signs bearing Chinese characters (Figure 2.14), the screen caricature of Mandarin that fills the background of the soundtrack during the interior shots of the restaurant, and the enigmatic appearance of the medallion followed by Sen's murder, all of these elements frustrate the white male viewer's ability to produce meaning and derive pleasure. It is only when Donegal Dawn enters the frame that a definitive knowledge of the Chinese as evil or monstrous begins to unfold, and with it a sense of visual pleasure. For Dawn's entry into the narrative affords the white male spectator the opportunity to project his look on to his like, his screen surrogate Dawn, the white male protagonist who controls events in the film through his powers of deduction.[31] However, before this opportunity for visual pleasure occurs, the white male spectator is subjected to visual unpleasure, the surveillant look of the Chinese Other that threatens abduction and murder of the white man and his agents.[32] This mode of looking becomes part of the film's visual iconography signifying Chinese and is first deployed in the opening scene at the restaurant in the previously discussed series of shots and reverse shots between the white man's agent, Sen, and his assassins. Once Sen has been dealt with, Rande, Doverscourt and Brandhma are subjected to the threatening surveillant look of Chinese men and subsequently kidnapped. Although the Police Commissioner is also watched by followers of the Black Robe, he remains, thanks to Dawn's powers of perception, secure. These images of a threatening Chinese field of vision suggest a racial imbalance in looking: the white man is subject to the disciplining gaze of the Chinese man. However, this is a false economy of looking deployed by the film narrative to conceal the active white phallocentric looking of the camera and the spectator that determines the Chinese man as abject monster and the white man as human in *Secrets of Chinatown*. It is also important to remember that male Chinese looking at Zenobia emanates from the imaginations of white men, Newmeyer and Morton. In this sense Chinese looking in *Secrets of Chinatown* is a projection of white sexuality on to Chinese as a way for whites simultaneously to represent and dissociate themselves from their own 'dark' desires.[33]

Detective Donegal Dawn's knowledge of the Chinese Other introduces a discourse of white male power, knowledge and pleasure into the film narrative. As Dawn informs Rande, he 'knows these Chinese'. Dawn shares his knowledge with the spectator and the Commissioner, in part, by passing for the monstrous Other. The curious scene in which Dawn attends his meeting with the Commissioner in black face, disguised as an 'Oriental', is important to the film narrative's attempts to restore the phallocentric white symbolic order disturbed by the Black Robe's looking at whiteness, and the 'theft' of Zenobia. Passing as Other, Dawn will become the eyes of white Vancouver or the white spectator, eyes that return the threatening looking of Chinese men and see through the 'mysterious Orient' to apprehend and solve the monstrous secrets of Chinatown. In his passing for Other, Dawn assumes what Dyer calls 'the position as the universal signifier for

Figures 2.14–20 Secrets of Chinatown
(1935)

humanity. He encompasses all the possibilities for human existence, the darkness and the light' (1997, 28). The darkness of Dawn's makeup, black turban and cape, here associated with the dark, the nefarious 'nature' of the Chinese Other, is, however, potentially confusing in terms of its visual signification (Figure 2.15). Morton and Newmeyer's concept of 'Oriental' is fairly vague and dependent on an audience's equally vague and naive understanding of 'Oriental' as anything non-white, non-Christian and non-Western. Only within the closed system of the film's racist and simplistic iconography of 'Oriental' can Dawn's ridiculous attempt to approximate Chinese register successfully. The minimal accoutrements of difference required to transform Dawn into 'Oriental' reinforce the film's notion of the white man's easy mastery of and superiority over the Other. The pleasure the white man derives from passing as Other, for being both dark and light, is enunciated in the death threat Dawn makes to the Commissioner while cloaked as Oriental. In Oriental drag, and with an Oriental accent, Dawn suggests that the Commissioner will soon be visiting the dead Dr Lem Yet Sen. Immediately following the utterance of these comments, Dawn removes his Oriental accoutrements (excepting makeup) and laughs at the joke he has played of the Commissioner's fear of the Other, a fear dependent on and perpetuated by a white performance of a white stereotype of Chinese. Ironically, Dawn's self-conscious performance of the Chinese Other can be read allegorically as a sign for the film narrative's white production of Chinese through costuming and lighting. A Caucasian actor, Harry Hastings, who becomes the white fantasy of the monstrous Oriental Other through makeup, costuming, lighting and dialogue, plays the role of the Black Robe/Chan Tow Ling. Following his successful passing as Oriental for the Commissioner, Dawn holds forth on Chinese religious practices, revealing the significance of the Lao Tse medallion, the film's harbinger of death and disappearance: 'It seems they didn't bow down to the magic eye. Lao Tse, the ancient seer, the father of a strange devil worship. He lived on the side of a mountain where they came to worship. Lao Tse, it seems they didn't bow down to the magic eye.' Drawing on the historical secrecy of Taoism, the film pathologizes the Chinese as devil worshippers by wilfully distorting Taoist teachings into the sinister ritualistic practices of the Occult.[34] Moreover, within the value system of *Secrets of Chinatown* Chinese religion is dismissed as holding no intellectual or spiritual value; it is merely, according to Dawn, 'a great screen of mysticism', a 'black magic' organized by 'a sinister evil mind' to 'cover up some ghastly traffic in human souls'.

Active white male looking at the passive (because structured as monster by a white camera eye) Chinese man is an aspect of what Rony calls ' "seeing anthropology" that involves a search for the visual evidence of the pathological' (1996, 161). Once Dawn is on the case, his forays into Chinatown strip back the layers of this (in Dawn's terms) 'hidden world' to reveal visual evidence of the 'pathological' Chinese. In the Temple of Lao Tse, Dawn and, through his visual agency, the viewer see a room full of hooded and robed Chinese chanting, and bowing down to an idol of Lao Tse that dissolves into the figure of Zenobia (Figures

2.16–2.18). The horror of the scene – the white woman subjected to the looking of the Oriental Other – is registered through reaction shots showing Dawn recoil in shock. Rande, the film's white male hero who rescues Zenobia from the monstrous Other, also serves as, in Mulvey's terms, 'the bearer of the look of the spectator' (1989b, 20). Looking through Rande, the spectator sees Zenobia as a fetish object desired by the Other. However, it is also through Rande that the spectator learns the sinister secret of her soul's enslavement to the Other, sees the Other unmasked and destroyed, and subsequently sees the restoration of the white woman as the white man's object of desire. The restoration of the white phallocentric symbolic order is initiated when Rande disappears with Zenobia into the 'hidden world' of Chinatown through the grotto housing the idol of Lao Tse. Thus Rande inserts a white male presence into the space of the Chinese Other and challenges the Other's power over the white woman. When he is in the 'hidden world' Rande pretends he has been assimilated into the ways of Lao Tse and passes for one of the cult. Interestingly enough, only the heroic white man is represented as strong enough to resist the 'black magic' of Lao Tse, while criminal white men such as Brandhma and white women such as Zenobia prove to be weaker beings who cannot resist the spell of the Other. The very presence of a white man breaks the spell of the monstrous Chinese Other, and Zenobia soon tells Rande: 'I am awake now, you have broken the spell. I love you.' Shortly after recovering the white woman and reinstalling her in the symbolic order as the materialized enjoyment of white male looking, Rande unmasks the Black Robe as trusted police operative Chan Tow Ling, confirming the film narrative's racist construction of the Chinese as a monstrous infection of the national white body. Surrounded by Dawn and the police who have arrived to rescue Rande and Zenobia, the Black Robe swallows poison. As he dies, he makes a speech of contrition honouring Donegal Dawn as a 'brilliant man' and the white police force as 'very kind'. Visual pleasure here is derived from the knowledge of the Other gained by the white male detective work that results in his unmasking, his veneration of his white oppressors and his destruction. The very last shot of the film – Zenobia and Rande, kissing in a recessed grotto behind an altar – refers back to the earlier scene in the Vancouver temple where the grotto housed the idol of Lao Tse through which Zenobia materialized for the visual pleasure of Chinese men. Here the statue of Lao Tse, and with it the threat of miscegenation, is displaced by the white heterosexual couple (Figure 2.20). What the film misrepresents as the racial imbalance of Oriental men looking at a white woman is eradicated in these final shots where the white phallocentric phantasy is realized and a vicious visual pleasure produced through the death of the Other, and the re-establishment of patriarchal hegemony over white women. As Rande tells the Commissioner and Dawn in the film's last lines of dialogue, the white man has 'things well in hand'. Entertainment or (after Dyer) the social construction of happiness in this film is enacted through the death of the Chinese Other. In this sense the narrative of *Secrets of Chinatown* reflects Rony's contention that the archetypal narrative forms of the horror film are related structurally to ethnographic cinema narratives where the monster first appears (the murder of Sen), is discovered by human protagonists (Dawn and Rande) and ends with a confrontation between human and monster where the monster dies (Rande and the Black Robe) (1996, 163).

In *Secrets of Chinatown* the phallocentric white Anglo-Canadian nation is predicated both on the castrated (because looked-at) white woman, Zenobia, and on the raced Other, who is constructed as less than human, less than the white man. But *how* do we see Donegal Dawn, Rande and castrated Zenobia as *normal* in relation to the Chinese as *pathological*? What visual codes structure our vision of white male, white female and Other? Principally, the *mise-en-scène* devices of lighting, costuming and set design structure *how* spectators see racial and gender alterities on film. Cinema, as a medium of light, privileges a hierarchical and ideological representation of whiteness as humanity through chiaroscuro (from the Italian *chiaro* = bright, *oscuro* = dark), the composition of light and dark in a shot (Dyer 1997, 83, 115). As Dyer argues, the translucence of film, the projection of light through celluloid 'permits a construction of the human person that discriminates between those who have a large amount of light shining through them and those who have next to none – the radiant white face and the opaque black one' (1997, 115). Traditionally, radiant white light is associated with enlightenment and superiority, while darkness is associated with base values and an absence of morality in western visual culture. With the exception of the Caucasian actor playing Chan Tow Ling, who is lit by the same overhead high-key lighting as Zenobia and Doverscourt in the curio shop scene, light does not fall on Chinese and whites evenly in *Secrets of Chinatown*. Light does not shine through the spectre of the Chinese man who threatens Zenobia through the window of the curio shop, just as it does not shine through the hooded and robed members of Black Robe's followers who stand in for Chinese. Dawn (when he is not in black face), Rande and the Commissioner, however, although dressed in dark suits are lit from above in most scenes and their faces are luminescent with light. The spaces of the Chinese Other – the basement temple in Vancouver and Black Robe's cave hideout on Vancouver Island – are constructed through lighting and set design as dark subterranean repositories of evil inhabited by black robed figures whose costumes reflect very little light. By contrast, Zenobia, the stolen white woman imported into these dark spaces, glows with radiant light (Figure 2.19). High-key lighting, and a highly reflective, white bridal-like 'Oriental' costume produce in the figure of Zenobia what Dyer calls the glow of white women in cinema that signifies ethereal qualities and a superior moral position that, in the case of Zenobia, threatens to be compromised by her placement in 'Oriental' darkness (Dyer 1997, 122, 130). Zenobia's white full-length gown and 'Oriental' headdress resemble a western wedding ensemble and suggest that as the Eye of Lao Tse she is wedded to darkness: however, her embrace of Rande in the film's final shot dispatches this spectre of miscegenation and affirms reproduction of the white nation. Zenobia's head-to-toe luminescence marks and naturalizes her as the woman displayed; she is produced to be looked at by the determining gaze of white men. *Secrets of Chinatown* represents the non-white subject only in terms of its function to the white subject. In this film the monstrous non-white subject, Black Robe/Chan Tow Ling, played by a white actor, is clearly a means of producing a knowledge of the white self as superior to white phantasies of the 'Oriental' Other.[35]

Of Japanese Descent: An Interim Report

Not unlike Chinese Canadians, the Japanese in Canada were represented historically by white Canadians as a threat to the white body of the nation. Public discourse racialized the Japanese body, transforming it into a loathsome stereotype designed to produce fear in white men. In the early 1900s the Japanese body was dehumanized by the British Columbia press as a 'machine' requiring less sustenance and pay than the labouring bodies of white men, and therefore a threat that could displace the white labouring body (as quoted in Adachi 1991, 65). Newspaper editorials, such as this from the *Daily Province* (9 September 1907), promulgated the rhetoric of the yellow peril consuming whiteness: 'We are all of the opinion that this province must be a white man's country . . . We do not wish to look forward to a day when our descendants will be dominated by Japanese or Chinese, or any colour but their own . . . We are an outpost of the Empire, and that outpost we have to hold against all others' (quoted in Adachi 1991, 63). The Reverend H. W. Fraser, in a public speech that Ken Adachi suggests was instrumental in inciting the violent anti-Japanese riot of 7 September 1907, raised the spectre of the 'pulpit', a sign of the white Christian nation, 'in the hands of the Japanese' and pleaded for a 'White Canada' (Adachi 1991, 63). The riot of 1907 adumbrates the hostility directed towards Canadians of Japanese descent following Japan's attack on Pearl Harbor in 1941. At this point, however, a virulent white racism didn't manifest itself just in newspaper editorials and random acts of violence but in racist Orders in Council, state legislation that stripped Japanese Canadians of their human rights, revoked their citizenship, confiscated and liquidated their property, forcibly removing them to internment camps in the interior of British Columbia in the name of national security.[36] National security in this context is a signifier for a racist phantasy of a white nation predicated upon the containment and subordination of racial difference. Japanese Canadians threatened the security of this white nationalist phantasy, they did not pose a threat to the security of the allied war effort.[37]

What had been posited by white racist public discourses as the problem of Japanese Canadians is 'solved', temporarily, by Orders in Council removing them from the terrain of the national. However, the end of the war renders the 'solution' untenable by abrogating the 'threat to national security' rationale and raising human rights questions sparked by the death camps of Nazi Germany. In August 1945, the NFB and the Canadian government's Department of Labour issued a propaganda film – *Of Japanese Descent: An Interim Report* (O. C. Burritt) – that sanitizes the fascistic racism practised by white Canada while continuing to stoke the white nation's racist insecurities through a documentary reframing Japanese Canadians as a dangerous problem to be solved. Under the guise of documentary realism – Grierson's creative factuality – *Of Japanese Descent* provides a visual historiography rationalizing the state's Orders in Council while rehabilitating internment camp as relocation camp. In the evolutionary paradigm of the ethnographic film, *Of Japanese Descent* represents evacuation and internment as a necessary relocation of Japanese Canadians to a healthier environment facilitating their improvement through assimilation. The film enacts this narrative trajectory by delineating what it constructs as essential differences between Japanese Canadians and Anglo-Canadians as these are articulated by images associating whiteness with hygiene and progress and Japaneseness with squalor and arrested development. Other sequences emphasize the value of Japanese labour, and the Anglo-Canadian education Japanese Canadians are receiving in the camps. *Of Japanese Descent* circulated at a critical time when the King government was anxious to create a receptive response to its policy of dispersing Japanese Canadians east of the Rockies.

The film's narrative is structured, in part, by a white male voice-over track that silences Japanese Canadians by appropriating them as signifiers in a white nationalist discourse naming them as the enemy of white Canadian nation. Establishing medium shots of Japanese businesses are interpreted for the white viewer as a threat to Canada and the allied war effort: 'But the outbreak of war brought to new prominence the fact that nearly all of the 23,000 [Japanese Canadians] lived, worked and had their small businesses inside the Western number-one defense zone.' Japanese Canadians are the observed, the spoken-for, in *Of Japanese Descent*; the status of speaking subjects is withheld from Japanese Canadians who are not interviewed but transformed into material to be mastered and organized by O. C. Burritt, the NFB and the Ministry of Labour. In the film's second sequence the NFB's discourse on the Other fractures the Japanese-Canadian community along the lines of hygiene, stating that while 'some had adopted Canadian ways and lived a healthy life in good surroundings', others 'lived crowded into houses where health conditions were below the standard'. The standard here is associated with 'Canadian ways' and the narrative's assumption that white Canada holds a monopoly on health. During the voice-over long shots of modest but respectable suburban homes are displaced by long shots of ramshackle homes and apartments. As this sequence continues it constructs most Japanese Canadians as abject figures living in inhuman conditions. Medium shots of the weather-beaten and dilapidated buildings that comprise a Japanese-Canadian fishing village are interpreted for the viewer as 'buildings entirely unsuitable for human use' where a 'very large proportion' of the 23,000 lived. This voice-over elides information that might explain the disrepair of the buildings, notably that owing to evacuation and internment they have been uninhabited for three years. Burritt (the director) cuts from shots of the deteriorating buildings to close-ups of filth and debris floating in stagnant water, images that are exploited by the voice-over to 'document' what the film purports to be the sorry state of Japanese-Canadian living before evacuation and internment: 'Sewage disposal was elementary in the extreme. And the unsanitary conditions resulting were the cause of much poor health.' This particular representation is in line with how Rony sees the construction of the Ethnographic on film as lacking civilization and technology (1996, 7). The improvement of Japanese Canadians through evacuation and internment is emphasized by Burritt in a striking jump cut from the close-up shot of filth and debris in the fishing village to a brightly lit sequence of shots depicting the Rocky Mountains and crystalline mountain waters, sites of internment. The cut is narrated by the voice-over track: 'In 1942 it was decided that all people of Japanese racial origin should be removed from the coastal defense zone to new locations in the interior of British Columbia and other parts of the Dominion.' The violence to the Japanese-Canadian community enacted by this decision and registered in Joy Kogawa's novel *Obasan* (1983), Michael Fukushima's animated film *Minoru Memory of Exile* (1993), Anne Wheeler's *The War Between Us* (1995) and Mieko Ouchi's *By this Parting* (1998) is repressed in *Of Japanese Descent* by Burritt's transition from what he represents as the unhealthy, 'inhuman' conditions of Japanese Canadians before internment to the healthy 'human' conditions Japanese Canadians enjoy after their imprisonment. The voice-over continues to stress the health benefits of what it insists are relocated and not interned people. New Denver is described as one of 'the healthiest spots' with an excellent beach 'available for swimming and sunning with beneficial affects to health'. In this way, white Canada's undemocratic human rights crime against its citizens of Japanese racial origin is re-visioned as a benevolent intercession providing salvation for Japanese Canadians. Consider the voice-over's narration of shots of smiling tuberculosis patients in various stages of recovery at a specially built sanitarium:

> Relocation has resulted in an improvement in the general health level. Before the evacuation from the coast, tuberculosis was known to exist among the Japanese and medical measures against it were carried out. However, the true extent of the widespread ravages of the disease went unreported to the proper authorities until the relocation. Then so many cases were detected it was necessary to build this sanitarium to fight tuberculosis alone. In addition regular hospitals were built or expanded. Thus, quite a large number of the brightest men and women will have a chance for life that they would not otherwise have had.

Here internment is a corollary for development. Shortly after these references to Asian disease and white health, the film narrative refers back to the unsanitary sewage disposal of the fishing village that existed when Japanese Canadians had freedom of movement by offering evidence of the 'improvements', such as the construction of a septic tank, that are available to Japanese Canadians under internment. *Of Japanese Descent* is organized tropologically around what Roy Miki refers to as 'the regulatory lexicon of "yellow peril"'. The film demonizes

71

the 'Asian' body as an object that could potentially infect the white body of the nation: 'The demonization of the "asian" body, a white supremacist projective field of anxieties and animosities, evoked the forces of mis-rule threatening to "mongrelize" the white body of "civilization"' (Miki 1998, 185). *Of Japanese Descent* represents the Japanese-Canadian Other as deliberately withholding information pertinent to the health of the white nation; it is only after relocation or internment that the white authorities detect the 'diseased' 'Asian' body and neutralize the Japanese-Canadian 'threat' to white Canada. This propagandist rhetoric supports the exclusionist ideology promulgated by prominent politicians such as federal Cabinet Minister Ian Mackenzie, who promised to resign if his government allowed the Japanese to remain in British Columbia (Adachi 1991, 292–3).

Ernst van Alphen writes that under nationalism descriptions of the Other, such as those of Japanese Canadians found in *Of Japanese Descent* are 'phantasms of the potential enemy, not interpretations of a real one in any sense' (Van Alphen 1991, 2–3). The title of Ken Adachi's important study, *The Enemy that Never Was*, reflects this phantasmic quality of nationalist alterity, as does Prime Minister Mackenzie King's 1944 admission that 'no person of Japanese race born in Canada has been charged with any act of sabotage or disloyalty during the years of war' (quoted in Adachi 1991, 276). Produced at the height of John Grierson's influence at the NFB, *Of Japanese Descent* is a Griersonian documentary *par excellence*. It attempts to predispose and shape the citizen subject's sphere of understanding to the Canadian state's policies of evacuation, internment and dispersal; it does not attempt to represent Japanese Canadians, only enemy aliens, spectral figures of Japanese descent. *Of Japanese Descent* is the type of 'propaganda' or 'public information' that Grierson described as one of 'the most powerful forms of directive statesmanship' (quoted in Morris 1987b, 38). Grierson goes on to write that in propaganda 'the place of the educator and the artist in society changes entirely to one of definite *social constructiveness*' (emphasis added). Therefore the phantasm of the abject, diseased, alien of Japanese racial origin is invented, is in Grierson's terms part of 'the patterns you put upon events and the patterns which, so to speak, you impose on the spectator's mind' (quoted in Morris 1987b, 38–9).

In a 1940 essay on film, war and propaganda, Grierson maintains that there are 'two sides to propaganda, and two sides to the film at war':

> The film can be mobilized to give the news and the story of a great historical event. In that sense our aim was to use it for all it was worth to secure the present. But my hope has been that the film would also be used more and more to secure the future and serve the still wider needs of people of Canada. War films, yes, but more films too, about everyday things of life, the values, the ideals which make life worth living. I hoped that we could use the film to give visual significance to the words of the Canadian Prime Minister [King] when he said that the spirit of mutual

tolerance and respect for fundamental rights are the foundation of the
national unity of Canada.

In that way I have thought to rescue from these barren days of trouble
something we could hand to the future.

(Grierson 1966, 226)

Of Japanese Descent embraces both of these notions of securing the present and
the future, though probably not along the lines Grierson was consciously thinking in 1940. The film tells the story of a war on the home front against what it
constructs as an enemy alien to secure the present and future of Canada for white
Canadians exclusively. The everyday values, the ideals of Canada Grierson refers
to, are distilled here as a unifying white nationalism that is predicated on the
manufacturing, persecution and disenfranchisement of a raced Other. This is the
visual significance given to Prime Minister Mackenzie King's hypocritical
gesturing towards 'mutual tolerance and the respect for fundamental rights', a
tolerance and respect regulated by race.

Of Japanese Descent is part of an ISA, the NFB, that interpellates Canadian
national subjects as white English speakers and disciplines them to see Japanese
Canadians as 'less than' Canadian. The film provides at least three categories of
representation where the Japanese Canadian is a figure estranged from full
national belonging: the enemy alien discussed above, a source of cheap labour
and an approximation of the white Anglo-Canadian national subject. Shots of
Japanese-Canadian men logging and working in a lumber mill are narrated by a
voice-over track explaining the importance of Japanese-Canadian labour to the
Canadian war effort: 'With the country at war the demand for wood products in
industry and the armed services grew beyond all peace-time levels. Thus, the
small number of operations near the various centres were expanded into a full-
scale business, the lumber produced helping to supply the country's war-time
needs.' The narrative goes on to represent this employment as a service provided
for Japanese Canadians, the type of work that along with highway construction
keeps these men 'occupied'. The paternalism of the voice-over track reduces
these Japanese Canadians to troublesome children who require supervision. This
ideological work represses the fact that these men are incarcerated against their
will, and that the overwhelming majority of them were in gainful employment
before the Canadian state terminated it with internment. Also elided from the
narrative are the economics of Japanese-Canadian labour. Fuel cutters were paid
22½–40 cents an hour and were required to purchase their own food and clothing from local merchants at what were usually higher prices than elsewhere
(Adachi 1991, 259).

The film's attempts to represent internment as a space where citizens of Japanese racial origin are transformed into loyal Canadians through assimilation is
undermined by the cautionary note it ends on. In a way not dissimilar to their
signification in Bird's film, Anglo-Canadian education and the uniform of the
Wolf Cubs and Boy Scouts become markers of the Canadian state's assimilating

discourse on the Other in *Of Japanese Descent*. Shots of schoolchildren are inter-preted for the viewer by the voice-over track: 'Education in the centres is carried on very much as it is in the rest of Canada.' A series of shots of the Tashme Wolf Cub pack and Boy Scout troop create a relationship between the uniform and the loyalty of the boys wearing it, visualizing them as Canadian subjects of the British Empire. Burritt cuts from a series of medium close-ups of boys in Scout uniforms to a series of extreme close-ups on uniform details such as the arm patch stating the name of the troop, 'Tashme 1' and the lettering over a boy's uniform pocket that reads 'Boy Scouts – Canada'. These images, followed by images of young men playing baseball and Canadian football, represent to the white viewer the detour through the Anglo-Canadian Other taken by the Japanese-Canadian male in the course of his 'Canadianization', his identification as Canadian. These shots work also to allay fears of an unassimilable Japanese cultural difference that might have been raised by an earlier sequence depicting women in kimonos practising a traditional Japanese dance honouring departed ancestors. This, the only visual irruption of Japanese cultural difference in the camps documented by Burritt, is neutralized, not only by the later shots of the Cubs, Scouts and athletes but by a cut from a medium close-up of two women dancing, which in turn cuts to a long shot of the Rockies and then back to two consecutive close-up shots of a Japanese paper lantern, one side emblazoned with the Union Jack, the other with the Rising Sun. The chain of signification established by this sequence of shots sug-gests a Canadianization of Japanese Canadians as British subjects by juxtaposing them to the Canadian Rocky Mountains and depicting the sign of British imperial authority, the Union Jack inscribed on a sign of traditional Japanese culture, the paper lantern. The film's subsequent closing shots and voice-over track, however, militate against a reading of the preceding shots of the Cubs, Scouts and athletes as signs for successful Canadianization, revealing this process to be only an approximation or mimicry of the Canadian national subject; Japanese racial origin remains written on the body and is reframed as a serious problem that remains unsolved. A series of medium long shots and medium shots of school-age Japanese-Canadian children are narrated to represent the future problem the Canadian state sees Japanese Canadians posing to Canadian nation-building: 'Like people all over the world there are the good, the bad, and the indifferent. The problem they represent has been solved only temporarily by the war. The ultimate solution will depend on the measure of careful understanding by all Canadians.' Despite apparent 'rehabilitation' of the 'enemy alien' through assimilation, the film ends on a cautionary and ominous note, constructing Japanese Canadians as an ongoing threat to a white Canadian social order.

Once again white Canadian nation in its attempt to isolate, assimilate and expel otherness from the white national body for ever alters that body. *Of Japanese Descent* is a discursive formation produced by an official national cinema, the NFB, that documents both the Japanese-Canadian presence and the failure of state legislation to erase that presence. Japanese Canadians constituted an insol-uble problem, for white nation-building in 1945, a matter of belonging to a national community that continued to be negotiated by the successful campaign for redress that resulted in the federal government's 1988 apology and reparation payments to surviving internees of the camps. The jeopardy in which racialized internment placed Japanese Canadians belonging to an imagined Canadian national community still resonates for Canadian film-makers such as Michael Fukushima, Mieko Ouchi and Anne Wheeler. All three film-makers produced films on the subject for national ISAs entrusted with representing the nation to itself, the NFB and the CBC, during the 1990s.

Historically, ethnographic cinema in Canada is part of a national cinema that has been deployed to construct racial and ethnic hierarchies of belonging to the nation. Those who are ethnographized by the nation's cinematic apparatus are set apart from the imagined national community of white Anglo Canada, or, in the case of *Of Japanese Descent*, expelled from it. Under the guise of education and entertainment Canadian ethnographic cinema laid down the co-ordinates of a white Anglo nation, offering spectators the vicious pleasure of consuming stereotypes of its cultural and racial Others.

3

PRODUCING A NATIONAL CINEMA

> National cinemas are simultaneously an aesthetic and produc-
> tion movement, a critical technology, a civic project of state, an
> industrial strategy and an international project formed in
> response to the dominant international cinemas (particularly
> but not exclusively Hollywood cinema).
>
> Tom O'Regan, *Australian National Cinema*

Previous chapters have engaged the civic project of an embryonic Canadian
national cinema, namely white Anglo-Saxon colonization or nation-building, and
addressed issues of aesthetics and production movements through ideological
readings of melodrama, ethnographic documentary and feature. This chapter will
grapple with the political economy of Canadian film production and the emergence of funding structures that supported, in the first instance, a bicultural
feature-film industry, and in the second more racially and culturally pluralist
fields of vision. The evolution of the state's funding of, and intervention in,
Canadian film production will be delineated in the context of British and
American hegemony, an economic dependency on the British and American
industries that undermined the development of a Canadian feature-film industry.

Although Ernest Shipman was busy producing such features as *Back to God's
Country* (David M. Hartford 1919), *The Man from Glengarry* (Henry MacRae
1922), and *The Critical Age* (*Glengarry School Days*) (Henry MacRae 1922), and
Canadian International Films produced the commercial and critical failure *Carry
On Sergeant* (Bruce Bairnsfather 1928) at a cost of $500,000, what semblance
there was of a feature film industry in Canada was in a state of dissolution in the
years following the First World War. The Dominion government's creation of the
Exhibits and Publicity Bureau in 1918 (the Canadian Government Motion Picture Bureau after 1923) locked Canada, for the most part, into the production of
documentaries promoting tourism and trade. What passed for the state's industrial strategy for Canadian film production emphasized the documentary at the
expense of the feature, a policy that would continue under Canada's first Film
Commissioner, John Grierson, when the Canadian Government Motion Picture
Bureau was absorbed by the National Film Board in 1941. Grierson's emphasis
on documentary was rewarded with the critical and commercial success the NFB
enjoyed during the Second World War with the *World in Action* and *Canada*

Carries On series. One postwar film produced towards the end of the *Canada Carries On* series, *Peoples of Canada* (Stanley Jackson 1947), is read here with reference to the National Film Act's remit to the Board 'to produce and distribute and to promote the production and distribution of films designed to interpret Canada to Canadians and to other nations' (quoted in Magder 1993, 52). The desire to produce fiction features, however, proved overwhelming to film-makers developing their craft, and in the early 1960s the NFB flirted briefly with feature-film production. Responding to pressure from commercial producers, and associations of professional film-makers, the Canadian state eventually broadened its industrial strategy to include feature-film production. The government created the Canadian Film Development Corporation in 1967 (Telefilm Canada after 1984), and developed funding structures such as government loans, subsidy, and tax deductions to facilitate investment in Canadian feature-film production. These measures provided the foundations for the emergence of two very different national cinemas: Québécois and Anglophone Canadian cinemas.

LEGISLATING A NATIONAL CINEMA

In Chapters 1 and 2 we looked at films produced by a variety of funding structures: private sector investment, corporate sponsorship and direct investment from the Canadian state. *Back to God's Country* was financed, in part, by Calgary investors who incorporated themselves as Canadian Photoplays in 1919 (Morris 1978, 105). Kenneth Bishop raised money for the production of *Secrets of China-town* by convincing British Columbians to invest in Commonwealth Productions (Morris 1978, 189). The CPR is a major funding structure for early Canadian film production, playing a role in which it stands in for the state to finance national film projects. *An Unselfish Love*, for example, is part of a campaign to attract immigrants from the United States for Canadian nation-building and colonization in Alberta, while *Saving the Sagas*, sponsored by the CPR and produced by its film subsidiary (Associated Screen News) for the National Museum of Canada, documents the 'disappearance' of the colonized First Nations who stand in the path of white nation-building. *Nation Building in Saskatchewan: The Ukrainians, Hot Ice: The Anatomy of Hockey. Canada's National Game* and *Of Japanese Descent: An Interim Report* are funded by direct investment from state agencies, the Saskatchewan Department of Education, the Canadian Government Motion Picture Bureau and the National Film Board of Canada respectively. Following the First World War, government-sponsored documentary films promoting tourism and trade, as well as industrial shorts, comprised the vast majority of Canadian film production.

Unlike Britain, France, Germany and the United States, which tabled and implemented legislation in the 1920s to assist and protect the development of feature-film production, Canada failed to take action in these areas. Peter Morris argues that Canada's lack of a centralized studio system and the federal and provincial governments' failure, in the 1920s, to 'legislate effective protection and support for the production, distribution, or exhibition branches of the industry' arrested the development of a Canadian feature-film industry (1978, 238). Moreover, the 1920s marked the American industry's vertical integration; the maximizing of profits and control of the market through corporate ownership of production, distribution and exhibition. This made it very difficult for Canadian independents to secure distribution and exhibition in a domestic distribution and exhibition system that was dominated by monopolistic United States interests. As Ted Magder notes, however, there was not a broad-based popular Canadian interest in developing features at this time. Many Canadians profited from the government's failure to introduce protectionist legislation. The main concern of Canadian exhibitors and theatre owners closely allied with Hollywood was 'ensuring a stable supply of popular films; the national origin or cultural content of the films they exhibited was of little consequence from their perspective' (Magder 1993, 25). Another major obstacle to feature production was the nature of the Canadian domestic market: small and scattered, it could not support a profit-making feature-film industry, therefore the prohibitive expense of foreign distribution would have been necessary for financial success (Magder 1993, 26).

The foundations of Canadian film policy are utilitarian: they do not engage the art of cinema so much as they exploit its communicative function to develop trade and commerce. The Canadian Government Motion Picture Bureau (founded in 1918 as the Exhibits and Publicity Bureau), the world's first state-sponsored production unit, was 'designed to be a very important adjunct towards the development of Canadian trade'. Sir George Foster, architect of the Exhibits and Publicity Bureau, envisioned the cinematic representation of Canada's resources as 'an inducement to capital to come to this country' (quoted in Magder 1993, 28). Unfortunately, by the mid-1930s the CGMPB was in trouble; the quality of its productions had deteriorated, as had its distribution network, while the onset of the depression first froze the Bureau's budget to $75,000 and then cut it to $45,000 per annum (Magder 1993, 50).[1] Canada's largest privately owned production company, Associated Screen News, was, like the CGMPB, engaged solely in the production of non-fiction shorts (27). Most of the features viewed by Canadian audiences were from Britain or Hollywood. In the 1930s public debate about Canadian film culture centred more on what was perceived by commentators as the disturbing preference of Canadian audiences for American films over Empire or British productions than it did on the concept of domestic production which was, for the most part, dismissed as financially reckless.[2] James A. Cowan, writing in *MacLean's Magazine*, declared that Canadians would be better off investing their money in 'peanut plantations' than in the production of Canadian features (Cowan 1930, 83). Cowan's response to the threatened inculcation of Canadians by American screen values is to 'create a strong public demand for British films' (84). On the cultural work of cinema as an art form representing Canadian communities and their experiences to

Canadians, the only concession Cowan recommends is that it 'should be possible to include a Canadian note on almost all programmes and without resorting to cumbersome legislative machinery' (84). This resistance to legislating a Canadian feature-film industry into existence is an attitude that would prevail until 1967 and the establishment of the Canadian Film Development Corporation.

ESTABLISHING THE NATIONAL FILM BOARD OF CANADA

The decline of the CGMPB prompted the government to invite John Grierson, the founder of the British documentary movement and a Scot who was responsible for the film unit of Britain's Empire Marketing Board, to study the state of Canadian film production and make recommendations that would revive it. Among Grierson's recommendations were: that the Canadian government should create a committee that would monitor Canadian film policy and advise the Minister of Trade and Commerce; that all government film production should be centralized under the auspices of a Government Film Officer; that film distribution should be centralized and further developed and that a more sophisticated and comprehensive sense of propaganda should be developed.[3] At Grierson's insistence, legislation based on his recommendations was drafted, tabled and passed as the National Film Act on 2 May 1939. The National Film Act gave the National Film Board the authority to 'initiate and promote the production and distribution of films in the national interest and in particular to produce and distribute and to promote the production and distribution of films designed to interpret Canada to Canadians and to other nations' (quoted in Magder 1993, 52). The position of Film Commissioner was first offered to E. A. Corbett who, as director of extension for the University of Alberta, set up an extensive film network servicing the rural areas of the province. After Corbett refused the position, John Grierson was approached and accepted. Early on in his tenure at the board Grierson recommended the dissolution of CGMPB. It was disbanded in 1941, leaving the NFB with sole responsibility for government film production (Magder 1993, 53).

Following the absorption of the CGMPB by the NFB, the vision of Grierson worked to delay the development of a feature-film industry. Very much concerned by Canada's dependency on US film culture, Grierson complained 'when it comes to movies we have no emotional presentation of our own. It is another nation's effort and pride we see on our screen, not our own. We are on the outside looking in' (Grierson 1944, 55). Grierson's strategy to remedy this cultural deficit, however, is not for Canadians to produce Canadian features in Canada but for those interested in feature production to leave the country and make their 'Canadian' film in New York or Hollywood (59); Canada will produce documentaries. Of course, Grierson's rationale for his 'If you can't fight them, join them' philosophy is the difficulty in competing with Hollywood production values and distribution networks (58–9); however, his strategy of documentary production for Canada is also based on his personal dislike of the feature format. The feature film holds little value for Grierson, who sees it as a low, escapist cultural form catering to the 'moods of relaxation', a cultural form he likens to 'dance halls' and 'the dope sheets of sensational newspapers' (63). Grierson imagined a more erudite, formally instructional Canadian national cinema.

Under Grierson's direction, the NFB developed two commercially and critically successful documentary series during the Second World War, *Canada Carries On* and *World in Action*, which were both distributed theatrically and played in 90 per cent of Canadian theatres (Jones 1981, 36). *Canada Carries On* (1940–51) was designed to represent Canada's contributions to the Allied war effort to a domestic audience and covered both the home front and the European and Pacific theatres of war. By 1944 it reached two and a quarter million Canadians through theatrical and non-theatrical distribution. One of the most important components of a national cinema, the construction of a national audience, was developed by the NFB during the war years with the establishment of rural travelling cinema circuits, which brought NFB films to small communities across the country. Ninety-two rural cinema circuits reached approximately a quarter of a million people a month by 1945 (Evans 1983, 162).[4] Additionally, the NFB built a national audience by developing alternative exhibition windows for individuals and groups that were made accessible through volunteer projectionists and the twenty regional film libraries the board had established by 1942 (Jones 1981, 37). This linking of a diverse and dispersed population by cinema is conceptualized instructively for us by Shohat's and Stam's adaptation of Anderson's work on horizontal comradeship: 'The cinema's institutional ritual of gathering a community – spectators who share a region, language, and culture – homologizes, in a sense, the symbolic gathering of the nation. Anderson's sense of the nation as "horizontal comradeship" evokes the movie audience as a provisional "nation" forged by spectatorship' (1994, 103).

By way of ascertaining how the NFB represents Canada to Canadians and who constitutes this horizontal comradeship or imagined national community during this period I will look at one of the later *Canada Carries On* films, *Peoples of Canada* (1947). I have chosen one of the later films for analysis, as it indicates a shift in the series' emphasis away from the war towards addressing peacetime nation-building and Canada's place in the new world order. Moreover, this film reflects Grierson's ideological brand of national cinema, the propagandist bent he advocated for NFB films that would interpellate national subjects, films that in Grierson's words 'cover the whole field of civic interest: what Canadians need to know and think about if they are going to do their best by Canada and by themselves' (1944, 64). Shohat's and Stam's notion of community as spectators who share a region, language and culture must be qualified when applied to the diverse linguistic and cultural groups forming Canadian audiences in general and *Canada Carries On* audiences in particular. All of the major films in the series were translated into French (Grierson 1944, 36); however, they were first written and produced by Anglophones for an Anglophone Canadian audience. A shared pan-Canadian culture inside Québec and shared language and pan-Canadian culture across Canada's diverse regions outside of Québec were part of what the *Canada Carries On* series attempted to create in its 'symbolic gathering of the nation'.

Peoples of Canada

The title *Peoples of Canada* (1947) signals the film's investment in forging a nation through spectatorship. *Peoples of Canada* lays down the co-ordinates for horizontal comradeship, who belongs to the Canadian nation and who does not as envisioned by Stanley Jackson and the NFB in 1945 and 1947.[5] European 'discovery' of Canada as a New World territory initiates the film's narrative which is then structured around 'progress': white exploration and enterprise in exploiting a resource economy and building the nation, and a delineation of the variant ethnic groups that contribute to that construction. An establishing extreme long shot pan of an empty forested shore colludes with the imperialist myth of virgin, empty land as does the accompanying voice-over track: 'European explorers first walked through the silent forests five hundred years ago.' However, a shot of a buckskin-clad First Nations man in a canoe abrogates this mythology. At this point the voice-over does not acknowledge the First Nations presence that is registered visually, but continues to narrate the exploits of Europeans who were 'lured' into the territory from their search for the Orient by 'the wealth of furs'. As this line of voice-over is completed, a sequence of three shots is initiated to construct a relationship between two iconic signs for Canada: the beaver and the 'Indian'. Cuts are made from the medium long shot of the First Nations man in the canoe to a medium close-up shot of a beaver jumping into the water and then back to a medium close-up of the First Nations man landing on shore. This sequence marks the white nation's appropriation, manipulation and translation of the Aboriginal Other into a signifier of the white nation's inheritance. Through cutting that associates the Native in his natural habitat with the beaver in its natural habitat (an icon for Canadian nation), the Native is reduced to flora and fauna pressed into service to signify the white nation. Half-way through this sequence the voice-over narrates European penetration of First Nations territory: 'soon the primitive trails of the new continent, known for centuries only to the Red Man and the Eskimo led the European through unmapped country as he braved hardship and danger for the rich reward of furs'. The 'Red Man' is represented here only to be disposed of by colonization or settlement. The narration and image perform the work of relegating First Nations peoples and cultures to the historical past where white men, not 'Red Men', braved great hardships to build the fur trade economy which formed the basis for Canada's development. The invaluable and integral participation of First Nations in the development of the fur trade is elided. Furthermore, First Nations are not represented in the next sequence depicting European ethnicities living in, and contributing to, the nation in the film's narrative present. The film's only other reference to Canada's First Peoples occurs later on in a shot of a slack-jawed Inuk staring skyward, supposedly awed by the white man's aeroplanes in a sequence narrating the 'rediscovery of our northland'. Again, the voice-over fails to reference this man whose territory is being explored and exploited. Visually, he stands outside of the film narrative's construction of peoples of Canada; he is reduced to a signifier for north, part of the natural terrain that forms 'our northland' in the white imagination. The collective first-person possessive 'our' also subordinates him to the white imagination and cinematic apparatus that, after Fuss, limits the cultural signification of the colonized, to this decontextualized – because removed from an Inuit context and inserted into a white one – slack-jawed caricature of the primitive.

Having introduced and dispatched the 'Red Man' to (after Rony) a displaced temporal realm separated from Europeans, the film narrative proceeds to introduce the 'peoples of all races' who 'have added their achievements to Canada's history'. The voice-over's usage of 'races', however, proves to be erroneous at best, disingenuous at worst, as the sequences that follow the voice-over limit themselves almost exclusively to the representation of European ethnicities that in the rhetoric of the film narrative stand in for all the 'races' comprising the 'Peoples of Canada'. The first sequence representing Canada's white nation-builders consists of an enumeration of German, French, Dutch and Scottish immigrants, their immigration history and the trades they brought to Canada. For example, a voice-over describing the Germans as 'skilled carpenters', shipbuilders and fishermen is accompanied by contemporary shots of their descendants practising these trades. After a brief sequence dealing cursorily with Québécois contributions to agriculture, the arts and politics, and another referencing the development of the lumber and farming industries in eastern Canada, the film addresses the settlement of the prairies by Ukrainians, Doukhobors ('the Doukhobor is one of Canada's hardest workers') and Hutterites ('among our most progressive farmers'). We are told that these groups 'beat the stubborn land by working together'. This voice-over narrates shots of Eastern Europeans working co-operatively to clear the land of trees. At pains to represent how the work of building the nation forges individuals from diverse groups into unified national subjects, the film, in its attempt to forge an imagined community of spectators, simultaneously recognizes and elides the diversity of Canada's peoples. The voice-over 'And on the streets of every small town across the prairies the crowds speak a dozen languages' marks the diversity of Canadians, yet the accompanying close-up shots of storefront signs register ambivalently. Inserted in the montage of signs representing central and Eastern European family named businesses is a sign bearing the name 'Wong's Café'. Whereas the film provides signifieds – visual representations of Ukrainians, Germans etc. – for the European storefront signifiers, in the case of Chinese the film narrative is haunted by the absence of a signified; it fails to represent Chinese people visually, reducing them to the signifier Wong's Café. Central and Eastern European involvement in the physical clearing of the land and settling aspects of nation-building are privileged above the contributions of Chinese and other racialized groups to this process. The sequence dealing with the construction of the national railway deploys shots of white labour building the unifying steel spine that unite the nation from coast to coast, but fails to provide images or voice-over narrative acknowledging the project's dependence on poorly paid and ill-treated Chinese labour. In the discursive organization of the film Chinese contributions to Canadian nation-building are reduced to serving Chinese food to white Canadians. This selective mapping of ethnic and racial groups' contributions to nation-building creates a hierarchy of peoples of Canada. Although *Peoples of Canada* legitimizes specific *ethnic* differences amongst Caucasians, its representation of *racial* differences remains conflicted and for the most part limits or elides the signification of racialized groups as peoples of Canada. For example, visual evidence of racial diversity in human form is limited to a matter of seconds when a shot of a Sikh man crossing a street in Vancouver is used to punctuate a voice-over proclaiming, 'Canada was ready to take her place in the world family of nations.' The Sikh presence in Vancouver, while it is acknowledged visually (albeit fleetingly), is not narrated by a voice-over explaining the history of Sikh immigration or the contributions of Sikhs to Canadian culture.[6] Although African Americans from Oklahoma contributed to Canadian nation-building by actively participating in founding the towns of Maidstone and Wilkie in Saskatchewan and of Junkins, Breton, Clyde and Amber Valley in Alberta, *Peoples of Canada* represses these contributions by limiting its narration of nation builders to white settlers.[7] The film narrative's offering to its audience of specific cultural co-ordinates that it categorizes as representatively Canadian further restricts the imagined community that *Peoples of Canada* projects on to the screen and hails or recruits from its audience. In a transitional sequence between the film's delineation of Canada's social terrain and its representation of the nation's physical landscape, voice-over and image prescribe 'the look and feel of things Canadian: hot summers, the sparkle of winter, hockey night, the excitement of a rodeo, a cricket match, the Orangeman's annual parade, a busy weekday street, or the strict observance of the Sabbath'. Each verbal cue of the voice-over is accompanied by a shot of white Canadians celebrating these co-ordinates of national culture, these 'things Canadian'. This monochromatic shot composition constructs a symbolic white ownership of these cultural co-ordinates. Moreover, while the images of a rodeo or summer, winter and hockey, potentially constitute 'things' many Canadians might identify with, cricket and the Orangeman's annual parade are culturally specific. The Orange Parade raises the spectre of white Anglo-Celtic Protestant national hegemony in Canada, and most certainly is not a co-ordinate for identification with the nation for French Canadians, Catholics, Canadians of Asian descent and Canada's First Nations.[8] *Peoples of Canada* constructs a horizontal comradeship of whiteness that excludes racialized Others from entering into the symbolic gathering of the nation constructed by state-funded national cinema. In this way we can understand Balibar's argument that:

> *Every social community reproduced by the functioning of institutions is imaginary*, that is to say, it is based on the projection of individual existence into the weft of a collective narrative, on the recognition of a common name and on traditions lived as the trace of an immemorial past (even when they have been fabricated and inculcated in the recent past). But this comes down to accepting that, under certain conditions, *only* imaginary communities are real.
>
> (Balibar 1991, 93)

The social and physical landscapes of the nation are brought together in the next section of the film narrative which charts how white enterprise has harnessed Canada's natural resources, industrialized, and carved out a viable and dynamic economy that exports Canadian resources globally. Here *Peoples of Canada* structures the imagined community along the lines of a national economy, interpellating national subjects as those participating in the economic project of commodifying and selling the nation. However, the signification of those contributing to this economic project is limited – with the exception of a fleeting glimpse of an African Canadian working on an aeroplane assembly line – to the labouring bodies of white men working in the lumber, mining, construction, petroleum, shipping and manufacturing industries. The industrialization of Canada during the war years is represented by shots of ships and aeroplane manufacturing which are narrated by the voice-over: 'the industrial and mechanical skills developed during the war years are already serving to rebuild the peace-time economy'. Part of this new technological sophistication in rebuilding the peace-time economy is used to revisit the narrative of discovery referenced in the film's establishing shots. The 'new timber and mineral land, the North' is the subject of the white nation's colonizing gaze at mid-century. Aerial shots of this northern terrain, combined with shots of white engineers surveying the landscape, and bulldozers clearing brush, rock and soil for the construction of the Alaska Highway, represent the mastery of the white nation of the south over this northern territory. The film invites readings of white internal colonialism, by invoking the tropes of discovery and figuring the north as a new frontier ripe for resource exploitation: 'here one of the world's richest known sources of radium and uranium, key to atomic energy has been uncovered. This is pioneer country still in the stage of discovery and development.' Furthermore, the shot of the Inuk supposedly awed by the superior colonizing technology of the white nation (included in this sequence but referenced earlier in my argument) constructs a colonizer/colonized binary. Shots of bulldozers and graders building an air base and a plane taxiing for takeoff precede the shot of the Inuk, structuring our understanding of his passive subservient position in this new world order. This is the type of binary that a film such as *Map of the Human Heart* (Vincent Ward

1992) or a television series such as *Nunavut* (Zacharias Kunuk 1996) attempts to interrogate.

The film's final sequence is composed of a voice-over articulating the issues of racial and cultural alterity that the film narrative has gestured towards, yet failed to reregister fully, and a series of shots that further frustrate the signification of the voice-over's proclamation of the nation's racial differences. 'During the war,' the voice-over narrates, 'Canada developed more than ever the tradition of working together for the common good. Tolerance of others' ideas, understanding among different nationalities, compromise between differing points of view. These have always been necessary to maintain unity in a far-flung country of many racial origins.' The tension between diversity and homogeneity is palpable in the voice-over itself, which speaks on the one hand of 'the common good' and 'unity' and on the other of tolerance for differing nationalities, racial origins and points of view. Accompanying shots of white male farm labourers harvesting the nation's crops work to abrogate the voice-over's declaration of racial pluralism. Similarly to the shots of children allegorizing the product of nation-building – white settlers – in *The Wheatfields of Canada*, shots of white school-aged children at play in the closing sequence of *Peoples of Canada* constitute the film's projection of Canada's future as a white nation. The voice-over narrating these shots stresses the significance of the 'co-operative' aspects of Canadian nation-building for 'our' children while the proceeding voice-over invokes the 'pioneer tradition of mutual understanding' as the nation's inheritance and a model to be employed as a search for understanding among the nations of the world. Unfortunately, the inheritance left by the pioneers or white colonists fostered a type of unequal understanding that worked to excommunicate non-whites from the nation through legislation such as the Indian Act, and Orders in Council interning Japanese Canadians and stripping them of their citizenship. The tolerance of cultural Others claimed for Canada in the voice-over remains the empty propaganda of a film that would construct Canada as a democratic model for harmonious race relations, yet refuses to represent the racial Other as Canadian. Although the film narrative recognizes the many racial origins composing the peoples of Canada abstractly at the level of the voice-over, it simultaneously elides these differences at the visual level in the name of homogeneity. Here the NFB fails miserably in its remit to represent Canada to Canadians by erasing 'peoples of Canada' – First Nations, Chinese, Japanese, and African Canadians – and their contributions to the national collectivity, but succeeds in promulgating the propaganda of fictive ethnicity. The raw footage of *Negroes* (1944), an incomplete NFB–Crawley Films co-production for the NFB series *People of the Maritimes*, indicates that there was at least some attempt by the Board to represent the nation's racial diversity. However, the film's aborted status and the fact that the other three films in the series – *Men of Lunenberg*, *The Acadians* and *The Gaels of Cape Breton* – were completed raises questions about whether or not race was a factor in closing down production on *Negroes*.[9]

If *Peoples of Canada* does what Grierson believed NFB films should do, namely tell Canadians what they need to know and think (1944, 64), it tells them to know and think whiteness as a collective identity. It would take forty-six years before the NFB would shift its institutional structure to fund the representation of racial difference as an identifying co-ordinate of Canadianness under the New Initiatives In Film programme of Studio D.

Although distributed in Great Britain, New Zealand and Australia, *Canada Carries On* was produced more for the domestic market, while *World in Action* targeted a more international audience with distribution in the United States, Latin America, Great Britain, New Zealand, Australia, India and South Africa. Gary Evans suggests that by 1944 NFB material reached an average of forty to fifty million people a week (1983, 224–5). As early as 1941, the NFB gained international recognition for the *World in Action* film *Churchill's Island* (1941) which won the Board its first Academy Award for best documentary film (Evans 1984, 139). The wartime success of the NFB, however, dissipated with the end of hostilities when NFB films disappeared from American screens and from many Canadian screens (Magder 1993, 61).

POSTWAR SCHEMES AND DEPENDENCY

As Peter Morris observes, Grierson's 1944 pipe dream about munificent American assistance in producing features with Canadian subject matter anticipates the 1948 Canadian Co-operation Project (Morris 1986, 18). Magder describes the Canadian Co-operation Project as a strategy for inducing American producers into 'establishing a quasi branch-plant feature film industry' in Canada (1993, 71). The goals of what was to become the Canadian Co-operation Project were delineated in a 1948 memo from Eric Johnston of the Motion Picture Association of America to J. J. Fitzgibbons, President of Famous Players. Among these stated goals was a desire to increase coverage of Canadian subjects in American newsreels; to have short films made about Canada by the US film companies; to insert some Canadian sequences in US feature films; and to make a series of radio recordings by US stars extolling the virtues of Canada as a vacation land (Magder 1993, 72).[10] Although this policy was designed ostensibly to address Canada's trade deficit with the United States, its underlying purpose was to encourage US investment in Canada by ensuring that American box office receipts earned in Canada were repatriated unobstructed by protectionist tax legislation (74). Not surprisingly, this policy which ran until 1957 did nothing substantive to alter the status quo in Canadian cinemas, where 75 per cent of Canadian screen time was devoted to US films, another 20 per cent to British films, and the remaining 5 per cent to Western European films (75).

Concerns about the ramifications for Canada of a growing US cultural hegemony led to the establishment of the Massey Commission, a federal government inquiry into the state of Canadian arts and culture. The Massey Report found that the penetration of American capital and culture deformed and inhibited the

production of Canadian culture, and recommended state-sponsored development and protection for the arts in the face of 'a vast and disproportionate
amount of material coming from a single alien source'. The Commission argued
that the millions of dollars being spent by the federal government to 'maintain a
national independence . . . would constitute nothing but an empty shell without
a vigorous and distinctive cultural life' (quoted in Magder 1993, 82). The ramifications of Canada's failure to develop a feature-film industry are noted in the
Commission's Report, which points to the dominance of Hollywood film as an
American cultural form that 'refashions us in its own image' (quoted in Magder
1993, 83). Pierre Berton's *Hollywood's Canada* (1975) provides an informative
survey of the 575 Hollywood films with Canadian settings produced between
1907 and 1956. These films 'refashion' Canada as cinematic Canadas with American landscapes, inhabited by the people and values of America's dominant white
culture. Margaret Atwood is very much aware of this phenomenon of cultural
deformation when she figures the Hollywood film western as a vehicle for American cultural imperialism in her poem 'Backdrop Addresses Cowboy'. In
Atwood's allegory, Canada is personified as the female backdrop to the American
cowboy. The cowboy signifies American popular culture as an invasive discourse
that displaces indigenous cultural forms, and 'litters' the Canadian imagination.
As the backdrop informs the cowboy: 'I am the space you desecrate / as you pass
through' ([1968] 1991, 70–1). This isn't to suggest that Canadian features
weren't being produced by the commercial sector in the immediate postwar
period; they were. However, Canadian features such as *Bush Pilot* (Sterling
Campbell 1946), *Forbidden Journey* (Richard Jarvis and Cecil Maiden 1949) and
Now That April's Here (William Davidson 1958) were viewed by very few Canadians owing to the American monopoly on distribution and exhibition in a territory Hollywood considered part of its domestic market (Morris 1980, 9).[11]
Although the Massey Report delineates the problematic of the American film
industry's cultural hegemony in Canada, as Magder observes, it offers no mech-
anisms to alter the situation (1993, 84). Developments at the NFB, however,
worked towards addressing the issues of American dominance in North America
through more politically engaged film-making and experiments with feature-film
production in French and English.

Québécois film-makers at the NFB began to shift towards a more *auteur-*
centred or director-centred aesthetic with the development of lightweight
cameras and synchronized sound that marked the *Cinéma direct* movement's
minimalist approach. These technical innovations enabled film-makers in Québec
to produce personal, spontaneous, unscripted, short documentary films informed
by and focused on the Quiet Revolution: Québec society's shift from a rural
culture dominated by the Catholic church to an urban one heavily invested in the
state and moves towards independence from Canada. Through *Cinéma direct*
spontaneous events and real people's lives became the basis for filmic production.
As Michel Euvard and Pierre Véronneau argue, French-speaking directors in
Québec saw the direct method as a means of constructing community by

representing the Québécois to themselves.[12] Responding to the Massey Commission's recommendations for increased French language production, a Francophone production unit within the NFB was finally established in 1964. None the less, some Québécois film-makers saw the Board's role in Québec as a colonial one that conflicted with their aspirations for self-determination and viewed its refusal to permit feature production as restricting their freedom of expression. The response of Pierre Juneau, the Director of Production for the French language unit, to the published protestations of five of these film-makers (Jacques Godbout, Gilles Carle, Claude Pérron, Denys Arcand, Gilles Groulx) confirmed their perceptions of the NFB as a restrictive colonial power structure. Juneau reprimanded and demoted the outspoken film-makers and imposed restrictions on the *auteur* elements of future French language documentaries (Clandfield 1987, 42).

A burgeoning Québécois nationalism is palpable in *Pour la suite du monde* (Pierre Perrault 1963), a film focusing on the rural traditions of Québec, and *Québec – USA ou l'invasion pacifique* (Michel Brault and Claude Jutra 1962), an urban work framing the influx of American tourists into Montreal as a peaceful invasion. According to Euvard and Véronneau, Perrault saw his film about the reconstruction of a dormant Beluga whale fishery by the fishermen of l'Ile-aux-Coudres as a symbolic narrative in which 'a dispossessed and humiliated people is once again invited to become a people by rediscovering its past and roots' (Euvard and Véronneau 1980, 83).[13] Brault's and Jutra's film shows a sophisticated cosmopolitan city with a rich historical past and distinctive, vibrant cultural present that have survived the oppression of British conquest, Anglo-Canadian and neo-American colonialism.[14] Perrault, Brault and Jutra clearly see filmmaking as a nation-building project, in this case the construction of the contested nation, or imagined community of Québec.

English-language production was also experimenting with the direct style in the fourteen shorts produced by Studio B for the *Candid Eye* (1958–9) series; however, unlike their Francophone colleagues, they resisted making films identifying with a national community (Euvard and Véronneau 1980, 79). David Clandfield describes the *Candid Eye* series as 'naïve observer films' where a 'detached, ironic observer registers surface impressions of a myth-laden aspect of Canadian life, in order to de-mythicize and de-dramatize it, but without analysis or critique' (Clandfield 1987, 26). *The Days Before Christmas* (Macartney-Filgate *et al.* 1958), for example, was shot in Montreal during the pre-Christmas shopping frenzy by several cameramen working without a script. Another Macartney-Filgate project, *The Back-breaking Leaf* (1959), documents the labour of tobacco pickers in southern Ontario. The most successful and best-known film to come out of Studio B's experiments with the direct method is *Lonely Boy* (Wolf Koenig and Roman Kroitor 1961), a *cinéma-vérité* style film representing several days in the maelstrom of fame and adolescent adulation experienced by teen singing sensation Paul Anka.

THE NFB AND FEATURE PRODUCTION

In the early 1960s the NFB began to produce its first feature films, *Drylanders* (Don Haldane 1963), a fiction feature, and Pierre Perrault's *cinéma direct* project *Pour la suite du monde* (1963), a documentary feature. *Drylanders*, which has already been examined at length in Chapter 1, tells the story of white invader-settler pioneers in Saskatchewan, while *Pour la suite du monde* focuses on the re-enactment of a traditional whale hunt in a small village on l'Ile-aux-Coudres. Both films were originally conceived as one-hour television dramas; however, as both completed projects exceeded the one-hour television format, the NFB released them theatrically (Magder 1993, 99). *Pour la suite du monde* garnered critical praise at Cannes, while *Drylanders* generated healthy box office receipts through its distribution deal with Columbia pictures (100). The trend in feature production continued with such notable features as *Nobody Waved Goodbye* (Don Owen 1964), *Le chat dans le sac* (Gilles Groulx 1964), and *La vie heureuse de Léopold Z* (Gilles Carle 1965). All of these features were produced by the enthusiasm of their directors and were not shot with the approval or knowledge of the Board (Magder 1993, 100). The NFB attempted to assert control over its directors by keeping a tighter rein on budgets and discouraging *auteur* projects such as the three films mentioned above (100–1). These restrictions resulted in the disaffection of some of the Board's best film-makers, who left the NFB to work on their own features. Claude Jutra took a temporary leave from the board in 1962 to work on *À toute prendre* while Pierre Patry left the Board to found Coopératio, a co-operative production company that produced seven films between 1963 and 1967.[15]

FUNDING DIFFERENCES AT THE NFB: REGIONALIZATION, STUDIO D AND NEW INITIATIVES IN FILM

The representation of differences from an Ottawa-centred vision of a homogeneous national community began to receive funding with the establishment of the French-language production unit in 1964 and the development of regionalization, a decentralization of production at the NFB that began in 1965. Regionalization attempted to reconfigure 'national' as a category by focusing on the local and specific in Canada's diverse regions. According to Ronald Dick, Colin Low, who developed regionalization for the NFB, felt that English-Canadian film-makers at the Board emphasized the totality of a pan-Canadian cinema at the expense of the diverse 'parts that made the whole meaningful'. As Dick puts it, Anglophone Canadian film-makers depended on craft to construct their coherent and unitary Canada. 'They knew how to shoot and splice together with great art the most splendid scenes taken from coast-to-coast to suggest a pan-Canadian reality', but often times failed to capture the specific, the local, the regional co-ordinates composing the 'pan-Canadian reality' (Dick 1986, 110). Peter Jones, the NFB's regional production representative in Vancouver, also resists viewing the nation through the master code of a pan-Canadian totality in a letter he writes to a senior executive at the NFB's Montreal headquarters: 'We are *not* all identical from coast to coast and the government that understands this will be a strong government with widespread support in the country' (quoted in Dick 1986, 119). However, diversity was ultimately still structured around the sub-suming unity of the original nation-building project that Grierson saw the NFB forging. For example, Don Hopkins, the Ontario Studio's executive producer, delineates regionalization's emphasis on 'individual origins' as a way of more effectively 'telling *the truth* of the country to ourselves'; however, it is still a singular truth of the nation as a collectivity that is sought (emphasis added: quoted in Jones 1981, 181).

Colin Low and Dick see Low's *Challenge for Change* programme (1969–80), a series of social action films that targeted minority and disadvantaged groups around the country, as a catalytic precursor for the Regional Programme he later developed for the NFB (Dick 1986, 112). The earliest moves toward decentral-ization of production, however, were made by Grant McLean, who established regional offices in Halifax, Toronto, Winnipeg and Vancouver in 1965 (Jones 1981, 177). At this stage the regional offices were to act as observation stations, collecting production ideas that would be sent back to NFB headquarters in Montreal (Jones 1981, 178). These offices, excepting Vancouver which remained intact, were closed because of financial cuts in 1968, but reopened as regional studios in 1976 (Jones 1981, 179). A Northwest Studio was established in Edmonton in April 1980. The philosophy behind the decentralization of pro-duction is summarized in the NFB *Annual Report* for 1976–7: 'the objective of this policy, in keeping with the role of the NFB, is to provide each region the opportunity to interpret a regional subject to a national audience or national subject from a regional point of view' (quoted in Dick 1986, 122). To these ends the project was extended to include French regional offices that were opened in Moncton, Toronto and Winnipeg to represent the French-Canadian experience outside of Québec (Dick 1986, 125). Regional film-making, however, was regarded with scepticism by the upper management at the NFB, which Dick suspects was structured by a 'literalist' brand of nationalism 'which wants to see everything in an obvious Pan-Canadian frame of reference and submerge debate in celebration' (Dick 1986, 129).

State funding of regional images of difference from the universalizing pan-Canadianism of earlier NFB films was extended to the funding of images of gen-der difference in 1974 with the founding of Studio D, the first publicly funded women's production unit in the world. This effort to shift away from the histor-ically male gaze of the NFB (*Careers and Cradles*, 1947; *Is It a Woman's World?*, 1956) and provide women access to the cinematic apparatus and the production of their own images was, as the studio's founding executive producer, Kathleen Shannon, put it 'in the national interest . . . so that we may have complete women as role models rather than dependent, shrill, frivolous stereotypes' (quoted in Anderson 1996, 176). Shannon, who honed her skills writing and producing the *Working Mothers* series (twelve films) in the *Challenge for Change* programme, draws a correlation between the representation of regional and gender differences from a homogenizing pan-Canadian cinema: 'Both the regions, and women, have distinct constituencies, to whom we must respond, even when their demands are different from those of an hierarchical institution where we are outnumbered as part of a large homogenized English Production Branch' (quoted in Anderson 1996, 179). An early Studio D project, *Great Grand Mother* (Anne Wheeler, Lorna Rasmussen 1975), is a co-production with Edmonton's Filmwest Associates which brings together the retrieval of prairie and women's history. As Elizabeth Anderson's reading of this film suggests, 'In its attention to regional history and specificity, and, most importantly, to women as historical actors, *Great Grand Mother* countered earlier homogenized and male-orientated versions of Canadian history' (Anderson 1996, 172). Studio D's remit was not only to make interventions in a patriarchal cinematic tradition by restoring images of women to a history that had repressed them, but to also train women to produce their own images. A 1976 NFB document delineates the remit of the Women's Studio:

> Studio D is a filmmaking unit within English production at the National Film Board of Canada. It provides a forum for women filmmakers.
>
> Studio D brings the perspective of women to all social issues through the medium of film, promoting personal, social and political awareness.
>
> Studio D addresses the specific information needs of women audiences.
>
> Studio D provides an opportunity for women to develop and express their creativity in film, and to move into filmmaking occupations that have been dominated by men.
>
> Studio D provides an environment where women can work together in a collective atmosphere of mutual support.
>
> (quoted in Anderson 1996, 169)

The tone and style of the films produced during Studio D's first decade were shaped by Shannon's work on *Working Mothers*. As Anderson observes, the Studio D aesthetic came to reflect Teresa de Lauretis's conceptualization of a specific 1970s social realist film-making that 'pushed for immediate documentation for purposes of political activism, consciousness-raising, self-expression, or the search for "positive images" of women' (Anderson 1999, 48; De Lauretis 1988, 288–9). Studio D's social interventionist work was successful in provoking community discussion and in garnering critical prizes. *I'll Find a Way* (Beverly Schaeffer 1977), *If You Love This Planet* (Terri Nash 1982) and *Flamenco at 5.15* (Cynthia Scott 1983) were all awarded Oscars (Clandfield 1987, 32).

Despite the successes of Studio D, its universalizing tendencies frustrated its ability to represent a broad spectrum of Canadian women's experiences. In its first twelve years Studio D failed to recognize its own essentialist construction of gender as one subsuming the differences of sexuality, race and class that cut across any monolithic imagining of woman. As Anderson notes, Shannon's acute awareness of the NFB's subsuming of the tensions between 'equality and difference, unity and diversity in its construction of "unity in diversity"' does not prevent her from homogenizing women's experiences through a white, heterosexual, middle-class camera eye (Anderson 1996, 180). In this sense then, Shannon's Studio D with its brand of what Anderson calls 'integrative feminism' constructed its own 'unity in diversity' paradigm where differences among women were absorbed by the larger project of a national woman's studio (122). It was this problematic of representation that led to the creation of the New Initiatives in Film programme (NIF 1991–6) under the tenure of Rina Fraticelli, who replaced Shannon as executive producer of Studio D in 1987 following the latter's retirement in 1986.

New Initiatives in Film restructured Studio D by making representations of the ethnic and racial diversity of women's culture in Canada a major component of the studio's production. Fraticelli worked with Sylvia Hamilton, a Black filmmaker and race relations worker from Nova Scotia, to design a programme that would 'address the under-representation of Women of Colour, and Native Women in Canadian film' (Anderson 1999, 51–2). The 1992 NFB document articulating the objectives of the revamped Studio D reflects this corrective paradigm shift from a homogenized white heterosexual image of woman to more pluralistic understandings of women's experiences:

> Our chief objectives are to support women of diverse backgrounds and regions of Canada who wish to speak on film in their own voices; to produce and distribute films which analyze and challenge the influences which limit women's potential; and to influence social, political, economic and environmental realities by bringing feminist visions to all issues. Designed to engage audiences, provoke discussion and raise consciousness, Studio D films are conceived as tools for change and empowerment.
>
> (quoted in Anderson 1996, 272)

Films such as *Sisters in the Struggle* (Dionne Brand and Ginny Stikeman 1991) and *Forbidden Love: The Unashamed Stories of Lesbian Lives* (Lynn Fernie and Aerlyn Weisman 1992) mark a departure from the representations of white liberal, heterosexual middle-class women that characterized the first twelve years of Studio D films. *Sisters in the Struggle* charts Black women's struggles against racism over a period of twenty years and indicts the mainstream feminist movement itself as racist, while *Forbidden Love: The Unashamed Stories of Lesbian Lives* explores the lesbian bar culture in Canada during the 1950s and 1960s. Budget cuts at the NFB contributed to the closing of Studio D in March 1996. The extraordinary international success the NFB has enjoyed throughout its evolution was marked on its sixtieth anniversary in 1998 when the Museum of Modern Art in New York mounted a major retrospective of classic NFB animation and documentary films, and the Academy of Motion Picture Arts and Sciences in Los Angeles hosted a retrospective of eleven Oscar-winning NFB shorts and sixty-three nominated pieces.

STATE INTERVENTION: THE LEGISLATION OF A CANADIAN FEATURE-FILM INDUSTRY

While the NFB struggled with feature-film production and representations of diversity, the commercial sector continued to grow and lobby for government intervention in the Canadian industry. Commercial sector production for television increased dramatically during the 1950s, so much so that by 1957 there were approximately sixty production companies in the country as opposed to just under half that number in 1952 (Magder 1993, 92). Much of this vitality in television production was due to American-sponsored shows which, similarly to the 'quota quickies' of the 1930s discussed in Chapter 2, were designed to circumvent British quota restrictions through production in Canada. Crawley Films, established in 1939, was the major private producer in the industry carving out a market niche for itself as the leading producer of industrial-sponsored short subjects such as *The Loon's Necklace* (1949) sponsored by Imperial Oil. Crawley was also involved in the production of two television series, *Royal Canadian Mounted Police* and *St. Lawrence North* (Magder 1993, 93). Not unlike other film-makers in Canada, F. R. (Budge) Crawley, founder and President of Crawley Films, was seduced by feature production and developed the French-language feature *Ville jolie* (1963) and the English-language feature *The Luck of Ginger Coffey* (1964). Whilst the former was a critical and commercial failure, the latter received encouraging reviews but did not turn a profit. Following these two costly experiences in feature production, Crawley returned to television and short subject production (Magder 1993, 93). Crawley's failure in feature production underscores the non-viability of a Canadian domestic feature market in the early 1960s. As Magder asks, if a 'well-capitalized and able producer' such as Crawley could fail, what were the chances of success in feature production for any independent producer (94)? The formula for success pursued following Crawley's unfortunate experience was for Canadians to make US-style films that targeted a North American market (95). There were, however, individuals and organizations within the industry who resisted this harmonizing of Canadian feature production to a US aesthetic and market value. Both the Association professionnelle des cinéastes (APC) established in 1963 and the Anglophone Association of Motion Picture Producers and Laboratories of Canada lobbied the government for state support of a commercial feature-film industry in Canada (102). In a 1964 brief to the federal government the Directors Guild of Canada

(DGC) also pushed for state intervention in the production of features, making a case for their economic importance for trade, tourism and employment. The DGC brief stressed the contribution that features would make to the expression of a national identity and recommended that the government should develop, among other things, a government-backed loan system for feature production, a tax on the rental receipts of foreign companies that would be transferred to a domestic production fund, and a plan to secure distribution of Canadian features through Canadian-based distribution companies (109–10). Partly in response to pressure from these organizations, the Interdepartmental Committee on the Possible Development of Feature Film Production in Canada was established in 1964, and on 8 October 1965 the committee spoke the words that film-makers in Canada had been waiting to hear for decades: the 'Government has decided there should be a feature film industry' (quoted in Dorland 1998, 99).[16] Distribution and exhibition of Canadian features would continue to present a major obstacle to Canadian film-makers in the 1960s, 1970s, 1980s and 1990s as they had in the 1920s, 1930s, 1940s and 1950s. Recognizing the American monopoly on distribution and exhibition in Canada, the Committee commissioned the economist Otto John Firestone to conduct a study, 'Film Distribution, Practices, Problems and Prospects'. Completed in 1965, Firestone's study is not a ringing endorsement for feature-film production in Canada. Citing the 80 per cent of Canadian film distribution controlled by American interests, Firestone notes that there is not an international demand for Canadian feature films (Dorland 1998, 105). He goes on to recommend that, if a feature-film industry is to be successful in Canada, the films it produces must be 'internationally oriented' using 'proven success formulae with a freshness of approach relying on top stars and first-class producers with world-wide reputations, assisted by and associated with Canadian artists, professional and technical personnel' (quoted in Dorland 1998, 108). In short, Firestone advocates a Canadian feature-film production model that would mimic Hollywood. Taking into account the importance of distribution, the Interdepartmental Committee recommended the establishment of 'a Canadian film development corporation . . . to promote the overall development of a feature film industry in Canada' (quoted in Dorland 1998, 110). The Committee stressed that 'the cooperation of major distribution companies [read, American distribution companies] is a necessity for the development of the industry and Canadian feature films must be given fair and equitable treatment in distribution and exhibition, particularly in Canada' (quoted in Dorland 1998, 110). The Corporation would manage a 'revolving fund of $8.5 million' that 'would be established from consolidated revenue and an additional $1.5 million would be appropriated for the initial five years for making awards and grants' (Dorland 1998, 110). In February 1967 the Canadian Film Development Corporation Act passed into legislation, and the CFDC was established with a $10 million remit to invest in Canadian feature films.

In the early 1970s the CFDC invested in such Canadian classics as *Goin' Down the Road* (Don Shebib 1970), *The Rowdyman* (Peter Carter 1972), *La vraie nature de Bernadette* (Gilles Carle 1972) and *Kamouraska* (Claude Jutra 1973). From 1971 on, the CFDC placed a ceiling of $300,000 on big productions; however, there were exceptions to this rule as is evidenced in its investments in Claude Jutra's *Kamouraska* and Ted Kotchef's *The Apprenticeship of Duddy Kravitz* (1974) (Magder 1993, 138, 152). Distribution remained a major obstacle for the industry. Although Canadian features were now being produced thanks to CFDC moneys, these films were not seen by the Canadian public because of the US monopoly on theatrical distribution in Canada. In 1972 the Toronto Filmmakers Co-op sent a brief to the federal government recommending that it should impose a 15 per cent Canadian content quota on all commercial exhibitors (144). As Magder notes, however, Canadian exhibitors were not having any of it (145). Like their counterparts throughout the history of Canadian cinema, 1970s exhibitors regarded film as a business and not a nation-building project that would facilitate the expression of an imagined community. The response of the Secretary General to the Co-op's brief was unsubstantive and ineffectual. Not surprisingly, distribution continued to be a substantial impediment to the screening of Canadian movies in Canada, so much so that a newly formed lobby group, the Anglo-Canadian Council of Canadian Filmmakers (CCFM) representing several professional organizations and close to three hundred film-makers, singled it out as one of the causes for what it perceived as the failure of the CFDC. In a 1974 presentation before the Standing Committee on Broadcasting, Film and Assistance to the Arts, Pete Pearson, a director and chairperson of CCFM, criticized a system which spent $20 million of Canadian taxpayers' money to produce Canadian films yet failed to get these films widely distributed and exhibited in local cinemas:

> The film distribution system doesn't work. In 1972, less than 2 per cent of the movies shown in Ontario were Canadian, less than 5 per cent in Québec, the supposed bedrock of Canadian cinema.
> The film exhibition system doesn't work. The foreign-dominated theatre industry grossed over $140,000,000 at the box office and is recycling only nickles and dimes into future domestic production.
>
> (quoted in Magder 1993, 153)

Of course one obvious response was the imposition of quotas; however, the Canadian government was anxious not to upset the major players in exhibition and distribution (153). So, although the CFDC went on record as supporting quotas in 1974, the Department of Finance and the Treasury Board maintained that Canadian films had to be successful in the marketplace on their own (154). To placate the concerns of the CCFM, while avoiding a conflict with exhibitors and distributors, Secretary of State personnel developed the concept of a voluntary quota. As Magder explains, Famous Players and Odeon agreed to a 1973 deal whereby 'feature films produced or dubbed in English were to be guaranteed two weeks screen time in either Toronto, Vancouver, or Montreal. If successful, the films were to be given wider release' (156). In the introduction to his book *Canadian Dreams and American Control: The Political Economy of the Canadian Film Industry*, Manjunath Pendakur's comments on the ineffectiveness of protectionist Canadian policies provide a useful context for understanding the dynamic at play in the formulation of the voluntary quota policy:

> Protectionist Canadian policies do not attempt to overthrow foreign ownership and control of the Canadian economy. They are merely aimed at restructuring the relationship between foreign and indigenous capital in order to provide for greater participation for certain indigenous capitalists. In other words, these continuing conflicts between various sections of capital remain cast in the general framework of American hegemony in Canada.
>
> (Pendakur 1990, 34)

The voluntary quota system was viewed as a failure by 1975 when Secretary of State Hugh Faulkner lamented a policy that did not grant adequate exposure to Canadian films 'particularly in theatres with favourable locations' (quoted in Magder 1993, 160). Faulkner's alternative to the original voluntary quota system consisted of two parts, the first of which was a tax deduction permitting investors in an eligible Canadian feature to write off 100 per cent of their investment in the first year. Eligibility was limited to films of seventy-five minutes in length, where the producer and two-thirds of the creative personnel were Canadian and 75 per cent of the technical work was undertaken in Canada (160). None the less, this was still a voluntary scheme, without a tax levy mechanism to collect money from distributors' receipts for transfer into indigenous Canadian feature production. By 1977, Secretary of State John Roberts had drafted a policy with more political and economic teeth than Faulkner's alternative. Roberts's policy proposal imposed a 10 per cent tax on distributors' gross receipts. This would have meant a transfer of approximately $6 million from American distributors' earnings to Canadian feature production (167). The Finance Department and, not surprisingly, the Canadian Motion Picture Distribution Association greeted the Roberts proposal with entrenched resistance, and the initiative died on the table (168).

THE TAX-SHELTER BOOM AND CANADA'S HOLLYWOOD FEATURES

The Tompkins Report of 1976 emphasized the commercial, Hollywood aspect of the feature-film industry as an export industry (Magder 1993, 161). The report, therefore, pushes the Canadian industry towards making Hollywood-style films, films 'with a mass audience appeal beyond the boundaries of any one country', films which 'subsequently [return] a gross revenue well above production costs . . . A film such as *Jaws* is a classic example of this trend' (as quoted in Magder

1993, 162). As Magder notes, this attitude is a throwback to Grierson's 'if you can't beat 'em join 'em' ethos regarding Hollywood feature films (164). The Tompkins Report recommendations sacrifice cultural specificity of a Canadian national cinema for generic, North American – read Hollywood – projects to secure wide distribution and exhibition through US-owned companies. The late 1970s increase in feature production due to tax-shelter legislation developed under the assumption that Canada would become a Hollywood North producing features that could turn a profit in the United States, producing films for American audiences. This emphasis on the American market, of course, favoured the production of English-language films, as good risks for CFDC investment. Among the films produced during this period are *Meatballs* (Ivan Reitman 1979), distributed in the US and Canada by Paramount and grossing $40 million in 1979, *Murder by Decree* (Bob Clark 1979) and *The Changeling* (Peter Medak 1980). Distributed by 20th Century-Fox, *Porky's* (Bob Clark 1981) is the most successful of all tax-shelter films, grossing $11 million in Canada and $152 million worldwide in 1982 (Magder 1993, 197). Around this time the CFDC backed away from its nationalist remit to represent Canada to Canadians. As Michael McCabe, chief executive officer of the CFDC, stated in a 1980 interview, 'too often we hid behind our nationalism to protect mediocrity' (quoted in Magder 1993, 169). The CFDC's *Annual Report* for 1978–9 reflects this ideological shift, stating that the success of the 'cultural objective' was dependent on commercial success and that the production of films for a small elite couldn't possibly support a feature-film industry (quoted in Magder 1993, 183). The University of Toronto's Institute for Policy Analysis criticized the CFDC's tax-shelter incentive as having a 'perverse effect on Canadian film culture . . . Increased production budgets require larger foreign sales (which essentially means US sales) in order to have the slightest chance to recoup their costs . . . It may therefore be argued that one result of the expanded investment fostered by the tax shelter has been a reduction in "truly Canadian" films' (quoted in Magder 1993, 190). As Wyndham Wise observes, 'A handful of unscrupulous tax-shelter producer/entrepreneurs, with the assistance from short-sighted policy-makers and indifferent politicians took a distinctive, yet fragile national cinema, and in less than a year-and-a-half turned it into a full-blown, branch-plant industry' (Wise 1999, 24). Wise also suggests that the generous terms of the tax-shelter legislation sent the wrong signal to greedy producers and entrepreneurs who could walk 'away from their films with a great deal of money "off the top," no matter how much the film lost at the box office' (23).

For all of the shortcomings of the tax-shelter period in CFDC history, it did, as Magder points out, help to develop a cadre of skilled technicians and crews as well as establishing the careers of producers such as Robert Lantos, whose Alliance Communications became a major player in production and distribution (Magder 1993, 192). Moreover, some films made during this period, such as *Les bons débarras* (Francis Mankiewicz 1980), *Les Plouffe* (Gilles Carle 1981) and *The Grey Fox* (Phillip Borsos 1982) did represent Canada to Canadians. The much-admired *Grey Fox* proved an exception to the rule representing overt Canadian content in a Western genre that garnered critical praise, and American distribution through United Artist Classics. In response to criticisms that the tax-shelter boom had failed to produce 'truly Canadian' films, the Minister for Communications, Francis Fox, adjusted the criteria for what constituted a Canadian film, insisting that the roles of director and screenwriter be filled by Canadians to meet eligibility for capital cost allowance tax deductions (Magder 1993, 198).

TELEFILM CANADA

Increasingly television, both domestic and overseas, was providing an outlet for Canadian feature films, while the 60 per cent Canadian content regulations governing television broadcasting between 6 p.m. and midnight established a market and demand for Canadian programming (Magder 1993, 213). This shift towards television production and the increasingly close relationship shared by television and film are reflected in the renaming of CFDC as Telefilm Canada in 1984. According to its official website: 'Telefilm is one of the government's principal instruments for achieving its cultural objectives, including telling Canadian stories to Canada and the world.'[17] Of course, Telefilm faced the same major challenge as the CFDC, namely negotiating the American monopoly on distribution and exhibition in Canada. The 1980s saw two landmark attempts to invoke protectionist legislation that would limit both US domination of Canadian screens and the repatriation of profits by US-based distribution and exhibition companies. The province of Québec, with its dynamic film industry and receptive audiences for Québec cinema, attempted to challenge the American monopoly with the passage of Bill 109 in 1983. Bill 109 stipulated the following: only an enterprise having its principal establishment in Québec would be granted a general distributor's licence and, more importantly, all distributors in Québec would be required to reinvest at least 10 per cent of gross revenues in Québec-based productions (Magder 1993, 219). The Motion Picture Association of America regarded the legislation as draconian and, through its spokesperson Jack Valenti, threatened to pull its films out of Québec. The main concern of the US industry was what it referred to as the 'domino effect': the spread of protectionist legislation from Québec to other territories; the MPAA was not about to let Québec set a precedent it would have to deal with at future GATT meetings. A compromise was reached between the government of Québec and the American majors whereby the clauses in the legislation requiring reinvestment in Québec productions were deferred for future negotiations (224). Following the lead of the Québec government, the government of Canada attempted and failed to develop legislation that would retain 7 per cent of the US industry's revenues in Canada for Canadian-owned firms (224). The bill was killed off in the lead up to the Free Trade election of 1988 (225).

Clearly, Telefilm could not depend on the negotiation skills of Canadian politicians to create a more receptive environment for Canadian films in North America. Therefore, more money was invested in production and in distribution and marketing. In 1986 a $65 million Feature Film Fund was launched to support the work of Canadian film-makers. Despite this influx of money and the critical and commercial success of Canadian films such as *Le déclin de l'empire américain* (Denys Arcand 1986), *Loyalties* (Anne Wheeler 1986), *Un Zoo la nuit* (Jean Claude Lauzon 1987), and *I've Heard the Mermaids Singing* (Patricia Rozema 1987), poor distribution continued to limit the number of Canadian screens showing Canadian films. The major American distributors have been, as Magder notes, reluctant to carry Canadian product. Consequently, 95 per cent of Canadian films are distributed by Canadian firms that lack the extensive distribution systems of the American majors (Magder 1993, 216). To remedy the problem of distribution Telefilm initiated a Feature Film Distribution fund in 1988 that 'offers Canadian distribution companies a line of credit to ensure that Canadian films have the greatest possible market access'.[18] In 1998 Telefilm and the Canadian Television Fund invested $35 million in the production of feature films. Additionally, Telefilm provided approximately $15 million to support the distribution, marketing, and national and international promotion.

Of course, with the proliferation of exhibition windows such as home videocassette recorders, DVD players and cable and satellite feeds into the home, distribution has been transformed from a monolithic theatrical enterprise into a wider-ranging system. Most Canadians view Canadian films not in the cinema but via broadcast, videocassette or DVD. As Colin Hoskins, Stuart McFadyen and Adam Finn report on the research of David Ellis (1992): 'A Canadian movie attracting 30,000 in cinema attendance can be expected to attract about 100,000 on pay-per-channel TV (although pay-TV is found in only 10 per cent of Canadian cable homes), about 150,000 on home video, and 1 million on broadcast TV (two showings of 500,000 each)' (Hoskins, McFadyen, Finn 1997, 96). Hoskins, McFadyen and Finn, however, note one factor Ellis fails to take into account, the extent to which the marketing and publicity surrounding cinema exhibition 'creates a demand for the film in later exhibition windows' (96). Moreover, according to Elizabeth McDonald, the president of the Canadian Film and Television Production Association, Canadian feature films pull 40 per cent of their revenues from pay television (Gasher 1996, 23). Twenty-seven years after the establishment of the CFDC, Canada, through the work of the CFDC and Telefilm, had a thriving independent production industry that was beginning to wean itself from direct government investment (Dorland 1998, 145).

CO-PRODUCTION

Some of Telefilm's success can be attributed to its development of innovative industrial strategies such as co-production, which was used to circumvent the US monopoly on distribution and gain access to new markets for Canadian films. As early as 1962 Guy Roberge, chairman of the NFB, was exploring the possibilities of co-production with Britain and France on behalf of the Government of Canada (Dorland 1998, 83). As Dorland notes, the federal government's decision on 28 May 1962 to pursue co-production possibilities with France and Britain marked the state's initial step into private feature-film production (84). The first co-production pact was signed with France on 11 October 1963 (87). Increasingly co-productions are 'a key component of Canadian film and television production. They are a favoured method of penetrating new markets and facilitating project financing.'[19] Telefilm Canada sees co-production as 'a tool to finance high-quality products for distribution in the global market place'.[20] As literature posted on Telefilm's website notes, a co-production deal increases the production values of a project from an average budget for a Canadian feature-film deal of $2–3 million to $6–12 million.[21] Over $500 million was generated by co-productions in 1997. Between 1994 and 1999, 230 projects had been co-produced between Canada and foreign partners, generating production activity worth some $1.6 billion.[22] By 1998 Canada had forty-four co-production treaties in force with fifty-two countries, including Algeria, Argentina, Australia, Belgium, Brazil, Chile, China, Cuba, Czechoslovakia, Denmark, Finland, France, Germany, Greece, Hong Kong, Hungary, Iceland, Ireland, Israel, Italy, Japan, Luxembourg, Malta, Mexico, Morocco, Netherlands, New Zealand, Norway, Poland, Romania, Russian Federation, South Africa, South Korea, Spain, Sweden, Switzerland, United Kingdom, Venezuela and Yugoslavia.[23] CINAR Films, Nelvana Ltd and Alliance Atlantis constitute Canada's major co-production companies. Among some of the more successful co-productions of recent years are *Black Robe* (Bruce Beresford, Canada/Australia 1991), *Map of the Human Heart* (Vincent Ward, Canada/Australia/France/United Kingdom/United States 1992), *Zero Patience* (John Greyson, Canada/United Kingdom 1993), *Le confessionnal* (Robert Lepage, Canada/France/United Kingdom 1995), *Margaret's Museum* (Mort Ransen, Canada/United Kingdom 1995) and *The Red Violin* (François Girard, Canada/Italy/United Kingdom/ United States 1998).

Co-productions, however, certainly don't represent a panacea for the Canadian film-maker; they bring with them not only bigger budgets but, as director Anne Wheeler related in a 2000 forum on film production in Canada, potential compromises that could dilute the Canadianness of a production. Discussing the exigencies of finding production moneys in Canada Wheeler introduces the international co-production alternative:

> If I try to go international, they'll say the story is too Canadian. I've gotten that. On a bigger budget like that you have to have an international star, and you start playing this whole game of trying to get the star attached to the project and then maybe they want to change the actual location. At one point this [particular project] was supposed to be

shot on Vancouver Island at the turn of the century in the opium days of Victoria. Gee, the closest possibility I came to getting it made was in Ireland, and it was going to change the story significantly, so I refused to do it, I said no I won't tell that story in that way.

Echoing Wheeler's comments, director Gary Burns, speaking at the same forum, suggests that it is getting 'harder and harder to make a purely Canadian film financially' and that most people he knows in the industry are 'moving toward international co-production'.[24]

It has taken several decades, and trial and error experiments with industrial strategies, but Canadian national cinema now includes an internationally successful and healthy indigenous feature-film industry. *I've Heard the Mermaids Singing* (Patricia Rozema 1987) was awarded the Cannes Prix de la jeunesse and grossed $2.5 million in the United States. Denys Arcand's *Le déclin de l'empire américain* (1986) and Atom Egoyan's *The Sweet Hereafter* (1997) were both nominated for Oscars and awarded prizes at Cannes. The success of Canadian features, and a perception that they have potential to act as a national unity strategy, prompted Heritage Minister Sheila Copps to propose the creation of a Canadian Feature Film Fund in 1999 that would contribute $50 million to what the federal government already spends on film financing, establishing a film fund worth $100 million. This new money would raise the average budget and number of Canadian films and fund distribution, promotion, translation and training.[25] Despite these successes, the fact remains that approximately 2 per cent of Canadian cinema screens reflect Canadian images back to their audiences.[26]

One company that contributed, perhaps more than any other, to the commercial viability of Canadian cinema in an international market was Robert Lantos's Alliance Communications Corporation, now, after a 1998 merger with Canada's number two media company Atlantis, Alliance Atlantis. The distribution problem that had plagued independent producers in the past was overcome by Alliance, thanks to investment from Telefilm and the business savvy of Lantos which made Alliance one of the twelve largest entertainment companies in the world on the basis of revenues.[27] A producer of film and television products ranging from Atom Egoyan's *The Adjuster* (1991), *Exotica* (1994), *The Sweet Hereafter* (1997) and David Cronenberg's *Crash* (1996) to internationally successful television series such as *E.N.G.* (sold to sixty countries), *Due South* (sold to over 150 countries) and *North of Sixty* (sold to thirty-six countries), Alliance was the major player in Canadian production and distribution of film and television, with a 75 per cent share in one of the country's largest distributors, Cineplex Odeon Films. This position is now occupied by Alliance Atlantis, which had projected revenues of approximately $750 million in 1998–9. Although, as Brian D. Johnson reports, some smaller companies questioned the wisdom of continued public subsidy for such a prosperous corporation, Lantos rationalized Telefilm Canada's investment by citing the profits the Crown Corporation derived from Alliance projects: 'There's no need for Telefilm in a David

Cronenberg film . . . but that doesn't mean that they shouldn't be involved. They will make money on *Crash* and they made money on *Exotica*. I think it's fair for them to not only subsidize but also to reap the benefits of the filmmakers they nurture and actually make profits' (quoted in Johnson 1996, 54). Public funding, however, Lantos acknowledges has been crucial to his success (54).

The Canadian Film Centre has pulled together funding from private sector and government sources to produce a number of short films and features. Founded by Academy-Award-winning director Norman Jewison in 1988, the Canadian Film Centre has become an indispensable national institution for the training and nurturing of screenwriters, directors, producers and editors. The Centre is sponsored by some of Canada's top corporations such as the Royal Bank of Canada, Viacom Canada and Molson, and film and television companies such as Global and Alliance Atlantis. In collaboration with film unions, and with financial support from all levels of government and from the corporate sector, the CFC has produced such successful Canadian features as *Rude* (Clement Virgo 1994) and *Cube* (Vincenzo Natali 1997) and counts directors John Greyson, Don McKellar and Mina Shum among its graduates. Vincenzo Natali's science-fiction thriller *Cube* experienced phenomenal success in international markets earning $10.3 million in theatrical release in France and becoming the number one video rental in Japan.

The political and economic structures shaping a Canadian national cinema have shifted from the early entrepreneurial cinema of *Back to God's Country* and the racially exclusive and utilitarian impulses of commerce and trade that drove documentary film production under the CGMPB and the first two decades of the NFB to a politically engaged documentary and feature-film production that often work to interrupt and challenge earlier cinematic imaginings of Canada as a patriarchal white Anglo-Saxon nation. Some symbolic gatherings of the nation that might be formed through spectatorship are now informed by the co-ordinates of difference produced by Studio D's New Initiatives in Film programme, the NFB's Aboriginal Programme, and the commercial sector of the industry, which has, with the support of Telefilm Canada, produced such transgressive features as *Masala* (Srinivas Krishna 1991), *Double Happiness* (Mina Shum 1994), *Sam and Me* (Deepa Mehta) and *Rude* (Clement Virgo 1994) to represent diasporic identities and race relations in Canada through multicultural fields of vision.

4

NARRATING NATIONS/
MA(R)KING DIFFERENCES

Nations have died . . . from the moment that they began to
dream the dreams of others, from the moment that they have
proved themselves unable to create their own mythology . . .
We, in Canada, have often been ashamed of our own mythology, of our own domestic heroes, and we have been quick to
mimic the fads of other lands. And so, with the cinema, we have
lived by proxy, for the last sixty years.

Guy Côté

EXTERNAL AND INTERNAL COLONIALISM

Guy Côté's comments, taken from a May 1964 speech to the Canadian Society
of Cinematographers, describe the ramifications for Canadian national cinemas of
an American 'cultural colonialism' (quoted in Dorland 1998, 123). Canada's
cultural representation of its national self is bound up in its construction of a
colonizing American Other, in this case the industrial Other of Hollywood. Representations of a harmonious relationship between the two countries, often celebrated in the world's longest undefended border, belie the history of physical and
economic incursions across that very border. American troops invaded Canada in
1812, and American capital, facilitated by Sir John A. Macdonald's National
Policy of 1879, created Canada's US-driven branch plant economy.[1] The Trudeau government's attempts to regain control of Canada's economy produced
the Foreign Investment Review Agency, which was created in 1973 to monitor
foreign takeovers of Canadian companies, and the National Energy Programme of
1980, a nationalist policy that sought to gain 50 per cent control over Canadian
resources. The failure of both of these projects was marked by the Mulroney
government's negotiation of the 1987 Free Trade Agreement (FTA), which
worked towards the elimination of tariffs to harmonize further the economies of
Canada and the United States. The North American Free Trade Agreement
(NAFTA) of 1994 saw Canada's full entry into globalization's post-national
world. Twelve years after the FTA was signed and five years after NAFTA, direct
American investment in Canada was in excess of $800 billion, and, according to
Peter C. Newman, Canadians now controlled a smaller segment of their 'pro-
ductive wealth than any other industrialized country on earth' (Newman 1999,

51). Clearly, as we saw in the Hollywood monopoly on Canadian domestic film distribution and exhibition discussed in Chapter 3, American economic hegemony in Canada has serious consequences for domestic cultural production. Drawing a direct correlation between what they read as an erasure of Canadian cultural identity and increasing American domination of Canadian cultural production, the Canadian Film and Television Production Association warned in 1991 that 'If Canada hopes to survive as a sovereign nation, it must take steps to repatriate its culture' (Harris 1991, C1). By 1995 Newman was writing about the Americanization of Canadian cultural institutions such as the national newspaper the *Globe and Mail* which had recently appointed an American, Roger Parkinson, as editor. Newman concludes from this appointment and others that 'the message is clear: to run a cultural institution in Canada requires no knowledge of country or people, but instead of how to tickle the bottom line' (Newman 1995, 40).

Increasingly, some Canadians feel they are being assimilated into a dominant United States monoculture. In a 1999 poll of twelve hundred Canadians conducted by the national newsmagazine *Maclean's* and the CBC, 50 per cent said they felt they were becoming more like Americans (Wood 1999, 22). With three-quarters of their books, 98 per cent of their cinema screen time and 90 per cent of their television programming and recorded music originating from foreign, largely American sources, it is not surprising that Canadians feel as if they are being taken over by what the narrator in Margaret Atwood's 1972 novel *Surfacing* referred to as the 'disease' (Atwood 1972, 7) from the south, 'the machine' of a colonizing American culture that 'takes a little of you at a time' leaving only a shell (165).[2] What is somewhat alarming, however, is that, despite Canada's domestic and international market successes in literature, popular music, and cinema since 1973 – due in part to federal and provincial policies funding and protecting cultural production – Canadians continue to register the homogenizing effect of a US-dominated global culture.[3]

Whilst American cultural and economic colonialism figure large for Canada, Anglophone Canadian cultural colonialism has, historically, thwarted the self-determination of Québec as a nation. From the perspective of Québec separatists, Québec constitutes a national community trapped within the Canadian nation by an accident of history, the conquest of New France by Britain on the Plains of Abraham in 1759. British victory initiated the twin processes of anglicization and Québécois resistance, with power differentials very quickly manifesting themselves around linguistic and cultural differences. English became the language of commerce and politics while the Treaty of Paris (1763) excluded 'Roman Catholics' – read French Canadians – from public office (Francis *et al.* 1992a, 167). Pressure exerted by French Canadians for a society that would recognize their customs and usages helped to form the Québec Act of 1774, which reintroduced French civil law to the colony and permitted Roman Catholics to hold office (Francis *et al.* 1992a, 174).[4] Although these aspects of the colonial legislation suggest a progressive British attitude toward the Québécois, secret instructions accompanying the Act ordered the governor to consider the gradual introduction of English civil law, and advocated the subordination of the Catholic church and suppression of religious orders (175). This duplicitous and assimilationist discourse set the antagonistic tone that shaped French–English relations for the next two hundred years. During the nineteenth and for most of the twentieth century the Québécois majority were second-class citizens in their own province. In the 1950s Québécois comprised the lowest-paid ethnic group in Québec (Francis *et al.* 1992b, 396). The marginalized position of the Québécois began to shift, under the leadership of Premier Jean Lesage (1960–6) whose Révolution tranquille or Quiet Revolution brought about rapid, non-violent change to make Québécois *maîtres chez nous* or 'masters in our own house'. In addition to seeking further autonomy for Québec from Ottawa, Lesage continued the secularization of the province initiated by his predecessor Maurice Duplessis and also created the Ministry of Cultural Affairs to protect and promote Québécois literature, cinema, visual arts, theatre and music. Ottawa responded to Québec's demands for autonomy through the Royal Commission on Bilingualism and Biculturalism (1963–9), which recommended the federal government's official recognition of French language and culture. The Trudeau government passed the Official Languages Act in 1969, enshrining French and English as the nation's official languages.[5] These changes to the status quo, however, were not substantive enough to satisfy Québec nationalists who sought to secede from Canadian federalism, nor were they radical enough to satisfy extremist nationalist groups such as the Front de libération du Québec (FLQ), which waged a terrorist campaign to overthrow the capitalist regime of federal and provincial governance that, in its view, exploited and oppressed Québécois labour. Despite, or perhaps because of, the violence of the October Crisis – the 1970 FLQ kidnapping of the British Trade Minister James Cross and provincial cabinet minister Pierre Laporte, and the execution of the latter – Québec and Ottawa continued to renegotiate the terms of federalism, often around language legislation and the 1982 Constitution Act which Québec refused to sign.[6] In 1980 the nationalist Parti Québécois government launched the first of two unsuccessful referenda to obtain a mandate for negotiating Sovereignty Association: political sovereignty for Québec combined with an economic association with the rest of Canada.[7] Over the last four decades, Québec has increasingly resisted dreaming the federalist dream of nation and Québec film-makers have refused to live by proxy; conversely they have focused on creating their own national mythology, their own national cinema. Simultaneously, film-makers in Anglophone Canada were also developing their own distinctive national mythology for the cinema.

Differences between Canada's two 'founding nations' and their cinemas prompted Québec critic Gilles Marsolais to write of a Canadian cinema composed of two divergent cinemas, 'Canadian' and Québécois (quoted in Leach 1984, 100). There are, however, dynamic moments of intersection and imbrication where a comparative context is essential for any consideration of what

Bhabha has called the 'impossible unity' of nation, for any substantive engagement with the impossible unity of a Canadian national cinema (Bhabha 1990, 1). This chapter locates those moments in 1960s meditations on nationalism by Michel Brault and Claude Jutra from Québec and Joyce Wieland from Anglophone Canada (Ontario), and in representations of Anglophone and Francophone 'nations' in genre texts, and in films representing the FLQ crisis of 1970.

ETHNIC AND GENDERED NATIONALISMS

The signifying practices of Michel Brault's and Claude Jutra's *Québec-USA ou l'invasion pacifique* (1962) and Joyce Wieland's *Patriotism, Part One* (1964), and *Reason Over Passion* (1967–9) work to construct, respectively, Québécois and Anglophone-Canadian national identities around tropes of nationalist struggles against historical and contemporary formations of imperialism. Whereas *Québec-USA ou l'invasion pacifique* presents a homogeneous Québécois ethnicity standing in resistance to the aggressive overtures of eighteenth-century British imperialism, twentieth-century Anglo-Canadian dominance and twentieth-century American neo-imperialism, Wieland's films figure Canada as a bicultural colonial space gendered variantly as male and female and subject to the violence of an aggressive US neo-imperialism. Although not unaware of Québec nationalists' perception of Anglo Canada as a colonizing force, Wieland's Canadian nationalist and feminist film project of the 1960s, aside from peripheral references to Québec nationalism in *Reason Over Passion*, was an anglocentric one that did not engage the irony of Anglo-Canada's doubled position of colonizer/colonized.[8] I will argue that, for all their attempts to transgress and denaturalize dominant mythologies of identity, Wieland's two films and *Québec-USA* re-inscribe Canadian identity as a white subject by creating exclusionary national narratives.

Patriotism, One and *Reason Over Passion*

Visual artist, experimental film-maker and putative mother of the feminist avant-garde in Canada, Joyce Wieland figures Canada as a passive male complicit in his rape by a US neo-imperialism in the stop-motion *Patriotism, One*, and as a series of idealized signifiers which fail to signify, perpetually displacing each other in the experimental film *Reason Over Passion*. A film Wieland refers to as a technically bad experiment with animation,[9] *Patriotism, Part One* depicts an army of phallic, bun-clad wieners marching on a vulnerable sleeping white male body, naked save for a sheet. During the advance of the hot dogs, the American flag jumps out from under the sheet, forcing the wieners out of their buns and wrapping itself around them before disappearing under the sheet to continue the attack. Although the man awakens to give the hot dogs a look of incredulity, he appears

106

powerless to halt what Lee Parpart reads as a sexually exploitative assault (Parpart 1999a, 257). The film ends with a shot of the man in bed with a smile, the spent wieners, Old Glory and a pile of destroyed hot dog buns. In this light-hearted, and by early twenty-first-century standards hackneyed, allegory of US neo-imperialism the hot dog is not just a sign of a US culture passively consumed by Canadians, but rather a phallic sign of a penetrating US multinational capitalism. Simultaneously, given the ephemeral, junk-food connotations of the hot dog, the film represents an ironic destabilization of what Parpart refers to as phallic nationalism (253).

This film is important to an understanding of Wieland's imagining of Canada as female. Not unlike Atwood's gendered allegorizing of the relationship of Canada to the United States as that of a feminized backdrop to a Hollywood cowboy,[10] Wieland came to envision Canada as female and its 'defacto colonial ruler, the United States' as male (258). Wieland's film's playing out of this gendered dynamic of imperialism through the sign systems of phallic and feminized masculinities raises the problematic undermining such essentialist constructions as gendered nations. On the one hand, Wieland's representation of Canada as a passive white male could be read as an ironic appropriation and troubling of a patriarchal tradition in which woman is constructed as the symbolic bearer of the nation but denied any meaningful access to national agency.[11] On the other, it can be read as a re-inscription of binaries refusing woman's complicity with the structures of the patriarchal state.[12] The exchange between the white male and the wieners of *Patriotism, Part One* invokes an untenable symbolic compartmentalization of Canada along gender lines. The collusion of patriarchal state and corporate structures for mutual satisfaction (the US wieners and the white Canadian male) suggests an exploited national community that is female, at a distance from and therefore not complicit in the selling out of Canada to US concerns, or Canadian nationalist imperialism directed at First Nations. Acknowledging white women's subordination to white men and the 'borrowed' power imperial women had over colonized men and women (as missionaries, teachers, nurses etc.), Anne McClintock has argued that white women were 'ambiguously complicit both as colonizers and colonized, privileged and restricted, acted upon and acting' (1995, 6). Moreover, 1960s and 1970s nationalist white feminist representations of Canada as a feminized victim of imperialist activities work to displace the real historical, and contemporary, subjects of imperialist aggression in Canada, First Nations.[13]

Part of what Wieland considered her ongoing role of feminizing national symbols,[14] *Reason Over Passion* is an experimental nationalist road film (an experiment in nationalisms) cross-cutting idealized signifiers for Canada – the national flag, images of Prime Minister Pierre Elliott Trudeau – with coast-to-coast shots of regional landscapes. The establishing shot, a flickering image of the Canadian flag punctuated by the stereotypical audio cues for Canada of a snowstorm's howling wind announces representation of the nation as the subject of Wieland's film. The travelogue begins with shots of the Atlantic Ocean against the Cape

Breton coast accompanied by the strains of bagpipes, and continues east to Québec. After Québec, we encounter Trudeau in the film's centre section, his visage and words effectively displacing Ontario, before we travel through the prairies and end our journey in Vancouver with what Regina Cornwell describes as a postcard shot of a steamer (1977, 288). During this trans-Canada trek, computer-generated permutations of Trudeau's words 'reason over passion' flash over the onscreen images. Flickering shots of the dotted line of a highway or of the landscape flying by from a train window remind the viewer of the technology required to traverse such a vast and geographically diverse terrain. Deliberately avoiding representations of the people who live in what the camera represents as an empty country, Wieland provides idealized signifiers, such as a statue of Robbie Burns, the sound of bagpipes, the Union Jack and the *fleur de lis* flag of Québec to designate the specific, exclusionary strands of national ethnicity and colonial history forging her imagined community.

Along the way, Wieland's handheld camera captures reflections in train and car windows of the woman making the images while the soundtrack records a woman's voice amidst a cacophony of industrial noise. Wieland thereby sutures herself and the viewer into the self-reflexive process of making the nation, of feminizing the cold rationalist Trudeau vision of 'reason over passion', described by Linda Hutcheon as a 'male power slogan' (Hutcheon 1989, 38). Trudeau's description of his writing – '*La raison avant la passion; c'est la thème du tous mes écrits /* Reason over passion; that is the theme of all my writing' – provides a point of intervention for Wieland's film. Made at the height of Trudeaumania – a national fascination and identification with the young, progressive Liberal Justice Minister that resulted in his election to the office of the Prime Minister in 1968 – *Reason Over Passion* translates Trudeau's mode of self-expression into a national motto, the vision of a national icon, and interrupts, appropriates and ironically reconfigures his words and image of 'reason' so that they are displaced by Wieland's passion. Trudeau's rational thought is relocated in a field of passionate images of the landscape and incongruous soundtrack noises that work to undo reason. Reason is ironized in the 537 permutations of Trudeau's words inscribed on the film stock by what Hutcheon refers to as 'reason's instrument', the computer, which literally disassembles his text into collections of meaningless letters floating senselessly above Wieland's images of the nation (Hutcheon 1989, 87).

Reason Over Passion presents the viewer with idealized signifiers which attempt to refer back to the material signified of a Canadian nation, but are quickly displaced by others which seek to perform the same work. Before considering such signifying practices in the film, semiotics requires further elucidation. In the introduction to a collection of essays on semiotics or the science of signs, Marshall Blonsky draws on the work of Wlad Godzich and Umberto Eco to conceptualize the Saussurian sign as:

> a recognition marker, an expression, a signifier. It is correlated by a
> culture (and this correlation is a code) to items of the culture's contents

(the signified, the form of content). A theory of codes results and also a theory of sign production; that is, a theory of signification systems, of ideological functioning.

(Blonsky 1985, xvi)

For example, in Wieland's film the idealized sign of Pierre Trudeau's pro-filmic photographic image is composed of a signifier and signified. In the first or denotative order of signification, the iconic signifier Trudeau refers back to the signified of the man Pierre Trudeau, the Prime Minister of Canada. In the second or connotative order of signification the metonymic signifier Pierre Trudeau stands in for Canada, a part is made to stand in for a whole; the leader stands in for the nation. Here we see the correlation of the signifier by a culture's myth-making agents; through the myth of Trudeaumania, a young, handsome, dynamic leader with a vision becomes associated with the abstract imagined community of Canada. The collision of the first two orders of signification produces a third, ideological, order of signification in the viewer. In this intersubjective interpretation, the signifier Trudeau refers back to the signified of a strong federalist vision of a bicultural and bilingual nation that would peripheralize regional and cultural differences in the name of national unity. This signification of Trudeau as nation is then interrupted by the national flag, another idealized signifier for Canadian nation that attempts to refer the spectator back to the impossible, because indeterminant, signified of Canadian nation. The signifying chain Wieland constructs through her cutting and combining of signs continually defers signification of nation, brings into question how a nation signifies. However, despite this gesture toward the indeterminacy of nation, and her emphasizing of nation as an experiment in making meaning through the genre of experimental film, Wieland reduces Canadian nation to tensions in signification located amongst Anglo-Celtic, Anglo-Saxon and Québécois white settler ethnicities as these are represented in the film in bagpipes, the statue of Robbie Burns, the Union Jack, the *fleur de lis* flag and an audio track of a French lesson. Wieland's film privileges white liberal feminist concerns about imperial and patriarchal oppressions at the expense of First Nations and Canadians of colour, thus displacing them from the terrain of the national; the film's idealized signifiers fail to refer back to the material reality of these Canadians. In this respect Wieland's two avant-garde films, aside from their feminist politics, are, surprisingly, in line with the basic 'founding nations' co-ordinates of the NFB's *Peoples of Canada*; both films address and construct an infrangible we of white invader-settler 'founding' nations.

Québec-USA ou l'invasion pacifique / Visit to a Foreign Country

Michel Brault and Claude Jutra, two of the most influential figures of Québec cinema, collaborated on this NFB project early on in their careers. They would

later work together as, respectively, cinematographer and director on the celebrated *Mon oncle Antoine* (1971), while Brault would go on to direct *Les ordres*
(1974) and photograph the much-loved *Les bons débarras* (1980), and Jutra
would make the acclaimed *Kamouraska* (1973). Brault and Jutra share with Wieland a desire to articulate national identity through nationalist responses to
imperial colonialism, and like Wieland exclude First Nations and people of colour
from their imagined community. Despite this common characteristic, Brault's
and Jutra's documentary representation of Québec's status as a contested
imagined community within Canada was produced by a structure of Canadian
federalism (the NFB) designed to promote national unity, and provides a sharp
contrast to Wieland's experimental Anglo-Canadian documentary representation
of nation. Unlike Wieland's films, Brault and Jutra produce a linear narrative
told through image, voice-over and interviews which construct their province as
a pseudo-national French-speaking community under attack in North America.

Québec-USA ou l'invasion pacifique (1962) is a film structured around representations of Québec's difference from Anglo-Canada and the United States.
The territorial, linguistic and cultural borders separating Québec from the
United States and Anglo Canada are made clear to the spectator in the film's
establishing shots depicting what the male French-speaking voice-over narrates as
a US tourist 'invasion' of the province. The idea that the province is a separate
country from English-speaking Canada is marked in the politics of translation
which rewrite the title of the English language version of the film as *Visit to a
Foreign Country*. As the vast majority of the NFB's audience is English-speaking,
this translation performs the ideological work of disciplining Anglo-Canadian
spectators to view Québec as territory as foreign to them as it is to American
tourists, the narrative agents through which they view Québec in this film. Composed of five distinct sequences – the opening border sequence; a language lab
sequence promoting Québec as an international centre for French culture and
language; an African-American tourist sequence; a military performance by
French-speaking soldiers in British uniforms; and a sequence where US sailors
make overtures to Québécois women – the film speaks its difference to anglocentric North-American cultures, and Anglophone spectators in the Québécois
accent of the male voice-over that narrates the English version of the film.

A province that will not forget its cultural and colonized past, Québec's official
motto is '*Je me souviens*' (I will remember); Québec's French language and
culture will not be forgotten, nor will its occupation by the British nor its invasion by the Americans. All of these cultural memories – language, English domination and the threat of American invasion – are central to the film narrative's
construction of Québec in 1962. The film's very first lines of voice-over frame
Québec as a cultural space subject to, yet dynamic enough to survive, aggression.
In narrating the shots of Americans crossing the border, the voice-over correlates
the influx of American tourists with the historical fact of American incursion into
the province: 'In 1775 their forefathers led by General Montgomery marched
into the province of Québec. They didn't get anywhere.' Similarly, subsequent

110

shots of a US naval vessel and disembarking American sailors, contemporary signs of a global US cultural and military hegemony, are countered by signs marking the preservation and perpetuation of French-Canadian culture, a large language laboratory where French is being taught to English speakers. The ability of Québec to compete successfully with American popular culture is communicated through the soundtrack. American big band music interrupts the centuries-old habitant folk music of the title sequence to accompany shots of the ship and sailors. However, the habitant folk music of Québec returns to interrupt the American music and punctuate a cut away from the American presence to the waterways and highways of *la belle province*. The language lab sequence affords the voice-over opportunities to articulate the importance of Québec as a founding nation in the contemporary power structure of Canada where French is spoken by the Prime Minister and is 'bound to be useful' 'no matter what your occupation'. On the one hand, the film anticipates the developing bicultural and bilingual vision of the federal government, yet on the other it challenges this national vision by producing Québec as monocultural, Francophone, imagined community. This is the Québec presented to an African-American tourist couple in the next sequence.

The American presence reverts back to tourism with the introduction of an African-American couple who is taken on a tour of Québec City by a male Québécois youth. Anticipating Québec separatist Pierre Vallières's representation of the Québécois as an oppressed minority, 'les nègres blancs', Brault and Jutra construct a questionable equivalence between the positions of Québécois in Canada and African Americans in the US (Vallières 1968, 26). A shot of the African-American couple driving by the Plains of Abraham, site of the British victory over the French, is narrated as 'One minority guides another past the Plains of Abraham'. While Québécois did find themselves discriminated against in their own province, important material differences between their situation in Canada and that of African Americans in the US, such as the legacy of slavery – segregation and lynchings – militate against such easy comparisons. The African-American tourist sequence plays an important role in establishing what Balibar contends is the 'long "pre-history"' generating a national formation, that produces 'the people' of Québec (Balibar 1991, 88). A tracking shot of a public garden in which plants have been arranged to spell out '*Je me souviens*' is one of the first sites taken in by the tour and establishes the remembering of the 'pre-history' of Québec that this sequence will focus on. The tour taken by the African Americans, and the question and response session with their guide are structured, by the film-makers, to produce a *pur laine* Québec. The tour guide explains that the Québécois are a people whose land was 'taken' from them by the English in 1759, ignores a question about the English-speaking 'natives' of Québec, and to the question 'Do you have any Indians in Québec now?' replies 'No'. In this way – remembering and forgetting – the film negotiates what Balibar terms the fundamental problem of the nation, the production of the people. *Québec-USA ou l'invasion pacifique* produces 'the effect of unity by virtue of which the people will appear, in everyone's eyes, "as a people", that is, as the basis and origin of political power' (Balibar 1991, 94). An ethnically based, homogeneous, *Québécois*, imagined community is produced by evacuating First Nations, Anglophone Quebeckers and Quebeckers of colour from the socio-political terrain of this, in the film's English title's terms, 'foreign country'. The film's interpretation of the province's 'prehistory' suggests that, if the British General Wolfe had been indisposed that day in 1759, French political power would have been more broadly established by the now of the film's present, and 'many of these tourists might already be French speaking'. In the discursive organization of the film, the British conquest and subsequent Anglophone domination are accidents of history.

That the Québécois are 'the people' whose self-determination has been thwarted by English domination is communicated by the directors in a sequence where shots of French soldiers dressed in the red tunics and bearskin hats of English troops are cross-cut with shots of a child reading *Gulliver's Travels* and illustrations of Gulliver on his back, tied down by the Lilliputians. These images and their voice-over narration provide the film's most pointed political commentary. As the soldiers drill and are photographed by tourists, the voice-over interprets the shots for the viewer: 'You may see a display of military might anywhere, but only here will you be able to see French-speaking soldiers disguised in English uniforms performing a borrowed ceremony for the benefit of American cameras.' The image of Québécois parading around in English uniforms is denaturalized here as an official performance of belonging to an other imagined community, Anglo-Canada, and recalls the film narrative's anterior signs of Québec's invasion and occupation by American tourists, US sailors, and the British conquest on the Plains of Abraham. Fast-motion photography of the drilling also works to denaturalize it and render it a ridiculous, fraudulent dance. The contemporaneous oppression of Québec's self-determination is emphasized by a cut from the colonized French-speaking soldiers in English uniforms to an illustration from *Gulliver's Travels* of a regiment of Lilliputian soldiers marching beside a captive Gulliver. The collision of images suggests an allegorical reading where English Canada stands in for the Lilliputians that would restrain a Québécois Gulliver. Cross-cutting between the boy reading and the soldiers drilling emphasizes this allegory, while an excerpt from Swift, read aloud by the boy via voice-over narration, makes a bid for a more autonomous Québec: 'He could not imagine of whom we were afraid or against whom we were to fight and would hear my opinion whether a private man's house might not be better defended by himself.'

The film's final sequence revisits its opening *l'invasion pacifique* or peaceful invasion of US sailors on shore leave in Québec City to reiterate that Québec is resilient and savvy enough to survive the aggressive overtures of Anglophone Others. This is achieved through a gendered narrative construction of image and voice-over where woman stands in for Québec and the sailors constitute a phallic US nationalism. Shots of sailors making overtures to women on the city's boardwalk are narrated by a refrain of voice-over narration from the beginning of the film: '200 years ago the Americans sent their strongest troops, they didn't get very far. Today they send their smartest sailors. They get further.' At this juncture a cut is made to a shot of a sailor assisting a woman whose high heel is caught in the boardwalk. Several shots of sailors propositioning women are followed by a voice-over: 'it is hard to say which is the winner, our Québec girls are pretty good at strategy.' At this point we cut to a shot of a Québec girl who rejects a sailor's invitation for a date. Not unlike Wieland's gendered representation of Canada, Brault's and Jutra's representation of Québec as a white woman rebuffing the advances of a neo-imperialist United States elides the province's history of imperialist aggression against First Nations, something that irrupts in Alanis Obomsawin's film *Kanehsatake: 270 Years of Resistance* (1993).

GENRE TEXTS

If genre is, as Stephen Neale argues, 'difference *in* repetition' (Neale 1980, 50), that is the reworking, extension and transformation of the normative codes of a genre, then a consideration of Anglophone-Canadian and Québécois translations of the dominant Hollywood cinema's normative genre codes can reveal national differences in narrative significations (Neale 1990, 58). Genres are components of what Neale calls, after Christian Metz, the mental machinery of cinema: 'a machine for the regulation of the orders of subjectivity' (Neale 1980, 19).[15] Canadian and Québécois productions of the melodrama, the road movie and the western constitute different modes of signification from their Hollywood counterparts and therefore produce different functionings of subjectivity, 'moving the subject differently in their various semiotic processes, producing distinct modes of address' (Neale 1980, 25).[16] For example, while a Québécois family melodrama such as *Mon oncle Antoine* (Claude Jutra 1971) may play on the essential elements of its industrial Other, the Hollywood melodrama, its mode of address is inflected by the specificity of Québec culture, society, politics and economics, as well as the director's and cinematographer's aesthetic sensibilities. So, while it exploits audience expectations that have, largely, been forged by Hollywood – the victimization of the powerless by a corrupt social system as this is represented through family relationships[17] – *Mon oncle Antoine* addresses its audience via narrative co-ordinates demarcating the power differentials between French and English, management and labour, working class and bourgeoisie, and cinematographer Michel Brault's haunting representation of physical and social landscapes. Although Neale's argument for difference in repetition is focused on Hollywood cinema, it has a particular resonance for Canadian cinemas in English, Québec, Australian and New Zealand cinemas where difference in repetition is complicated by a desire to communicate national and cultural differences to the dominant Hollywood cinema through Hollywood narrative systems. As Tom O'Regan writes, such national cinemas and their film-makers 'indigenize genres' (O'Regan 1996, 1).[18] Canadian and Québec cinemas rework and transform Hollywood genres that have a currency with global and domestic audiences to tell or sell Canadian and Québec stories. In this way, we understand Neale's point that 'genres are systems of orientations, expectations, and conventions that circulate between industry, text, and subject' (Neale 1980, 19). This section considers Canadian and Québec indigenizations of the family melodrama, the road movie and the western with reference to the following films: *Mon oncle Antoine*, *Les bons débarras* (Francis Mankiewicz 1980), *The Adjuster* (Atom Egoyan 1991), *Le confessionnal* (Robert Lepage 1995), *Margaret's Museum* (Mort Ransen 1995), *My American Cousin* (Sandy Wilson 1985), *Highway 61* (Bruce Macdonald 1992), *Goin' Down the Road* (Don Shebib 1970), *The Grey Fox* (Philip Borsos 1982) and *Road to Saddle River* (Francis Damberger 1997). Indigenization is structured through cultural and national inflections of the genre, but also by what Neale refers to as genre specificity, 'exclusive and particular combinations and articulations of elements' and 'the exclusive and particular weight given in any one genre to elements which in fact it shares with other genres' (Neale 1990, 22).

MELODRAMA

As in Chapter 1, I am concerned here with the family melodrama, a genre where plots revolve around the powerless, and their victimization by a corrupt social order as this is represented through family relationships (Elsaesser 1974, 514–15). A genre that tailors 'ideological conflicts into emotionally charged family situations' (Elsaesser 1974, 516), the popular family melodrama 'facilitates conflict and negotiation between cultural identities' (Gledhill 1987, 37). These are the elements given exclusive or particular weight in the films under consideration. Family melodramas, as we saw in Chapter 1, negotiate the space between the home and the community, and the family's classed, raced and gendered positions within these two spheres. As Hayward has suggested, in melodrama the family becomes the site of patriarchy and capitalism and therefore reproduces them (Hayward 1996b, 200). The present analysis will pay close attention to cinematic constructions of the home, site of the family, as a symbolic structure of identity, its *heimlich* (canny, homely, familiar) and its *unheimlich* (uncanny, alien, unknown) properties.[19] In her perceptive and cogent reading of colour spectrums in Robert Lepage's *Le confessionnal*, Erin Manning locates the home – as identity – within the discourse of the *unheimlich*, suggesting that its continual alteration changes the 'configurations of inclusion and exclusion at the level of larger "homes" such as nation-states' (Manning 1998, 63). For Manning's term nation-state, I will substitute nation or imagined community, to adapt her conceptualization of the home as an allegorical sign of the melodramatic text's relationship to the world outside the text, the national communities outside the film.[20] For it is this world outside the film upon which the success of melodrama is dependent; as Gledhill argues, 'the melodrama has power only on the premiss of a recognisable, socially constructed world. As the terms of this world shift so must recognition of its changing audiences continually be re-solicited' (Gledhill 1987, 37). This re-soliciting of the audience brings us back to Neale's conceptualization of film narrative as processes of production and structuration in and for a subject (Neale 1980, 25), that is the distinct modes of address through which genres hail their audiences as subjects.

Mon oncle Antoine

Mon oncle Antoine (Claude Jutra 1971) tells a story of Québec in the 1940s by juxtaposing the family of asbestos miner Jos Poulin to the extended bourgeois family of Antoine, a shop owner and the town undertaker. Antoine's household is composed of his wife Cecile, his nephew Benoit, Carmen, a shop girl who lives with them and Fernand the shop clerk. The establishing shots of Jutra's film structure audience understanding of the social terrain that will alienate asbestos miner Jos Poulin from his work, himself, his home and his family by addressing the specificity of labour-capital relations in the province during this period. Long shot pans of a mining town give way to lyrical long shot pans of the surrounding mist-shrouded landscape until the camera comes to rest on an asbestos mine. This shot dissolves into another pan of the landscape that moves in to offer a close-up of a cascade of asbestos being spewed out of the mine (Figure 4.1). A cut from a low-angled shot of the mine and the falling asbestos – suggesting the mine's domination of the town – to a red truck introduces us to one of the miners, Jos Poulin. A heated reprimand he receives from an English-speaking representative of the company prompts Jos to quit the mine, and leave his family to work as a lumberjack. However, before we learn the full extent of Jos's alienation and his plans to quit the mine, Jutra cuts from another shot of cascading asbestos to Antoine, Benoit and Fernand working at the funeral service of another miner. Although this miner's cause of death is never stated explicitly, Jutra's collision of shots suggests that the mine is the cause of death, perhaps through asbestosis.

Having demonstrated visually that this is a capitalist landscape that consumes labour, and that this consumption feeds the bourgeoisie as this is represented in Antoine's funeral business which disposes of the consumed labour, Jutra cuts back to Jos and other miners drinking at a local bar. The graffiti read by Jos as he relieves himself at the urinal works to re-solicit the audience for a Québécois melodrama by naming the specificity of the corrupt social order victimizing the powerless in Québec, the Union Nationale government of Maurice Duplessis. From Jos's subjective camera perspective the viewer reads the name of the Québec Premier Duplessis in the same visual field as a caricature of Adolph Hitler, and crude drawings of a woman's open legs and a penis. This association of Duplessis with the obscene, exploitation and fascism on the toilet walls of a working-class bar invokes the history of his harsh dealings with striking asbestos

Figures 4.1–2 Mon oncle Antoine (1971). © National Film Board of Canada, 2001. All rights reserved

miners. The graffiti and Jos's pissing against the wall indicate the pitiful attempts at resistance to the corrupt social order available to the disempowered miners. Labour unrest in Québec's asbestos country in the 1940s and early 1950s became the focus of a social activism that later manifested itself as the Quiet Revolution and eventually brought down the Duplessis regime. Jos returns to his friends, proclaiming that he will not be another victim of the mine, naming and indicting the social structures that work to oppress and alienate him: 'the hell with them, the English . . . the undertaker, the priest the boss, the whole bunch . . . I'm getting the hell out.'[21]

Reading against the grain of Janis Pallister's (1995, 237) depoliticized analysis of the film privileging Benoit and his adolescent rite of passage, I agree with Bruce Elder that Jutra, by framing his narrative with signs of the social and industrial conditions of the time, signals the political implications of the film (Elder 1977, 195). Of, course, Pallister is quite right to read Benoit as the focus of the film; however, we know him only in relation to the frames that precede and follow him, i.e. in the context of the field of social relations in which Jutra places him. Capitalist industry and the Roman Catholic church constitute the disciplining and omnipresent power structures regulating the subject formation and social relations of the townspeople, and also work diegetically, visually to forge a relationship between the rebellion of Jos and Benoit's developing resistance to the mine, the church and Antoine.

Following Jos's decision to stop 'licking [the] arse' of the power structure, he bids farewell to his children and walks away from his home and family. The transition from Jos's narrative to Benoit's is affected by the following series of shots: a cut away from Jos's departure to long shots of men going to work in the mine, a long shot pan to the church followed by a zoom to a medium close-up of the exterior of the church and a cut to the interior where Benoit is stealing the Host. Even when the mine is not present visually, it haunts the narrative. For example, a piercing siren warning of an imminent blast interrupts the sequence where the community gathers at Antoine's shop to buy their Christmas gifts with

116

their pay packets from the mine. The dominance and power of the church, the mine and Antoine's shop are interrupted and denaturalized by Benoit's developing recognition of them as corrupt. Through the gaze of Benoit we see the priest surreptitiously drinking the Communion wine, Antoine's boorish consumption of food and drink at the home of the bereaved Poulins, and finally we see the pathetic charitable efforts of the mine's boss who denies his workers a rise, but throws Christmas 'trinkets' at the townspeople from his carriage. It is at this point that Benoit acts out and marks his public rejection of the social order by throwing snowballs at the boss.

As Elder notes, Benoit's actions constitute an important contrast to the parallel Jos Poulin narrative. Poulin returns home from the forest to an oppressive reality he is incapable of changing, his son's death, in Elder's terms a defeat, while Benoit's awakening to the social conditions around him provides him with the means for a potential victory over the forces of oppression (Elder 1977, 198). Elder's interpretation is an allegorical one that reads melodrama's structuring of ideological conflicts through family scenarios; in this analysis Benoit stands in for the people of Québec and the collective awakening that facilitated the Quiet Revolution. Allegory here performs the ideological work of constructing 'the people' of Québec as an ethno-national group, Québécois, producing a *pur laine* Québec that, similarly to the vision of *Québec-USA*, excludes First Nations, Anglophones and Quebeckers of colour.

One important aspect of Benoit's awakening, absent from Elder's reception of the film, is the boy's complicity, as an agent of Antoine and the bourgeoisie, with the structures that oppress the Poulins, as Jos delineates these at the beginning of the film; Benoit works as an altar boy, and a shop and funeral assistant to Antoine. This complicity becomes clear to the audience and to Benoit when his recklessness results in the loss of Marcel's body. Following the ill-fated trip to the Poulin home, Benoit's understanding of his own home and family is altered. Antoine's inability to help Benoit retrieve Marcel's casket characterizes the elder man as a drunken, impotent fraud in Benoit's eyes. Upon his return, Benoit is confronted with an *unheimlich* secret of the home when he discovers the duplicity of Fernand and Cecile whose lovemaking cuckolds Antoine. Jutra, however, represents the home as an *unheimlich* structure of identity throughout the film. Home for Benoit – *le magasin général* – is a site where the reproduction of capitalism is staged, a location of commerce hailing the community as consumers and wage slaves. Carmen is a wage-slave farmed out to Antoine by her father who visits at Christmas not to see his daughter but to collect her wages. Home or *le magasin général* is an ideological space where Roman Catholicism and capitalist consumerism intersect and are focalized through the concept of the family, which is itself, in Athusserian terms, an ISA. The disciplining Roman Catholic model of the ideal family, the Nativity scene, is represented as commodity by its placement behind Antoine's shop windows (Figure 4.2) alongside other commodities such as the wedding veil purchased by a young woman during the Christmas Eve shopping sequence. Antoine sells the consumer goods necessary

Plate 2 Mon oncle Antoine (1971). © National Film Board of Canada, 2001. All rights
   reserved

for the social construction of family under Roman Catholicism and capitalism.
The consumption of these products is tantamount to the consumption of the
dominant ideology and, after Marx, enacts the reproduction of social relationships. Religion and its attendant social rituals, weddings and funerals, work to
mask political struggle between labour and capital for all but Jos Poulin. Poulin
sees the capitalist production of the mine and the social structures which naturalize it, the church and *le magasin général* as a death-dealing matrix which he
refuses to buy into. The Poulins are never depicted in town or in Antoine's shop.
As Jos informs his friends in the bar scene on the occasion of another miner's
funeral at the beginning of the film, 'Twenty-five years of rotting away there . . .
same thing will happen to you bunch of idiots, not me I won't end up that way.'
Jutra denaturalizes this matrix for his spectators not only through Poulin's alienation but also through an ironic inversion of the Nativity and Benoit's shifting
subject position.

   By the film's final shot Benoit has moved out from behind the glass of
Antoine's store, where he participated in the unveiling of the Holy Family to
waiting consumers, to a position outside the Poulin home where he looks
through the window to view the Poulin family gathered around the open casket
of their dead son Marcel. The relationship between the Holy Family celebrating a
birth and what Heinz Weinmann refers to as the Québec family mourning a

118

death (Weinmann 1990, 88) is anticipated by Cecile when she remarks to Carmen that the Jesus of the Nativity 'had an accident, we dropped him'. Having witnessed the shortcomings of the status quo of Duplessis's Québec – Antoine, the Priest and the mine boss – Benoit, and through him the viewer, is confronted by an allegoric tableau of its victims, those whom it dropped.[22] Weinmann reads this final shot as the death of adolescence for both Benoit and for Québec. The shifting subject position of Benoit – from adolescent naivety to a cynicism directed at oppressive power structures – reflects the shifting subject position of Québec, the reconfiguration of social relations that will result in the Quiet Revolution and the social and political turmoil that will explode in the FLQ crisis of 1970.[23]

Read allegorically, the Poulin home – a space from which Jos is alienated by the mine, and the site of his son's death – and le magasin général – the site where inequitable social relations are reproduced – represent the unheimlich oppression within a larger 'home' structure, Québec.[24] Simultaneously, this recognition of the unheimlich, the final shot from Benoit's perspective of the exploited classes, marks a move towards the heimlich of Québec as 'home', as this will develop in the struggle of Québécois to be maîtres chez nous or masters in (their) own house. As the social reality of Québec shifts, directors like Jutra rework the mental machinery of genre to resolicit their audience as members of the Québec nation. Mon oncle Antoine provides its 1971 audience with a historical context for the social and political unrest of late 1960s and early 1970s Québec nationalism, it addresses a community that increasingly imagines itself as a nation by representing the pastness of that nation. I am using national pastness here in the Wallersteinian sense as 'a central element in the socialization of individuals, in the maintenance of group solidarity, in the establishment of or challenge to social legitimation' (Wallerstein 1991, 78). Despite Pallister's insistence on privileging Benoit's rite of passage above what she terms the incidental political allegory of the film, Mon oncle Antoine, like most melodrama, works as Gledhill argues 'less towards the release of individual repression than towards the public enactment of socially unacknowledged states, the family is a means not an end' (Gledhill 1987, 31).

Les bons débarras

Francis Mankiewicz's 1980 melodrama tells the story of a precocious child, Manon, whose obsessive, frustrated love for her mother Michelle motivates her designs to remove rivals for her mother's affections – her mother's boyfriend Maurice and her alcoholic and meningitis-damaged uncle Ti-Guy. Manon is sick of these 'morons' and is horrified by the news that Michelle is pregnant with a 'baby Maurice'. Manon's desire for her mother, her determination to have her mother to herself, on her own terms, is made clear in the child's promise to Michelle: 'If I can't have you, I'll steal you.' By the end of the film Manon has realized her desire: Ti-Guy, whom she wishes would get drunk and crash into a

Plate 3 Les bons débarras (1980). 'If I can't have you, I'll steal you.' © Filmopticon
International Inc. 2001

tree, dies after driving his truck off an embankment in a drunken stupor, while
she steals Michelle away from Maurice by claiming, falsely, to be the victim of his
sexual advances. Both Weinmann and Pallister read the tempestuous relationship
between mother and adolescent daughter as an allegory for Québec's struggle
towards political maturation; however, their interpretations are nuanced differently. Where Pallister sees a subliminal reference to 'the emergence of young
Québec, and its ambivalence toward as well as revolt against the greater mother-
land, anglophone Canada' (1995, 246), Weinmann is willing to see more overt
political connotations which he reads through what he views as the film's prescient release date, two months before the 1980 referendum. For Weinmann, in a
very general sense, the film reflects Québec's extrication or *débarassé* of itself
from childhood (1990, 93). More specifically, he sees in Manon's frustrated love
for her mother, the frustrated love of the Québécois for Québec. Hearing an
echo of '*le quasi hymn national du Québec*' in the refrain that is sung to Manon
three times by her family – '*Ma chère Manon, c'est à ton tour de te laisser parler
d'amour*' – Weinmann concludes that *Les bons débarras* is a testimony of French
Canada's love for Québec during its '*passage difficile*' (1990, 97). While some
viewers might find tenuous Weinmann's decoding of Manon's and Michelle's
relationship as representative of a passionate move by Québécois to steal their
country away from an Anglo-Canadian federalism, it is significant to an understanding of the role reception plays in constructing a national cinema. A desire to

see the nation in cinema, to see cinema as a national object at a critical juncture in Québec's struggles towards political independence, is present in both Weinmann's and Pallister's responses to the film. In this way the reception of the film by a cultural elite engaged in the production of meaning plays an integral role in what Shohat and Stam term 'the cinema's institutional ritual of gathering a community', in forging identifications between spectator and nation through the screen of cinema (1994, 103). Again, as it did in *Mon oncle Antoine*, allegorical encoding and decoding flatten out the diversity of Québec, limiting identifications between spectator and screen to a white *pur laine* collectivity in *Les bons débarras*.

Although an element of melodrama – Québec as the powerless victim of a corrupt Anglo-Canadian federal system – is present in Weinmann's and Pallister's responses to the film, the negotiation of conflicted cultural identities that characterizes the popular family melodrama is perhaps most usefully read through the film's engagement with class. If part of reading a film is, after Fredric Jameson, reading the 'political unconscious', 'unmasking cultural artifacts as socially symbolic acts', perhaps the most striking representation of Québec nation in *Les bons débarras* is class disparity, the poverty of Michelle and her family that Mankiewicz juxtaposes to the affluence of Mme Viau-Vachon (Jameson 1986, 20).[25] The film's opening title sequence delineates a field of unequal social relations in rural Québec. Mankiewicz zooms in from a macrocosmic long shot of autumnal colour – the collectivity at a distance – to focus on a town, then cuts to a microcosmic series of shots of the police officer, Maurice, making his way towards Michelle's home. The camera finds Michelle, Manon and Ti-Guy in front of their ramshackle house loading a great pile of wood into the back of a van, their dog barking madly at the blaring siren of Maurice's cruiser (Figures 4.3–4.4). After Michelle and Maurice make arrangements for a date later that evening, the camera tracks Michelle's van as it leaves her property. At this point, the title appears and a jump cut is made to the terrace of Madame Viau-Vachon's bourgeois home, while the barking of the dog gives way to classical music. The fracturing of Québécois ethnicity by class is represented by Mankiewicz through the structure of the home, its *heimlich* and *unheimlich* properties. The characters themselves recognize class difference through their relationship to and alienation from property. As Michelle explains to Maurice, all she has is her family: 'What else can I talk about, my millions? They're all I have. I'm no Viau-Vachon. All Dad left me was an old snow plow and a half-paid house the bank would love to foreclose on.'[26] To return to my discussion of the opening sequence, it, much like the establishing shots of *Mon oncle Antoine*, structures its audience's understanding of Québec through inequitable social relations as these are constructed through a dialogue between two homes, between the working poor of rural Québec and the province's bourgeoisie. The shots of Michelle's and Viau-Vachon's homes are composed in very different ways. Contrasted to the relatively short takes of lumber debris, disorder and the barking dog soundtrack of Michelle's home are slow pans demarcating the elegant order of Viau-Vachon's residence, accentuated by

Figures 4.3–7 Les bons débarras (1980).
© Filmopticon
International Inc. 2001

strains of Puccini. The exterior pan takes in a brightly lit glass patio table, on which sits a crystal pitcher of orange juice and potted flowers (Figure 4.5). As the camera continues to pan to the right, these *heimlich* properties of *maison* Viau-Vachon are interrupted by audible signs of what is, to the bourgeois lady of leisure, the *unheimlich* – labour – the unloading of fuel for Mme Viau-Vachon's fireplace by Michelle, Manon and Ti-Guy. The shot continues to pan to the right and up over the wall of the terrace to reveal the family at work, as the classical music fades from the soundtrack, privileging the acoustic signs of labour (Figure 4.6). After several shots of the family working, a cut is made from an altercation between Manon and Ti-Guy to a slow interior pan of Viau-Vachon's home that is marked by the soundtrack's return to classical music. Retracing the movement of the exterior pan, the camera pans to the right to take in various *objets* including a sofa upon which sit Manon and Ti-Guy (Figure 4.7). A cut is made to the scene they are observing, Mme Viau-Vachon telling Michelle about her interior-decorating plans, and Michelle's negotiation with her for the number of cords to be purchased. A subsequent cut to the van on its return journey is followed by a cut to an interior shot of the bare two-by-fours and plywood constituting the walls of Ti-Guy's room at Michelle's house. This cross-cutting of shots establishes the dialogue between Michelle's and Viau-Vachon's homes that charts irruptions of class which contribute to the transformation of the *heimlich* properties of both homes into the *unheimlich*.

For Manon the canny, familiar or homely (*heimlich*) features of her home are limited to the few moments of intimacy she shares with her mother while the uncanny, alien or unknown (*unheimlich*) elements of the home present themselves in the bank's potential to foreclose on Michelle's mortgage, and in the persons of Ti-Guy and Maurice who alienate Manon from her mother. Viau-Vachon's home also plays an important role in constructing Manon's home as *unheimlich*. The economic solvency of Manon's mother and her continued ownership of the family home is dependent on people like Viau-Vachon and her class through the purchase of wood. Moreover, Mankiewicz's positioning of the Viau-Vachon home in relation to Manon's opens up a space through which Manon and the spectator perceive a material lack between the two homes. Viau-Vachon's home is the site of an economic transaction between Manon and Madame that reproduces inequitable social relations. When Manon visits Viau-Vachon to collect payment for the wood, she is told to wait while Viau-Vachon completes a telephone call with her lover. While waiting for the woman she refers to as 'rich bitch', Manon reads the well-lit and richly appointed home, decoding the *mise-en-scène* of the shots framing her for the spectator:

> Great love story
> Great music
> Great paintings
> Great books
> Fat cats, look at that!

With this last line of dialogue Manon names the class structure that holds her at the limit of access to these material signs of bourgeois culture.[27] Manon's recognition of class difference marks a further transformation of her own home into the *unheimlich*; she attempts to fill the material lack of class difference with alienating signs of the bourgeois home – the studded dog collar that she steals from Viau-Vachon and Viau-Vachon's hard-cover copy of *Wuthering Heights*. The appropriation of these objects, signs of the limits to material culture imposed by class, and their translation into Manon's home environment constitute an attempt to recuperate the *heimlich* of her own home that the exposure to Viau-Vachon's home had interrupted.

Ti-Guy also perceives his lack in terms of material bourgeois culture as it is

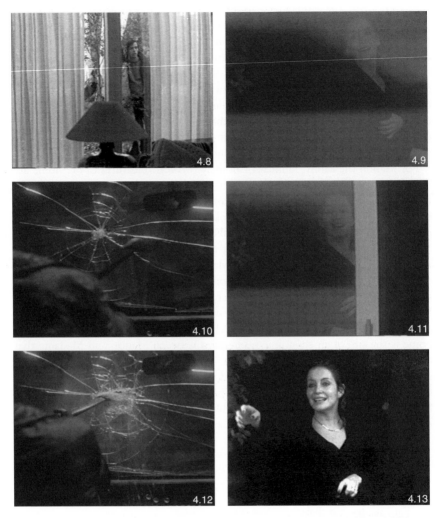

Figures 4.8–13 Les bons débarras (1980). © Filmopticon International Inc. 2001

reflected back to him through the *unheimlich*, alienating glass of Madame Viau-Vachon's home. As he gazes longingly through the glass panel at Viau-Vachon conversing with Manon, he recognizes that he does not register for Madame as anything other than labour (Figure 4.8). The glass panel holds him at the limits of bourgeois culture, thwarting his desire for Viau-Vachon and the material culture she represents. His *anagnorisis* produces actions that work to do violence to the glass barrier of class boundaries. Attempting to step out of his social class, Ti-Guy returns to maison Viau-Vachon dressed in his best clothes and carrying what he believes is the currency for entry into this rarefied world, the studded dog collar he has stolen back from Manon's dog Princess. In this manner, he

Figures 4.14–16 Les bons débarras
(1980). © Filmopticon
International Inc. 2001

attempts to recast himself in the discourse of the *heimlich*, as he believes it to be
understood by Viau-Vachon. Madame Viau-Vachon, however, does not respond
to his raps at her door and he finds himself once again reduced to a voyeur,
separated from Viau-Vachon and her world by sliding glass doors as he watches
her swim in her indoor pool. Ti-Guy's attempt to translate himself into Viau-
Vachon's *heimlich* order is read by Viau-Vachon as an irruption of the *unheimlich*
when she discovers him on her property later that evening. In a drunken stupor,
Ti-Guy, studded collar in hand, chases after Viau-Vachon, who flees in terror to
the safety of her home. For Viau-Vachon, Ti-Guy's actions represent a violent
transgression of class boundaries. Viau-Vachon's fear and revulsion structure
Ti-Guy as part of the *unheimlich*; it is his vision of himself through her eyes as
abject that prompts his suicide. Shots of Ti-Guy in his van perched on the top of
an embankment are intercut with subjective camera shots of a slow-motion fantasy sequence in which Viau-Vachon steps out of her pool, opens up her sliding
glass doors and beckons Ti-Guy to join her. Mankiewicz cross-cuts a medium
shot of Viau-Vachon sliding the door open with an over-the-shoulder shot of
Ti-Guy smashing his van window with an axe, destroying the reflective surface
that obstructs his desire (Figures 4.9–4.15). In his suicidal fantasy Ti-Guy breaks
down the barriers of class and his brain damage to enter into the world of Viau-
Vachon. The fantasy scenes of him running towards Viau-Vachon in slow motion
are intercut with long shots of his van accelerating over the embankment where it
crashes in a smoking heap on to the highway below (Figure 4.16).

Despite the film's final homely or *heimlich* shot, a tight close-up of Michelle half asleep in the arms of Manon, the *unheimlich*, or the truth that ought to remain repressed, has come to light for the viewer: the dysfunctional and damaging structure of social class that fractures Québec. Mankiewicz's film, through the mental machinery of the family melodrama genre, reveals Québec as a 'home' place haunted by the *unheimlich* of class disparity. While a Hollywood family melodrama such as *Mildred Pierce* (Michael Curtiz 1945) negotiates social class through a mother–daughter relationship, its Hollywood aesthetics and American context regulate an order of subjectivity that is foreign to Québec. Mankiewicz's film produces that difference in repetition that Neale argues is genre, he indigenizes Hollywood melodrama through a mode of address that speaks from the socioeconomic and cultural landscape of Québec to Québec in a naturalistic cinematography and acting style that eschew the dramatic excesses of Hollywood productions.

Un zoo la nuit and *Léolo*

With two films, *Un zoo la nuit* (1987) and *Léolo* (1992), writer/director Jean-Claude Lauzon takes the Québec family to new extremes of dysfunction while troubling the *pur laine* collectivity haunting previous Québécois melodramas. A story of conflict between father and son, *Un zoo la nuit*, like the other Québécois family melodramas we have looked at, has been read allegorically as a representation of a conflicted Québec. Henry Garrity sees the father, Albert, and the son, Marcel, as 'signifiers of old rural and new urban Québec' (Garrity 1995, 81). In this allegory, however, the fictive ethnicity of a *pur laine* Québec is interrupted by Lauzon's introduction of an ethnic Other, the developing Italian community that displaces Albert from his home. For old Québec, ethnic difference constitutes irruptions of the *unheimlich*, the haunting of the home structure of Québec nation by its ethnic others. The eponymous Léolo of Lauzon's 1992 film also troubles any assumptions that Québec is composed of *pur laine* ethnicity. Léo rejects his Québécois ethnicity, insisting that his birth was the result of his mother's accidental sexual contact with imported tomatoes laden with the semen of an Italian farmer. With this sensational claim, Léo attempts to rationalize changing his name to Léolo. Again, family dysfunction – a brother's obsession with weight training, Léolo's sexual congress with a piece of liver, his sisters' various mental illnesses, his father's obsession with the family's bodily functions, and his grandfather's violence and paedophiliac predilections – drives the plot of this film. At one point Léolo, blaming his family's psychoses on his grandfather, tries to hang the old patriarch in his morning bath. As Geoff Pevere observes, 'in Léolo the family is a place of grotesque repression and displacement, where nothing, not even those rare good things, promise transcendence' (Pevere 1992a, 24). Given these problems, it is not surprising that Léo rejects his Québécois birthright in favour of an Other identity. The title of Pevere's review – 'Family ties: Québécois Film-maker Jean-Claude Lauzon Already Knows Canada Is a

126

Dysfunctional Family' – registers the desire to read cinema as a national object, allegorizing the film as a national narrative. For Pevere, *Léolo*, like so many Québécois films offering family as a 'microcosm of identity', begs to be read as a 'political metaphor' (24). Pevere reads the dysfunction of Léolo's family as Lauzon's expression of Canadians' discomfort with the 'idea of national family', its failure to represent them 'in this time of profound national redefinition [the lead up to the 1992 Referendum]' (24). In this particular melodrama the dysfunctional national family is pathologized as insane.

Le confessionnal

Set in 1952, against the backdrop of Alfred Hitchcock's filming of *I Confess* (1953) in Québec City, and in 1989, Robert Lepage's *Le confessionnal* (1995) tells the tragic story of another dysfunctional Québec family. Lepage cuts back and forth between the events of the past which shape the experiences of the Lamontagne family's two sons in 1989. The 1989 narrative is driven by the twinned desires of Marc and Pierre, brothers by adoption, to determine the identity of Marc's father, something shrouded in the family history of 1952. Melodrama's allegoric turn, the working through of macrocosmic national narratives through microcosmic family ones, is, as the film's press kit indicates, very much a part of *Le confessionnal*. The press kit invokes a quotation from Lepage as the 'thesis' of the film: 'Quebec lives continuously with its past' (*Le confessionnal* Press Kit 1995, 10). This marketing of the film as a narrativization of Québec nation indicates the producers' awareness of an audience expectation that cinema will represent the nation in some form. The character Manon's comment – 'in order to know where you are going in life, you have to know from whence you came' – speaks, as the press kit notes, to Marc and Québec City, but also to a larger Québec, the cultural and historical Québec nation framing the narrative of the Lamontagne family (10). The first lines of dialogue in the film, Pierre's voice-over narration of the establishing shots, delineates the overlapping relationships between the past and present for Québec and the Lamontagnes: 'In the city where I was born, the past carries the present like a child on its shoulders.'[28] This collective remembrance of things past also evokes, as did *Québec USA*, the province's official motto 'Je me souviens' (I will remember). Lepage's film narrative turns on the haunting of the present by familial and national pasts, and is far more critical of that past than *Québec-USA*. Pierre's 1989 utterance is accompanied by the onscreen image of a bridge, signifying his voice-over narration as the film's diegetic bridge to the past. Pierre's narratorial bridge links the 1989 shot of the bridge and the 1989 locus of his utterance to 1952, the year Pierre's family moved into the house next door to his aunt Jeanne d'Arc. A cut from the Lamontagne home in 1952 to shots of the Québec City premiere of Hitchcock's *I Confess* is punctuated by Pierre's revelation of three events marking the life of Québec City in 1952: the arrival of television, Maurice Duplessis's re-election as Premier and the presence of Hitchcock and company for the production of *I*

Plate 4 Le confessionnal (1995). © Cinémaginaire Inc. 2001

Confess. These three events mark the foundations of the secularization of Québec, setting the stage for Lepage's cross-cutting between the old provincial, Catholic Québec of 1952 and the modern, secular Québec of 1989, a cross-cutting representing the becoming of Québec nation. Of course, this cross-cutting also stands in for the becoming of Pierre. As his voice-over narration tells us, he is at the Hitchcock premiere, 'cosy' in his mother's womb. Pierre's development and search for family identity is thus paralleled to the secularization or modernization of Québec. The arrival of television in Québec brings greater access to ideas outside the orthodoxy of the Catholic church, while Duplessis's second and third terms marked the beginnings of the Québec state's assertion of its authority over the Catholic church and are precursors of the dramatic change Jean Lesage would bring with the Quiet Revolution (1960–6). Finally, Hollywood's arrival in Québec is, for Lepage, a pivotal sign of the province's transition to modernity: 'Imagine . . . An insular society of French origins, and what is more, Catholic, turned inward upon itself, witnessing the arrival of the great Hollywood machine. In a symbolic manner, it can involve the transition to modernity, with all the re-questioning which that involves' (quoted in *Le confessionnal* Press Kit 1995, 6). References to both Duplessis and Hitchcock's presence in Québec frame the film; both are invoked as agents of secularization in the establishing shots, and in the film's second last sequence where Pierre's father tells Hitchcock of Duplessis's condescending and cynical perception of the Québécois electorate.[29] The conflicted signification of Duplessis and Hitchcock as agents of secularization – potentially liberating but also threatening – becomes clear in this scene. While Hitchcock and Hollywood are representative of modernity and liberalism, their presence in Québec is, similarly to the presence of the American navy in *Québec-USA*, also a sign for Americanization. Duplessis's legacy is not just initiating secularization but, as is referenced in *Mon oncle Antoine*, his corrupt government's attempts to smash labour unions.

The film's principal site of the past haunting the present is the Lamontagne home to which Pierre returns in 1989 to settle the affairs of his recently deceased father. The *unheimlich* of the home, the repressed which ought to have remained hidden, manifests itself in Pierre's father's affair with Rachel, his wife's sister, a relationship that gave birth to Marc and drove Rachel to suicide. The uncovering or revelation of this uncanny secret is anticipated in the first interior shots of the home's dark, stagnant living room into which Pierre introduces light by opening shutters, and in the bleeding through of the non-secular past into the secular present as this is represented by the ghostly traces of family photographs that reappear on the living room wall throughout the film. Pierre, paradoxically, mines the past for Marc's father, but also represses it through his removal of artefacts, such as family photos – including one of Aunt Rachel – and the crucifix from the wall, and by his continuing efforts to paint over their silhouettes which bleed through each layer of paint he applies to the wall. The wall, like Québec itself, is a palimpsestic text where the past intermingles with the present, structuring our understandings of both. For Erin Manning, the seeping through of the wall's yellow paint, a colour she associates with homosexuality and Marc and Massicotte, 'demonstrates how difficult the transition into the secular is for a society that has based its cultural practices on the conservative discourse of the Catholic church' (Manning 1998, 54). Manning argues that in Lepage's film yellow signifies the 'fear of otherness and difference', it is 'the stain of a conservative nationalism which marks the norms in a community that believes it has discarded the oppression of religion' (54). The oppression of religion, however, continues to haunt the present. In Manning's reading of the film, the community constructs the pregnant and unmarried Rachel as a deviant in 1952 and does the same in 1989 to her son Marc, a gay prostitute, contributing to both of their suicides (57). This co-existence of past and present is communicated visually by Lepage in some brilliant flashback and flashforward transitions within the same shot. The flashback is a device Christine Gledhill associates with the circular thematic and narrative structure of the melodrama (1985, 80). Lepage's film circles around the theme of secularization or modernization in Québec, measuring these processes through the past and present of the Lamontagne family. The camera pans from the secular 1989 space of Pierre's father's funeral in an empty church to the non-secular space of 1952 and a full church. The device of the pan stands in for the becoming of modern Québec, its transition from a Catholic to a secular society, and simultaneously questions the completeness of the transition by reinscribing traces of Catholicism in the present. The Catholic church is the space that the film always returns to, and this return constitutes Lepage's

Plate 5 Le confessionnal (1995). © Cinémaginaire Inc. 2001

requestioning of the past, the film's archaeological dig into the foundations of the Québec social text to understand the present. Pierre returns to the Catholic church and its archives in an attempt to discover the identity of the priest who baptized Marc, a man who was rumoured, incorrectly, to be Marc's father. Pierre's visit to the church is introduced by a transition from 1952 to 1989 within a continuous shot. A tracking shot of a visibly pregnant Rachel walking down the aisle of the church in 1952, attempting to hide her swollen belly from the moralizing stares of the parishioners, cuts to a continuous pan following a young priest in 1952 as he walks behind the altar, emerging into the sacristy as an older man for a 1989 meeting with Pierre. In this uninterrupted pan, the past walks into the present to facilitate the decoding of that present. Although the 1989 priest can't tell Pierre the identity of the baptizing priest, his explanation for why he cannot provide this information narrates the relationship between the Catholic past and the secular present of the Québec social text. 'During the ecumenical revival of the Sixties many young priests became more socially involved. A number of them left the priesthood.' Massicotte is one of these priests, a homosexual and high-ranking government bureaucrat who appears to have embraced the secular. However, the 1952 priest Massicotte, who performed Marc's baptismal, and heard Rachel's confession, co-exists with the 1989 government bureaucrat, now Marc's lover. The ideology of the Catholic past structures Massicotte in the supposedly secular present; he will not break the silence of the confessional by revealing the identity of Marc's father and is therefore unable to alleviate Marc's pain in 1989.

The family melodrama – seen here in ideological conflicts between Catholic and secular worlds that get played out through the Lamontagne family tragedy,[30] the representation of the family as the site of woman's sexual repression under patriarchy (Paul's abusive and exploitative relationship with Rachel), and the film's negotiation of the social crisis introduced through modernization or secularization – is indigenized by Lepage through his intertextual, metacinematic references to Hitchcock. Modernity, long associated with the death of God, comes to Québec, in the symbolic field of Lepage's film, in part, through the presence of the Hollywood production machine, and its representation of Québec for a global audience. The film's establishing shots of a Québec City audience watching the premiere of Hitchcock's *I Confess* are metacinematic: they foreground the act of viewing and focus our attention on the cinematic apparatus. These shots and subsequent sequences of Hitchcock shooting scenes from *I Confess* denaturalize cinema as the production and consumption of images, and signal to us that Lepage's film is to be read in the light of this self-referential knowledge and in the context of Hitchcock's film. The social crisis of Québec secularization signified through the interpersonal relationships of the Lamontagne family gets externalized in Lepage's translation of the melodrama into a Québec context. Lepage not only juxtaposes his postmodern aesthetic to Hitchcock's modern one, he juxtaposes the cinema, as a sign for the secular, to the Catholic church as a sign for the non-secular. In *Le confessionnal*, the cinema is the only space aside from the Catholic church where the Québec collectivity gather for cultural ritual. Cinema becomes a place for secular worship. The church, an ISA involved in the production of Catholic subjects, is displaced by the cinema, a secular ISA also involved in the production of subjects. This representation of the church and the cinema as competing ISAs is perhaps most visible in Marc's baptismal sequence. The baptismal sequence conflates the Roman Catholic and cinematic production of subjects. Hitchcock waits for baby Marc to stop crying in the sacristy so that he can shoot a scene in the sanctuary in silence. The baptism performed by the priest is a religious rite that produces Roman Catholic subjects; it is a ceremony that reproduces the Catholic family by forging identifications between man, woman, child and Catholicism. Cinema – Hitchcock's finished product – also hails or recruits subjects, forging identifications between spectator and screen.[31] This is not to suggest that these identifications – between family and Catholicism, between spectator and screen – are stable; it is precisely the instability of identification that Lepage's film charts. As we know from our previous applications of Fuss's concept of identification – 'the naming and entry of history and culture into the subject' (1995, 3) – identifications 'reverse and disguise themselves, to multiply and contravene one another, to disappear and reappear years later' (2). This process is perhaps most palpable in Massicotte's identification with the church through his vows as a priest, his reversal of that identification through his homosexuality and secular lifestyle, and its reappearance years later when he makes a renewed identification with Catholic doctrine in his observance of the sanctity of the confessional. Collectively, Quebeckers' identifications with Québec as a Catholic and secular society are subject to the same kinds of contradictory shifts. Manning, quoting Fuss, reads identification as the mechanism in Lepage's film that keeps identity at a distance, thereby thwarting a totalizing Québec identity (Fuss 1995, 2; Manning 1998, 51). Manning argues that in response to the past's haunting of the present, or what she calls 'spectrality', 'characters in Le Confessionnal are forced to make a necessary transition from identity (relegation to the strict codes of religious discourse) to identification (the threatening unspeakable world of desire, homosexuality, and difference)' (1998, 51). Moreover, the identifications we watch a 1952 Québec audience make with Hitchcock's psycho-thriller or melodrama representation of a contemporaneous Québec will shift as the social landscape of Québec and audience expectations are transformed over time, shifts that will require the resoliciting of audience Lepage attempts in his film. Lepage sutures frames of I Confess into Le confessionnal, literalizing Neale's definition of genre as 'repetition in difference'; Lepage reworks, extends and transforms the normative codes of the Hollywood melodrama or psychological thriller by redeploying Hitchcock's film in the cinematic field of irony that is Le confessionnal.

Le confessionnal invokes a dialogic relationship between itself and I Confess in the establishing shots where Hitchcock's film of modernity is placed beside Lepage's postmodern aesthetic. With the suturing in of the opening and closing shots of Hitchcock's film in close proximity to the opening and closing shots of his own film, Lepage creates the illusion that both films are running alongside each other, commenting on each other. The cinema screen becomes a palimpsestic text; not unlike the Lamontagne living room wall, it becomes a field of doubled representation where an anterior cultural text is re-evaluated. Hitchcock's film is a continuous, determinant narrative that, aside from the director's trademark cameo walk-on appearances, makes no reference to itself as cinema. *I Confess* perpetuates the social economy of classical Hollywood narrative cinema where familial bonds are developed through the construction of the heterosexual couple, and in this way maintains the metanarratives or master codes brought into question in Lepage's discontinuous, fragmented, indeterminate, self-reflexive film narrative. Roman Catholicism and classical Hollywood melodrama have more in common than one might expect: ideologically both structure the subject as heterosexual, promote gender fixity and reproduce the family. Hitchcock's narrative represents a testing of the sanctity of the confessional – will Father Logan break the silence of the confessional to save his life? – and a priest's vows of celibacy – will Father Logan come between Mme Grandfort and her husband? At the end of the film, however, any threat to the established orthodoxy is dismissed. Father Logan is cleared of murder without rupturing the secrecy of the confessional. In the film's second last scene Mme Grandfort looks away from Father Logan, embraces her husband and asks to be taken home. In addition to telling the story of Father Logan, Hitchcock's film also performs another cultural narrative: the story of the dominant industrial Other's – Hollywood's – representation of Québec, a story of cultural imperialism, an Americanization associated with the modern.[32] A montage of shots comprising the film's establishing sequence constructs Québec as a semiotic field signifying the historical, the colonial, the claustrophobic, the Catholic. Shooting in black-and-white Hitchcock introduces his audience to the 'Old World traditions'[33] of Québec with a low-angled, cantered night shot of a statue of Québec's seventeenth-century Governor-General Frontenac dwarfed by the Château Frontenac. A low-angled medium long shot of the fortress wall surrounding Québec City continues this signification of colonial history, suggesting a closed, provincial society living in the historical past. Intercut with these shots are medium and close-up shots of One Way traffic signs in narrow claustrophobic streets which, through cutting, eventually point to a low-angled long shot of a Catholic church, and ultimately to the corpse of Monsieur Villette the murdered blackmailer. In this way Hollywood represents Québec to Quebeckers and to the world as a museum piece frozen in time. Here Hollywood cinema's regulation of the orders of subjectivity is structured around compulsory heterosexuality, and strict adherence to the religious order as these are performed, through an English-language film narrative, by Hollywood stars Montgomery Clift, Anne Baxter and Karl Malden.

While Lepage plays on these co-ordinates of Old Québec, by splicing some of Hitchcock's shots into *Le confessionnal*, he also troubles them through his parodic dialogue with *I Confess*. Lepage omits Hitchcock's shots of fortress Québec and the Catholic church, substituting his own images of cinema spectatorship at the Hitchcock premiere. These differences, along with his shooting in colour and in French, with Québec actors in the lead roles, produce a mode of address distinct from Hollywood's *I Confess*.[34] Lepage's family melodrama resolicits his audience with a self-reflexive emphasis on the processes of identity production, and in this way interrogates not only Hitchcock's black-and-white binaries of Québec identity but also the naive impulses of any national cinema that would produce a constant, totalizing, exemplary 'pastness' in the interests of maintaining 'group solidarity' (Wallerstein 1991, 78). While Lepage's film pays homage to Hitchcock, mimicking scenes such as the shot in *Psycho* where blood runs down the drain,[35] it is also a self-consciously revolutionary text that reworks what it reads as the tyrannical discursive weight of *I Confess*.[36] Through Hollywood's monopolistic global distribution system Hitchcock's film becomes tyrannical; its 1952 representation of a provincial, closed Catholic society becomes the dominant global cinematic referent for Québec. In contrast to *I Confess*, *Le confessionnal* directs a postmodern incredulity towards metanarratives or totalizing systems, like the compulsory heterosexuality of melodrama, through Massicotte and Marc, and the value of a confessional silence that destroys both Marc and Rachel.[37] Whereas Hitchcock's film narrative is determinate – the murder of Villette is solved, Father Logan will continue the work of the church, and the Grandforts' marriage is made sound – Lepage's film is marked by a postmodern indeterminacy. Although we discover the identity of Marc's birth father (Paul), in the final analysis cultural identity, Québec identity, is revealed as transitory, indeterminate, something that is provisional, manufactured by the church, Hollywood, Québec film-makers. What Lepage offers is not, strictly speaking, an oppositional discourse to Hitchcock. Lepage's film is not a set of stable codes of identity for a Québec national cinema but a semiotic field invested in representing the shifting, contradictory and unstable identifications made by an imagined community over time. For example, Lepage does not represent 1989 Québec as a completely secular, open, modern society, the antithesis of Hitchcock's 1952 Québec. Lepage's Québec represents the ongoing process of becoming, a becoming that is always-already informed by the past. This becoming, the transition from Catholic to secular, is marked by Lepage in the temporal transitions that take place within continuous shots discussed earlier, but also in the traces of Catholicism that haunt the secular world. The confessional box, the film's iconic sign of Catholic community, is present in 1989, but not in its 1952 formation. The only confessional boxes present in 1989 are associated with sexual practices: the booths in which Marc's ex-wife Manon table-dances are referred to as confessionals. Formerly a ritualized space of containment in which Rachel confesses her sin of adultery before a male priest, the confessional becomes a ritualized space for the performance of female sexuality for the male gaze. This transformation of the confessional troubles any suggestions that Québec has broken free of its Catholic past. The violence of blasphemy – naming the space of vice after the space of absolution – indicates that the Catholic past is very much present as a spectral trace of sexual repression that the present reacts against. Similarly, patriarchy under Catholicism, what Lepage represents as the oppressive system of confessional which destroys Rachel but saves Paul, is transformed but still present under a secular patriarchal economy of gender inequity where Manon performs for male gratification. In these ways Lepage offers an alternative to both Hollywood classical melodrama and what Manning refers to as 'a secure home-based and nationalist cinema' (1998, 51). For Lepage the purity of a 'nationalist' cinema is mythology; *Le confessionnal* is an eclectic film influenced by a Hollywood cinema that the director reworks and translates into the contexts of Québec culture and politics to tell a Québec story. This indigenization of genre is not just the domain of the director but, as *Le confessionnal* demonstrates, involves viewing practices. Hitchcock's *I Confess* becomes for the Lamontagne family a touchstone of cultural memory that acts as a narrative route to Québec cultural history and family history in Pierre's correlation of Hitchcock both with Duplessis and with the events that shook the Lamontagne family in 1952. Cinema and the home place, cultural and family memory, collide on the living room wall of the Lamontagne residence toward the end of *Le confessionnal*. The wall, a site where the *unheimlich* of family memories bleeds through into the present, is transformed into a surface resembling a cinema screen when Pierre applies a final coat of blue paint. Unlike previous scenes where the ghostly traces of old family photographs bleed through the paint, the blue wall becomes luminous, eventually dissolving into a cinema screen on which appears the final shot of Hitchcock's *I Confess*. The dissolve from the home place to the cinema returns us to where we began our journey through cultural and family history, the premiere of *I Confess*, and emphasizes the relationships between the cinema and subject formation, cultural memory and family memory. Hitchcock's complaints to his assistant as he leaves the premiere about cuts made to his film at the request of the church remind us that the process of indigenization is political, signifying in complex ways, and is not always about liberating local culture from the hegemonic codes of Hollywood.

Margaret's Museum

Not dissimilar to the ideological conflict played out between an Anglo-managerial class, its French-Canadian agents and labour in *Mon oncle Antoine*, *Margaret's Museum* (Mort Ransen 1995) represents class conflict in an Anglo-Protestant managerial class's exploitation of Catholic Highland Gaels' labour for the extraction of coal on 1940s Cape Breton. The cost of mineral extraction on Cape Breton, where class division is structured, in part, through linguistic and religious differences, is the same as it was in Québec, the lives of the exploited classes. Lee Parpart's 1999 essay on the film reads Cape Breton as subject to a type of internal colonialism similar to that which structures Québec. Parpart, however, is careful to note an important distinction between the two spaces, namely that, for many in Western and Atlantic Canada, Québec is an economic component of Central Canadian capital, a core to Cape Breton's periphery (1999b, 66).[38] In *Margaret's Museum* the Anglo-managerial class, agents of Central Canadian and foreign capital, constitute melodrama's corrupt social order vicitimizing the diasporic Scots-Highland community we view through the lens of Margaret and her family.[39] *Margaret's Museum* represents a flip-side of family melodrama's historic project of the bourgeois family's ascendancy: the cost paid by the working-class family for that ascendancy (Gledhill 1985, 74). Allegorically, the film also tells the story of another historic project, a Central Canadian nation-building dependent on an inequitable federalism exploiting Atlantic Canada. In these ways Ransen's film indigenizes family melodrama by producing different functionings of subjectivity to address class struggle and internal colonialism in Canada, thereby creating a mode of address distinct from Hollywood family melodrama's fixation on a bourgeois American nation. Granted, he accomplishes this through a Canada–UK co-production, and the casting of two British actors, Helena Bonham Carter and Clive Russell, in the lead roles, and Canadian actors Kate Nelligan and Kenneth Welsh in supporting roles, but Ransen is a pragmatist when it comes to box office returns. On the casting of Bonham Carter, Ransen comments, 'It isn't really a level playing field in Canada and the only way you can draw attention to your film is to hire a high-profile cast. It's almost impossible to score at the box office without stars' (quoted in Randoja 1995, 30).

Similar to the signification of the home in *Mon oncle Antoine* and *Les bons débarras*, the home sites in *Margaret's Museum* comprise structures through which social class is staged. Margaret MacNeil's family home is a generic structure owned by the mining company. The home of the mine manager is a far larger and more elaborate building where Margaret performs domestic labour and her brother Jimmy works as a dance instructor for the manager's daughter. The third home featured in the film, a structure built from derelict mining company buildings by Neil Currie, Margaret's husband, represents a failed attempt to undo the rigid structures of class that lock people into the categories of labouring tenant or property-owning bourgeoisie. Ultimately, this home site becomes Margaret's Miner's Museum, a memorializing space where the material violence of class struggle is exhibited through the pickled organs of her brother, husband and grandfather that comprise Margaret's show 'The Price of Coal'. Peter Urquhart and Lee Parpart note how Sheldon Currie's screen adaptation of his story and novel privileges the love story between Neil and Margaret over labour issues, and in this way dilutes the film's engagement with the politics of class.[40] None the less, I will argue that this shift does not evacuate class politics from the film narrative. Whilst the film adaptation elides the strike present in the novel, the *unheimlich* of a cannibalistic corporate capital that devours labour haunts the screen, structuring our understanding of the film's social relationships. As Margaret and her mother agree, the mining company has transformed the community into 'buzzards' who 'feed off each other'. This observation is made with reference to the deathwatch Margaret's mother keeps on the elderly mining

Plate 6 Margaret's Museum (1995). Margaret MacNeil (Helena Bonham Carter).
Courtesy of Glace Bay Pictures Inc.

widows to determine her own position on a waiting list to collect on her late
husband's pension. The subordinate relationship of the Gaelic community to
Central Canadian and foreign capital is marked in the three mine cave-ins punc-
tuating the film which maim and kill the community's men and, significantly, in
the home place where violence to labour is made most palpable. Paradoxically,

Plate 7 Margaret's Museum (1995). Catherine MacNeil (Kate Nelligan). Courtesy of Glace Bay Pictures Inc.

violence is made visible in the film's representation of *heimlich/unheimlich* tensions, the irruptions of *unheimlich* truths in the field of the *heimlich*, homely discourse that would work to repress the violence of capitalist mineral extraction and its attendant work of internal colonialism assimilating Cape Breton's Gaels. In *Margaret's Museum* the very foundations of the *heimlich* homely home contain the secrets of its other, the *unheimlich* haunted home where what is naturalized as the MacNeil family home is in fact an alienating structure of capital, an asset of the mining company. The foundations of this home are *undermined*, quite literally, by the company's extraction of coal. As Jimmy explains to his girlfriend, the next-door counterpart to the MacNeil tenement home has disappeared, has been consumed by the landscape of industrialized capital resulting from the company's subterranean tunnelling. The MacNeil home is haunted by the violence of the pits as this is represented in the absent presence of Margaret's father (the scene where she polishes his whisky glass), and the figure of the castrated male, Neil and Margaret's grandfather.[41] In true melodramatic form, Neil, fired from another mining operation for speaking Gaelic, and the grandfather, dying from black lung that renders him mute and paralytic, are men alienated from capitalist production, relegated to the domestic sphere, in a sense feminized. And this I believe is central to an understanding of the apparent shift from novel to film of which Urquhart is so critical. 'Labour and class', he writes 'are much less important concerns in the film' (1999, 17). It is not so much that labour and class are 'less important concerns in the film', rather the film's interest is in tracking the displacement of alienated labour into the domestic sphere through melodrama to make visible the destructive ramifications of an alienating system of production on family members, on the women who must negotiate alienated labour in its displaced, domestic context.[42] When the mine kills Margaret's brother and father, she and her mother are left to bury the bodies of alienated labour. Margaret and her mother also provide round-the-clock care for the dying grandfather, whose lungs need to be cleared perpetually because of the coal dust he has inhaled during his working life in the mine. Based on her own experience and the experiences of the community, Margaret's mother discourages her daughter's budding relationship with Neil, convinced that 'He'll dig coal and make [her] cry', two things that come to pass. In this scene the mother, by way of sketching Margaret's future if she marries a miner, encapsulates woman's collective experience of alienated labour in a Cape Breton mining town: 'You'll lose two sons to a shoe factory in Boston and three to the pit. One'll die with the lungs, one from a fall of stone, and one'll get shot in the face makin' a speech durin' a strike.' In melodrama the alienated labour of capitalist production does violence to the home, the domestic space of reproduction and the family, by repressing sexuality and demanding woman's self-sacrifice.[43] In *Margaret's Museum* Neil's unemployment prompts Margaret to insist that he use a condom as they cannot afford to have children. Offended by Margaret's request, Neil leaves her bed and spends the evening playing his pipes in the rain in protest. The next morning he is dressed for work in the pit, a decision that causes Margaret to leave him, temporarily, for fear that he will make her a widow; his subsequent death in the mine deprives her of a family.

Part of the representational work accomplished by Ransen's film is a denaturalizing of the violent deaths that the coal industry naturalizes as an inevitable part of the coal extraction process. On two occasions Margaret notes attempts to hide the violence mining does to the bodies of its victims. Speaking of the deaths of her father and brother Charlie David, Margaret observes: 'they never opened the coffins as though we had no right to see them all torn up'. She also asks Neil 'why'd they go to all the trouble to bring up the bodies just to bury them again, as though nothing happened?' While the referent of 'they' is ambiguous here, other references to an all-powerful and oppressive 'they' peppering the film's dialogue contextualize these utterances within a shifting register of Anglo-centric, socio-economic, political power ranging from imperial England to internal colonialism as practised in Canada, and the contemporaneous agents of this oppressive Anglo elite, the mining company. Addressing Margaret's grandfather, Neil's usage of 'they' invokes a history of English attempts to erase Gaelic culture and oppress and exploit Gaelic people stretching back at least as far as the Highland Clearances that brought the first Scottish Highlanders to Cape Breton: 'We love you Donald, all you've got in your head are a couple of old tunes you can hardly remember, that your sons barely know, and that your granddaughter doesn't know at all. They took your language, and your music and your songs, and all they left you with was a shovel.'[44] Neil's speech act conflates the historical processes of an internal colonialism's assimilation within the UK with the contemporaneous and oppressive processes of an Anglo/Central Canadian system of coal production, and a continued assimilation and internal colonialism in Canada.[45] Similarly, Margaret's uncle, Angus, in a drunken song of despair, links the contemporaneous situation of Gaels in 1940s Canada to that of the Highland clans defeated by English troops at Culloden: 'seventeen hundred and forty five hardly half of us left alive / in nineteen hundred and forty four half in the pit half in the fucking war'. Explaining the song to his niece, Angus says, 'they killed us Margaret, at the battle of Culloden and one way or another they're still trying to pick us off'. Again, Angus's speech acts, much like Neil's, invoke a history of cultural erasure practised by a 'they' signifying, concomitantly, the troops of English imperialism and the Anglo/Central Canadian elite managing the Atlantic Canadian or Scottish labour in the pits.

The most arresting refusal of the company's naturalizing of industrial deaths is enacted in Margaret's transformation of the company-owned family home into a mortuary where she bears witness to the company's violence to the bodies of her men, surgically removing her husband's and grandfather's lungs, and her brother's penis. Emerging from the company tenement covered in blood, Margaret makes visible the *unheimlich* of labour's violent death under capital that the community and company work to repress through the illusion of the *heimlich* home, which Margaret's actions reveal to the camera as a death trap, a slaughterhouse financed by the blood of the family. Margaret's Miner's Museum exhibition of male body parts floating in formaldehyde preserves the material effects of capitalist production on labour that conventional museums would repress. As Parpart suggests, Margaret's is an 'anti-folkore' museum, a counter-discursive formation interrupting the region's museums' dominant visual iconography of pans, shovels and masks – the tools of coal extraction – by inserting the human price paid for coal extraction (1999b, 71).[46] Significantly, the violence of capital-ism's relationship to labour is staged in the home Neil built, a sign of both the failure and success of his separatist stance, his attempts to remain outside of and resistant to the political economy of the mine. Although Neil eventually responds to the mining company's interpellation of him as disposable labour, his wife redeploys the derelict materials of the company that he had reconfigured into property or home to structure a resistance narrative. Margaret translates materials formerly facilitating Central Canadian nation-building into a context where they house a discourse signifying the exploitation and inequity upon which that national construction is based.

Intertwined with capital's violence to labour is its erasure of cultural difference; the home place is haunted not only by the *unheimlich* of class violence but also by the *unheimlich* of a Gaelic culture and ethnicity that an Anglo/Central Canadian capital disciplines its labouring subjects to repress. As evidenced by Neil's dis-missal from another mining operation for speaking Gaelic, capitalism structures its Scottish labourers as English speakers, denying them an identity outside of the world of work in an attempt to reduce them to a generic, undifferentiated labour pool devoid of a collective cultural identity outside of mineral extraction. By making it an obstacle to employment, the mining company calls the value of Gaelic language into question, so much so that Margaret's mother, a descendant of Gaelic speakers, reads it as the foreign, abject language of drunken old men when she returns home to find Neil and other Gaelic speakers singing and drink-ing in her living room. Neil interrupts the dominant ideology by valuing the Gaelic language and culture and (re)introducing them to those, such as Marga-ret, who have been assimilated by the dominant Anglo-Canadian culture. In this way Neil's presence marks the return of the repressed, haunting the family home with what is strangely familiar but has become alien; he offers a human identity to workers and their families that has been erased by a dehumanizing and alienating mode of production. Through the actions of Neil and Margaret which denatural-ize the inequitable and exploitative relationship between capital and labour, between Central and Atlantic Canada, Ransen's film reveals one of the hidden foundations of Canadian social relations, the inequities of social class structuring belonging to and produced by Canadian nation.

The Adjuster

Unlike most classical postwar Hollywood family melodramas whose challenges to the status quo were realized not through radical aesthetics or overt ideological transgressions but through academic analysis, *Margaret's Museum* and *The Adjuster* (Atom Egoyan 1991) integrate a self-conscious critique of the domin-ant culture into the discursive structure of their narratives.[47] Both films denatural-ize the relationships between things that stand in for the relationships between people under capitalism; they reveal, in Marx's terms, an alienating commodity fetishism that interrupts and mediates social relations between people.[48] As Terry

Eagleton argues, commodity fetishism has ideological consequences, one of which is that 'the real workings of society are thereby occluded: the social character of labor is concealed behind the circulation of commodities, which are no longer recognized as social products' (1991, 85). Whereas *Margaret's Museum* unveils the alienating and deadly workings of capitalist production concealed behind the circulation of commodities through Margaret's exhibit 'The Price of Coal', *The Adjuster* self-consciously exploits the melodramatic tropes of home and family (*heimlich*) to reveal the commodifying impulse (*unheimlich*) driving North American suburban culture. *The Adjuster* makes visible the sterility of a family and home life that are themselves becoming commodities, and thus structures of alienation under late capitalism. Egoyan's celluloid family live in a model demonstration home, on a stretch of waste ground, the empty lots of the failed suburban development for which their residence acted as an advertisement. Dotting this desolate landscape are billboards selling suburban life by offering up images of homes and families as commodities (Figures 4.17–4.18). The 1950s-style graphics and colour separation of these images mark them as redolent of the suburban expansion experienced by Eisenhower's America and its obsession with appearances. However, the billboards' location on a waste ground that, at times, is manipulated by shots of hovering seagulls to resemble a garbage dump, indicates their poverty, their failure to refer back to a material referent in contemporary Toronto where the film is set. The smiling faces of the billboards' nuclear families are absent from Egoyan's neighbourhood. Egoyan's suburbia is the Eisenhower dream turned inside out, a nightmare vision where the *heimlich* discourse of suburban home or family is haunted by the *unheimlich*: hard-core pornographic films, voyeuristic masturbators and film-makers, and the spectre of destruction by fire.[49] As with the previous films in this section, I want to read *The Adjuster* as a family melodrama with a focus on the home site. In this case my reading will be framed by the concept of commodity fetishism and Mulvey's understanding of the domestic sphere as the location of commodity consumption (1989d, 76).

Cross-cutting between three home sites in the film's establishing shots introduces the staging of bourgeois social class through the buying power of the home's inhabitants, and the alienation produced when things structure human interaction. In the opening sequence we move from the 'model' suburban home of Noah Render, an insurance adjuster, and his wife Hera, a film censor, to the suburban home destroyed when the camera follows Noah to a house fire to meet a client, Arianne. Egoyan cuts from a shot of the adjuster introducing himself to Arianne, to Bubba and Mimi performing one of their fantasy scenarios in a subway car for Hera, in this instance a sexualized transgression of class boundaries. As Bubba sums it up later in the film, he and Mimi have all the material things they desire, but don't really know what it is they want. They attempt, unsuccessfully, to reach beyond things, and interact with people through performance. Bubba, who lives in a mansion, masquerades as a dirty, homeless man who masturbates an affluent stranger, Mimi, under the gaze of Hera. Eventually we

Figures 4.17–21 The Adjuster (1991).
Courtesy of Johnnie
Eisen, © Ego Film Arts

follow Bubba and Mimi, still in costume, to their estate where a chauffeur-driven limousine drops them off.

Juxtaposed to these three home sites – Noah's 'model' suburban home, the suburban home ravaged by fire and Bubba's mansion – is the transient non-home site of the motel where Noah's clients, refugees from suburban infernos, live. For these people, displaced from the suburban dream, the discourse of commodity fetishism has been interrupted. This destruction of commodities and the centre of their consumption, the home, can, potentially, reveal how relationships between things are substituted for human relationships between people. However, Noah's job as an adjuster is to work towards the repression of this knowledge. The suburban insurance claim is a semiotic system inscribing the substitution of new commodities for destroyed ones, not just to provide such basic amenities as shelter but to restore the performance of social class. Tim, one of Noah's clients, sits in his motel room surrounded by things, his stock, the lamps he has salvaged from his fire-ravaged home, a suburban space that doubled as his place of business, a retail outlet for household lighting. In the series of medium shots and close-ups composing this sequence, illuminated by the many lamps which threaten to displace the characters from the room, the mediation of people's relations by things is made abundantly clear to the viewer. Things, the lamps, dominate the visual field, while the dialogue paradoxically disavows and acknowledges the commodity fetishism signified by the excessive *mise-en-scène* (Figure 4.19). In response to Noah's assurances that his claim is being processed as quickly as possible, Tim thanks the adjuster for being so caring, to which Noah replies, 'I deal with people.' A disciplining consumer culture ideology conceals from Tim and Noah what is revealed to Egoyan's audience through the director's manipulation of *mise-en-scène* and dialogue: things form the foundation of Noah's caring. He does not care about people, rather his investment is in their things, he restores an economy where things structure human relations by placing a dollar value on commodities destroyed by fire, magically reconstituting the use-value of the suburban dream destroyed by fire. Even Noah's sexual activity with Arianne is punctuated by dialogue urging her to complete her list of things for the expedition of her claim. However, Arianne, surveying the charred wreckage of her suburban home, is beginning to see beyond the surface of household commodities and through the dominant ideology of consumer culture of which Noah is both agent and captive. Part of Noah's social role is to adjust the perception of his clients to ensure that they do not suspend their belief in suburbia's ability to produce meaning. Where they see meaningless, twisted skeletal remains of suburbia, he attempts to realign their vision so that they see the potential to rebuild their lifestyle, 'to return things to normal' through commodity consumption. For Arianne 'normal' in the rhetoric of the suburban insurance claim is a term that fails to signify. As Noah explains it, normal in this context 'is whatever you think you need to make you feel like you are functioning in the right way'. Ironically, the fire itself, its destruction of things, may be what Arianne required to feel as if she is functioning in the right way. Arianne's experience of suburbia is a stultifying one; she watched passively as a spark from an electrical short circuit set fire to her house. Asked by Noah why she looked on as the fire consumed her home, she replies, 'something had to change, so I watched as it did'. Arianne's desire for liberation from the weight of commodity consumption, symbolized in the destruction of its centre, the suburban home, anticipates Bubba's torching of the Render's 'model' home.

The *unheimlich*, stultifying, alienating properties of home and family as commodities that Noah is unable to recognize in his work as an adjuster are brought home to him and his family, and the viewer, incrementally, as the narrative develops. The first interior shots of the Render home, a scene between Noah and Hera set in their bedroom, are haunted by the soundtrack's strangely familiar, yet unrecognizable muffled grunts and groans of the *unheimlich*. We learn later that these are the noises of violent hard-core pornography emanating from the living room where Hera's sister Seta views pornographic videotapes recorded surreptitiously by her sister at the Censor Board. Whereas the postwar family melodrama of Hollywood cinema represses the primal scene, absenting graphic sexuality from the home, Egoyan's melodrama marks the aural materialization of the repressed; we don't see the video images, we hear the soundtrack. Hera's job as a censor and her decision to bring pornographic video materials into the home raise important questions about woman's position in the home and family in the context of melodrama, the *unheimlich* of home as a patriarchal structure of female containment. Discussing melodrama and the genealogy of the woman's movement from 'near silence' towards speech, Mulvey argues that this process is 'negotiated primarily by the figure of the mother as "signifier of censorship"' (1989d, 76). As an 'essential adjunct to bourgeois marriage', the domestic is 'associated with woman, not simply as female, but as wife and mother' (69). The intertwined roles of wife and mother constitute what Mulvey refers to as the double helix of woman's silence in melodrama: 'the mother who represents the silence imposed by censorship and the mother's own containment and restraint within the language of patriarchal domination' (76). In postwar Hollywood melodrama the mother figure's censorial role is realized in her work as guarantor of the home's moral decency and privacy; she is, as Mulvey puts it, 'as essential a defence against outside incursion or curiosity as the encompassing walls of the home itself' (69). The double helix of woman's silence undergoes a shift in the character of Hera, whose censorial role becomes literalized and relocated outside of the home. She is a film censor whose importation of her work from the public sphere into the domestic sphere invites outside incursions and the curiosity of voyeurs into the home. In Egoyan's extension and reworking of the codes of the postwar Hollywood family melodrama, his indigenizing of the genre, the mother is no longer defender of the home and its respectability but, as alienated labour, an agent of its deterioration. While Hera, not unlike the mother of classical melodrama, still experiences a form of patriarchal silencing – Noah's refusal to hear her – she departs from the traditional mother figure by playing a silencing role outside the home, deciding what viewing materials will be available to the consuming public.

Mulvey's reflections on postwar Hollywood family melodrama suggest that the arrival of the television within the suburban home 'within censorship', by which she means the codes governing what was appropriate for broadcast, challenged the separation between public and private. Public events such as the early 1950s broadcasting of the House Un-American Activities Committee hearings, were brought into the privacy of the home (Mulvey 1989d, 76). For Mulvey television represents the 'apotheosis of the home as point of commodity consumption within capitalism under the aegis of the housewife' (76). In Egoyan's film it is the technology of the video camera, with which Hera tapes porno films, and the VCR, on which Seta watches them, that blur public and private. It is the production and consumption of pornography, a commodity that can stand in for, or structure human sexual relations, that contributes to a dissolution of the Eisenhower-era myth of the sexless, happy and healthy nuclear family. The television, formerly the conduit through which televisual products in the vein of *Leave It to Beaver* entertained and structured the family of the 1950s, is in Egoyan's film the technology that delivers the sexual fantasies and moral decay of suburbia repressed by shows such as *Leave It to Beaver*.

The voyeurism associated with Seta's viewing of pornographic films initiates a series of sequences exploring the uncanny of the watcher being watched, and by extension the voyeurism of cinema spectatorship, and the commodity fetishism of cinema. Hera's introduction of pornographic materials into the home space attracts the attentions of a Peeping Tom who masturbates against the Renders' window while watching Seta watch a porn film. The Peeping Tom is another sign for the dissolution of a tyrannical American myth of suburbia extending from the 1950s Eisenhower era and into contemporary Canada. In an earlier sequence, a long shot of the Peeping Tom figure leaning against one of the 1950s-style billboard tableaux of home and family, watching the Render home and family, constructs him as someone who has been interpellated by this emptying advertising myth. He is the dysfunctional, alienated neighbour produced by a consumer culture where things mediate human relations; the Renders become objects for his self-gratification. The family itself becomes the object of a pornographic, voyeuristic, and ultimately commodifying desire as this is realized in Bubba's fetishization of the Renders and their home. Egoyan cuts from the Peeping Tom sequence to the sequence where Bubba, after photographing the exterior and interior of the Renders' home and clandestinely snapping Hera, her son Simon and sister Seta while they sleep, strikes a deal with Noah to rent his home and members of his family for the production of a film. Bubba's film translates the moral guarantor mother of 1950s family melodrama into a sexual predator who serves prepubescent boys birthday cake in her bra. With Bubba's and Noah's economic transaction the family becomes a thing, a commodity mediating the relationship between the two men. Bubba's alienation from himself and others grows over the course of the film as the sexual fantasies he and Mimi pursue fail to bring him satisfaction. He attempts to buy relationships with people in an unsuccessful move to undo his sense of alienation, thereby reducing people to things and further alienating himself.

The production of Bubba's film makes visible the processes of cinematic production, drawing attention to cinema itself as a commodity, a thing that structures or mediates relationships between people. A series of metacinematic shots of klieg lights illuminating the home exterior, and interior shots exposing boom mikes, cameras, cables, production assistants and the dolly track laid down on the house floor to facilitate tracking shots, reveal the Render home as a film set, a construct where suburban family life will be reproduced for consumption (Figures 4.20–4.21). Egoyan's auto-referential gesture of allowing his audience to see the technology that has produced *The Adjuster* interrupts the reality effect of the cinematic apparatus and invites a questioning of the staging or cultural pro-duction of the suburban family. If the excessive *mise-en-scène* of domestic space in the Hollywood family melodrama is representative of the interiority or human emotions of its protagonists, then the Render 'model' home's synecdochic signi-fiers such as the faux-model home book prop signify an emotional investment in surface appearances behind which the empty value of suburban life is con-cealed.[50] For the Render home is not a home at all, it is, according to Egoyan, 'an archetype – the *idea* of a house' (Johnson 1991, 68). And the cultural and economic value of this archetype of home and family life has been produced, in part, by Hollywood's idealized televisual and cinematic representations of sub-urban life consumed by Canadian spectators who then attempt to reproduce or perform this American fantasy, only to discover its meaninglessness. In Bubba's film narrative, which, significantly, becomes indistinguishable from his lived experience, the failure of suburbia as a system of meaning results in his suicide and the destruction of the commodified home or set, the sites where a sub-urban consumer culture are reproduced. As Bubba explains to Noah before he turns the adjuster's home into his funeral pyre: 'the character in this film, the person who is supposed to live here, decides that he's going to stop playing house'.

Unlike most classical Hollywood melodramas, which Neale argues suggest not a crisis of the legally established social order 'but a crisis within it, an "in house" rearrangement', *The Adjuster* suggests a crisis of this order itself in the literal bankruptcy of the suburb developers and the destruction of the suburban home (Neale 1980, 22). In Egoyan's film the suburban home, a sign of the dominant social order and economic system of consumer culture, is revealed as an alienat-ing structure of late capitalism, a nodal point in a discourse of commodity fetish-ism that does psychological violence to those it recruits. The identification made by Egoyan's characters with the signs of an Eisenhower-era domesticity offered to them as commodity through billboard tableaux of the family are represented as tragic misrecognitions. The increasing incursions of the world of work into the domestic sphere, and the ramifications of this collision, radically alter understand-ings of the home space under late capitalism. The definition of the bipartite split between work and family that Chuck Kleinhans's essay on melodrama and the family under capitalism argues is unique to capitalist social organization is troubled by Egoyan's film (Kleinhans 1978, 41). If the family under capitalism is the 'center of personal life, the primary institution' through which alienated labour acquires, in Kleinhans's words, personal happiness, love and fulfilment, then its commodification, and the transformation of the home site, locus of the family, into a site of industrial production in *The Adjuster*, leave no space for the individual's definition of meaning and purpose outside of production systems. Commodification's abrogation of the home and family as institutions facilitating personal fulfilment marks the home and family as fetishized objects in Egoyan's film. *The Adjuster* brings together both Marxist and Freudian concepts of fetish-ism. As Laura Mulvey explains it, 'the obvious link between [the] two concepts of

Plate 8 The Adjuster (1991). Bubba (Maury ChayKin) producing the family. Courtesy of Johnnie Eisen, © Ego Film Arts

fetishism is that both attempt to explain a refusal, or *blockage*, of the mind, or a phobic inability of the psyche to understand a symbolic system of value within the social and psychic spheres' (Mulvey 1993, 8). In this case, the characters' inability to understand how a suburban system of value, centred on the commodification of the home, structures their interpersonal relationships. Noting the significant differences between the two concepts, Mulvey writes: 'The Marxist concept is derived from a problem of inscription: that is, the way in which the sign of value is, or rather fails to be, marked onto an object, a commodity.' As we have seen in our reading of *The Adjuster*, 'it is in and around the difficulty of signifying value that commodity fetishism flourishes'. In contrast, the Freudian fetish is 'constructed from an excessive, phantasmatic inscription: that is, the setting up of a sign, which is of value only to its worshippers, to conceal a lack, to function as a substitute for something perceived as missing'. The family and domesticity as spaces of meaning and fulfilment are 'missing' in the world of Egoyan's film; therefore a desire for the physical home as commodity is substituted by Bubba, the Peeping Tom and Noah to conceal this lack.

THE ROAD MOVIE: *MY AMERICAN COUSIN,*
HIGHWAY 61, GOIN' DOWN THE ROAD

The road movie, a Hollywood genre synonymous with American culture and society becomes, perhaps surprisingly, a fertile field for the ironic interventions of Canadian film-makers who hijack this cinematic vehicle for the expression of a rebellious American freedom to visualize Canadian road adventures. Steven Cohan and Ina Rae Hark write in the introduction to *The Road Movie Book* that in its staying power the road movie is 'like the musical, or the Western, a Hollywood genre that catches peculiarly American dreams, tensions, and anxieties, even when imported by the motion picture industries of other nations' (1997, 2). Although *My American Cousin* (Sandy Wilson 1985) and *Highway 61* (Bruce McDonald 1992) trade subversively on American popular culture to create a space for Canadian popular culture products, the dreams, tensions and anxieties of both films are peculiarly Canadian. *Goin' Down the Road* (Don Shebib 1970), while it shares some structural elements with the Hollywood road film – male bonding through automotive technology – represents a specifically Canadian road of economic migrancy and regional disparity. All three films, however, possess the essential ingredient of road movies, they forge a travel narrative out of what Cohan and Hark describe as 'a particular conjunction of plot and setting that sets the liberation of the road against the oppression of hegemonic norms' (16). Wilson's and McDonald's films in their appropriation and redeployment of the Hollywood road movie reveal Sandy and Pokey as Canadians whose subjectivity is ordered, in part, by a dominating US popular culture industry. In this way, not dissimilar to Atwood's representation of US popular culture incursions across the border and into the Canadian imagination, *My American Cousin* and *Highway 61* act as resistance narratives critiquing the excesses of a seductive US popular culture hailing or recruiting Canadian audiences through Hollywood cinema and popular music.[51] Both films engage Guy Côté's contentions that the death of nations is cultural and develops from the moment they begin to 'dream the dreams of others' and that 'we in Canada have been quick to mimic the fads of other lands' (quoted in Dorland 1998, 123). Although Wilson's Sandy and McDonald's Pokey dream the dreams of an American Other, their creators' parodic mimicry of Hollywood cinema deflates these identifications as misrecognitions in the directors' production of an Anglo-Canadian mythology through indigenizing re-codings of an exported Hollywood genre. Wilson's and McDonald's difference in repetition reworks the Hollywood road movie's normative code of 'projecting American Western mythology onto the landscape traversed and bound by that nation's highways' to represent Canadian negotiations of American popular culture that produce Canadian cinematic culture (Cohan and Hark 1997, 1).

My American Cousin

While the road that brings Sandy's American cousin Butch to Canada, and the candy-red Cadillac he drives, constitute engines which fuel the plot of *My American Cousin* (Sandy Wilson 1985), the film's status as a road movie is unstable; it is a road movie shot through with elements of the family melodrama. Unlike such Hollywood road pictures as *Easy Rider* (Dennis Hopper 1969) or *Thelma and Louise* (Ridley Scott 1991), the bulk of screen time in *My American Cousin* is devoted not to the road trip through the United States but to the ramifications for Sandy and her family of Butch's arrival in 1959 British Columbia. The only roads Sandy sees from Butch's car are local, Okanagan ones; however, the car and the road are central elements structuring the film narrative. They facilitate Butch's escape from and return to the US and Sandy's desire to escape from a Canadian space where, she thinks, 'nothing ever happens'. Butch and his car represent the materialization of the American music and cinema – the space where something always happens – consumed by Sandy and her girlfriends.

Before reading the film's representation of the Canadian negotiation of the American, it is necessary to delineate the signification of allegorical stereotypes in *My American Cousin*. Sandy's family relations allegorize Canada's colonial relations to Britain, historically, and the United States, contemporaneously. Sandy's grandmother is a caricature of an English aristocrat living in the colonies: she presides over high tea, and disciplines her granddaughter to speak the 'Queen's language' the way it was 'meant to be spoken', with an upper-class English pronunciation. The cadence of Kitty's and the Major's speaking voices reveals Sandy's parents to be diluted versions of the grandmother. However, the dominance of English influence is giving way in the film to American influences. Butch's arrival and the teenage rebellion he brings with him interrupt Englishness as a normative cultural code at Paradise Ranch. Butch and his parents, Al and Dolly, constitute allegorical stereotypes of an affluent, loud, superficial, materialist, and immature America. Wilson's self-conscious use of such one-dimensional cartoon characters exploits what Richard Dyer terms the 'boundary maintenance' mechanism of the stereotype, maintaining a pejorative and reductive American difference from the Canadian (Dyer 1984, 29). In this way Wilson produces a counter-narrative to Hollywood cinema's practice of either not representing Canadians and Canadian experience at all, or constructing a celluloid wilderness populated by mad trappers, lumberjacks, saloon girls and singing mounties, stereotypes that, collectively, become the privileged cinematic sign for Canada in Hollywood productions such as *Rose Marie* (Mervyn LeRoy 1954).[52] *My American Cousin* plays Canadian and American allegorical stereotypes, or what critic Joanne Yamaguchi reads as 'two sets of cultural conditions', off each other (Yamaguchi 1989, 71). The film's first sequence reveals the Major slumped over his adding machine, a 'number cruncher' struggling to keep his cherry business in the black. These establishing shots of Canadian economic instability open up a space for American investment, a space that the Major's American counterpart,

Plate 9 My American Cousin (1985). Butch (John Wildman) and Sandra (Margaret Langrick). Courtesy of Kirk Tougas © Okanagan Motion Picture Co.

Al, attempts to fill at the end of the film. 'What's a place like this worth?' Al asks upon arriving in the Okanagan. Despite the Major's complaining that Al always has to put a price on things, he doesn't say no immediately to Al's offer of investment capital to convert the ranch into a tourist resort for Americans. This exchange acts out Canada's conflicted relationship to the United States, its resentment of, but dependence on, American investment. The codes of *mise-en-scène* – the major is costumed in a khaki British colonial-style tunic, Al in cowboy hat and boots, cigar firmly planted in mouth – combined with dialogue about a potential economic relationship between the two men provide the textual triggers which alert the viewer to the allegorical resonance of this scene. The Canadian is the colonial accountant, the American the enterprising entrepreneur-cowboy on the continually expanding American frontier in this signification of Canada's branch-plant economy. The mothers too are played off of each other: as Yamaguchi observes, Kitty is the refined, subtle, sensible mother, while Dolly resembles a faded Las Vegas showgirl more concerned about the well-being of her Cadillac than her son's welfare (71). Al's and Dolly's son Butch's sense of self has been shaped by Hollywood cinema: he is a screen stereotype of a self-centred American masculinity, most obviously the James Dean character in *Rebel Without a Cause* (Nicholas Ray 1955), a film that Shirl informs him hasn't yet played in the Okanagan. The car race sequence from *Rebel Without a Cause* is relocated in a field of irony in *My American Cousin* where Butch's car, the sign of a phallocentric symbolic order in *Rebel*, becomes feminized in Wilson's film as an object of male desire Butch steals from his mother. Wilson's seemingly light-hearted play with American stereotypes is making a rather serious point: it renders visible the potential for American popular culture to interpellate greedy, self-obsessed subjects, like Al, Dolly and Butch.

If Sandra's parents and grandmother are the allegorical figurations of an anglo-centric colonial Canada, then Sandra herself allegorizes an adolescent Canada coming of age at mid-century, shifting her gaze from the UK to the US. Allegor-ically, Canadian nation as read through Sandra is gendered female, while the US as read through Butch is gendered male. In the 'golden summer of 1959', Sandra is in the process of constructing herself as a young woman. She accomplishes this, in part, by making an identification with the United States, through her relation-ship to the Hollywood images of femininity and masculinity she covers her bed-room walls with, and through her relationship to Butch. The detour Sandra takes through the American Other to define, in Fuss's terms, a 'fictive sense of self' is an allegorical staging of the detour Canada takes through the American Other to define itself (1995, 143). However, it is important to note that similarly to the other family allegories cited above, the Sandra/Butch allegory does not represent a one-to-one correspondence between characters and nations. As Theresa Kelly's reading of Walter Benjamin's *Trauerspiel* notes, 'allegorical images posit some-thing like an impervious, material cover whose gesture toward some "other" cannot be read as the spiritual thing itself' (1997, 256).[53] So, while the film narrative is coded allegorically, embedded within that allegorical code is the dis-continuous nature of allegory that, as Paul Smith argues, 'remarks the irremedi-able distance between representation and idea' (Smith 1982, 105–6). That is to say there is an inherent discontinuity between Sandy and Butch as characters in a film narrative and the nations of Canada and the United States, a discontinuity structured by the ambiguity of allegorical signification itself, and the arbitrary and variant decoding of the characters by spectators. Despite her assessment of Butch as 'a little conceited and immature', Sandy simultaneously maps on to Butch the aura of glamour and excitement she associates with Hollywood and American popular music. When she rides in Butch's Cadillac, listening to 'Sea Cruise' on the radio, Sandra, temporarily, lives the dream of the American Other. An earlier scene in which Sandra practises kissing by pressing her lips to her reflected mirror image most effectively demonstrates the identification she makes with Butch and through him the United States. Addressing herself as Butch before kissing her reflection, Sandra displaces her own mirror image with the projected spectacle of her American cousin, misrecognizing the American Other for the Canadian self. Sandra's desire for excitement, for things American, is the impetus behind her failed plan to escape the boredom and rules of Paradise Ranch for California with Butch. Her desire for the US Other and its Hollywood representations, one of which, James Dean, her cousin misrecognizes himself for, is, however, conflicted by her determination to represent herself. The camera Sandra uses to photograph her family and Butch at the beginning of the film, her control over the field of representation, may be read as a self-reflexive sign of a developing Canadian film industry struggling to represent Canadian experiences in a medium dominated by the United States. Sandra's camera is analogous to Wilson's own cinematic apparatus and its production of *My American Cousin*.[54] Sandra also controls the field of representation that is *My American Cousin* as the film's homodiegetic narrator; we know Butch and the world of Paradise Ranch through her voice-over narration of her memories and reconstructions of scenes from which she was absent. The allegorical structure of the film, its acting out of Canada's and the Canadian film industry's coming of age, is reflected in the film's narrative trajectory which builds towards the Dominion Day Dance and the steady deflation of the American Other. Revealed as a lazy coward afraid of work, rattlesnakes and heights, Butch is finally reduced by the Canadian boy Lenny to a 'tough punk in a fancy car trying to pick up chicks' during their fight at a dance celebrating Canada's birth as a nation.

Not unlike allegory in *Mon oncle Antoine* and *Les bons débarras*, the allegorical impulse in *My American Cousin* runs the risk of flattening out belonging to Canadian nation into an identification with a white subject, something films like *Honey Moccasin*, *Masala* and *Rude* unveil as a misrecognition. The juxtaposition of these films and their representations of racially diverse Canadas to Wilson's film is informed by Fuss's instructive understanding of identification as: 'a process that keeps identity at a distance, that prevents identity from ever approximating the status of an ontological given, even as it makes possible the formation of an *illusion* of identity as immediate, secure, and totalizable' (1995, 2). Our detour through the American Other with Sandra suggests that the white American is for the white Canadian a misrecognition which, once revealed, makes possible the illusory and totalizing 'authentic' identity of a white Canadian nation allegorized by Sandra and her family. Such a reading belies the web of complex significations interrupting any one to one correspondence between object and idea, between the cinematic sign for Canadian nation and its multiple and conflicting material signifieds. Sandra's identification with the American Other, however, will have a resonance for most Canadians who are structured as desiring subjects of a dominant American popular culture, the monopolistic distribution systems of which displace Canadian popular culture products. Hollywood's global monopoly on cinema disciplines Canadian directors who wish to represent Canadian experiences to a wide audience of Canadians to take a detour through the American industrial Other. These directors seek to divert the Canadian spectator's gaze from the US to Canada by using codes of the Hollywood industry that are familiar to Canadian audiences whose expectations of cinema are shaped by Hollywood genres. Wilson makes an anti-road movie about the road not taken to the United States. Sandy's road of liberation from the hegemonic norms of parental control takes her not to the United States but into town for the evening before returning her to the Major and Kitty. At the end of the film Sandra is left in a cloud of dust at the gates of Paradise Ranch watching as Butch is driven home to California by his mother.[55]

Highway 61

In contrast to Butch's south–north border crossing, Bruce McDonald's 1992 film charts a north–south border crossing following the road exploits of two Canadians, Pokey Jones and Jackie Bangs, as they travel Highway 61 from Pickerel Falls, Ontario, to New Orleans pursued by an American who believes himself to be Satan. Chris Byford writes of this Canadian detour through the American Other: '*Highway 61* makes it quite clear that our particular context always/already includes American popular culture' (1998, 17). Similarly to Sandy who considers leaving what she sees as the boredom of Paradise Ranch behind for the excitement of the United States, Pokey dreams of escaping what he perceives as the cultural backwaters of Pickerel Falls for a place where he can play his coronet. As he informs Jackie, 'New Orleans, the birth place of Jazz, Louis Armstrong . . . Buddy Bolden, a chance to walk down those legendary streets, a chance to drive down the highway, hear the music, meet the people, see the people, see America, it's a dream come true.'

Both Sandy's and Pokey's dreams of elsewhere are structured by the soundtracks of their lives and their respective film narratives, which, like Canadian radio, are dominated by American pop music. The dream of elsewhere is a dream of America that is, as Byford puts it, always-already part of the Canadian psyche. The presence of America in the Canadian popular imagination is ironized by McDonald's exploitation of the road movie genre to tell Canadian story and the visual transition device of the spinning red, white and blue barber pole outside Pokey's barber shop in northern Ontario. An extreme close-up on the spinning colours is used twice in the opening sequence to effect transitions between shots. The spinning red, white and blue field of colour, a visual reference to the American flag and by extension American popular culture, is not immediately recognizable as a barber pole until later when it is revealed as such in close-up and medium shots. Similarly, American popular culture, the presence of its iconography in physical and psychic Canadian landscapes, can become naturalized and is not always readily recognizable as something foreign. The punctuation of the opening sequence with the swirling, brightly lit and seductive spectacle of what constitutes a sign, in the context of this film narrative, for American advertising delineates the presence of America in Canada. Byford reads the barber pole as a marker for the existence of the US 'at least in an encapsulated form in the very heart of the Canadian Shield' (1998, 16).

This US presence contributes to the interpellation of Pokey and Jackie. Although the more worldly of the two, Jackie – a roadie for a rock band who has travelled in the US and doesn't share Pokey's naive romanticized vision of the country – is formed, in part, by a knowledge of Hollywood films. After stealing cocaine from the band she is touring with, Jackie goes 'on the lamb'. She appropriates the body of an unfortunate youth as a mule to smuggle the drug into the US with the assistance of an unsuspecting Pokey whom she cons into driving herself and the body she claims as her brother's to New Orleans. Not dissimilar to Wilson's Butch, McDonald's Jackie Bangs is a stereotype of Hollywood cinema, in this case a *femme fatale* amalgam of Bonnie Parker (*Bonnie and Clyde* 1967, Arthur Penn) and Lulu (*Something Wild* 1986, Jonathan Demme), an outlaw figure whose knowledge of drug and gun culture has led at least one Canadian critic to mistake her for an American.[56] However, as the close-up of the American border guard's computer monitor informs us, Jackie's citizenship is Canadian; she is a Canadian character (self)constructed from American materials, the materials of a road movie sub-genre, the Bonnie-and-Clyde film. Ian Leong, Mike Sell and Kelly Thomas see this sub-genre as typically featuring 'two young people who fall in love, speed away from home in a stolen car, shoot guns, make love, and get caught' (1997, 72).

McDonald and his characters, however, negotiate the Hollywood Bonnie-and-Clyde film with, after Neale, a difference in repetition. 'Canadians confronted with American movies make a different meaning and make meaning differently because of our knowledge of America and our knowledge that we are not American', writes José Arroyo in his thoughtful consideration of colonialism and Canadian cinematic culture (1992, 78). Arroyo makes his comments in the context of a discussion of how Canadians see Hollywood films, but his ideas are useful for working towards an understanding not only of how Canadian spectators introject Hollywood cinema but of how they project it on to lived experience, and creative projects such as Canadian feature film. Adapting feminist critic Mary Ann Doane's concept of gender masquerade and female spectatorship to theorize Canadian viewing practices, Arroyo argues that, although Canadians

Plate 10 Highway 61 (1992). © Shadow Shows 2001

comprehend Hollywood cinema as if we were the intended audience, we understand that we are not addressed directly. In this way, Arroyo suggests, we constitute an absence, a gap that demands a realignment: 'When watching American films we too have to put on a masquerade, re-align our cultural identity so that that gap, which is the result of being Canadian watching films as if we were Americans, can be bridged' (1992, 78). In the characters of Jackie and Pokey we can see a transposition of this masquerade to lived experience, and in the creative project of *Highway 61* we witness McDonald's projection of a Canadian understanding of American cinema on to Canadian feature-film production, where a different meaning of the Bonnie-and-Clyde road film is produced by its detour through the Canadian Other. In McDonald's film two young people speed away from home in a car that is not stolen but with a body that is, smuggle drugs, shoot guns, make love and get caught, not by the law as in the Hollywood paradigm but by themselves. Ironically, *Highway 61* represents the seduction of Canadians by Hollywood's construction of a peculiarly American freedom associated with a culture of sex and guns. Upon his initial discovery that Jackie had purchased a gun with the money she stole from the Watson family, Pokey registers his disapproval: 'great you're going to end up dying in slow motion'. Pokey's/McDonald's invocation of the final slow-motion gun carnage sequence from *Bonnie and Clyde* articulates the Hollywood solution to the Bonnie-and-Clyde road film, getting caught by the law in a hail of deadly bullets, and adumbrates a Canadian solution of catching the self. After being forced at gunpoint to have sex with Jackie, the Canadian who masquerades as the film's sign of American outlaw culture, Pokey takes the gun Jackie fired to mark their sexual climax and begins taking random shots at road signs from the couple's speeding vehicle. The seduction of the Canadian by American cultural forms now complete, McDonald begins to unwork the American paradigm his film is in dialogue with by creating moments in which Jackie and Pokey become cognizant of their misrecognition of the American Other for a self. After Satan, also known as Mister Skin, destroys Pokey's car, Pokey renounces Jackie's 'carefree criminal lifestyle', declaring, 'I'm not a criminal, I'm a musician.' Jackie responds by short-circuiting Pokey's detour through the American Other: 'you're no fucking musician! You're a barber, a small-town barber, a Canadian!' Although spat out like insults, the words 'barber', 'small town' and 'Canadian' prompt Pokey to acknowledge their resonance for him: 'yeah, maybe I am and maybe that's where I belong'. Jackie has her anagnorisis when she uses her gun to prevent the cocaine from being removed from her dead mule, electing instead to set the corpse adrift in a Louisiana bayou. After a brief, silent ceremony in which Jackie places a flower and one of her earrings on the coffin and tenderly pushes it downstream, she submerges herself under the muddy waters, surfacing to the strains of Pokey's coronet to enact what Pevere describes as 'a form of born-again, moral baptism' (1992b, 36). Instead of ending with its principles dying in a hail of bullets as per Hollywood, McDonald's indigenization of the Bonnie-and-Clyde road movie ends with its Canadian principles emerging out of their

Hollywod image prisons. The escape from the hegemonic norms of small-town Ontario becomes an escape from Hollywood cinema's overdetermined American subjectivities. This decolonizing of Canadian cinema through a subversive dialogue with Hollywood is furthered by McDonald's self-reflexive homages to Canadian film in *Highway 61*. Pevere claims McDonald's film as one of the most 'self-consciously "Canadian" features' ever produced, noting its 'checklist of signature English Canadian concerns and clichés' including references to the road in Shebib's *Goin' Down the Road*, and the coffin on the move in Jutra's *Mon oncle Antoine* (1992b, 36).

An examination of the red, white and blue barber pole and the scenes associated with it provides greater insight into McDonald's decolonization of the Canadian imagination in *Highway 61*. The barber pole is a floating signifier in the film; a marker of US popular culture at the beginning of the film, it re-emerges towards the end of the film transformed into an identifying marker of Canadian experience. A close-up on the red, white and blue pole outside of Pokey's barber shop is structured by the voice-over narration of Satan as a sign of an aggressive, if laughable, US cultural and economic neo-imperialism that presides over the exchange of a Canadian soul for a clichéd dream of American popular and consumer culture: 'Wanna be rich? Want your own TV series?' These questions invoke the discourse of American television advertising consumed by most Canadians on a daily basis. A cut from the pole to a medium shot of Satan reveals this American devil as a second-rate salesman with slicked back hair in a cheap suit offering Pokey's French-Canadian pal Claude life in the United States 'on a yacht the size of a football field'. Claude, however, as Pevere notes, is the quintessential Canadian 'hoser' who is ready to sell his soul for beer but settles for a mickey of American bourbon (1992b, 36). While this scene allegorizes the economic and cultural seduction of Canada by the United States, its destabilizing irony undermines constructions of Canada as the noble victim of an evil empire in its signification of a weak-minded Canadian populace complicit in its subjection to a banal tabloid joke, a sociopath who thinks he is an omnipotent Beelzebub. The barber pole, the film's sign in Canada for US advertising that sells American consumer and popular culture, becomes in the United States a sign for Pokey's identity as a small-town Canadian barber. He advertises himself as 'Pokey Goans, the barber, direct from Canada' when he markets his services to a gang of bikers on the road in Louisiana. Moreover, shots of Satan surrounded by his melting polaroids, Jackie in the drug house, Pokey walking the streets of New Orleans that precede the bayou funeral are intercut with shots of the barber pole. In this montage of shots, the last of which is a close-up on the melting polaroid of Ronald Quarry, the youth who sold his soul to the American Satan, the doubled ironic vision of McDonald becomes apparent. The barber pole, a sign of US advertising associated with Mr Skin's sales pitches and Quarry's selling of his soul to American interests is also an identifying marker of Pokey's Canadianness. The shifting register of the barber pole marks the transforming, introjective and projective powers of Canadians confronted with American culture; Canadians receive and make meaning differently. In this context the red, white and blue barber pole's presence in the Canadian cultural landscape is analogous to Hollywood's presence in the Canadian imagination where a genre narrativizing US experience is received and re-produced transformatively as a cinematic expression of Canadian experience. McDonald's film takes Hollywood cinema, a device of cultural colonization, and transforms it into a representational system enacting an oppositional narrative of cultural decolonization.

Goin' Down the Road

Produced and released at the height of Anglo-Canadian nationalism, Don Shebib's *Goin' Down the Road* (1970), Canada's original road movie, figures significantly in a Canadian film criticism which has given and continues to give the film an iconic status as the foundational text for Canadian cinema in English. Shebib's film undeniably marks a renaissance of Canadian feature film-making in English; however, to claim that it represents the 'beginning' of English-Canadian national cinema, as Christine Ramsay does in her citation of contemporaneous reviews of the film, is to deny the international success of *Back to God's Country* (1919), the work of early documentary film-makers, the NFB and the efforts of Sterling Campbell (*Bush Pilot* 1946), Budge Crawley (*The Luck of Ginger Coffey* 1964) and David Secter (*Winter Kept Us Warm* 1965), amongst many others, that forged the foundations of a Canadian national cinema in English (Ramsay 1993, 32).[57] As Ramsay's analysis of criticism on Shebib's film indicates, most critics, from Margaret Atwood to Robert Fothergill, have concentrated on what they perceive as the 'loser' or in Atwood's terms 'victim' paradigm,[58] where the failure of the film's principals Pete and Joey is read allegorically as Canada's failure to throw off its status as a cultural and economic colony of the US. Fothergill decodes Pete's and Joey's failure as acting out what he describes as Canada's perpetual younger brother role to the United States (Fothergill 1977). Ramsay frames her own reading of the film around marginality and masculinity, drawing an insightful comparison between the construction of the nation and masculinity. She argues that *Goin' Down the Road* became a touchstone of Canadian film scholarship, not because of its representation of the quintessential Canadian loser or victim but because of its 'empathetic engagement with marginality' (1993, 45). Chris Byford dismisses this claim, citing Shebib's insensitivity to marginality in what he contends are the film's 'gross stereotypes' and 'misinformation'. According to Byford, Shebib's film caricatures Maritimers such as Pete, whose application for a job that he is 'woefully unqualified for' creates a stereotype of Nova Scotian labourers as 'either rather dense' or 'quite delusional' (Byford 1998, 12). The present reading, while negotiating the critical work of Byford and Ramsay, focuses on Shebib's indigenization of the Hollywood road movie into a Canadian narrative form. The narrative trajectory of *Goin' Down the Road* is plotted not along the south–north or north–south crossings of the forty-ninth parallel that shaped the road action of *My American Cousin* or *Highway 61* but along the east–west movement of two Cape Bretoners, Joey and Pete, toward Central Canada and what they hope will be economic and social success in Toronto. Similarly to *Margaret's Museum*, Shebib's film narrativizes the disparities in region and social class that frustrate an equitable belonging to Canadian nation. Unlike Ransen's film, however, *Goin' Down the Road* reveals Nova Scotia's culturally and economically marginal position within the nation through a defamiliarizing journey into the symbolic and material source of Eastern Canada's alienation, Toronto, the corporate headquarters of the Central Canadian capital that, as we saw in *Margaret's Museum*, has profited from the exploitation of generations of Cape Bretoners.[59]

As is the case with most road films, the road in *Goin' Down the Road* offers only temporary liberation from oppressive hegemonic norms that re-materialize upon arrival; Pete and Joey become prisoners of their social, economic and regional identities in Toronto. The film's establishing shots of disused railway tracks, a derelict mine, an abandoned house and rotting fishing vessels define the economic and social decay of Cape Breton before Shebib cuts to shots of Pete and Joey escaping this graveyard of dead industries for the promise of the West. These opening shots are structured by Canadian singer/songwriter Bruce Cockburn's eponymous song as a lament for a disappearing way of life. Joey's departure is narrated by a lyric referencing the disappearance of the region's fishermen: 'But they couldn't compete with the company fleet / Now it's welfare relief or go West.' A cut to a low-angled close-up shot of the highway's broken lines speeding by before the camera marks a shift on the soundtrack from Cockburn's lament to up-tempo acoustic and electric guitars and initiates a series of shots signifying the freedom of the road: Pete and Joey drinking beer in the speeding convertible; Pete and Joey laughing and conversing. A flat tyre, perhaps the film's first foreshadowing that the road west might not be the route to self-empowerment imagined by the protagonists, provides Pete with an opportunity to spin Joey a romantic narrative proclaiming Toronto as the salvation of alienated Eastern Canadian labour.

> Christ, Joey, I'm not working in any more canneries. That's why we left. You'd be working for a buck and a quarter an hour for the rest of your life . . . Oh listen Joey it's going to be so different. There you can get all kinds of jobs, not just sweat and dirt all the time, and the places you go, we're going to hit some nice spots, have us some good times.

Pete's and Joey's quest is predicated upon their successful performances of a patriarchal masculinity. Toronto is gendered female, framed by Shebib as an object of Eastern Canadian male desire that must be conquered. Joey structures our understanding of a tracking long-shot of the Toronto skyline through this gendered paradigm: 'Hey Pete, there she is, doesn't she look good?' That they imagine Toronto as a feminized object over which they will obtain sexual mastery becomes clear in the very next lines of dialogue: 'Look out Toronto here we come . . . Hide your daughters, lock your doors cause we're about to drop our drawers.' However, their failure to penetrate the economy of Toronto and Toronto's subsequent consumption of them as a source of cheap labour is adumbrated in the cut that is made at the end of this line of dialogue from a medium shot of their speeding car on its way into the city, to an aerial shot of the car travelling down a Toronto street where it is dwarfed to insignificance by the skyscrapers of the city's financial and commercial institutions. Following this shot, Pete and Joey end up spending the night in a Salvation Army hostel, after they are rejected by Pete's aunt and uncle, a Cape Breton migrant couple who have secured a place in the suburbs of middle-class Toronto. The car, the means of their escape, is paradoxically a sign of their failure to escape their economic, social and regional identities. A rusting hulk of automobile inscribed with hand-painted text reading, 'My Nova Scotia Home', Pete's 'dreadful car', as his aunt calls it, continues to define him and Joey after they arrive in the city. Ramsay interprets the night spent at the hostel as the deflation of Joey's and Pete's 'fantasy of empowerment and independence and the beginning of their emasculation' (1993, 42). Timothy Corrigan sees such a 'destabilization of male subjectivity and masculine empowerment' as characteristic of the road movie genre (1991, 145). This destabilization or emasculation builds throughout the film, with the car, traditionally a sign of phallic potency in the Hollywood road movie, constructed here as an obstacle to Pete's successful performance of masculinity with Nicole Morin, a sign with the potential to betray his emasculated economic status. His co-workers from the bottling plant tell him that he can't use that old 'heap' for his date, offering him one of their cars, and suggesting he purchase new clothing.

The disciplining cultural and social norms of Central Canada contribute to the emasculation of Pete and Joey, locking them – and, allegorically, Eastern Canadian labour – out of equitable belonging to the nation. This refusal of equality in belonging is communicated visually in Shebib's play with a hierarchical shot composition that makes visible and reifies social class. Shebib shoots the phallic towers of Central Canadian capital from angles that do violence to the stature of the Eastern Canadian male labourer. The aerial shot of the office towers marking the insignificance of Pete's and Joey's arrival in the city from the perspective of corporate Toronto is revisited in Pete's arrival at the base of an office tower for a job interview with an advertising firm. However, this low-angled close-up shot, foregrounding the back of Pete's head as he looks up at the skyscraper stretching out of the frame, impresses upon the viewer the inaccessibility of corporate Canada to Pete; the office tower is a structure of capital and consumer culture that stretches beyond Pete's vision and understanding. Although he ascends the tower, his lack of both education and an advertising background cost him the job and prompt the interviewer to ask him, 'Whatever possessed you to come here looking for a job?' Pete's naive response is that he has watched plenty of television commercials 'down home'.

This scene in the advertising executive's office is, according to Byford, one of the film's more problematic moments of signification. For Byford, the scene constitutes an offensive stereotyping of migrant Nova Scotian labourers that militates against Ramsay's organization of the film around empathetic representations of marginality. Byford argues: 'to posit that a Maritimer with Pete's background would be so gullible as to travel to Toronto in search of such a position is to insult the intelligence of all such migrant workers within Canada' (1998, 12). Ramsay, on the other hand, reads the scene as contributing to an empathetic engagement with regional marginality in the context of an internal Central Canadian colonialism. For her, Shebib uses Pete's origins to articulate the differences between 'the Maritimes and Canada's imperial centre, Toronto' (1993, 40). She suggests that the job interview scene reveals 'that higher education was not only not available to Pete but also unnecessary in order for him to perform the only available Maritime work in the canneries, on the docks, or in the mines of Cape Breton' (40). Both Byford and Ramsay make important and insightful points which, taken together, flesh out the conflicted signification of this scene, something that may be traced, in part, to what both note is Shebib's own conflicted understanding of his characters. In an interview with P. M. Evanchuck, Shebib mistakenly identifies his protagonists as 'Newfies' whom he and most viewers wouldn't really want to speak to in real life (Evanchuck 1973, 14, quoted in Ramsay 1993, 41). Ostensibly Shebib's film sets out to represent the plight of two Cape Breton migrant workers sympathetically; however, at times such as this his Central Canadian cinematic apparatus unwittingly re-inscribes his cultural bias, limiting the bounds of a sympathetic, much less an empathetic, signification. Ironically, the interview scene enacts a critique of Central Canadian capital's cultural and economic hegemony over Eastern Canadian labour, while simultaneously revealing the film-maker's unknowing complicity with this ideological structure. Clearly Shebib is irretrievably inside, is a subject of, the dominant ideology he seeks to critique and ends up re-producing and re-circulating images which reify the social and economic subject positions of Eastern Canadian labour from the perspective of Central Canadian capital. This is not to deny the film's sympathetic impulses, its attempts at intervention in and subversion of a cultural field interpellating Eastern Canadians as peripheral and subordinate members of Canadian nation; rather my aim is to work through the problematic in the film narrative's signifying practices that Byford's and Ramsay's readings demand, and thus recognize how a dominant ideology regulates the representation of its others.

The alienation of Eastern Canadian labour is made clear enough in the migrant roles of Joey and Pete at the beginning of the film, while the alienation of Eastern Canadian labour from a Canadian nation defined through the economic and cultural power of Central Canada is delineated in the downward spiral of transient jobs held by these two characters. Deflated by his job interview experience, Pete's dream of middle-class status is further eroded by the work he and Joey are forced to take on as labourers in a bottling plant, car wash attendants and flyer delivery boys. At the end of the film they become petty criminals who steal

Plate 11 Goin' Down the Road (1970). Reproduced by kind permission of Don Shebib

groceries and assault a clerk with a tyre iron, before hitting the road west to escape the law. As Martin Knelman writes, *Goin' Down the Road* provides a veritable case study of how people become criminals:

> Uprooted because of the country's failure to make one region as pros-
> perous as another, [Pete and Joey] find themselves stripped of the social
> customs and institutions that have always given them their bearings. In
> the big city, the dream that lured them away from home – the prospect
> of material heaven suggested by slick magazines and TV commercials –
> proves to be cruelly beyond their reach.
>
> (Knelman 1977, 101)

Although the film represents the material conditions which force people into crime it also risks aligning Eastern Canadianness with criminality.

Generically, *Goin' Down the Road* is a road film shot through with elements of the melodrama. The escapist fantasy of male bonding on the road in the absence of women morphs into domestic melodrama when Pete and Joey arrive in Toronto and acquire jobs, and when Joey acquires a wife. According to Cohan and Hark, this tension between the road and domesticity is part of the road movie's generic makeup where the road is defined as 'a space that is at once resistant to while ultimately contained by the possibilities of domesticity: home life, marriage, and employment' (1997, 2–3). Pete, Joey and Joey's wife Betsy form what Ramsay describes as a pseudo-family, with Pete becoming their sole source of financial support after Betsy becomes pregnant and the unemployed Joey spends his days in the apartment drinking and watching television (Ramsay 1993, 41). Not unlike the feminized male characters in *Margaret's Museum*, Joey is feminized by a capitalist system of production that relegates him to the domestic sphere, a space of stasis that is escaped, temporarily, by a return to the road. Pete reveals wage labour itself as a realm of stasis in his complaints about the meaningless tasks that he and Joey perform daily at the bottle plant: 'Well can't you see there ain't nothing happening? That everything keeps going around in the same stupid circle doing the same stupid thing over and over. And there ain't nothing happening? You can't see what you have done, there ain't nothing there. Don't you understand that?' Pete's account of work at the bottle plant also describes the limited structure Shebib offers to narrativize the lives of Eastern Canadian migrants: a stupid circle in which the principals do the same stupid thing over and over.

Despite the problems the film encounters in its efforts to represent marginality, it is important not to dismiss, *pace* Byford, Ramsay's persuasive argument that in *Goin' Down the Road* the nation's margins – 'its cheap migrant labor pool' – are 'foregrounded as the Canadian nation's enabling condition' (1993, 39). Shebib's recoding of the Hollywood road movie displaces the mythologies of an American landscape to privilege a representation, albeit a conflicted one, of social, cultural and economic marginalities of region that frustrate belonging to Canadian nation.

THE WESTERN: *ROAD TO SADDLE RIVER* AND *THE GREY FOX*

As noted above and in Chapter 3, the Hollywood western, a narrative articulating the aggressive and perpetual US expansionism of Manifest Destiny, is the film genre *par excellence* of US imperialism. With the exception of the more sympathetic or pro-Indian films produced in the 1920s and 1950s, and later films troubling white American imperialism such as *Little Big Man* (Arthur Penn 1970) and *Dances With Wolves* (Kevin Costner 1990), the western naturalizes the extension of the Republic's borders westward and the assimilation or destruction of whatever or whomever is in the path of expansion, usually Native Americans. *The Far Country* (Anthony Mann 1954), starring Jimmy Stewart, takes the American ideology of Manifest Destiny north-west, extending US sovereignty beyond the forty-ninth parallel. Stewart plays an American Marshall who arrives in the Dawson City of 1898 to stake his claim, only to find a lawless town, a lone incompetent mountie, and a very high body count. The film ends with the mountie deferring to Stewart, whom the townspeople elect as sheriff. In the closing shot Stewart pins a tin star to his chest, becoming a symbol for American law and order in Canadian territory. The ideological function of these images is fairly transparent. This final shot, together with all the film's preceding shots, regulates an order of subjectivity where the spectator is disciplined to see the United States as a strong and righteous country that sometimes must expand its frontier to bring morality, law and order to other lands that are bereft of such uniquely American commodities, usually at the invitation of the other country's inhabitants.[60] Hollywood produced its own series of pseudo-Canadian westerns via the mountie movie, a sub-genre of the western. As Pierre Berton suggests, in these films the mountie was little more than a US sheriff in a red tunic (Berton 1975, 121). However, it wasn't just Hollywood that was producing western-themed pictures set in Canada: *Back to God's Country* (1919) and *Cameron of the Mounted* (Henry MacRae 1921) with their saloon scenes, gunplay and frontier locales might be considered two of Canada's earliest home-grown westerns.

As the western has historically been one of the most popular of Hollywood genres, and, as I have argued, the Hollywood genre of American cultural imperialism *par excellence*, it is not surprising that other national cinemas appropriate it. The best-known and most commercially successful of these appropriations are of course the Italian westerns of Sergio Leone and Sergio Corbucci starring Clint Eastwood. Christine Gledhill notes the transgressive nature of these films which, she suggests,

> clearly mark a challenge to the dominance of Hollywood over genre production, complicating the question of the relation of genre motifs to the culture which produced them, and demonstrating the work of translation and transformation that goes on between cultures, especially in the cinema.
>
> (1985, 71)

More recently, two Canadian films, *Road to Saddle River* (Francis Damberger 1993) and *The Grey Fox* (Philip Borsos 1982), have drawn on the Hollywood western genre self-consciously and parodically, challenging Hollywood's dominance of the genre by using it to narrativize Canadian stories. Both films make auto-referential play with codes and conventions of the Hollywood western: the outlaw as hero, the conflict between the laws of civilization and the brand of outlaw masculinity they threaten to contain. The protagonist of Borsos's film, Bill Miner, is an American outlaw who flees from American law-enforcement authorities into Canada. The outlaw hero of Francis Damberger's film is a late-twentieth-century Eastern European immigrant to Canada, Cowboy Kid, who escapes the domestic tyranny of his uncle and aunt for the homosocial world of the cowboy: the Hollywood western myth of Saddle River that he seeks on the road west to 1990s Alberta. Self-reflexivity is a quality that marked the western from its beginnings (Gallagher 1986, 204, 208); however, the self-reflexivity of both Damberger's and Borsos's films foregrounds Canadian acts of viewing and translating, indigenizing a Hollywood genre; a difference in repetition emphasizing cultural difference.

As much as these two Canadian films signify through their generic difference in repetition, they, like Hollywood westerns in general, address a male problematic.[61] The discourse of masculinity promulgated in westerns constitutes what Australian sociologist R. W. Connell terms a disciplining exemplary masculinity (Connell 1995, 214). Connell comments that his own masculinity was formed in part by replaying the images of North American frontier warfare between 'Cowboys and Indians' that he consumed in the South Pacific through imported comic-book and Hollywood images (185–6).[62] Similarly, after Byford, the laws or codes of masculinity circulating in the Hollywood western are always-already part of the Canadian popular imagination. Therefore the various antimonies among them – individual/community, freedom/restriction, tradition/change, east/west – that Neale sees as focusing on the body of the male western hero to 'articulate the space of the functioning of what is defined in the genre as the Law, and the space which is defined as outside it, as Other' structure both Damberger's and Borsos's films (1980, 58). For Neale, the body of the hero is located within a series of other bodies (Indians, outlaws, townspeople) across which the opposition between Law and Other is delineated (58). This opposition is also marked 'across a spatial economy whose polar instances are natural landscape on the one hand and the township/homestead on the other' (58–9). Neale emphasizes the dynamic location of the body of the hero at the point of intersection, 'oscillating' between these oppositions (59), and this is precisely where Borsos and Damberger locate their heroes.

Road to Saddle River

The body of Cowboy Kid, the Eastern European immigrant hero of *Road to Saddle River* (Francis Damberger 1993), is situated within a series of other bodies, a series of typologies of masculinity. These range from the metacinematic bodies of the Hollywood stereotypes of celluloid Cowboy and Indian that appear at various points in the film, structuring the narrative and signalling the film's awareness of itself as cinema, to Rango and the four travelling companions Cowboy Kid meets along the Trans-Canada highway in search of Saddle River. Alienated from his job as butcher's assistant to his uncle, Cowboy Kid develops an alternative reality based on his obsessive identification with Rango, a fictitious star of Hollywood westerns. All of the dialogue spoken by Cowboy Kid is either pulled directly from Rango or is Rango-inspired. A meal with his aunt and uncle in their claustrophobic home in an eastern Canadian city sets in motion a series of events that prompt Cowboy Kid to abandon the restrictions of urban life for the wide open spaces of the West. Deeply entrenched in commodity fetishism, the workaholic uncle and his wife articulate the warped understanding of quality of life offered by consumer culture in North America. 'In this country,' says the uncle, 'they have something what they call quality of life. The more harder you work, the more quality of life you can buy.' Illustrating her husband's rationalization of the work ethic to maximize a quality of life that is equated with conspicuous consumption, the aunt gestures towards commodities such as 'magic hamburger machine, microwave, colour TV' that can be accumulated through labour. If he fails to invest in this 'quality of life' his uncle threatens to send him back to the Old Country. Cowboy Kid, however, will have none of this; he pushes himself away from the table and escapes a stultifying domesticity through Damberger's Rango, a parodic homage to the Hollywood western *Shane* (George Stevens 1953). Cut-aways from Cowboy Kid pushing himself away from the table to a black-and-white medium close-up of Rango, Damberger's version of Shane, and back to a medium close-up of Cowboy Kid gazing at the cinema screen communicate the identification Cowboy Kid makes with the Hollywood cowboy (Figures 4.22–4.23). As Cowboy Kid looks on in rapt enjoyment, Rango (played by Damberger) speaks from the screen for both of them, articulating an aversion for homesteading and domesticity: 'no place for my kind here'. When Lance – Damberger's version of Joey from *Shane* – asks Rango where he will go, the cowboy star's response provides Cowboy Kid with the narrative of the westerner, an exemplary narrative of masculinity that will carry him away from his role as a wage slave in the East to freedom in the West: 'West, a place called Saddle River. A place where the grass is green and the river runs clear and there's blue sky as far as the eye can see. I'm gonna get some land and build a ranch . . . A man's gotta do what a man's gotta do.' On his way home from the cinema, Cowboy Kid is nearly hit on the head by a saddle that falls from the sky. The saddle is, of course, the materialized sign of the visual pleasure he receives from the Hollywood western, and our first sense of the ontological collision Damberger's film enacts between the worlds of cinema and lived experience. Rejecting the bourgeois values of the East, and armed with the words of Rango and an icon of western cowboy mythology, the saddle, Cowboy Kid begins hitch-hiking west along the Trans-Canada highway. He is soon picked up by Sam, a would-be real estate entrepreneur who is heading west to start over after his wife leaves him and his house is repossessed. As they continue west they are joined by an East German traveller, Dieter (who hopes to marry a Canadian so that he can stay in the country), Norman Many Heads, a First Nations Elvis devotee on a vision quest, and, finally, Louis, an old Alberta ranch hand.

Cowboy Kid's identification with Rango and his appropriation of the Hollywood image of the cowboy – he identifies himself as 'Cowboy' to Sam – shapes the questing narrative of the film. Ostensibly, all of the characters who climb inside or on top of the yellow Honda get caught up in Cowboy Kid's search for the mythical Saddle River. He recites Rango's description of Saddle River to Sam and to Norman Many Heads, who, in exchange for tobacco, promises to lead the white men to this Hollywood construction. Each man, however, understands the road to Saddle River, and what it represents, very differently. For Sam, Saddle River signifies as a real estate commodity, a potential golf course development. He advises Kid to secure the mineral rights to Saddle River. This elicits a Rango

Figures 4.22–6 Road to Saddle River
(1993). © National Film
Board of Canada, 2001.
All rights reserved

response: 'Where there is gold there is blood.' The advice and response invoke the theft of land and mineral rites from North America's indigenous peoples that marked the westward expansion of the frontier in the nation-building projects of both the United States and Canada, and is the subject of Hollywood westerns. For Norman Many Heads, who tells Cowboy Kid that he can take him to Saddle River but 'cannot show [him] the way', and who later admits to his father that he has no idea where Saddle River is, the road to Saddle River becomes a personal vision quest on which he meets his spirit guide, the talking buffalo. For Dieter the road to Saddle River becomes a route to matrimony and Canadian citizenship through his union with a Hutterite woman at the end of the film. Cowboy Kid himself, the interlocutor of the Hollywood westerner narrative, uses it to forge a

Plate 12 Road to Saddle River (1993). Francis Damberger on the set of *Road to Saddle River* with Cowboy Kid (Paul Jarrett) and Norman Many Heads (Sam Bob). © National Film Board of Canada, 2001. All rights reserved

narrative route away from his mundane existence and, paradoxically, away from the Hollywood stereotypes of 'Cowboy' and 'Indian'. As much as he pursues these stereotypes, his real-life experiences distance him from them. These variant translations of the Hollywood westerner narrative by Damberger's characters recall Arroyo's comments about Canadians producing different meanings through their introjection and projection of Hollywood film (1992, 78). Norman Many Heads, for example, misrecognizes Hollywood cinema and popular music star Elvis as his spirit helper; however, he does not understand Elvis as an acculturating figure he is disciplined to imitate. Conversely, he reads Elvis as advocating Native empowerment. In Norman's vision, Elvis tells him to 'get up an' wiggle your bum and show the white people what you think'. Damberger, not dissimilarly to McDonald, projects a Canadian understanding of Hollywood cinema on to Canadian feature-film production, where a different meaning of the western and road film is produced by their detour through a Canadian Other. Damberger's film is a late-twentieth-century western shot through with elements of the road picture where, once again, genres designed to map US territory and mythology represent Canadians in Canadian landscapes negotiating Hollywood's myths of the US.

The yellow Honda is a mechanical horse in Damberger's film, literally saddled and ridden by both Norman Many Heads and Cowboy Kid. It is the road that is privileged in Damberger's title, a title emphasizing process, a journey without arrival. The road to Saddle River as parodic process denaturalizes masculinity as a ritual performance disciplined by what Teresa de Lauretis theorizes as the social technology of Hollywood cinema.[63] Through Damberger's parodic reframing, Hollywood stereotypes of the 'Cowboy' (or male adventurers) and 'Indian' collapse under their own excess. The 'great white hunters' encountered on the prairie by Kid, Sam and Norman are not the resourceful, self-reliant heroic male adventurers of the screen western who roam the open range on their own terms, but 'weekend warriors', urban professionals whose performance of masculinity is temporal and foregrounded through *mis-en-scène*. Damberger's modern-day outlaws require costumes – camouflage gear – and props – a generator and microwave oven – to enact their masculinity. Moreover, the machismo of the great white hunter stereotype is ironized by its prey; in Damberger's film it is not wild beasts that get caught in the cross-hairs of the hunters' rifles but the signs of Sam's failed domesticity, his wife's Wedgwood china. Here, the idea of outlaw is reduced to a joke. The attempts of a dentist and lawyer – agents of a social status quo – to 'get away from it all', to stand outside the law, are compromised by their dependence on electricity and microwaves, two signs of late-twentieth-century consumer culture and domesticity. In this film the landscape marking the Hollywood western – the wide open range – is also ironized through a visual pun. A shot of a kitchen range with its oven door wide open against a background of wide open prairie range constructs a tension between the hyper-masculine, open world of the cowboy and the kitchen as the absent presence of a domestic or feminine closed space that haunts the western.

The masculinity of the armed 'Indians' encountered by the 'Cowboys', Kid and Sam, is revealed as a ritualized, self–reflexive and ultimately parodic performance of the Hollywood western's representation of Aboriginal masculinity as predicated on acts of savage violence against white men. Ironically, but not surprisingly, it is the performance of white cowboy masculinity that is dependent on this construction of Aboriginality. Damberger's 'Indians' are savvy readers of the Hollywood western, and highly attuned to the racist preconceptions of First Nations masculinity it has formed in spectating subjects such as Cowboy Kid and Sam. The parodic context of Damberger's unworking of the pejorative Hollywood representation of Native American masculinity is triggered for the spectator through an ironic juxtaposition of soundtrack music. While Hollywood's hackneyed approximation of Native American music marks the appearance of Damberger's 'Indians' onscreen, the ability of this music to signify Native culture is immediately brought into question by the tapes of authentic First Nations music played by the Native characters for Sam and Kid. This crisis in signification contextualizes Damberger's re-staging of Hollywood's 'Indian' masculinity for an audience who insist on projecting those dehumanizing images on to Native subjects. Informed that they are trespassing on Native land, Kid and Sam revert back to the cosmology of a Rango western to negotiate their predicament. Recalling the colonizing frontiersman's use of alcohol to manipulate First Nations into ceding away their title to land, Sam offers the Native characters beer while Kid chimes in, 'we bring wampum'. As they sit around the fire, Cow-boy Kid quotes Rango invoking the fictive white colonial discourse of Native American masculinity: 'An Indian is not warrior till he kill and take scalp.' Decod-ing these signs of the Hollywood western that are being mapped on to them, the two Native characters begin to act out the racialized and imagined gender roles their guests desire to view. One man pulls a knife on Sam and jokes with him that it is a good thing his hair is too short to scalp. The parodic register of this performance is marked in the Native character's subsequent use of the knife to gesture toward a case of beer, his laughter and his next line of dialogue: 'Pass me another beer eh?' This utterance resonates with the stereotypical Canadian 'hosery' made famous by the Mackenzie Brothers' Great White North on *SCTV* (the CBC satirical television series). Although the Native characters self-identify as warriors, this is part of a rhetorical strategy colluding with, and then dismiss-ing, the stereotyping generated by Kid and Sam. These Native men are hired by the government to make war on the gopher population. In this self-deprecating joke about their warrior status, the men reveal why they are armed and reference the internal colonialism of a government that regulates First Nations subjectiv-ity. Sam, however, continues to frame his conversation with these men around armed conflict, conquest and subjugation: 'Just think, if like you guys had won the war we probably wouldn't be sitting here having a beer right now.' This bigoted compulsion to see the Aboriginal Other through the binaries of colonizer/colonized is punished in Damberger's film: white racist fantasies of the Aboriginal Other as exoticized savage are made material for these white 'cow-boys' through parodic performance. Kid's and Sam's disciplining of the two Native men to 'imitate the colonizer's version of their essential difference' pro-duces a situation where the two white men are stripped naked and tied to a stake on the prairie in the Native characters' parodic mimicry of Hollywood 'Indians'' savagery (Fuss 1995, 146). As Judith Butler reminds us in her discussion of parodic gender performances, 'parody by itself is not subversive'. She cautions that some repeated performances 'become circulated and recirculated as instru-ments of cultural hegemony' (Butler 1990, 139). However, Damberger's film, through its ironic juxtaposition of soundtrack music, and its culturally savvy Native characters whose performance turns racist gender stereotyping against itself, does effectively disrupt the racialized colonial discourse of 'Indian' masculinity.

Cowboy Kid's gender identity is foregrounded as performative and parodic in the scenes where we witness his introjection and projection of the over-determined 'Cowboy' masculinity offered by Hollywood's Rango. The obsession with Rango is unveiled as a masturbatory adolescent fantasy, in the sequence following Kid's reverential cinema spectating. Soundtrack noises of squeaky bed-springs moving rhythmically, and a close-up on the expression of disgust on Cowboy Kid's aunt's face as she listens to this noise with her ear pressed against his bedroom door, suggest that he is masturbating. A cut-away from the door reveals Kid naked, astride the saddle, his hands grasping the phallic pommel, a cowboy hat perched on his head (Figure 4.24). This is Damberger's deflating reformulation of Hollywood's solitary outlaw hero, an adolescent 'jerk-off'. Although both Sam and Cowboy Kid live up to the Hollywood stereotype of the outlaw in their transgression of territorial fences in favour of the open range, these transgressions are punished. As referenced above, the trespassing on First Nations territory meets with a humiliating punishment produced by their own racist imaginings of 'Indian'. Sam's and Cowboy Kid's destruction of a rancher's fence sees them surrounded by cattle and paying off the damage to the fence by doing the physical labour of contemporary cowboys. In the course of this work which involves castrating and branding cattle, Cowboy Kid's fears of castration by an authentic referent for Rango, the contemporary ranch hand or cowboy whose ritual performance of masculinity is more convincing or seamless than his own, announce themselves in a daydream. This is not the brand of outlaw masculinity modelled by Shane or Rango.

The viewer of *Road to Saddle River* is disciplined to decode its narrative in the light of other films, just as Cowboy Kid is disciplined by the Hollywood western to measure his own performance of masculinity continually against Rango's. This comparative viewing constitutes parody's ironic 'transcontextualization'. As Linda Hutcheon explains it, 'a critical distance is implied between the background text being parodied and the new incorporating work, a distance usually signaled by irony' (Hutcheon 1985, 32). We have already witnessed this critical distance in the ironic dialogue Damberger creates between his representation of Natives and Hollywood's screen caricatures of Aboriginality. The parody of *Road to Saddle River* asks us to decode the film's narrative in the context of a certain type of Hollywood western, a western that Damberger delineates generically through his overt references to *Shane* in the Rango footage viewed by Cowboy Kid. The *mise-en-scène* and dialogue of the scene between Rango and Lance echo the *mise-en-scène* and dialogue of the scene between Shane and Joey: in both films the hero rides off alone, disappearing west into the empty 'never-never land' of the frontier. *Shane* has been read as a classical formulation of the Hollywood western, and is taken by Damberger to be representative of the type of cinematic text his film parodies.[64] The impressionable naive boy who idolizes Shane, or in Damberger's scenario, Rango, is, in *Road to Saddle River*, inscribed as the male spectator of westerns, our narratorial agent Cowboy Kid. Though a grown man, his appellation is kid, and he, like Joey in *Shane*, wants to play Cowboy. The idealized simplicity of *Shane* that Thomas Schatz attributes to the perspective of Joey is referenced in *Road to Saddle River* through Cowboy Kid's perspective (Schatz 1981, 55). However, this naivety is tempered by the latter film's overriding ironic commentary that Kid is an underdeveloped adult whose sense of masculinity is mediated by a masturbatory fantasy fuelled by American comic books and films. Damberger's celluloid 'Cowboy' and 'Indian' who appear in the film's establishing shots circulate in the fantasy world of the male viewer of Hollywood westerns, in the alternative reality of Cowboy Kid. However, the power of these figures to invade lived experience is made very clear in the sequence of shots where the saddle from the land of celluloid dreams materializes in Kid's lived experience (Figures 4.25–4.26). Initially, the celluloid 'Cowboy' and 'Indian' are confined to a discreet visual field of prairie badland landscape where they continually attempt to best each other. However, when the 'Indian' steals the 'Cowboy's' saddle and throws it off a cliff in a daytime shot, it appears in the next scene falling from the night sky into the world of Cowboy Kid. The surreal nature of this sequence is communicated to the viewer through the cartoon-like sound effects that punctuate the theft and disposal of the saddle. In one crucial shot the celluloid 'Cowboy' rides along the Trans-Canada highway in the same frame as the yellow Honda, while in another the celluloid 'Indian' plays violin as the car speeds by in the background. Damberger's film delineates the collision of lived experience with an alternative cinematic reality that interrupts and structures understandings of the social terrain for impressionable viewers like Cowboy Kid. For Kid the celluloid 'Cowboy' stands in for the spirit helper Norman Many Heads told him would come to help him realize his identity as a Cowboy. It is the celluloid 'Cowboy' who appears to Kid when he is unconscious and tells him 'You wanna be a "Cowboy," you've got ride the bucking horse,' something Kid fails to do at the rodeo. By the film's closing sequence, however, the Hollywood spirit helpers – celluloid 'Cowboy' and 'Indian' – are displaced in favour of the wild horse and talking buffalo that appear to both Cowboy Kid and Norman Many Heads. This coda of shots attempts to negotiate the conflict and enmity between Europeans and First Nations signified in the figures of Hollywood 'Cowboy' and 'Indian' by intercutting shots of Kid and Norman working together to break in and saddle the wild horse with shots of the celluloid 'Cowboy' and 'Indian' locked in a death struggle. Norman's placement of the iconic saddle on the wild horse, and Kid's mounting and riding of the horse, bring together Hollywood cinema and lived experience in a manageable way; Kid, with the help of Norman, successfully rides the bucking horse that is the Hollywood western genre. In this Canadian indigenization of the genre, Kid's Cowboy and Norman's Indian are pictured travelling together with the buffalo and horse on the banks of a river, possibly the mythical Saddle River. This tableau shot dissolves into a long shot of open prairie at sunset, across which dances the celluloid 'Indian' playing the violin. In Damberger's parodic inversion of the western, the final image is not the lone 'Cowboy', sign of colonization, riding into the sunset on an empty plain devoid of the continent's indigenous peoples. The film's final image is given over to the 'Indian' dancing on an empty plain devoid of the colonizer. Granted, this ending is, perhaps, overly optimistic to the point where it could be argued that it masks the pain and suffering of colonial contact for First Nations. However, Damberger, who does represent internal colonialism as demeaning through the government programme that employs Natives to kill gophers, is using the western, for so long a genre celebrating white victory over a colonized Aboriginal population, to forge a more equitable cultural construction of First Nations relations to white Canada. Although undeniably romantic, and somewhat naive, the closing shots of the film echo old cow hand Louis's words to Cowboy Kid: 'It ain't what it is, it's what could be.'

The Grey Fox

Although he constructs a dialogue between *The Grey Fox* (1982) and *The Great Train Robbery* (Edwin S. Porter 1902), Philip Borsos's film is not as overtly or playfully parodic as Damberger's. The early history of the western genre is traced in the very first frames of *The Grey Fox* incorporating footage from an unknown silent western,[65] and again in Bill Miner's viewing of *The Great Train Robbery* in a Washington state cinema. In this way Borsos prefaces the main action of his film with a foregrounding of the act of viewing. His film's auto-referentiality draws spectators' attention to their own process of consuming images, something Tag Gallagher argues *The Great Train Robbery* does in the scene where the bandit fires at the audience in close-up, shooting outside the space of the movie's diegesis (Gallagher 1986, 204). Borsos's suturing of this footage from *The Great Train Robbery* into his own film creates parody's transcontexualizing moment where the audience is asked to decode *The Grey Fox* in the context of Porter's silent classic. By cutting from the train-robbing bandit of Porter's film to Bill Miner's face illuminated by the reflected light of this image from the cinema screen, Borsos signals to his audience his film's interest in the cinematic representation of the outlaw in the western. He locates the body of the hero, Bill Miner, in, after Neale, a series of other bodies, including the metacinematic body of Porter's bandit, to delineate an opposition between Law and Other, what lies outside of Law. In addition to the body of the celluloid outlaw, Borsos positions Miner's body in a field of criminals – the young ex-con who accosts Miner in the saloon, Shorty Dunn and the tubercular Louis – and townspeople – Kate Flynn, the newspaper editor and Sergeant Fernie, the film's sign of Canadian law. However, it is Miner's moment of identification with Porter's celluloid outlaw figure that inspires him to rob a train, an event that structures the proceeding action of the film. Borsos unveils cinema as a technology of gender, in a chain of signification that links the beam of light projected through the celluloid image of a train robbery to the light of a train, implicating the film in the social construction of Bill Miner. A cut is made from the light of the projector beam illuminating the frames of *The Great Train Robbery* to the light of an oncoming steam-driven car illuminating Miner. This shot subsequently gives way to a shot of Miner at railway tracks watching the light of an oncoming train that illuminates his face. Of course Bill Miner's is already an outlaw masculinity when he is released from San Quentin, in the words of the film's intertitle, 'into the twentieth century'; however, in this sequence of shots we can see how the cinematic apparatus informs his self-representation as an outlaw in the new century, his movement from stagecoach heists to train robberies.

As much as it is marked by his exposure to *The Great Train Robbery*, Miner's outlaw masculinity is also a departure from that Hollywood construction of the

violent, killer bandit, a difference in repetition from the Hollywood western that
Borsos effects through the representation of Miner as the 'Gentleman Bandit' in
Canadian territory. Borsos's protagonist oscillates between the oppositions of
Outlaw and urbane gentleman, between Bill Miner, criminal, and George
Edwards, Miner's alias, prospector. It is as George Edwards, opera lover, that he
romances Kate Flynn, the local photographer and turn-of-the-century feminist.
Flynn is, in the social context of her times, an outlaw, a gender outlaw who flouts
social law. She is a type of female westerner. Revelling in her unmarried status,
Flynn leaves the East to become a female adventurer in the West. In Kamloops
she owns and operates her own photography business and attempts, unsuccess-
fully, to publish letters to the editor in the local newspaper advocating equal pay
for equal work. Her passion, she tells Miner/Edwards, is to record social
injustices with her camera. As Blaine Allan observes, Miner's relationship with
Flynn transforms her into 'an adorer', his adventure outside the Law becomes
hers when she discovers his true identity and, as the intertitles at the end of the
film indicate, gives up her life in the West to travel with him to Chicago and then
Europe.[66]

Borsos indigenizes the Hollywood western, by transporting the narrative of
the outlaw westerner from the American West to the Canadian North-west, a

Plate 13 The Grey Fox (1982). Philip Borsos on the set of *The Grey Fox* with Richard
Farnsworth in costume as Bill Miner. © Mercury Pictures, 2001

space that is, unlike the western US of Hollywood myth, characterized by civility and the order of law. Based on the true story of Bill Miner, an American citizen who fled authorities in the US to perpetrate Canada's first train robbery, Borsos's film, as Blaine Allan argues, is at pains to emphasize Miner's migration to Canada, marking the crossing of the border into Canadian territory three times to signify Canada as a space where difference is significant (Allan 1993, 73).[67] Miner, the American outlaw is, simultaneously, a figure of Canadian history, the nation's first train robber, something the provincial government of British Columbia commemorates with a plaque on the Trans-Canada highway near Kamloops. In the historical discourse of the province, in Frank W. Anderson's published history and in Borsos's film, Miner becomes indigenized, part of a Canadian myth of West. Part of this indigenizing process in the film involves delineating the difference in the social orders on either side of the forty-ninth parallel. As Allan notes, Borsos represents the US as a site of violence and lawlessness. Miner's barroom fight with the young ex-con in Washington, where the 'Gentleman Bandit' breaks a whisky bottle across the younger man's face and threatens him with a gun, and the failed train robbery that sees gunfire and a casualty are set in the US. Canada, on the other hand, is constructed as 'the peaceable kingdom' where despite his horse rustling, and Canadian train robbery, Miner is loved by all, including the local North West Mounted Police officer who continues to show him respect, even after his identity becomes known and he is arrested. After his trial and sentencing, the good people of Kamloops celebrate Miner as a hero, waving Union Jacks as a brass band plays him on to the train that will take him to prison in what amounts to a strangely pseudo-nationalist ceremony.

The indigenizing of Miner and the western genre undertaken by Borsos is not limited to his script, production and editing, but also takes shape in the film's casting and its resistance to the tax-shelter film formula of the late 1970s which saw pseudo-Hollywood product displace truly Canadian films.[68] The casting of Richard Farnsworth, a Hollywood veteran of westerns, as Bill Miner, might make it appear that Borsos was following the tax-shelter formula of, as Allan puts it, casting a 'second-rung US star in a Hollywood genre picture'. Allan argues, however, that by making border-jumping its subject matter *The Grey Fox* articulates its difference to pseudo-Hollywood productions of the tax-shelter era to tell what I would argue is a very Canadian story of negotiating American difference (Allan 1993, 74). Borsos's process of indigenization suggests yet another antimony to supplement the series of antimonies marking the western as a genre that Neale sees focusing on the bodies of the male western hero to 'articulate the space of the functioning of what is defined in the genre as the Law, and the space which is defined as outside it, as Other': American/Canadian (1980, 58). For it is American law, as represented in the body of Detective Seavey, the Pinkerton agent, that follows Miner across the border and regards Canadian law as Other, subordinate. Whereas Miner, an outlaw, is constructed as a sympathetic character embraced by Canadians as some kind of hero, the Pinkerton agent is clearly

Other, an arrogant, supercilious man whose interference in Canadian law enforcement earns him the disrespect and animosity of Sergeant Ferney. Ferney denies any knowledge of Miner to Seavey, and co-operates with this representative of American law in Canadian territory only grudgingly when he learns that his commanding officer in the North West Mounted Police has ordered that the American's wishes should supersede his own where the search for Miner is concerned. The villain of *The Grey Fox* is the film's sign of US expansionism, Detective Seavey. Far from celebrating the conventional Hollywood western's ideology of Manifest Destiny, Borsos's film uses Seavey to hold it up to ridicule, thus creating an order of subjectivity which resists the kind of US expansionist ideology promulgated by Jimmy Stewart's sheriff character in *The Far Country*.

RE-PRESENTING THE FLQ CRISIS

Representations of nationalist irruptions within Confederation constitute what might be considered a sub-genre of Canadian cinema, the film of contested nation. Films gathered under this category might include *Secret Nation* (Michael Jones 1992), a speculative fiction suggesting that a conspiracy to rig the 1948 referendum on Newfoundland's entry into Confederation circumvented the will of Newfoundlanders to remain outside of Canada.[69] Another possible title for inclusion in this tentative sub-genre might be *Kanehsatake: 270 Years of Resistance* (Alanis Obomsawin 1993) which narrativizes the Mohawk Nation's struggle for recognition of its sovereignty by Québec and Canada, something taken up in the next chapter on First Nations cinema. Films negotiating the most violent and tragic materialization of Québec nationalism – the FLQ crisis of 1970 – would, undoubtedly, compose an important component of the film of contested nation. All films of the contested nation sub-genre constitute what Bhabha calls the nation's 'counter-narratives', narratives that 'continually invoke and erase its totalizing boundaries' (Bhabha 1990, 300). Robin Spry's *Action: The October Crisis of 1970* (1973), Michel Brault's *Les ordres* (1974), Pierre Falardeau's *Octobre* (1994) and Robert Lepage's *Nô* (1998) all take the FLQ kidnappings of James Cross, the British Trade Commissioner, and Pierre Laporte, a provincial Liberal Cabinet minister, and the subsequent imposition of the War Measures Act (a declaration of martial law) by the Trudeau Liberals as points of departure to relate Québec's struggle for independence from Canada. These variant representations of the FLQ as agents of terror, misguided nationalist heroes forced into action by political, economic and social oppression, or bumbling performers in a political farce play on the history of Québec's colonial legacy. This history has produced an understanding of the people, *les Québécois*, as an oppressed community exploited by the English majority with the complicity of a French comprador class. These were the conditions of possibility that gave currency to the nationalist rhetoric of the *Parti Québécois*, and the armed revolution fomented by the *Front de libération du Québec* in the late 1960s. The generic codes of the films under discussion track how we as a nation (Canada) or as nations (Canada and Québec) have struggled to incorporate nationalist dissonance into a narrative of the nation(s) as: documentary fact (Spry), tragedy (Brault and Falardeau) and comic farce (Lepage). No matter how the films in question are inflected generically, they all draw on the pastness of the nation(s), on Québec's historical relationship to Canada, a conflicted and double-speaking structure delineating both Québec's position in a federation of provinces and its desire for independent nation status. Wallerstein's theory of pastness as 'a central element in the socialization of individuals in the maintenance of group solidarity, in the establishment of or challenge to social legitimation' is at work in Spry, Brault, Falardeau and Lepage (1991, 78). All four directors hail or recruit us, variously, as members of imagined Canadas and Québecs, drawing on the historical coordinates of these communities to maintain or contest our identifications as Canadian, as Québécois. Three of these films – *Action: The October Crisis of 1970*, *Les ordres* and *Octobre* – engage, to varying degrees, the visual historiography that is the documentary form (Nichols 1991, 177). Spry's *Action: The October Crisis of 1970* is an expository documentary, whilst Brault's *Les ordres* is a pseudo-reflexive documentary employing actors to recreate the experiences of fifty Québécois interned without charge under the War Measures Act.[70] Falardeau's *Octobre* incorporates elements of documentary film-making and the memoirs of one of the FLQ kidnappers of Laporte, Francis Simard, to recreate the events from the perspective of Laporte's abductors.

Action: The October Crisis of 1970

As Philip Rosen suggests, 'the concept of documentary as a mode of understanding the nature, potential, and functions of cinema and indexical representations, is in intimate ways intricated with the concept of *historical* meaning' (Rosen 1993, 65). Robert Spry is very much in the business of producing historical meaning: his 1973 film aspires, in Michael Renov's words, to replicate the 'historical real' of Montreal in October 1970 (Renov 1993b, 25). Spry reveals his perspective and the historical meaning he sought to produce in an interview with Alan Rosenthal: 'It looked as if I was now living in a police state and I knew whatever was going on had to be filmed' (Spry 1980, 248). Narrated from his personal perspective as an Anglophone sympathetic to the aspirations of Québec (252), Spry used his own voice on the film's voice-over track to give his film 'a certain fallible personal element' (253). I would argue, however, that *Action* still subscribes to what Nichols writes is a fundamental expectation of documentary, 'that its sounds and images bear an indexical relationship to the historical world' (1991, 27). These sounds and images are of course mediated, not only by Spry's selection, and editing of stock NFB footage, television news footage and the footage of three NFB camera crews assigned to record the crisis but by cameramen, NFB and television editors. Spry is very conscious of how, as Michael Renov writes of documentary practice, 'always issues of selection intrude . . . the results are indeed *mediated*, the results of multiple interventions that necessarily *come between* the cinematic sign (what we see on the screen) and its referent (what existed in the world)' (Renov 1993b, 26). This sensitivity to the exigencies of mediation produced one of the best-known sequences from *Action*, the exchange between Trudeau and a journalist where the Prime Minister, asked how far he will go with the use of repressive state apparatuses to protect the public from the FLQ, responds, 'Well, just watch me.'[71] This interview on the steps of Parliament had aired in a truncated version on the CBC evening news, distorting what had been a measured, ten-minute dialogue between the Prime Minister and the media about the pros and cons of suspending civil liberties into a soundbite where Trudeau is reduced to, in Spry's words, 'a blind raving fascist' (Spry 1980, 254). Spry included the unedited interview in his film 'so the people of Canada could see what had been done to Trudeau' through the editing process of television (254). *Action* provides at least one other, inadvertent, object lesson on the production of pastness through editing. In creating a historical context for the resonance of separatism for the people of Québec, Spry incorporates footage of Charles de Gaulle's infamous Montreal speech of 1967 in which the general shouts, '*Vive le Québec libre!*' (Evans 1991, 189–90). Unbeknownst to Spry, this footage from Jean-Claude Labrecque's film on de Gaulle deviates from the pro-filmic event it stands in for; the resounding cheer of the Québécois that this exhortation produces in Labrecque's film, and now in Spry's documentary, was, as Gary Evans's research reveals, a fabrication added to the soundtrack of Labrecque's film in post-production (1991, 190). This knowledge, as Evans points out, reminds us that 'in film as well as in print, it is the arrangement of facts that becomes history, not the facts themselves' (1991, 190).

Work on *Action* was initiated by Spry almost accidentally when he began assembling historical facts to create a five-minute introduction that would contextualize the October Crisis for his film *Reaction: Portrait of a Society in Crisis* (1973), a series of interviews with English-speaking Quebeckers about their reactions to the kidnappings, martial law, the mobilization of the army and the execution of Laporte (Spry 1980, 249). That introduction became *Action*. *Action*'s introduction arranges historical facts around the problematic of contested nation. From establishing aerial colour shots of Montreal in 1970, Spry cuts to a black-and-white long shot of the Heights of Abraham in Québec City where, Spry's voice-over informs us, the French were defeated by the English over two hundred years before the present narration of nation he is undertaking. Spry's narration of the Canadian nation marks its birth as an event dependent on the conquest of the French:

> It is over two hundred years since the English defeated the French here on the heights of Abraham in Québec City. It is over one hundred years since Canada became a nation, a nation which encompasses Québec. But Québec's French-speaking population has persistently survived as a living Francophone culture never forgetting that one day Québec

might become a separate French-speaking state free of outside domination.

The voice-over is punctuated by an additional audio track of battle noises and gunshots made audible at Spry's reference to the conquest. However, these aural signs belying the violence of empire or nation-building continue to be heard past the utterance of English victory over the French haunting Spry's reference to Confederation and Canada's encompassing of Québec. Through his manipulation of soundtrack and the establishing shots of *Action*, Spry troubles the dominant myth of Confederation as birthing a Canada of peace, order and good government. Spry's opening sequence suggests that the gunshots and battle cries of the Conquest never really faded away, but resonated well into the twentieth century where they are taken up by contemporaneous social actors in Québec City, Montreal and Ottawa. The history composing the film's introduction moves from the Conquest to chart periods of unrest in Québec from the 1940s and 1950s such as the Asbestos Strike (1949) and the Murdochville Strike (1957). Footage of these conflicts between labour and capital emphasize the socio-economic roots of a Québec nationalism reacting against a comprador class that, under Duplessis, we are told by Spry's voice-over, kept Québec 'rural, subjugated and poor'. By way of contextualizing the violence of October 1970, Spry provides footage of and commentary on such critical events as: the 1963–4 terrorist bombings, separatist resentment of and protests against Queen Elizabeth's 1964 visit to the province that culminated in the bloody confrontation between police and separatists that came to be known as *Samedi de la matraque* (the Saturday of the truncheon), the 1967 visit of Charles de Gaulle and his public support of an independent Québec, and the separatist attack on Trudeau and other dignitaries at the 1968 St Jean Baptiste Day parade. Spry also documents what was perceived by many in Québec as the failure of the democratic process in the province, namely the provincial election of 1970 which saw only 6 per cent of the seats in the legislature go to René Levesque and the Parti Québécois who had received 24 per cent of the popular vote.

Having set the stage for the kidnappings of Cross and Laporte, Spry assembles a montage of television and NFB coverage of the kidnappings, government reaction to the kidnappings, Laporte's execution and funeral, the imposition of the War Measures Act and the public debate about whether or not this suspension of civil liberties was warranted. Spry's documentary is structured by the opposing ideologies of two documents, the FLQ Manifesto and the War Measures Act. The FLQ Manifesto is a Marxist declaration of war on what the FLQ perceives as the capitalist and anglocentric system of governance that oppresses and exploits the people of Québec, while the Canadian government's response, the War Measures Act, is a document that gives repressive state apparatuses the powers to silence the dissenting voices of the FLQ and contain the violence that would give birth to a separate nation. The reading of the Manifesto on television was one of the few demands of the kidnappers met by the government and is included in its entirety in Spry's film. The Manifesto indicts the comprador class, what the document represents as 'the clique of voracious sharks' and 'big bosses' – political leaders that collude with Anglo corporate interests such as 'Steinberg, Clark, Bronfman, Smith . . .' – for its translation of the province into 'their hunting preserve for "cheap" labour and unscrupulous exploitation'. In the FLQ's words these oppressors are to be 'purged' from the nation of Québec.[72] Remarking on the sympathy with which the people of Québec received this document, Spry's voice-over argues that the Manifesto is a 'key' to the crisis.

The other 'key' to the Crisis is the War Measures Act, which unlike the FLQ Manifesto is not read aloud in the film but is the textual presence behind the shots of Québécois roused from their beds by the Canadian army in pre-dawn raids. The sweeping powers granted to the military facilitated the incarceration of some 450 citizens of Québec. Article 3 of the 'Regulations to Provide Emergency Powers for the Preservation of Public Order in Canada' declares the FLQ an 'unlawful association', thus rendering all of its members criminals. Article 5 of the legislation goes one step further, declaring that 'a person who, knowing or having reasonable cause to believe that another person is guilty of an offence under these regulations, gives that person any assistance with intent thereby to prevent, hinder or intefere with the apprehension, trial or punishment of that person for that offence is guilty of an indictable offence and liable to imprisonment for a term not exceeding five years' (quoted in Saywell 1971, 87–8). The very broad and subjective interpretation of the legislation by the military and provincial police read guilt by association, with the result, as we shall see in *Les ordres* and *Nô*, that many innocent people with separatist sympathies were wrongfully imprisoned. The shots in *Action* of Québécois being rounded up and forced into police vehicles troubles the War Measures Act's definition of police and military personnel as 'peace officers' and invites questions about who terrorized the people of Montreal in October 1970, the FLQ or the Canadian nation's security forces. These are questions that Michel Brault engages in *Les ordres*, a compilation of narratives told from the perspective of those who had their freedoms wrenched away from them.

Within and without Québec there was a vigorous interrogation of whether or not the Trudeau government was justified in enacting the War Measures Act. Spry includes footage of Tommy Douglas, the national leader of the NDP, criticizing the government's high-handed appropriation of such powers without going through Parliament, the first government in Canadian history to do so in peacetime. Following a montage of shots including Douglas's comments and of police and armed soldiers conducting searches without warrants and making arrests, Spry cuts to Trudeau's defence of the War Measures Act. In a nationwide television broadcast the Prime Minister argues that the sweeping powers of the legislation, including the suspension of Canada's Bill of Rights, are necessary 'to root out the cancer of an armed revolutionary movement that is bent on destroying the very basis of our freedoms'. Trudeau also notes that the government's action was invited by the city of Montreal and the province of Québec. These

Plate 14 Action: The October Crisis of 1970 (1973). © National Film Board of Canada, 2001. All rights reserved

invitations by Mayor Drapeau and Premier Bourassa were points of contention for critics in Québec. Claude Ryan, writing in the Québec daily *Le Devoir*, sug-gested that Bourassa's request subordinated his own government to federalist forces (quoted in Saywell 1971, 96). Similarly, René Levesque declared that the imposition of the War Measures Act at Bourassa's request meant 'Québec no longer has a government', that the Bourassa government was now 'no more than a puppet government in the hands of the federal leaders' (quoted in Saywell 1971, 96).

The anxieties felt by the Canadian state over representations of its handling of the FLQ crisis, and the ramifications these representations might have for the efficacy of federalism in Québec, are palpable in the institutional resistance Spry encountered in trying to make *Action*. Initially the National Film Board's English Language Programme Committee's response to Spry's request to shoot what was happening in the streets of Montreal was 'No, it's impossible' (quoted in Spry 1980, 248). However, when the French Unit gave a crew permission to shoot unfolding events for archival purposes, the Board's upper management, in the person of Sydney Newman, gave Spry the green light to shoot the interview footage that would become *Reaction* (248). None the less, the NFB sequestered the raw footage shot by its units for two years (248). Even after the completion of *Action* the film had to be vetted by the Secretary of State for clearance, and its ending altered before the NFB would release it (250). Spry's final voice-over narration – 'The question remains; will Québec separate?' – was edited out of the finished product.[73] Unlike most expository documentaries, Spry's first cut of the film does not pose a problem, Québec separatism, that will be 'solved' by the film narrative but leaves the fate of Canadian nation and Québec nationalism open-ended for the viewer. The potential resonance of an independent Québec created in the viewer's psyche by Spry's question is refused by an ISA of the federal government – the NFB – invested in Canadian national unity, invested in structuring spectators as unified Canadian subjects. The NFB's intervention is, however, a moot one; it cannot abrogate the preceding frames of film which signify Québec's resistant otherness to Canadian nation.[74]

Les ordres

Michel Brault's *Les ordres* (1974) documents the October Crisis from the perspective of those victimized by the War Measures Act, the innocent individuals who were arrested, incarcerated for up to ninety days and then released. Not dissimilarly to its initial opposition to Spry's documentary, the NFB rejected Brault's proposal for *Les ordres* in 1970. By 1973, however, Brault had secured a deal with Prisma Productions to produce his film independently. The day before shooting began on *Les ordres*, Spry reports that Brault watched an 'almost final-cutting copy of *Action* to remind himself of what had happened at that time and how it had felt' (Spry 1980, 249). The fact that *Action* served as a point of reference for Brault in his direction of *Les ordres* is significant given the hybrid-ized blending of documentary and fiction he creates with his own film. In interview Brault reveals how *Les ordres* was constructed from documentary materials: 'You could almost say that for *Les Ordres* I put on a documentarist's hat. I began with documents, with the words of others, I had people tell me what they had gone through, and I tried to recreate the impression they gave me of moments they had experienced' (Brault 1980, 43). Brault qualifies his remarks by stating

Plate 15 Action: The October Crisis of 1970 (1973). © National Film Board of Canada, 2001. All rights reserved

that, despite this process, his film is not a documentary, nor is it a 'fictional documentary'. 'Documentary is documentary, fiction is fiction,' argues Brault, 'you can't mix the two' (Brault 1980, 43). Many critics, however, have read the film as a hybrid of the documentary and fiction feature. René Rozon, reviewing *Les ordres* in 1974, refers to it as a 'fictionalized documentary' (Rozon 1974, 34). Brault engages in self-conscious play with the conventions of documentary film-making. He frames his film with text in the establishing and closing shots indicating that *Les ordres* is based on interviews with fifty of the 450 victims of the War Measures Act, signalling the documentary foundations of his film narrative to the viewer. The interview, documentary film's sign of oral history and truth claim, is deployed by Brault to foreground his film's re-creation of past events. The dialogue and action of *Les ordres* is interrupted by cuts to interviews Brault conducts with his actors about the characters they are playing. These interviews serve as self-reflexive markers of representation, drawing our attention to those interviews conducted by Brault in pre-production with the real victims of the War Measures Act these actors stand in for. In this way it may be useful to think of Brault's film as a form of the reflexive mode of documentary film-making Nichols describes where 'Actors help avoid difficulties that might arise with non-actors since their profession revolves around willingly adopting a persona and being available as a signifier in someone else's discourse' (1991, 59). The use of actors may also be an ethical move that protects the privacy of Brault's interview subjects.[75]

Les ordres follows the violence the War Measures Act does to the lives of five characters: Clermont Boudreau, a taxi driver, textile worker and trade unionist; his wife Marie; Jeane-Marie Beauchemin, a doctor; Richard Lavoie, an unemployed father; and Claudette Dusseault, a social worker, giving the impression of a point-of-view documentary. Brault's career as a director has focused on documenting the past of Québec, producing a visual historiography that in turn produces a people who have been structured by the oppressive dynamics of colonialism. Like his province whose motto is 'Je me souviens' (I will remember), Brault refuses to participate in the collective amnesia he believes Pierre Trudeau desired to cloak the War Measures Act in: 'Afterward Trudeau said we have to forget it and move on. That is the exact opposite of what we had to do. We had to understand what had happened or else we could never become anything. I wanted to give a voice to the people who had suffered the horror of this' (quoted in Conlogue 1999, R3). Giving voice to the historical oppression of Québec nation is what Brault has continued to do; his 1997 release *When I Am Gone*, a film inspired by the defeat of the separatist cause in the 1980 referendum, represents the failure of the 1838 Patriote Rebellion, the subsequent excommunication of the rebels by the Roman Catholic church and their execution by British authorities.[76] In many ways the more recent film about the nineteenth-century past revisits the work of *Les ordres*; in both films a French comprador class colludes with English governance to silence the dissonant voices of the oppressed.

As Rozon observes, aside from the text at the beginning and end of the film, there is a striking absence of tangible signs of the Crisis at the macrocosmic level in *Les ordres* – newsreel footage of Trudeau, direct references to the FLQ abductions of Cross and Laporte. Brault's film shows the ramifications of Trudeau's response to the FLQ on the microcosmic or domestic sphere of Québec. Although Trudeau is not present corporeally in the film, his Orders in Council are what drive the action of the narrative and his words comprise the very first shot of the film, preceding the title graphic *Les ordres*. Brault, however, does not select the Trudeau government's Orders in Council for the first shot of his film, but a quotation from Trudeau that allows the director to indict the Prime Minister and the Canadian nation with the Liberal leader's own words: 'When a given form of authority commits an injustice on a man, all other men are guilty, because they through their silence and their consent allowed the authority to commit that abuse.'[77] So, in quick succession we have the words of Trudeau, a long shot exterior of the tenement where Boudreau and his family live, followed by interior shots of the family at breakfast, the interview segments referenced previously, more shots of the interior followed by a cut to an exterior long shot of the tenement with text superimposed over the building describing how the War Measures Act imprisoned 450 Québécois. These shots establish the spectral figure of Trudeau, as a hypocrite whose brand of federalism, seen through the lens of Brault, does violence to the Québécois family and undercuts the democratic principles he espoused in 1958. For it is this very same tenement home that will be forcibly entered by the state, two of its occupants pulled away from their children and jailed on the Prime Minister's orders.

Through identification with the film's five principals, the spectator of *Les ordres* is disciplined to understand the police action of the War Measures Act as state terrorism, a form of class warfare. The class politics of the film resonate with the FLQ Manifesto's representation of Québécois as a cheap labour pool exploited by corporate interests. Three of the five individuals in the film who feel the full weight of Canada's repressive state apparatuses are engaged in activities to shift the status quo between capital and labour in Québec. Boudreau is a member of the cheap labour pool, someone who is suspended from his job because of his involvement with trade unionism. The social worker is depicted intervening in the eviction of a family and sees herself as someone who fights against injustice. Dr Beauchemin is a committed socialist who started a clinic for the underwaged. For Brault, the War Measures Act is nothing short of a declaration of war on the people of Québec. When Marie is arrested, her neighbour asks the police, 'Is it a crime to feed your kids and clean your house?' The film's narrative is organized around the process of criminalizing the five characters as enemies of the state. We watch Boudreau, Marie, Beauchemin and Richard going through the humiliation of being processed for incarceration in an underground parking arcade overflowing with detainees and later see them in despair behind prison walls. At one point a police officer informs Richard that he is just following orders, orders behind which, as Michel Brûlé argues, hide the 'characters' of the Prime Minister and the Minister of Justice (quoted in Pallister 1995, 323). Part of what makes this film so affecting is that, as Rozon has observed, 'the people we watch on the screen are being manipulated abusively by those very forces which are supposedly protecting them' (1974, 34).

Octobre

Pierre Falardeau's *Octobre* (1994) reconstructs the October Crisis from the point of view of the Chénier FLQ cell that kidnapped and executed Pierre Laporte. That Falardeau would depict this pivotal and tragic moment in Québec history from the point of view of the Chénier Cell was unacceptable to many in Québec and Canada, who regarded the Cell's members as murderers. Not unlike Brault and Spry, Falardeau had to negotiate the anxieties and political bias of cultural funding bodies ideologically opposed to this particular re-presentation of the October Crisis, a process that delayed production of the film for ten years. SOGIC, Québec's cultural funding and certification agency, although it initially accepted Falardeau's proposal for the film, ultimately refused to contribute to the financing of *Octobre*. In a passionate, if vitriolic, statement included in the film's press kit, Falardeau explains that the 'shithead' Charles Denis's patronage appointment as President of SOGIC by Premier Robert Bourassa was what killed any hope of provincial money going into *Octobre*.[78] Denis after all was Bourassa's press secretary during the 1960s and a former director of public relations for the Montreal Stock Exchange, a member of the comprador class attacked in the FLQ Manifesto. Eventually the NFB and Telefilm Canada agreed to finance the production of the film. A national uproar occurred, however, when it became public knowledge that Telefilm Canada had contributed $1 million to the film's budget. Senator Philipe Gigantes told the *Globe and Mail* that Falardeau's film was a 'scandalous' attempt 'to justify the killing of Laporte'. Gigantes was also outraged to learn that the NFB had paid $9,000 to Francis Simard, one of the FLQ terrorists involved in the murder of Laporte, for the film rights to his memoir *Pour en finer avec octobre* (*The Last Word on October*) (quoted in Canadian Press 1993, C1).

One element of Falardeau's project that many of his critics might have found disturbing was the documentary style in which this film is shot; it facilitates a rewriting of history that imbues the Chénier Cell with a humanity denied its members in the press coverage of the time. Falardeau responds to accusations that his film rewrites history in the Foreword he writes for the film's press kit. He argues that history 'must be re-written' as a matter of 'survival', for history 'as it is written by the Power Corporation mercenaries is not only a crime against intelligence but a suicidal attitude for our people to take'. This citation of a history written by the elite, the comprador class, is most likely a veiled reference to the history of the Crisis written by Gérard Pelletier, a Trudeau cabinet minister who published his version of the events of October 1970 in English under the imprint of McClelland & Stewart in 1971.[79] Notwithstanding Falardeau's overblown rhetoric, former FLQ members such as Pierre Vallières and Francis Simard have published alternative histories of the October Crisis.[80] What is significant about Falardeau's statement is its conceptualization of cinema as a technology for *le survivance*, a visual historiography that makes nationalist interventions into the discursive fields of Canadian and Québec histories to facilitate the cultural survival of the Québécois. In the case of *Octobre*, cinema becomes a technology of extreme nationalism that rationalizes the FLQ execution of Laporte. The film's establishing shots show two of the kidnappers placing Laporte's body in the trunk of a car and driving off into the night. At this point the screen fades to black, and white text from Albert Camus fades into the shot: 'Necessary and unjustifiable'. This sequence of shots sets the tone for *Octobre*, suggesting that the Chénier Cell had no choice but to kill Laporte. And this, argues Falardeau, is what makes his film a tragedy as opposed to a drama. In an interview with Maurie Alioff, Falardeau defines drama as a genre in which the hero must choose between good and evil, and tragedy a genre in which 'there is no good and evil. No one wins, no one loses' (quoted in Alioff 1994, 12). Many would take issue with this analysis; clearly, no matter what the genre of representation, Laporte loses based on the choice of murder made by the *felquistes*. In *Octobre*, however, the audience is structured by Falardeau's camera to identify with the *felquistes*, not Laporte. This is not to say that Laporte is not represented with dignity and empathy, he is; but the audience views him through the subjective camera perspective, and therefore nationalist ideology of the FLQ as it is represented by Falardeau.

Falardeau's emphasis, in the press kit, on the rewriting of history to re-establish 'truth' is reflected in his exploitation of documentary techniques to imbue *Octobre* with that sense of sobriety Nichols associates with non-fiction systems such as science, economics and politics (Nichols 1991, 3). Arguing that the documentary has a kinship to these 'discourses of sobriety', Nichols writes that 'discourses of sobriety are sobering because they regard their relation to the real as direct, immediate, transparent . . . They are the vehicles of domination and conscience, power and knowledge, desire and will' (Nichols 1991, 4). Falardeau is at pains to forge a transparent and immediate relationship between his film narrative and the events of October 1970. Co-ordinates of the documentary real are encoded into the film narrative from the first moments of the film's sound-track reproducing the voices of *le Québec libre* in the demonstration chant of '*le Québec pour les Québécois*'. These voices of contested nation which introduce the film could be recreations, but are very probably extracts from the sound archives of CKAC 730 Société Radio-Canada acknowledged in the film's credits. The other radio voices heard during the film on broadcasts charting the escalation of the Crisis are, on the other hand, most likely reconstructions, as the credits acknowledge four actors as '*voix radio*'. Moreover, Falardeau incorporates excerpts from Spry's documentary *Action: The October Crisis of 1970* to create an aura of reality for his own interpretation of events. Similarly, intertitles in the film's establishing shots structure the viewer to receive a narrative of documentary veracity: 'This film tells a true story based on respect for facts and people.' In this sense Falardeau's film creates what Nichols has called 'blurred

Plate 16 Octobre (1994). Pierre Falardeau with an actor in costume as a *felquiste* on the set. © Lion's Gate Films

boundaries', the blending of fact and fiction that trouble the production of meaning in contemporary culture. Nichols's description of this blurring is instructive for viewers of Falardeau's film:

> When a single idea about the nature of reality, a common set of shared values and collective purpose, does not prevail, a considerable blurring of previously more sharply maintained boundaries is in the offing. These blurrings of what used to be effective distinctions may not be simply logical confusions but the arena within which major political, or ideological, contestation occurs.
>
> (Nichols 1994, x)

The contested ideological ground of this film is whether the Chénier *felquistes* are cold-blooded brutes who murdered a man or courageous victims of the Québec social hierarchy forced into an impossible position by the state. The co-ordinates of the documentary real are deployed by Falardeau to undergird his re-creation of what, in Nichols's words, 'is not available for representation in the here and now': visual representations of events from the perspective of the FLQ (Nichols 1994, 4). The infusion of *Octobre* with elements of sobriety contributes a power and knowledge to representations of the FLQ, serving to rationalize their actions as those of desperate amateurs pushed too far by socio-economic and political conditions. At one point in the film, Falardeau has Laporte, the film's and the

FLQ's sign for a corrupt Québec elite, ask his nineteen-year-old *felquiste* captor, 'Why do you do this? I mean the FLQ, the violence?' The response of the young militant to Laporte, and Falardeau's to critics of the FLQ's tactics, follows: 'Because. It's the only way to change things. Otherwise nothing ever happens. You never listen.' Another sequence in the film lays part of the responsibility for Laporte's death with federal and provincial governments who refused to negotiate to save one of their own, while the kidnappers are portrayed as reluctant murderers forced into their crime by the intransigence of a heartless government.[81] A scene between the two *felquistes* who will murder Laporte structures the viewer to perceive them as kind, sensitive men, one of whom is apparently incapable of shooting his pet dog after it is run over by a car, men who on their first attempt to kill Laporte flee the room in terror. None the less, these men and their comrades keep insisting, as does the film, that 'we gotta do it', 'we have no choice'; they do kill Laporte off camera.

These representations of the Chénier Cell are very much at odds with how they figure in Spry's film. *Action* incorporates an interview with René Levesque, the leader of the nationalist Parti Québécois, who, when asked to comment on the death of Laporte on behalf of the PQ and in conjunction with the trade unions, says: 'We find something completely intolerable in Mr. Laporte's barbaric execution by people who have no sense of humanity, who don't reflect Québec ... if they did really reflect anything valid about Québec, I'd get away from here so fast, I'd never come back.' Levesque, however, does in this interview place some blame for Laporte's death on the shoulders of the Bourassa and Trudeau governments' hard-line response to the terrorists, something Trudeau rejects in Terence McKenna's recent documentary *Black October* (2000). In an on-camera interview with McKenna, Trudeau defends his government's hard-line strategy of non-negotiation with the FLQ, its refusal to release what he refers to as the 'so-called political prisoners': 'If we have to release common criminals who are being charged with manslaughter and murder because some guy is kidnapped, there will be no end of it.' In Trudeau's view negotiating with the FLQ would be tantamount to recognizing them as a 'parallel government'. Ironically, McKenna's film uses excerpts from *Octobre* as co-ordinates of realism to recreate the kidnapping and execution of Laporte for the viewer.

The variant re-presentations of the FLQ Crisis found in *Action*, *Les ordres* and *Octobre* are the results of historical constructions. This is not to suggest, as Hayden White writes of conflicting historical representations, 'that certain events never occurred or that we have no reasons for believing in their occurrence'. However, these films do constitute historical inquiries, and, as White argues, a 'specifically *historical* inquiry is born less of the necessity to establish *that* certain events occurred than of the desire to determine what certain events might *mean* for a given group, society or culture's conception of its present tasks and future prospects' (White 1986, 487).

Nô

Although Robert Lepage's *Nô* (1998) is also a type of historical inquiry that attempts to track the meaning produced by the events of October 1970, his locations for interpreting those events – Montreal and Osaka, Japan, in 1970 and Montreal in 1980 – and his choice of genre, comic farce, set his film apart from the previous three works. The action of *Nô* cuts between the Canadian pavilion at the 1970 World's Fair in Osaka where Sophie, a young Québécois actress, is performing in a French farce by Georges Feydeau and a Montreal apartment where her boyfriend Michel watches the events of the October Crisis unfold on television, and engages in terrorist activities with three *felquiste* colleagues. When she discovers she is two months pregnant, Sophie calls Michel at 4 a.m. Montreal time to inform him. Unfortunately, the conversation turns rancorous, and is cut short by the arrival of Michel's terrorist friends seeking refuge from the War Measures Act. Their inopportune knocking prevents Sophie from telling Michel of her pregnancy. Interpreting the 4 a.m. knock at Michel's door as evidence of a mistress, Sophie drinks too much and becomes involved with Walter, a married Canadian cultural attaché. The bedroom farce Sophie performs in – *The Lady from Maxim's* – begins to spill over into lived experience when Walter's wife Patricia and Francis Xavier, a young actor with designs on Sophie, discover the couple in Sophie's hotel room. Emphasizing life's imitation of art, Lepage has a door in the hotel room open to reveal the set of the Feydeau play. The opening and closing of bedroom doors, confusing coincidences and ironic misunderstandings that signify a comic bedroom farce in *The Lady from Maxim's* and in the

Plate 17 Nô (1998). © In Extremis Images

interactions of Sophie, Walter, Patricia and Francis Xavier reverberate in Montreal in Lepage's representation of nationalist politics as theatre. One of Michel's colleagues inadvertently uses a clock Michel has set to Osaka time as a timing device for a bomb. Ignorant of how his Osaka clock has been deployed, Michel engages his colleagues in a heated critique of the language used in the communiqué they will deliver to the press claiming responsibility for the bombing. According to Michel, his *felquiste* associates who are fighting for the liberation of a Québécois people and culture from Anglophone domination use syntax and phrases that 'just aren't French'. After rewriting the communiqué, Michel realizes that his Osaka clock has been used as a timing device for the bomb and he and his comrades flee the apartment seconds before the clock detonates the bomb. At this point their militant actions, as a member of the surveillance team across the street observes, literally blow up in their faces. It is not just the forces of separatism that are reduced to incompetent bumblers by Lepage; he metes out similar treatment to the agents of federalist authority. The farce of Osaka is played out in Montreal not only by Michel and friends but also by the two police officers monitoring Michel's residence from an apartment bedroom across the road from his building. Arriving on the scene to show the apartment to prospective tenants, the landlady opens the bedroom door to reveal the two cops frantically striking normalized poses in the room, one on the bed, one standing. These men are attempting to hide their surveillance work; however, the woman and the prospective tenants read their startled response to the opened door as efforts to conceal some kind of sexual liaison. Sophie eventually returns to her bombed-out basement apartment from Japan only to be arrested under the War Measures Act. As the police handcuff her she miscarries her pregnancy. At this juncture Lepage cuts from a low-angled close-up shot of blood running down the inside of Sophie's legs to Sophie and Michel watching television coverage of the results of the May 1980 Referendum to make a rather heavy-handed point about the failure of Québécois separatists to carry the embryonic Québec nation to full term.

Structurally, *Nô* moves back and forth between sites for the staging of nation. The World's Fair in Osaka is an international forum for the staging of national cultures in national pavilions; Lepage shows us both the Candian pavilion in which Feydeau's play is staged, and the Québec pavilion where Sophie and Walter party and where a distraught Francis Xavier wanders aimlessly through a slide show representing clichéd visions of rural Québec. The streets of Montreal become a space where competing nationalisms, Québécois and Canadian, are staged by the FLQ and the Canadian military. In the film's final Montreal 1980 sequence Michel and Sophie are both audience for the televisual staging of contested nation on the English-language CBC and French-language Radio Canada, and social actors in what Lepage constructs as the perpetual farce of nationalist politics in Canada. Commenting on the victory of the No forces that voted against separation, Michel compares the relationship between Québec and Canada to that of a couple: 'That's static, sterile. No one can seriously believe this has settled things. It's like a couple trying desperately to find shared ground or a common project. But it's sterile, there's no common identity.' Developing this analogy one step further, Sophie asks Michel if he is thinking of their relationship, and indeed he is. 'OK,' he says, 'we share a certain intimacy, certain values . . . but we don't have a project for the future.' The common project he envisions turns out to be a child, something that, unbeknownst to Michel, was lost ten years previously. The film ends with Michel trying to arouse what he refers to as 'voter interest' in Sophie for conceiving. Coding his overtures for procreating in the language of prospective referendum results, Michel asks if they could hope for more than a 50.5 per cent simple majority for the Yes, pro-separatist or pro-pregnancy forces, to which Sophie says 'maybe'. The final shots see Michel, 'campaigning' for his platform; the couple embrace and turn off live television coverage of No supporters singing *O Canada*. Like the first cut of *Action* Spry offered to the NFB, Lepage's film asks the question 'Will Québec separate?'

The film's proleptic cutting from the failed birth of Québec nation in 1970 to the failure of separation in 1980, and its very title, *Nô*, could be read as a No to this question. Lepage, however, disallows any definitive response to the question of separation, suggesting that the conditions of possibility for Québec independence have shifted radically from 1970, and that separation is still a possibility. These conditions of possibility are made material in the film through a referendum presided over by the nationalist Parti Québécois and through the changed life situations of Sophie and Michel. Arguing for the shared project of a child, and concomitantly the collective project of a nation, an independent Québec, Michel tells Sophie: 'It's not the same now. Ten years ago we were busy changing the world. We had no jobs, we had no money. Things have changed. You've a career, so do I. We've money.' Ten years previously, both characters were social actors involved in the production of a very different Québec. The colonial dynamic of Québec in 1970 is represented by Lepage through the roles of two separatists, Sophie and Michel. While the inept Michel almost blows himself up to liberate a colonized Québec, Sophie acts in a French farce to represent Canada at the World's Fair and climbs into bed with an agent of the Canadian federalist state, the cultural attaché, Walter. Venting her frustration at the cultural politics of colonialism, a drunken and exhausted Sophie explodes at dinner with Walter and Patricia, members of Québec's comprador class:

> Why did we bring a French director to Montreal so we'd use a French accent in a lousy French play to represent Canada at the World's Fair? I'll tell you why. We're colonized . . . Colonized, fuck!
>
> Yes, fuck! I said fuck! Makes me want to swear, fucking Christ to goddamn fucking shitting hell! Even General de Gaulle said 'Long live free Québec.' Fuck!

Under the auspices of a PQ government in 1980 the field of cultural production has shifted to the point where Sophie, a co-opted sovereigntist in 1970, and

Michel, formerly a failed revolutionary and writer, are no longer enemies of the provincial state but part of its cultural elite.

Lepage's emplotment of the October Crisis as comic farce does not, aside from incorporating television news coverage of events in the streets of Montreal, make any overt references to a purchase on documentary truth claims in the manner of Brault's and Falardeau's representations of the October Crisis as tragedy. Lepage sets his fictional story of Michel and Sophie against the real historical events of October 1970. This comic representation of what is represented in the other films as tragedy demonstrates White's contention that 'Narrative accounts of real historical events . . . admit of as many equally plausible versions of their representation as there are plot structures available in a given culture for endowing stories, whether fictional or real with meaning' (White 1986, 489). Whether tragedy or comedy, all four films endow the stories of October 1970 with a white subjectivity, thereby producing a misleading and ethnically specific meaning: the contested nation of Québec is composed of a *pur laine* Québécois people, while Canadian nation is composed of an Anglo-Celtic people and a Québécois people. This bicultural divide of the so-called 'founding nations' has been one of the dominant representational markers of Canadian nation since Lord Durham reported in 1839 that in Lower Canada he found 'two nations warring in the bosom of a single state'. Biculturalism is a representational system that performs the cultural work of forgetting the colonization of Aboriginal cultures upon which the 'founding nations' of both Canada and Québec are predicated.

Just Watch Me: Trudeau and the '70s Generation

Pierre Elliott Trudeau's development of the recommendations made by the Royal Commission on Bilingualism and Biculturalism (1963–71) helped to promote an understanding of Canada as a nation structured by the cultural dualism of English and French. For separatists, Trudeau, a Québécois whose vision of Canada took Québec's permanent membership in a federation of provinces as foundational, was anathema. Not surprisingly then, Trudeau's visual image and words have been imported into the project of signifying nation(s) on film more than those of any other Canadian leader. In Québec and Anglo-Canadian cinemas Trudeau's visual image and words come to stand in most frequently for either the imagined bilingual and bicultural nation (Joyce Wieland) or the oppressive embodiment of the War Measures Act that thwarted Québec nation (Spry, Brault, Falardeau). However, the range of significations performed by the sign Trudeau on film is not limited to his vision of a unified federation organized around two cultures or the legislative measures taken to secure this vision. For writer/director John Greyson, Trudeau's decriminalization of homosexuality makes the former Prime Minister a cinematic sign for queer nation and an object of gay sexual desire in *Uncut* (1998). None the less, it is as a signifier of biculturalism and bilingualism, a site where the two Canadas collide or coalesce, that Trudeau is most frequently deployed by Canadian film-makers. One of the most compelling examples of this practice is Catherine Annau's documentary *Just Watch Me: Trudeau and the '70s Generation* (1999). Annau's film assembles interviews with eight people ranging from Anglophones to Francophones, federalists to separatists, all of whom grew up under Trudeau and his vision of a bicultural and bilingual nation. The interview subjects relate how Trudeau's bicultural vision structured their own understanding of themselves as Canadians. During some of the interview sequences images of Trudeau dissolve into and out of the interview subjects' faces, signifying the identification they made with Trudeau. The film's opening shots establish its project of reading Trudeau as part of the national iconography that signifies Canada. Annau cuts from the introductory low-angled letter-box long shot of the Peace Tower in Ottawa to low-angled interior shots of the corridors of Parliament before cutting to Trudeau's angled portrait image reflected in a security mirror. We then cut to a long shot of the portrait, followed by two different tour guides who offer interpretations of this image in French and English. This series of shots associates Trudeau with other iconographic signs for Canadian nation, the very architecture of the national capital designed to signify the nation to the people. Parliament and Trudeau are also both producers of the people of Canada through legislation and image. Annau's film shows the people, Canadians, refracted through the prism of Trudeau's image and policies. The sense of self and national identity of many of the interview subjects is attributed to media images of Trudeau and participation in some of the cultural and educational programmes initiated by his government between Québec and Anglophone Canada. Interview subjects describe him variously as a father figure, a fantasy figure, an icon, an idol and a figure with which some of them grew disenchanted. John Duffy, a 1970s participant in a federally sponsored educational exchange with Québec, tells the camera that he thinks of Trudeau as having 'made' himself and other Canadians:

> Becoming an adult in Canada involves a bit of an Oedipal drama *vis à vis* what you think Trudeau made you. I had a pretty Trudeauvian and politicized identity formation in the 1970s. I bought into all that stuff. Even though I wasn't a supporter of Trudeau's, I still bought into it implicitly. Subsequently, I defined myself, in part, against some of that.

By 'all that stuff' Duffy refers to bilingualism and biculturalism as a structuring principle of Canadian identity, something he and other interview subjects see now as a dream that failed. From the perspective of the 1990s, Duffy sees multiculturalism, another Trudeau policy that grew out of the Royal Commission on Biculturalism and Bilingualism, as more important to a sense of collective Canadian identity than the dualism of the two founding nations model. An alternative view is espoused in the film by Evan Adams, a Salish First Nations man who was inspired by Trudeau's success as a bicultural leader to believe it possible that a Native person could one day become Prime Minister of Canada. This reading of Trudeau's concept of biculturalism and bilingualism is of particular interest to an understanding of the place of First Nations in relation to Canadian nation and the representations of First Nations on film and, more specifically, in the film of contested nation. The inspiration Adams finds in his identification with Trudeau and Trudeau's vision of the nation is at odds with many First Nations people who objected vociferously to Trudeau's 1969 White Paper. The White Paper proposed legislation that would reconfigure Canada's relationship to First Nations by abrogating any special status afforded Native peoples through treaty, making First Nations like all other Canadians. Trudeau believed, notwithstanding his enshrinement of 'founding nations' status, that any special status for a special group was unacceptable in a truly democratic society.[82] Some Native leaders, however, read the White Paper as an instrument of assimilation. The National Indian Brotherhood rejected the proposed legislation as 'a policy designed to divest us of our aboriginal, residual, and statutory rights. If we accept this policy, and in the process lose our rights and our lands, we become willing partners in culture genocide' (quoted in Dickason 1997, 364). Responding to the overwhelming resistance to the White Paper, Trudeau withdrew it in 1971 (365).

Here we can see the limits of bicultural and bilingual fields of vision to represent the complexity, diversity and continued internal colonialism that mark Canadian national cinemas. The Trudeau government's emphasis on political and ethnic tensions between the two so-called 'founding nations' promotes a dualistic mythology displacing the plight of the colonized First Nations and contributes to an atmosphere where Pierre Falardeau, a separatist whose films advocate *Québec libre*, can be unsympathetic to the situation of the Mohawk at Oka. Commenting on the Mohawk blockade of the Mercier Bridge during an armed standoff with the Québec provincial police and the Canadian army to protect their treaty rights and prevent a golf course from expanding through an ancestral burial ground, Falardeau says, 'If the problems hadn't been solved by the army, the people would have solved it themselves. The rifles weren't far away' (quoted in Alioff 1994, 13). The next chapter considers the variant ways in which white representations of First Nations, and First Nations cinema itself, negotiate this kind of murderous and antiquated colonial thinking.

5

VISUALIZING FIRST NATIONS

> If the problems hadn't been solved by the army, the people
> would have solved it themselves. The rifles weren't far away'.
>
> Pierre Falardeau

The racist discourse of Québécois nationalist Pierre Falardeau (quoted in Alioff 1994, 13) which others the Indigene nationalist as a target for violence is created and maintained, in part, through the circulation of representations that stereotype First Nations as intellectually challenged, blood-thirsty or Noble Savages, the fossilized remains of a culture that belongs to the historical past. For Ward Churchill, these types of literary and cinematic images constitute 'fantasies of the master race', the ironic title of his study examining the roles played by literature and cinema in the colonization of American Indians.[1] In her introduction to Churchill's book, M. Annette Jaimes characterizes such representations as 'weapons of genocide' (quoted in Churchill 1992, 1); they provide misinformation deforming human subjects with highly developed social, cultural, economic, agricultural and linguistic systems into non-human, primitive obstacles to colonization or settlement. The classical Hollywood western emplots genocide as a jingoistic and triumphalist narrative of conquest that gives birth to the white US nation. Although the narrative works to elide it, the film of contested 'Indian' nation is palpable inside the classical Hollywood western. The violence of Native Americans in classical Hollywood films, while it may be coded as a sign of savage bloodlust by the film-maker, signals an irruption of resistance to aggressive acts of invasion or settlement to the spectator who reads the screen oppositionally. Sympathetic depictions of the imperial violence waged against Amerindian nations come much later through the agency of a white character and camera eye in films such as *Little Big Man* (Arthur Pen 1970) and *Dances With Wolves* (Kevin Costner 1990).

I suggested that the circulation of vicious dehumanizing stereotypes provides cultural constructions of Aboriginality that contribute to a racist discourse advocating violence against First Nations and their resistance to ongoing dispossession. However, the construction of Aboriginal difference as abject and subordinate to white North Americans of European descent is inscribed not just in popular culture forms such as cinema, but in law. In the Canadian context,

196

Indian policy constructed a paternalistic relationship between the state and its wards, the Natives, who, in the colonial cosmology of the white invader-settler, had to be protected not only from certain aspects of 'civilization' such as liquor but also from their own 'heathen' cultural practices through the project of assimilation.[2] The reserve system was, as John L. Tobias notes, designed to serve as a social laboratory where Natives would be indoctrinated with European religious, cultural, linguistic and agricultural practices (1983, 41). As we saw in our discussion of *Saving the Sagas*, the Gradual Civilization Act of 1857, the Indian Act of 1876 and the Indian Act of 1951 are conflicted pieces of legislation that sought to 'protect' First Nations by erasing their identity through assimilation into invader-settler society, by erasing their status and rights as nations. The Indian Act and various amendments to it have ensured Canadian state regulatory control over First Nations. As Mohawk scholar Taiaiake Alfred writes, in Canada 'band councils, tribal councils, and the Assembly of First Nations are all creatures of the federal government' (Alfred 1999, 70). The Indian Act also defined Aboriginal identity through the mechanism of Indian Status.[3] Alfred calls for a return to traditional understandings of belonging to Aboriginal communities, arguing that it is 'the collective right of Native communities to determine their own membership' and that 'no other nation (or state or organization) has the right to force an identity on another nation' (86). The identity politics of decolonization and contested nations within Canadian nation are located in the very struggle to grasp terminology that effectively signifies Aboriginal identity in Canada.

I have been using the terms Aboriginal, Native, Amerindian, Indigene and First Nations to refer to the Indigenous peoples of Canada. First Nations refers to the various Aboriginal peoples of Canada who constituted sovereign nations at the time of European contact. The recent preference for this term is due largely to its re-inscription on the Canadian consciousness of the autonomy sought by Aboriginal Canadians in their ongoing negotiations for self-determination.[4] As Alfred notes, however, such potentially empowering terms as Aboriginal or First Nation can work in the service of a colonial Canadian state apparatus that wishes to project a myth of postcolonial autonomy on to a people who continue to be granted the authority to govern through the vestiges of a colonial power structure: 'a band council under the Indian Act' (Alfred 1999, 83). For Alfred, 'the only value in the word play is for white people, who do not have to face the racism built into the structure of their supposedly enlightened country' (83). At the risk of courting accusations of what Alfred terms the 'intellectual dishonesty' that is one of the 'essential elements of colonialism', I will continue to use First Nations as a signifier designating Canada's First Peoples in contexts where the refusal to acknowledge the rights of Canada's Indigenes by Canadian colonial state apparatuses is clear.

The system of internal colonialism that denies First Nations people sovereignty has produced a racialized and colonized community whose subaltern status is measured materially in a recent report of the World Health Organization indicating that '750,000 native people suffer poor health conditions and indicators show they are at greater risk of tuberculosis, diabetes, suicide, violent death and alcohol-related illness and injury than the general population' ('Warning' 1999, A9). Not surprisingly, given the failure of the colonial system to 'protect' the welfare of First Nations, Native leaders are working towards greater recognition of indigenous nationhood, towards various forms of self-government. Alfred cautions, however, that Natives need to ensure that they adapt traditional systems of governance and do not move towards forms of government that closely resemble Western notions of the state (1999, 56). For Alfred 'indigenous nationhood is about reconstructing a power base for the assertion of control over Native land and life' (47).

The ideological work of representation, as we have seen it in state-sponsored films such as *Saving the Sagas* (Marius Barbeau 1928) and *Peoples of Canada* (Stanley Jackson 1947), is central to creating a discourse of the vanishing indigene of prehistory that is antithetical to Alfred's vision of 'indigenous nationhood'. Such films, to use Alfred's words, 'allow the colonial state to maintain its own legitimacy by preventing the fact of contemporary indigenous nationhood to intrude on its own mythology' (1999, 59). These types of representations celebrate 'paint and feathers and Indian dancing, because they reinforce the image of doomed nobility that justified the pretence of European sovereignty on Turtle Island' (59). Although white attitudes towards Natives have changed somewhat since the release of *Saving the Sagas* and *Peoples of Canada*, the stereotypes present in those early state-sponsored ethnographic documentaries and in Hollywood films of the last ninety years are re-inscribed across a range of contemporary Canadian feature films written and directed by whites. In certain cases these paint and feather stereotypes are re-inscribed in an ironic field, as we saw in *Road to Saddle River*, so that they may be deconstructed by white film-makers with a sensitivity to the work of colonization and assimilation performed through the technology of the cinematic apparatus. Not all of these experiments in the deconstruction of stereotypes are successful as, for the most part, these white directors still end up constructing spectacle Indigenes from white cultural materials. The first section of this chapter considers the gaze through which the white camera eye apprehends the Aboriginal Other in five feature films produced in the 1990s: *Black Robe* (Bruce Beresford 1991), *Windigo* (Robert Morin 1994), *Clearcut* (Richard Bugajski 1993), *Map of the Human Heart* (Vincent Ward 1992) and *Dance Me Outside* (Bruce McDonald 1995). Made by white directors sympathetic to the plight of First Nations, some of these films inadvertently re-inscribe, while others critically examine, the problematic of Rony's ethnographic cinema as 'an instrument of surveillance as well as entertainment, linked like the written ethnographies of cultural anthropology to a discourse of power, knowledge and pleasure' (1996, 10). In other words, some of these films attempt to undo the 'whiting out' of the Indigene – the projection of white concepts and anxieties about the primitive on to the Aboriginal Other – effected by the white camera eye, while others contribute to this whiting-out process. The second part of this chapter considers the process of decolonization as practised by Native film-makers Alanis Obomsawin, Duke Redbird and Shelley Niro. Not only do Redbird, Obomsawin and Niro render the white invader-settler gaze visible, they interrupt and invert that gaze to observe the indigene self and white subject and reconstruct both from a First Nations perspective.

WHITING-OUT THE INDIGENE

Black Robe

Much was expected of Australian director Bruce Beresford's sumptuously photo-graphed and extensively researched $14-million Australian–Canadian co-production *Black Robe* (1991), widely received by mainstream critics as Canada's more sophisticated and sensitive *Dances With Wolves*.[5] Shot during the Oka land claims standoff between the Canadian army and the Mohawk peoples of Kaneh-satake, the film represents the foundations of a conflict that exploded during the summer of its production: seventeenth-century colonial contact between the French and the Algonquin and Mohawk nations. The film narrative of a journey into the heart of Huronia unfolds from the perspective of a Jesuit missionary, Father Laforgue, who sees his Algonquin guides and their enemy, the Iroquois (Mohawks), as doomed, if noble savages, succumbing to their own violence and white disease. Whilst critics such as Jay Scott reviewed the film in the *Globe and Mail* as presenting 'Indians' with 'sensitivity, sympathy and some ethnographic accuracy', First Nations and Native American responses to *Black Robe* registered disappointment. Reviewing the film for the Native magazine *Windspeaker*, Métisse critic and writer Marilyn Dumont warns her readership:

> If you go to this movie hoping that Natives will be portrayed in a just light you will be disappointed. You may even despair, for this film reconstructs a Jesuit perspective of first contact in 17th century New France and although native viewers may find this view disturbing, it is nevertheless convincingly and artfully rendered.
>
> (Dumont 1991, 13)

As the film represents First Nations from the perspective of the racist, 'civilizing' mindset of the Jesuits, accordingly, as Dumont writes, Indians are depicted as 'brutal, treacherous and cold. The Indians in fact, become the manifestation of the devil himself as they fornicate openly and delight in the torture of their enemies.' Bonnie Paradise, executive director of the American Indian Registry for the Performing Arts, saw the film as representing 'savage hostility – not our culture' (quoted in Thomas 1991, H5). A member of the Shawnee nation com-mented that Beresford's film 'gets caught up in the evil. There's still no balance in the portrayal of indigenous people' (quoted in Thomas 1991, H5). The savage hostility and emphasis on evil observed by both of these Native American viewers can be located in the scenes of brutal torture and death that punctuate the film's interactions between the Algonquin and the Mohawk, specifically the sequence where a young Algonquin child's throat is slit by a Mohawk. In this same sequence Father Laforgue has a finger hacked off by a Mohawk, and the Algonquin males, along with Laforgue, are forced to run a gauntlet of Mohawks wielding clubs.

More polemical in his response to *Black Robe* is Native Studies scholar Ward Churchill, who critiques the film as a weapon of genocide by comparing it to Nazi propaganda films such as *Der wiege Jude* (*The Eternal Jew*, Fritz Hippler 1940) (1992b, 24). Arguing that *Black Robe* sanitizes and rationalizes the genocide that was brought to Canada's First Nations through European contact, Churchill quotes *New York Times* reviewer Caryn James's understanding of the film as creating a respect for the sincere motivations of the colonist by criticizing 'cultural imperialism without creating villains' (quoted in Churchill 1992b, 24). As Churchill suggests, *Black Robe* is a film that repackages genocide for the consumption of white audiences, rationalizing the past without constructing whites as villains, but as well-meaning, if somewhat misguided people who believed they had the Natives' best interests at heart. However, the film is, he argues, replete with Native villains such as the bloodthirsty Iroquois and the malicious Montagnais dwarf shaman who plague Laforgue (23). Pointing to well-established anthropological sources indicating the matriarchal nature of Iroquois society, Churchill dismisses as invention the film's representation of Iroquois murdering child prisoners (23). Churchill argues that as Clan Mothers played decision-making roles regarding the treatment of captives, invariably children were adopted and raised as Mohawks 'rather than gratuitously slaughtered' (23). While the film plays up the 'savagery' of Indigenous peoples from the perspective of Laforgue, it fails, as both Churchill and Dumont note, to reference the 'savage' history of Laforgue's church which had tortured thousands of so-called heretics over the previous two centuries (Dumont 1991, 13; Churchill 1992b, 22). Since it is the perceived lack of civilization that constructs Native difference from Europeans as savagery to legitimize dispossession and the work of assimilation initiated by the Jesuits under the guise of salvation, a truly postcolonial film would not elide European 'savagery', as Beresford does here, but suture it into the film narrative to demystify how racial and cultural differences are culturally constructed to facilitate the subjugation of the Aboriginal Other in New France.

The process of whiting-out the Indigene by constructing spectacle screen Aboriginals from the materials of white fantasy is tempered somewhat by the casting of Aboriginal actors in some of the roles. August Schellenberg (Swiss/ Mohawk) plays the lead role of Chomina, while Chomina's wife is played by one of Canada's best-known and most accomplished Aboriginal actors, Tantoo Cardinal (Métisse). The film's cultural biases, its projection of white fantasies of Aboriginality, did not go unnoticed by Cardinal, who reportedly expressed her desire on set to work on a film that would make visible the matriarchal elements of Native culture (Gilmor 1991, 39). Acknowledging that the film has some authenticity deficits when it comes to the languages spoken by Native characters (Oji-Cree is substituted for Huron and Mohawk), Billy Two Rivers, who appears in the film as Ougebmat and acted as a dialogue coach during production, claims *Black Robe* gets closer to the truth than Hollywood productions (quoted in Thomas 1991, H5). However, Two Rivers's condemnation of Hollywood 'as a propaganda machine which justifies the seizing of our land under the guise of patriotism' finds a troubling resonance in Churchill's concluding assessment of the cultural work performed by *Black Robe*. For Churchill, *Black Robe* fails to offer a constructive redefinition of the roles of colonizer and colonized; conversely, he suggests, it says to its audience: 'Nothing was really wrong with what has happened . . . Therefore nothing really needs altering in the outcomes of what has happened, nor in the continuing and constantly accelerating conduct of business as usual in this hemisphere' (1992b, 24).

Despite good intentions, the Aboriginal Other of *Black Robe* is still filtered through layers of whiteness, before its pallid image is projected on to the screen. Brian Moore's novel *Black Robe*, the source text for the film, was based on Jesuit representations of First Nations found in the *Jesuit Relations*, colonial reports documenting the Jesuits' good works of assimilation through Christian conversion and language instruction. Producers of popular culture, Bruce Beresford and Brian Moore legislate the signification of an 'authentic' Aboriginality in *Black Robe*, as this is substantiated by claims of exhaustive research made by the film's press kit. The commercial and critical success enjoyed by both Moore and Beresford provides them with access to international marketing and distribution networks that circulate their representations of Aboriginality in a privileged trajectory that displaces First Nations self-representations while exploiting the global appetite for white 'Indian' stereotypes created by Hollywood.[6] When the voices of contemporary Natives question the veracity of the produced of the cinematic apparatus, they are structured by Beresford as the naive responses of romantics: 'I don't know why the Indians don't like to see themselves portrayed in that way. I think it has to do with some kind of romantic, liberal notions of a sort of utopia. It wasn't really like that' (quoted in Thomas 1991, H5). In this way white fantasies of the Native Other stand in for what it was 'really like' at Contact, and a hegemonic history told from the perspective of the imperial victors is perpetuated. The Native experience of colonization is appropriated and deployed as a tool of cultural colonialism, another natural resource that is exploited for profit.[7] Notwithstanding its postcolonial pretensions in representing colonial contact, *Black Robe* is a form of colonial discourse that is dependent on the stereotypes of the 'Indian' Other. In his reconsideration of the stereotype and colonial discourse, Homi Bhabha writes, 'the objective of colonial discourse is to construe the colonised as a population of degenerate types on the basis of racial origin, in order to justify conquest and to establish systems of administration and instruction' (Bhabha 1983, 23). Adapting its representations of First Nations from a novel based on the colonial discourse of the *Jesuit Relations* –

narratives that articulate the very systems of administration and instruction and degenerate types to which Bhabha refers – *Black Robe* re-inscribes the white colonial gaze on Aboriginal subjectivity to produce a narrative that, in Church-ill's words, rationalizes and redeems 'a process of conquest and genocide which had already transpired' (1992b, 24). *Black Robe* emulates colonial discourse, as Bhabha understands it, in the film's production of 'the colonised as a fixed reality which is at once an "other" and yet entirely knowable and visible' (1983, 23). Aboriginality is fixed and made knowable through the stereotypes of Chomina, the wise, noble and strong Indian of few words, the murderous Iroquois and the compulsively fornicating Pocahontas figure of Chomina's daughter, Annuka. This collection of caricatures reveals more about what David Lloyd terms 'the Subject that *judges*', in this case the white camera eye that defines *Black Robe*'s field of vision from the perspective of Laforgue, than it does about Native sub-jects. For this field of vision is, by Lloyd's definition, a 'racist vision' that sees 'an underdeveloped human animal whose underdevelopment becomes the index of the judging subject's own superior state of development' (Lloyd 1991, 74). In its attempt to represent colonization's violence to First Nations, *Black Robe* ends with a text indicating that the Huron conversion to Christianity resulted in their complete destruction by the Iroquois. Thus, the film inadvertently draws on and contributes to the discursive structure of the vanishing race stereotype upon which the genocidal project of colonialism in North America is predicated.

Windigo

If *Black Robe* shows us the beginnings of the French colonial regime, Robert Morin's *Windigo* (1994) represents its legacy, Native nationalism in Québec. The film's establishing shots feature media coverage of an armed standoff between the fictional Aki tribe and the *Sûreté du Québec* (Québec's provincial police force). Images of bulldozers, masked warriors behind barricades and flack-jacketed SQ officers inevitably conjure up media images of the 1990 Oka Crisis, the armed standoff between Mohawks and the SQ, which undoubtedly inspired Morin's film. Described by its press kit as making a 'plea in favour of the affirm-ation of the rights of nations and individuals' and read by *Variety* critic Brendan Kelly as 'supportive . . . toward first-nation gripes', *Windigo* attempts, unsuccess-fully, to forge a sympathetic field of vision through which the Aki contesting of Canadian governance may be read (Kelly 1994, 62). After Aki leader Eddy Laroche declares the unilateral independence of Aki territory from Canada and Québec, a team of negotiators representing the federal and provincial govern-ments as well as Native leadership is accompanied up river by a television crew to Laroche's armed stronghold deep in the heart of Aki territory. Not unlike *Black Robe*, the action of *Windigo* is filtered through a white narrative agency, in this case television reporter Jean Fontaine and his cameraman who interview mem-bers of the delegation, the ship's crew and eventually Eddy Laroche and his 'warriors'. They also record the various clichéd signs of primitive Aboriginality director Morin deposits along the route into Aki country. The voyage up river into the Indigenous world that Morin chooses as the structuring device of his narrative provides the first indication that the film will re-inscribe ethnographic cinema's racialized constructions of First Nations as 'always already primitive' (Rony 1996, 12) peoples of 'a displaced temporal realm' (8). The voyage up river away from civilization is a trope that evokes comparisons of Fontaine and his cameraman to Barbeau and MacMillan, who also travel along the river of time in 1927 to capture images of the primitive in *Saving the Sagas*. The comparison Morin is hoping we will draw, however, is just as problematic. The film's press kit tells us that 'Morin confronts us with stultifying Euro-american mythologies of the horror of the exotic, as he consciously plays with a tradition that runs from Conrad's *Heart of Darkness* to *Apocalypse Now*' (Lux Films Press Kit 1994). The African river that Conrad's Marlow travels towards the personification of unrestrained white imperialist evil, Kurtz, takes him on a journey away from civilization and back in time to the primitive world of the African Indigene. The intertextuality that Morin creates between his film and both Joseph Conrad's novella and Francis Ford Coppola's film is not parodic, it does not reconfigure racialized stereotypes of First Nations in a field of irony thereby destabilizing white fantasies of Aboriginal difference. Conversely, *Windigo* disciplines its viewers to read Eddy Laroche in the same light as Conrad's and Coppola's Kurtz, a white imperialist; it re-inscribes First Nations as disappearing exotic primitives who live in a displaced temporal realm. One of Eddy's warriors explains to a journalist, 'We are not just 300 kilometres away from civilization, we are 300 years away.'

The *mise-en-scène* of Morin's river voyage is coded with signs of a savage Abo-riginality, textual triggers signalling to the viewer that the present narrative is to be read in the light of Conrad's and Coppola's journey up river into the 'heart of darkness'. Both Conrad's and Coppola's significations of 'the heart of darkness' are ironized; the signified of 'heart of darkness' is found not in the 'primitive' indigenous peoples of Africa, or in Coppola's case Vietnam, but in the white Western European imperialist, Kurtz. Morin, however, by scripting the Abo-riginal Eddy to utter the famous last words of Conrad's Kurtz – 'the horror' – locates the 'heart of darkness' within the Aboriginal Other.

The 'dark heart' of Aboriginal savagery is presented to the viewer in the grisly scene of submerged plane wreckage. Zooming in from a long shot of the wreck-age to a close-up on a corpse floating under the surface of the water, Morin shows us the remains of a rival team of journalists who were flying into the Aki camp. Eerie white approximations of 'Indian' music that accompany these shots, together with Indian Affairs representative Côté's response to the crash – 'I will not negotiate with assassins' – structure the viewer's perception that Aki 'war-riors' have shot down the plane. The Native as murderous savage stereotype is re-inscribed again in an Aki 'warrior' attack riddling the delegation's ship and its captain with bullets. This sequence and the subsequent one where the ship's prisoners are taken as captives by the Aki echoes not only Conrad and Coppola

Plate 18 Windigo (1994). Robert Morin on the set. Courtesy TVA-International. Photo: Atilla Dory

but the narrative structure of countless Hollywood westerns where white invader-settlers are viciously attacked and imprisoned by barbarous savages. In Conrad's and Coppola's narratives, however, the Natives' actions are manipulated by the white imperialist; here they are the work of an indigenous leader, Eddy.

The slippage that occurs between a sympathetic representation of the violence internal colonialism has done to the Aki and a re-inscription of that violence through acts of racialized representation is found in the film's conflicted signifying practice. Morin's heavy-handed efforts to destabilize colonial stereotypes of First Nations are certainly apparent to the viewer. Through flashbacks from the perspectives of various passengers, Fontaine and his cameraman learn that white society has created the conditions of possibility for an Eddy, with Fontaine suggesting that some situations call for an avenging figure like Eddy. Perhaps the clearest example of the film's conflicted signifying practice is Fontaine's allegorical dream vision of relations between whites and First Nations. Fontaine dreams of a wild horse driven to madness by the savage beatings of its human owner. In his interpretation of the dream, the journalist emphasizes that the horse's madness is not the animal's fault, that the responsibility for its condition lies with the owner. After he relates the content of his dream, his colleague underlines its significance for the microcosm of Québec assembled on the ship: 'You have dreamed for all of us tonight.' That the horse is an allegorical signifier for First

204

Plate 19 Windigo (1994): Donald Morin as Eddie Laroche. Courtesy TVA-International. Photo: Attila Dory

Nations is confirmed in the last shots of the film, where, following a cut to black from Fontaine's failed attempts to summarize Eddy Laroche for his viewers, Morin cuts to a medium long shot of a wild horse at liberty, galloping through a dark forest. This trite representation of colonizer/colonized relations, while it indicts the cruelty of white imperialism and anticipates liberation from the colonial yoke, also evokes Lloyd's conceptualization of the racist field of vision. Here the horse stands in for the Native as 'an underdeveloped human animal' while Fontaine stands in for Lloyd's 'judging subject' who takes the perceived underdevelopment of the Native as an index of his own 'superior stage of development' (Lloyd 1991, 74). The sequence of shots also suggests that liberation for Eddy, for the Aki, is possible only through death.

The binary structure of the Native subject as inferior to the superiority of the white invader-settler subject undermines Morin's attempt to illustrate the ravages of internal colonialism on the Aki. Failing to represent the complex ways in which First Nations have negotiated white invader-settlers,[8] *Windigo* is dependent on the vanishing race trope of colonial discourse. In a regressive turn reminiscent of the images of the seventeenth-century smallpox-infected Hurons that *Black Robe* closes on, Morin depicts the Aki as a dying, diseased people who cannot survive in the late twentieth century. Just before his death Eddy tells the delegation, 'I am sick. We are all sick. We have chosen to die here rather than return to the world of the whites.' When Eddy tells Fontaine, a professional journalist entrusted with the responsibility of representing First Nations, that he had dreamed of 'transcending white representations so there would be no more scalping', we don't hear the voice of First Nations but that of Morin speaking through the Aboriginal subject. This laudable desire to transcend white representations is impossible in a film where 'authentic' Aboriginality is represented through savage rituals imagined by a white director and writer. According to Morin's creation, Eddy, to be truly Indian is to be essentially primitive. Towards the end of the film Eddy makes this point by cutting his thumb with a knife, rubbing his fingers in his blood, and looking up at an Aboriginal negotiator to tell him, 'You are too white to understand what is going on here.' What is perhaps most troubling about these images is that they are contextualized by a press kit that stresses the authenticity of the film's representations of First Nations. The producers want the media to know that four Natives contribute their 'very natural' talents to *Windigo* and that 'actual Native warriors round out the cast' (Lux Productions Press Kit 1994). However, these Natives are scripted by Morin to perform his vision of Aboriginality, they are bearers of meaning not producers.

Morin's images of First Nations are clearly racialized stereotypes. However, I do not mean to suggest that they are produced by a contempt for First Nations; rather they are produced from the consumption of white binary images of the Native as savage barbarian or noble savage. As Rony suggests, 'racialization is not necessarily the product of contempt. Notions of the native as pathological and savage often co-exist with images of the "noble savage"' (1996, 72). Morin, unfortunately, contributes to what Rony describes as 'the continued proliferation of images of indigenous people as spatially and temporally distant' (128). Sadly, Morin's mode of film-making 'sustains a denial of the history of native peoples' struggles against colonization and genocide, and their ongoing struggles for cultural identity against the forces of an image-hungry dominant culture which sees them as always already dead' (Rony 1996, 198).

Clearcut

Although ambiguous enough in its ironic representation of First Nations to give Ojibway writer and critic Drew Hayden Taylor the impression that it re-inscribes stereotypes, the problematic of whites reading their own anxieties and fears of the primitive through the Aboriginal subject is negotiated far more effectively in Bugajski's *Clearcut* (1993) than it is in *Windigo*.[9] While Bugajski necessarily re-inscribes white racialized constructions of Aboriginality in his appropriation of the colonizer's discourse, he does so in an ironic context where the sign systems of an ongoing colonialism are reconfigured to unmask colonial systems of representation as destructive for both colonizer and colonized. Unfortunately, irony is in the eye of the beholder, and not all viewers are going to decode the textual triggers Bugajski deploys to signify his doubled ironic vision. Bugajski represents the Native as a sadistic, violent and savage torturer Arthur who bites the heads off snakes and flays the flesh of the lumber mill manager; however, this representation is revealed to be a fantasy construction projected on to the Aboriginal subject by the white liberal lawyer Peter. Peter vents his own frustrations over his failure to negotiate successfully on the band's behalf by inventing the savage avenging 'Indian' figure of Arthur, who will do the violence to the logging company that refined, civilized, white Peter cannot. After Fanon, white man Peter projects his desires on to the Aboriginal, acting as if the Aboriginal really had them (Fanon 1967, 165). What is at stake in mining this bifurcated field of vision, in representing the tensions between white racist signifiers for First Nations and the material First Nations they stand in for, is that the white racist signifiers which refer back only to white racist imaginations will be read as referring to material signifiers of Native subjectivity. Franco-Métisse film-maker and cultural critic Marjorie Beaucage sounds the volatility of ironic inscription in the failure of an audience to de-scribe it when she writes '*Clearcut* makes the audience hate Natives' (Beaucage 1992, 28).

Clearcut, like *Windigo*, plays on contemporary struggles of First Nations against an internal colonialism that in its zeal to harvest resources disregards Native claims to territory. Bugajski's narrative begins as Peter Maguire fails to win an injunction prohibiting the clearcutting of forests on contested land claimed by an Ojibway band. Full of rage and hostility against the logging company, Peter tells tribal elder Wilf, 'Someone has to pay, someone has to hurt.' Suspecting that Peter's investment in the land claims case has more to do with himself and white liberal guilt than it does the Natives he represents, Wilf asks him, 'Who do you feel bad for, us or yourself?' This question is one of the first textual triggers alerting the spectator to the narcissistic nature of the film's narrative, its focus on Peter and the identification he makes with himself through First Nations cultures. Later Peter is invited to take part in an Ojibway sweat lodge ceremony to find insight into himself. Wilf counsels him to 'look inside for what you really want'. It is at this moment that Peter begins the journey into himself that will produce Arthur from his own psychic materials.[10]

Peter takes a detour through internalized white constructions of the Aboriginal Other to a fictive sense of self. During Peter's ordeal in the woods with Arthur and Rickets the mill manager, Rickets tells him that he is going Indian, that he is starting to resemble a Native. The spectator is disciplined to see Native culture through the agency of Peter, a white liberal sympathetic to the plight of First Nations. We see the spectacle Indigene Peter creates in the sweat lodge through subjective camera shots that cut between glowing rocks, rocks dripping with blood, rock face petroglyphs and images of Arthur in a loincloth emerging from water. The violence within Peter seems to summon up Arthur. Immediately following the spirit vision sequence of the sweat lodge, Bugajski cuts to a scene between Peter and Arthur, in which Peter expresses his desire to blow up the mill, tie the mill manager up and skin him alive. Later, when Peter's sleep is disturbed by revellers in the next hotel room, he wishes for a bomb. Subsequent to this utterance, Arthur appears as if conjured by Peter and puts an end to the noise next door by gagging and binding the noisemakers at knifepoint. Arthur's actions are highly performative; he narrates his performance of the exotic savage, drawing attention to how the colonizing gaze structures First Nations. When he first takes Rickets hostage he says to Peter, 'I could scalp him and be a real Indian. I should be a real Indian, shouldn't I?' As he ties up Rickets he asks him, 'Where's your daughter? I need a good fuck.' While he performs what he calls a 'de-barking' of the lumber mill manager's flesh, Arthur explains his actions to Peter: 'You wanted him hurt didn't you? Well, I am your friendly neighbourhood cruel Indian.' Bugajski's Arthur acts out the ramifications for First Nations of colonial systems of representation where, as Fuss writes, 'the colonized are constrained to impersonate the image the colonizer offers them of themselves; they are commanded to imitate the colonizer's version of their essential difference' (Fuss 1996, 146). Arthur self-consciously reflects back what Peter and the white world project on to him: scalping, raping, cruel savagery. Arthur is very much a creation of Peter and the white world as is indicated when Rickets demands of Peter, 'Can you handle *your* Indian?' Peter constructs his identity through the colonized as their protector; significantly he is addressed by his Native clients as the 'man who talks for us'. Peter is a white lawyer who, as an interlocutor, literally represents or stands in for the Aboriginal Other in a colonial system of representation, the justice system of the Canadian state.

In marked contrast to the press kit for *Windigo*, the press kit for *Clearcut* makes it very clear that Bugajski's film 'is not a native story' but 'the story of a white man entering a foreign landscape' (Cinexus Productions Press Kit 1993, 5). Adapted from M. T. Kelly's novel *A Dream Like Mine*, Bugajski's film, like the novel, offers whites their own reflection in the character of Arthur. In her discussion of white writers' appropriation of Native voice, Lenore Keeshing-Tobias commends Kelly for the respect he demonstrates in not using the Native voice to tell the Canadian story of a man who 'tragically falls victim to his own fears and expectations of what is "Indian"' (Keeshing-Tobias 1990, 176–7). As she says of the absent Native voice in Kelly's novel, 'the very element missing as it should be. Why? Because Canadians are staring themselves in the face.' Kelly and Bugajski know this, Morin does not.

Clearcut, however, not unlike *Windigo*, ends with the death of a Native, Arthur, who returns to the waters from which Peter saw him emerge by drowning himself in the lake. In an ironic reading of the film, the death of Arthur does not signify in the same way as the death of Eddy Laroche (a character Morin never acknowledges as a white projection of the Native) but as the death of a dangerous stereotype. For Arthur is, as the film's press kit indicates, and as Wilf tries to tell Peter, part man, part trickster-spirit of Ojibway legend, Wisakedjak. In the middle of the nightmare Peter is experiencing with Arthur, Wilf appears to tell him the story of Wisakedjak the deceiver who

> was told to teach man how to live in the right way, how to be able to get along with the creatures and the forest. But Wisakedjak made quarrels. He stained the ground with blood. They told him no more but he didn't

listen. Wisakedjak had to be stopped there was too much blood. He had become a victim of his own stupid ways. He had lost himself.

The white stereotype of the Native is also a kind of trickster figure, a deceiver who has caused blood to be spilled on the earth, a figure that has to be stopped.

Map of the Human Heart

New Zealand director Vincent Ward's British/Australian/French/Canadian co-production (1992) tracks the exploitation of resources in the Arctic and the assimilation of Aboriginal peoples through the love triangle of Avik, an Inuk, Albertine, a Métisse and Walter, an English imperialist.[11] Walter, a cartographer with the British Air Force, comes to the Arctic in 1931 to map it as part of the British Empire. While surveying the territory, he becomes friendly with a part-Inuit boy named Avik whom he subsequently diagnoses as tubercular and removes to a Catholic hospital and orphanage in Montreal where the young boy meets and falls in love with Albertine. Torn apart through the process of assimilation practised by a very severe nun who arranges for Albertine to be adopted by a white family, Avik and Albertine meet up again in London during the Second World War. Ostracized by his own people owing to his acculturation by white society, Avik begs Walter for work as a Bomber Command cartographer. When he arrives in London he meets Albertine, who is now Walter's lover and a map-reader at Bomber Command. Albertine is passing for white and sees Avik as a reminder of the Aboriginal heritage she has repressed.

Establishing aerial shots of ice floes and frozen white Arctic land mass communicate the film's organizing metaphor of cartography to its audience, as the camera maps the Canadian north. A powerful trope of colonial discourse, cartography is a signifying system where the land of the colonized Other, apprehended through the lens of the map-maker, is translated into territory possessed by the empire. The colonizer's mapping is not limited to the physical landscape; it includes the social and cultural mapping of the Indigenous inhabitants as Others who must be assimilated into the symbolic order of the colonizer through the disciplining doubled message of the Imperial Subject, in this case Walter: 'Be like me, don't be like me' (Fuss 1995, 146). As much as Walter encourages Avik and Albertine to be like him, he only allows them to approximate whiteness as a sign of their subjugation; he will not permit them to inhabit it (146). For Walter, Avik remains an Inuk in a British uniform and Albertine an exotic 'half-breed'. As he tells Avik at the end of the film, he views Avik and Albertine as precious objects, 'things' he does not want to lose. The colonized Other's potential inhabitation of whiteness, as we saw in our analysis of *Saving the Sagas*, would threaten to displace the power of the Imperial Subject which is dependent upon the construction of the colonized Other as savage. As Nederveen Pieterse writes, 'the savage is indispensable in establishing a civilization's place in the universe' (1991, 201).

Avik is mapped by Walter and the British Empire as savage. However, after his participation in white imperialism's mapping and fire-bombing of Dresden, Avik inverts the colonizing gaze by naming whites as 'cannibals' he didn't want to live among. The film represents white mapping as a violent commodification of the land. Mapped in 1931 by Walter with the assistance of Avik, the Arctic landscape of 1965, the film's present, has been transformed by thirty-four years of white oil extraction into a scarred, industrialized landscape that belches smoke and fire. Ward emphasizes the destructive nature of white mapping towards the end of the film by cutting from Avik's subjective flashback narrative of the flames of Dresden to the flames of the Arctic oil fields. Avik's telling to a contemporaneous map-maker in 1965 of the narrative that the white maps don't reveal provides a counter-narrative to imperial mapping by representing how imperial cartography reshaped the inhabitants of the territory. *Map of the Human Heart* charts the colonial contest as a whiting-out of the Indigene, a process that is reflected in Ward's use of dissolves into whiteness to affect transitions to the flashbacks and flashforwards that structure the narrative.

A blinding white fade-in marks Avik's first flashback to 1931 and his first encounter with Walter, an encounter that will place Avik and his culture under white erasure. The sequence of shots depicting the first contact between Walter and Avik signifies the violent ramifications of the colonial encounter for the Inuit. Ward cuts from an extreme close-up shot on Avik's face bouncing into the frame from below, to a shot of Walter's approaching plane, to an aerial shot of Inuit children holding a sealskin trampoline upon which Avik is bouncing. A cut is then made to a shot of the horizon with Avik's head bouncing into the frame as Walter's plane moves towards the camera, towards Avik. At this point Ward cuts from Avik's perspective to Walter's and we see the children scatter in the path of his plane, dropping the trampoline and abandoning Avik who lands upside down on his head. This scene constitutes a *mise-en-abîme* or mirror text, a reduplication of images or concepts referring to the textual whole. In this sequence of shots we have a blueprint for the entire film: the violence a mechanized white-invader-settler culture does to Inuit community and cultural practices as this is signified through the character of Avik whose contamination by white cultural practices leads to his expulsion from his own community.

The relay of looks between colonizer and colonized represented in this sequence of shots is revisited on several occasions in the film narrative, most notably in the scenes where Avik is learning to re-vision his own landscape through the technology of cartography. The lens of the survey equipment is a sign for the colonizing gaze that both Avik and Albertine are introduced to by Walter; through the agency of Walter they both learn to see from the perspective of the colonizer. It is no coincidence that the lens of the map-making equipment resembles the lens on a gun; the survey lens anticipates the lenses through which Avik will photograph bombing targets and through which Albertine will read enemy territory mapped by the cameras of Bomber Command. Avik, however, appropriates the imperial technology of Bomber Command to create a map of the human heart, in the aerial photograph of the horse through which he communicates his love to Albertine.

The cultural and social mapping of Aboriginality is also organized around a regime of surveillance. Infected by tuberculosis, which Walter calls 'white man's disease', Albertine and Avik are removed from their familial and cultural contexts and placed in the white environment of the Catholic hospital and orphanage where 'white man's medicine' is used to cure them. The prescription of white medicine, however, is both physiological and psychological. The psyches of Avik and Albertine are mapped by the Roman Catholic church, an institution which plays an integral part in colonization globally in its zeal to create an empire of the self-same: translating what it regards as heathen savages into Europeanized Catholics. The invasive internal mapping of Aboriginal subjectivity by the colonizing gaze is most effectively signified by the X-ray machine that so traumatizes Avik. Lured to a darkened radiology lab, Avik flees in terror when the doctor turns on the lightboards to illuminate X-ray images of lungs, ribcages and skulls. Albertine is also X-rayed and operated on as part of her treatment. The cure involves a whiting-out of their Aboriginal heritage. The nun teaches her charges that they may adopt white cultural practices and become Catholic or continue what she regards as their heathen uncivilized ways and be consumed for eternity in the flames of Hell. Avik is read by the nurse as a sign for the unassimilable. She tells him that if Albertine had not been adopted out to a white family he would have 'infected' her. The implication here is not just physiological infection but also a psychological one. The nun has told Albertine previously that she is not a 'savage', that she is not a 'half breed': 'If you don't behave like a half-breed girl, than anything is possible for you.' This white way of seeing the self is internalized by Albertine. She misrecognizes her self for the nun's and Walter's white projection, as she tells Avik in London: 'I'm not that half-breed girl anymore.' Moreover, the hospital signifies as a site for the institutional whiting-out of the Indigene in Ward's overdetermined *mis-en-scène*. The hospital set is brightly lit to emphasize its blinding white walls, the white uniforms of the staff and in one scene the white plaster cast that encases Avik as part of his TB treatment, a visual sign of a rigid and constricting white culture imposed on the Aboriginal.

Although *Map of the Human Heart* self-consciously charts the process of whiting-out the Aboriginal Other through assimilation, paradoxically it may also contribute to this whiting-out in its casting. Although Inuit actor Robert Joamie and Métisse actor Annie Galipeau play Avik and Albertine as children, Hollywood actor Jason Scott Lee and French actor Anne Parillaud play the characters as adults.[12] The casting of non-Aboriginal actors in lead roles in a film so clearly invested in representing Aboriginal alterities limits severely its ability to signify Aboriginal experience and belies its production of spectacle Indigenes from white materials. The experiences of Avik and Albertine are imagined by two white men, Vincent Ward and his screenwriter Louis Nowra. Although *Map of the Human Heart* attempts to represent an Inuit experience of colonial contact, one can't help but wonder if it constitutes the kind of representation Inuit film-maker

Zacharias Kunuk finds offensive: 'I get offended that every time there's a movie about the North there's always a Qallunaag (non-Inuk) who steals the subject, who's in the centre of the action while the Inuit take the backstage' (quoted in George 1997, B6). Kunuk's own representations of Inuit in his television series *Nunavut* focus not on white contact but on five Inuit families living traditional lives in 1940s Igloolik and are shot in Inuktitut. Kunuk's televisual narrative foregrounding traditional Inuit cultural practices is very different from Ward's feature film, which ends with the death of Avik, the ultimate whiting-out of the Aboriginal. Ward's Avik resonates with racialized properties reminiscent of Morin's Eddy, a noble savage corrupted by the white world whose death signals a failure of the Aboriginal subject to negotiate both worlds successfully. While it is important to document the ongoing residual violence of colonial contact for Aboriginal peoples and cultures as documentary film-makers Marjorie Beaucage (*Ntapueu ... I Am Telling the Truth*, 1997) and Alanis Obomsawin (*Kanehsatake*, 1993) have done, it is equally important to represent, as both Beaucage and Obomsawin do, living Aboriginal cultures working to negotiate and survive internal colonialism.

Dance Me Outside

Of the five films discussed in this section, Bruce McDonald's *Dance Me Outside* (1995) may, on first glance, be considered the most successful in unveiling romanticized and racialized images of First Nations as white projections, without re-inscribing them. Although *Dance Me Outside* includes a naive white character, Robert McVey, who tries to map his own fantasy of Aboriginality on to First Nations, McDonald's empowered, hip, Native characters are part of a living late-twentieth-century Native culture that is resilient enough to laugh at such a pathetic and impotent colonial gaze. Clarence Gaskill represents a foil to the well-meaning white liberal lawyer McVey who has married into a Native family. Gaskill, on the other hand, is a racist white punk whose internalization of colonial stereotypes of the Native Other motivates his murder of Little Margaret, an event around which the plot of *Dance Me Outside* turns. When Gaskill is released after serving a minimum sentence, he returns to the 'rez' where the young men of the community hatch a half-baked revenge plot to kill him. The young women of the community who slit Gaskill's throat to avenge the death of Little Margaret, however, pre-empt the men's plot.

Clearly McDonald sought to create a progressive film about life on a reserve that would negotiate racial tensions and represent Natives with dignity. The production seems to have the support of some major First Nations cultural producers: Métis film-maker and writer Duke Redbird acted as an associate producer and Cree writer Tomson Highway is thanked in the film's credits. McDonald cites the deconstruction of celluloid stereotypes as one of his goals in making *Dance Me Outside*: 'We were trying to bend and stretch and snap as many stereotypes as possible, while telling a good story.' He sees the Native characters of his film as 'a bit good' and 'a bit bad', but 'real' (quoted in McGovern 1995, 44). One of McDonald's actors, Adam Beach (Frank Fencepost), corroborates the director's claim of realistic Native characters: 'There's no problem here at all, unless it's with a very, very strict traditionalist. If this film was harsh in any way, I would have done something about it!' (quoted in Kirkland 1995, 59). The film's vaunted authenticity and perceived success in avoiding malicious stereotypes is all the more remarkable given its freighted source text, white author W. P. Kinsella's 1977 collection of stories set on Alberta's Hobbema reserve. Natives complained that Kinsella stole their stories and demeaned them by creating racialized characters to whom he attached the real names of Hobbema residents.[13] As Beach says of Kinsella's book, 'I think a lot of people who read it and are Indian feel a little stupid because of how it was written' (quoted in Kirkland 1995, 59).

In McDonald's film, however, it is the white characters' investments in racialized fantasies of First Nations that are represented as more than just a little stupid. McVey, who has married a Native woman, Illianna, reads Native culture as exotic and noble through the screen of popular culture images. To divert the sterile McVey's attentions away from his wife's conceiving a baby with Gooch, Silas and his friends get McVey drunk and provide him with a forum in which he can play 'Indian'. Under the guise of a naming ceremony, Silas and Frank crown McVey with feathers, paint his face and facilitate the exorcism of his inner white 'Indian'; naked and uttering primal screams, McVey proclaims himself the Wolverine. The sterility of this white fantasy of Aboriginality is signified through McDonald's intercutting of shots of McVey running through the woods with

Plate 20 Dance Me Outside (1995). Silas (Ryan Black) and Frank (Adam Beach). Shadow Shows 2001

213

shots of Illianna having sex with Gooch. The inherent racism that marks such imaginings of Native difference, however, has a darker side that materializes in Gaskill's and his sidekick's performances of the racist white stereotypes of 'Indians' they have internalized through Hollywood westerns. The first time Gaskill enters the frame, he pounces on the hood of Silas's truck making the clichéd war whoop noises of celluloid braves and pointing at Frank and Silas. However, it is Gaskill who acts the part of the bloody savage in his murder of Margaret; after Fanon he projects his murderous desires on to Silas and Frank, pretending that the Aboriginal subjects really have them.

Notwithstanding McDonald's stated goal of subverting stereotypes of Natives and Adam Beach's testimonial that the film is successful on this front, Terry Lusty, a reviewer for the Aboriginal magazine *Windspeaker*, argues that *Dance Me Outside* maintains stereotypes: 'There is hardly a scene throughout the entire 87-minute run of this flick which does not set apart Indians and their homeland as drinking, cheating, poverty-stricken, pool-playing racist people who have nothing better to do than tear around in old beat-up clunkers' (Lusty 1995, 18). Lusty is referring to Silas's and Frank's theft of McVey's car in the film's first sequence, and their translation of it into an old heap. Arguing that the 'rez' created by McDonald is a generality that, with some exceptions, no longer holds true, Lusty points to progressive reserves and Natives who are morally and socially adjusted and have new cars, and nice, well-furnished clean homes (18). Decrying what he sees as the film's failure to 'incorporate elements that have something positive to project about the social and cultural fabric of Indian country', Lusty asks: 'Where are the rodeos, pow-wows, round dances, tea dances, ball games, hockey games, schools with teachers and teacher-aides, churches, health clinics, talent contests, band meetings, etc., etc.?' (1995, 18). Lusty isn't the only critic who troubles the film's politics of representation. *Globe and Mail* reviewer Geoff Pevere suggests that one of the film's shortcomings is that 'it falls all over itself' in attempting to 'defuse' a 'minefield of representational objections – like the current one about white folk "appropriating" non-white stories' (1995, C2). According to Pevere, McDonald creates another kind of white spectacle vision of the Native by serving up 'irresistible pop confections' – 'the funkiest, funniest and most drop-dead gorgeous native characters we've ever seen' (C2). McDonald's whites – McVey, Gaskill and the police – on the other hand, writes Pevere, are 'turned into a gallery of one-dimensional cartoons' (C2). In this respect Pevere sees a 'full pendulum swing from the racist one-dimensionality of yesteryear to the anti-racist one-dimensionality of today' (C2). This reversal is not something John Kim Bell, founding president of the Canadian Native Arts Foundation and producer of the Aboriginal Achievement Awards, finds very troubling: 'For years and years we [Natives] have been portrayed as the bad guys. If it's suddenly reversed, well, too bad' (quoted in McGovern 1995, 45). Bell's comments raise an important point that Pevere's review fails to address: the power differential skewing the economy of cultural production in Canada and the United States in favour of the images of Natives produced and circulated by the dominant white cultural producers.

RETURNING THE GAZE: ABORIGINAL FILM-MAKERS AND DECOLONIZATION

Although McDonald's film might be more progressive than its predecessors by providing Aboriginal characters some much-needed depth, it remains a white vision of Aboriginal life in Canada. *Dance Me Outside* provides an all-too-clear answer to the questions that Native critic and writer Lenore Keeshing-Tobias asks about who determines what is ' "Indian," "too Indian," or "not Indian enough" ' for a global market hungry for images of Natives. Answering her own question, Keeshing-Tobias indicts the political economy of cultural production in Canada that privileges white representations of the Native over Aboriginal representations:

> It seems a host of non-Native professionals (publishers, editors, produ-
> cers, directors, and the like) have taken over the work of the missionary
> and the Indian agent. Like their predecessors, they *now* know best how
> to present the Native image, the Native perspective, never dreaming, of
> course, that it is really their own perspective.
>
> (1990, 175)

Part of the 'indigenous nationhood' that Alfred sees as 'about reconstructing a power base for the assertion of control over Native land and life' is also about asserting Native control over *representations* of Native land and life (1999, 47). As Marjorie Beaucage writes: 'Access to the tools of creation and self-representation is the beginning of self-determination. For too long our stories have been told by others and our dreams and visions misrepresented' (1992, 29). Towards this end the NFB has worked with Aboriginal communities across the country to develop an Aboriginal film community. Studio One, a Native produc-tion unit, was established in Edmonton in 1991 and replaced by the Aboriginal Filmmaking Programme in 1996. Unlike Studio One, which centralized produc-tion in Edmonton, the Aboriginal Filmmaking Programme is decentralized, pro-viding Aboriginal film-makers with access to NFB facilities across the country. Part of the Aboriginal Filmmaking Programme is devoted to training initiatives to 'increase the representation of aboriginal peoples in the Canadian film and television industry'.[14] The overall goal of the Programme is: 'To provide aboriginal film-makers with more equitable opportunities to make films, thus ensuring a more diverse spectrum of perspectives, visions and stories in Canadian cinema.'[15] Despite the NFB's designating of $1 million a year for NFB produc-tions or co-productions with independent Aboriginal film-makers, funding prob-lems still plague Native film-makers. NFB money is available primarily for the support of documentary, although other genres will be given consideration.[16]

215

This explains, in part, why there are so few fiction features produced by First Nations directors.

Isuma Productions' *Atanarjuat*, the first feature-length fiction film written, acted, produced and directed by Inuit in the Inuktitut language is an interesting example of the difficulties confronting Aboriginal film-makers who work outside of the documentary genre in a language other than English or French. *Atanarjuat* or *The Fast Runner*, directed by Zacharias Kunuk and based on a five-hundred-year-old myth, is described on the Isuma Productions website as 'an exciting action thriller which brings to the screen an historic legend of power, intrigue, love, jealousy, murder, and revenge told entirely from the Inuit point of view'.[17] Production on *Atanarjuat* was shut down in mid-May 1998 when Telefilm Canada failed to deliver completion money. Isuma's secretary-treasurer Norman Cohn believes *Atanarjuat* to be the victim of a two-tiered race-based funding structure: 'The second tier is aboriginal language low rent welfare ghetto, where the eligibility requirements are extremely low, but the amount of money is not enough to make a professional television movie' (quoted in Wilkin 1998, 9). As reporter Dwane Wilkin explains: 'While English and French language projects typically attract between $1 million and $2 million in production funding from CTCPF fund [Canada Television and Cable Production Fund], individual aboriginal-language film projects are limited to $100,000 subsidies' (Wilkin 1998, 9). Telefilm Canada, however, deny that racial or linguistic concerns played a role in their decision and that the failure of *Atanarjuat* to get completion money was due more to CBC's refusal to grant Isuma a licensing commitment for broadcast if that licensing money was to be used to trigger Telefilm money (9). The film went back into production in 1999 when Telefilm accepted the project for funding within the larger 'English' envelope of grant money (Soukup 2000).

The first NFB films produced with the active participation of First Nations were more concerned with the political utility of documenting ongoing colonial aggression than they were with representing stories from the oral tradition. Initial decolonizing steps towards self-representation and self-determination were taken in the Challenge for Change film *You Are on Indian Land* (Mort Ransen 1969). Although produced and directed by whites, *You Are on Indian Land* was made at the invitation of a Mohawk member of a First Nations film crew assembled by the Department of Indian Affairs and the Challenge for Change Programme, Mike Mitchell (Stoney 1980, 349). Mitchell wanted a film crew to document his band's blocking of the international bridge between Canada and the United States on the St Regis Reserve near Cornwall, Ontario. The Mohawks stopped traffic on the bridge to publicize how their rights to bring duty-free goods across the border from the US, as articulated in the Jay Treaty of 1794, were being violated by Canadian authorities. George Stoney, the film's producer, says the intent of the film was that 'the situation should be recorded from the Indian viewpoint' (350). Produced in collaboration with Mitchell and Noel Starblanket of Challenge for Change's Indian Film Crew and the people of Akwesasne

Mohawk Nation, *You Are on Indian Land* shows how repressive state apparatuses are deployed by federal and provincial governments to enforce colonial rule and ignore treaty obligations. Shots of Mohawks telling police that they are trespassing on Indian land where they have no authority give way to shots of mass arrests. The film's concluding sequence strikes a prescient note when Mitchell, addressing a representative of Indian Affairs, talks about broken treaty promises. According to treaty agreements, he says First Nations were 'obliged to cease making wars on the white man . . . We didn't break our side, we didn't go to war . . . yet.' In many ways *You Are on Indian Land* is the precursor for NFB films such as Obomsawin's *Incident at Restigouche* (1984) and *Kanehsatake: 270 Years of Resistance* (1993). By the time of the Oka Crisis, peaceful protests had failed to stop colonial encroachment on territory claimed by First Nations, and subsequent films document the escalation of resistance to internal colonialism. *You Are on Indian Land* and Obomsawin's films are highly politicized activist documentaries that dispel the myth of Canada as a postcolonial nation that embraces difference and human rights by locating the ugly and violent colonial reality confronting First Nations firmly in the Canadian nation's present.

Incident at Restigouche

Incident at Restigouche (1984) is a point-of-view documentary documenting two raids made on to the Micmac reserve at Restigouche by the Québec Provincial Police in June 1981 to enforce the provincial government's restriction of Micmac fishing rights. Obomsawin, an Abenaki film-maker, poet and singer, produces an oppositional discourse to the governing Parti Québécois's discursive formation of Micmac fishers as law breakers by contextualizing the conflict with historical materials substantiating the Mimacs' longstanding claim to the salmon fishery and its significance to Micmac cultural heritage and economy. *Incident at Restigouche* is an exercise in what bell hooks calls oppositional looking, a site of resistance to the white colonizing gaze of the Québec state that sutures the viewer into an identification with the Micmac subject position through interviews and subjective camera shots. Discussing the oppositional gaze of black female spectators, hooks writes: 'spaces of agency exist for black people, wherein we can both interrogate the gaze of the Other but also look back, and at one another naming what we see' (hooks 1992, 116). Obomsawin locates those spaces of agency for Native people in her documentary practice that interrogates the gaze of the Québec state through its repressive state apparatuses and names it as race-based police brutality. The film's opening sequence is composed of shots of black-and-white still photographs of the QPP in riot gear and wielding truncheons. The camera pans across several still images, before cutting to a medium close-up colour footage of an older Micmac man who voices his resistance, in Micmac, to the QPP: 'I draw the line for them not to come any further.' Obomsawin then cuts from this image of Micmac resistance back to a series of shots of the black-and-white still photographs, eventually zooming in on the truncheons held in the hands of the

217

QPP officers, before cutting to shots of Micmacs being subdued and arrested. From the film's very first frame, Obomsawin registers the oppressive presence of the QPP on the soundtrack through the acoustic signs of marching jackboots that punctuate the images of the police and the interview segment with the old man. Editing and sound effects discipline the spectator to see the QPP as agents of a repressive and fascistic regime. This sequence of shots representing the brutish power of the Québec state's internal colonialism and First Nations resistance culminates in an interview segment with a representative of the state, PQ Minister of Fisheries Lucien Lessard. Obomsawin uses this interview to structure her film, cutting back and forth from the main narrative of the raids to Lessard's reflections on his government's actions. The film's oppositional ideology, its return of the colonizing gaze that would structure Micmacs as nationless, cultureless, subjects of the Québec state is crystallized when the film-maker angrily confronts the Minister on screen with the hypocrisy and shortsightedness of his position on national sovereignty:

> When you came to Restigouche I was outraged by what you said to the Band Council. It was dreadful. The Chief said, 'You French Canadians are asking for sovereignty here in Québec. You are saying, "It's your country and you want to be independent in your country." We are surprised that you don't understand us Indian people and our sovereignty on our land.' And you answered 'You cannot ask for sovereignty because to have sovereignty one must have one's own culture, language and land.'

By the end of the interview and the end of the film, Lessard makes a personal apology for any problems his actions may have caused the Micmacs of Restigouche. His disregard for Native nationhood, as quoted by Obomsawin, however, is something First Nations and Obomsawin's cameras will negotiate again in 1990 during the seventy-eight days the Mohawks of Kanehsatake resist the aggression of the Sûreté du Québec (SQ) and the Canadian armed forces.

Kanehsatake: 270 Years of Resistance

Developing the documentary aesthetic of *Incident at Restigouche* – point-of-view documentary organized around interviews and footage of confrontation between Natives and the RSAs of internal colonialism – Obomsawin's *Kanehsatake: 270 Years of Resistance* (1993) interrogates the optics of colonialism and racism that saw the Canadian armed forces and the *Sûreté du Québec* pitted against the Mohawks. Before an analysis is presented of Obomsawin's film as counter-cinema resisting the hegemonic colonial discourses of Québec and Anglo-Canadian nations, some background on the complicated and vexed history of Mohawk land claims at Kanehsatake is necessary.

After they were dispossessed of their lands by the French Roman Catholic order of St Sulpice, the Mohawk nation is granted a plot of land at Kanehsatake by the French crown in 1716. Subsequently, secret negotiations between the French crown and the Sulpicians in 1717 erase Mohawk title to the land in favour of the Sulpicians. Neither the French crown nor the Sulpicians inform the Mohawks of this arrangement that effectively translates the Mohawks into tenants on the land of the Sulpicians. In 1840 the British crown confirms Sulpician title to what had been Mohawk territory. Tensions between the Mohawks and the Sulpicians continue until the religious order sells the land to the Belgian Baron Empain in 1936. In the 1930s residents of the town of Oka begin playing golf on the Commons area, a traditional gathering place of the Mohawks, which together with the sacred Pines area is eventually taken over by the municipality of Oka for the site of a golf course. Anticipating the proposed golf course expansion of 1990, the Mohawks resist the establishment of a golf course bordering their burial grounds in 1959.[18] Ultimately, the Mohawk cemetery is expropriated by the municipality. In response to Mayor Jean Ouellette's plans to build a luxury housing development and expand the golf course into what the Mohawks claim as their territory, some Mohawks begin a protest on the road running from the Pines to the golf course, a route they eventually block with barricades in June 1991. A force of about a hundred SQ officers mount a raid on 11 July on the Pines in which gunfire is exchanged and an SQ officer is shot and killed. Ballistics tests prove inconclusive and the identity of the party responsible for Corporal Lemay's death remains undetermined, with the SQ blaming the Mohawks and the Mohawks suggesting that Lemay was hit by SQ bullets or by his own recoil.[19] As Geoffrey York and Loreen Pindera suggest, the Mohawk warriors defending the Pines demonstrated great restraint when the majority of them chose not to open fire and mount a counter-attack. Following this skirmish and the arrival of more than a thousand SQ officers in Oka, Mohawk warriors blockade the Mercier Bridge and all highways leading from Kahnawake, a sister community to Kanehsatake. By 20 August the Canadian army is brought in to relieve the SQ at the Kahnawake and Kanehsatake barricades. The army begins its advance into Mohawk territory on 23 August. These armed incursions into Mohawk territory at Oka are not new, but part of a historical and contemporary practice of colonization. As Mohawk academic Donna Goodleaf and journalists York and Pindera indicate, the repressive forces of the Canadian state had violated the sovereignty of the Mohawks on several occasions, the most recent being an RCMP raid on Kahnawake in June 1988 (Goodleaf 1995, 31–2), the earliest a QPP raid on Oka in June 1877 (York and Pindera 1991, 81).

When Obomsawin first heard of the SQ's invasion of the Pines and the death of Lemay she was in the midst of working on another film, a project she abandoned to document the events at Oka. Working with a full camera and sound crew at the beginning of the standoff, Obomsawin found herself alone and shooting on video in the final days of the siege. So much footage was shot that her rough assembly of the film ran twelve hours after six months of editing; it took many more months to edit the material down to its final cut of two hours.[20]

Explaining her vision in the film's press kit, Obomsawin says, 'I wanted to show what Mohawk people were like and why they took the stand they did' (NFB Press Kit for *Kanehsatake* 1993, 2). This desire to represent Mohawk people involves oppositional looking that interrupts and reverses the white colonial gaze that is actively engaged in misrepresenting Mohawk people through the optic of colonial stereotyping. As Philip Rosen writes of politically committed film-makers, for Obomsawin 'the spectator can be defined as a terrain to be organized' (Rosen 1993, 77). Beginning with the interviews with Mohawk women Kahentiiosta and Ellen Gabriel, Obomsawin's point-of-view documentary sutures the spectator into the perspective of the Mohawks behind the barricades. The voices of Gabriel and Kahentiiosta narrate and contextualize the images of the SQ's attack on the Pines which is shot with a hand-held camera from the subjective camera perspective of the Mohawks, thereby making viewers subject to the violence of the SQ. This move initiates the reversal of the colonial gaze that Obomsawin's film takes up. Writing of Fatimah Tobing Rony's decolonizing film *On Cannibalism* in the context of reversing the gaze, E. Ann Kaplan articulates a process that describes Obomsawin's work in *Kanehsatake* where 'the gaze of the Other is turned with scorn on western colonial strategies, and the western viewer asked to identify with this gaze. In this process . . . the powerful subjectivity and agency of the non-western speaking subject is made material' (Kaplan 1996, 297). Obomsawin's Western viewer is asked to identify not only with the gaze of the Other that must negotiate the physical violence of colonialism, the SQ attack, but also with the psychic violence of colonial discourse, the white stereotype of First Nations, as it is negotiated by Obomsawin's cameras. The colonial construction of the Aboriginal Other as a bloodthirsty savage in *Black Robe* and *Windigo* and Hollywood cinema resonates in public understandings and media images of the Mohawk warriors as violent criminals, as terrorists. Goodleaf's chapter on the Kanehsatake crisis includes a list of headlines from the *Montreal Gazette* that she associates with the media's 'fabrication of images that were anti-Indigenous or anti-warrior in general', for example: 'Warriors Hold 6,000 Guns, $30 Million in Coffers', '14 Warriors on Barricades Face Charges in N.Y.: Official,' 'Police Union Warns Quebec: Let Us Act or We'll Put Out: Fed-up Surete Officers Want Army to Move in and Arrest "Terrorist" Mohawks and Rioters' (quoted in Goodleaf 1995, 67).[21] The Canadian Police Association produced a document, 'We Oppose Terrorism', that represented the Mohawk warriors as aggressors who 'ambushed' the SQ (Canadian Police Association 1990, 1). bell hooks's contention that 'one fantasy of whiteness is that the threatening Other is always a terrorist' provides an instructive contextualizing lens through which we might read whiteness, colonial stereotyping and the Aboriginal Other's return of the colonizing gaze in *Kanehsatake* (1992, 174). hooks argues that this white projection of the Other as always a terrorist 'enables many white people to imagine there is no representation of whiteness as terror, as terrorizing' (174). However, Obomsawin's film, as part of its undoing of the cultural construction of Mohawk warriors as terrorists, asks the white Western viewer to identify with the gaze of the Mohawk Other that reads colonialism as white state-sponsored terrorism. This is perhaps most clearly visible in the footage of women and children in the Pines just before the SQ attacked them or in the army's savaging of the unarmed Mohawks who walk out of the Treatment Centre at the end of the siege, a mêlée in which a fourteen-year-old girl was bayoneted by a soldier.

Obomsawin's interruption and reversal of the colonial gaze involves a denaturalizing of televisual representations that construct and circulate colonial stereotypes of Mohawks as violent warrior savages. According to freelance journalist Sandy Greer, 'the media's overall point of view was grounded in the institutional authority of government and law enforcement' (1994, 21).[22] Obomsawin documents and troubles that point of view in a powerful sequence of shots juxtaposing national television coverage of Québec Premier Robert Bourassa and Prime Minister Brian Mulroney maligning the Mohawks as undemocratic criminals to interviews with the victims of colonialism's repressive state apparatuses, the RSAs through which Mulroney and Bourassa govern. Bourassa's and Mulroney's soundbites are preceded by interviews with Mohawk negotiator Mavis Etienne, Gaston Tardif, Daniel Nicholas and Michel Trudeau. Etienne tells Obomsawin that she was arrested by the SQ and detained for five hours for being behind the barricades; none of the white negotiators who went behind the barricades were arrested. Gaston Tardif describes how he and some women he was escorting were strip-searched by the SQ in the street. Michel Trudeau, a white Quebecker misrecognized for a Mohawk by the SQ, relates how he was terrorized by officers who wanted to 'exterminate him'. When his young son arrives on the scene the officers apologize for their behaviour before accidentally discharging one of the loaded weapons they had been threatening Trudeau with into the ground. Daniel Nicholas recounts how he was physically assaulted by an SQ officer who punched him in the face, kicked him in the testicles and extinguished a cigarette on his stomach before dropping it down Nicholas's trousers. Responding to his recent experience at the hands of the authorities, Nicholas says, incredulously, 'and they calls *us* the savages'. At the breaking point, Nicholas tells the camera how he signed a blank confession to gain his release from custody.

Obomsawin cuts from this litany of human rights abuses to a medium close-up on Premier Robert Bourassa. Speaking at a press conference to address the demands of the Mohawks, he tells the media: 'The toughest challenge for any government in the western world, in our world is to defend democracy against people who do not believe in democracy.' A few frames into the press conference footage, Obomsawin makes a cut from the location shot of the press conference to its reception on a television viewed by warriors behind the barricades at Oka. A news anchor then introduces a clip of the Prime Minister by reporting that Mulroney praised Bourassa's government for the way 'it's been handling the situation in Oka'. The subsequent Mulroney soundbite questions the citizenship of the warriors and describes their actions as 'illegal'.[23] The dispossession of the Mohawk is, of course, 'legal' in the colonial context of Mulroney's utterance.

While the Mohawk viewers behind the barricades presumably read Bourassa's and Mulroney's statements as the rhetoric of internal colonialism, for some residents of Oka and surrounding area these statements could prove inflammatory. Street interviews with Oka residents indicate some support for the Mohawks and anger directed towards the mayor's proposed golf course development; however, an interview with two boys reveals that the dehumanizing colonial stereotype of the Mohawk warrior as dangerous, untrustworthy and supernatural has been internalized. One boy says of the Mohawks, 'They could be hidden in the forest. They could be hidden anywhere. You don't even see them.' While this description of the Mohawk warriors conjures up images of the colonial past and 'Indian' wars on white invader-settlers, the diegetic reality of the film posits the Mohawk territory and culture as under attack. The kind of white invader-settler perspective exemplified by the young boy, however, is what the Canadian and Québec governments allegedly hired the public relations firm NPR Inc. to produce.[24] The work of NPR Inc., the statements of Mulroney and Bourassa, the army's public relations video on the crisis, and media reports 'grounded in the institutional authority of government and law enforcement' (Greer 1994, 21)[25] are designed to perform the representational work of colonialism; it polices 'the boundaries of cultural signification, legislating and regulating which identities attain full cultural signification and which do not' (Fuss 1995, 143).[26] This imbalance in media coverage constructed from the white colonial gaze is interrupted in Obomsawin's reversal of that gaze through shots of an angry white mob at Chateauguay protesting against the Mohawk closure of the Mercier bridge to Montreal by chanting 'savages' and burning a Mohawk warrior in effigy.[27] In another incident shot at Chateauguay, Obomsawin records images of a mob of about three hundred white men and women throwing rocks at Mohawk vehicles carrying mostly women, children and the elderly away from the Kahnawake reserve, while the SQ look on, refusing to intervene. Obomsawin's voice-over narrates shots of large rocks smashing through windshields telling the spectator that one elderly man died of a heart attack following this ordeal. After zooming in through a shattered car window to a large rock on the car's rear seat, Obomsawin cuts to a medium close-up shot of a woman picking the rock off the seat and telling the camera in close-up: 'This is what they threw at my father, this is what hit him in the chest.' Obomsawin's voice contextualizes the shots, informing her spectators that this woman's seventy-seven-year-old father was seriously injured in the attack.[28] In another sequence of shots the spectator is forced to confront the violence of the Canadian army in close-ups on the bruised, lacerated and bloodied face of 'Spud Wrench', a Mohawk warrior beaten by Canadian soldiers. These three sequences, and the previously referenced interview segments, return the gaze, inviting the white Western viewer to identify with images of whites as terrorists while revealing the law as a social construction of the colonizer, a symbolic order used to define and subjugate the colonized as always-already criminal.

Kanehsatake offers a fuller signification of the warrior than the one legislated by the media, the federal and provincial governments, or the fictive representations of the warrior found in Morin's *Windigo*. In contrast to Morin's invented one-dimensional warriors who never really speak on camera unless it is to parrot the words of Eddy Laroche, and the warrior figures of the media, Obomsawin documents warriors interacting with their families and explaining their concerns for the survival of their people, their language and their culture. In an on-camera interview with Obomsawin, the warrior named 'Psycho' explains who the warriors are. In the Mohawk language he says they are the *rotiskentahkete*, 'the men' who must protect 'the people within'. Donna Goodleaf translates *rotiskentahkete* as 'those who carry the burden and responsibility of protecting the origins; or carry the burden of peace and justice' (Goodleaf 1995, 189).[29] Later in the film Obomsawin returns to her interview with 'Psycho' where he laments, patting his gun, that the only thing the governments understand is 'right here'. Continuing his discussion with Obomsawin, 'Psycho' articulates his motivation: 'The fish is dyin', the air is dyin', the plants are dyin', the animals are dyin'. We're not too far behind them as the Mohawk Nation.' Especially effective in returning the gaze are shots of warriors and their families sitting around a fire at night under attack from the army. Panning around the campfire, Obomsawin's camera cuts from fire-lit faces to focus on the casing from a flare lodged in the ground beside the fire while a small child asks her mother if it's a bomb. In another sequence of shots Loran Thompson teaches his children Mohawk language and stories until he is temporarily interrupted by the white noise of an army helicopter circling overhead. At one point in an interview with Richard Two Axe that is cross-cut with shots of the army using what can only be described as excessive force to subdue warriors and their families as they walk out of the Treatment Centre, Two Axe comments on the surprise of the authorities: 'When they found out that we were family people – they thought we were going to have records as long as our arm, there was families, husbands, wives, children. Who's going to leave their family behind?' These images of the army attacking Mohawk families combined with earlier shots of the SQ separating a Mohawk mother from her child at a road block, and the attack on women, children and the elderly at Chateauguay, reverse the white fantasy of the Aboriginal Other as terrorist to apprehend the white terrorism of internal colonialism.

Although I have focused on Obomsawin's deconstruction of the warrior-savage stereotype, the representation of Mohawk women in *Kanehsatake* is counter-discursive to the sexualized colonial stereotypes of the princess and the squaw served up in ethnographic films such as *Saving the Sagas* or features such as *Back to God's Country* and countless other historical and contemporary North American and European cultural products.[30] Unlike the licentious squaw caricatures of Barbeau's *Saving the Sagas* or Hartford's *Back to God's Country*, silenced signifiers in someone else's discourse, Ellen Gabriel and Kahentiiosta are given the space to voice their truths as empowered and articulate women who refuse the limits of internal colonialism, who refuse exploitation. Regrettably, however, the Oka Crisis inspired one film-maker to re-present the conflict as a sexualized pornographic contest predicated on colonial stereotypes of the Aboriginal. The producers of *Quebec Sexy Girls 2: The Confrontation* combine two colonial stereotypes – the warrior savage and the licentious squaw in one masked female figure who attempts to distract a Canadian soldier from his duty through sexual advances. Here the Native Other is made to signify as a sexually promiscuous and violent threat to the security of Canadian nation in a white phallocentric and racialized symbolic order. A still from the film published by the Canadian Press depicts an actress playing an Aboriginal woman clad in only a shirt, a camouflage mask and camouflage hat.[31] She stands opposite a Canadian soldier in camouflage combat gear played by Patrick Cloutier, a discharged Canadian soldier who served at Oka. Cloutier is reprising the role he played as a soldier in the defining media image of the Oka Crisis, a face-to-face standoff between a member of the Canadian army and a masked Mohawk warrior that circulated on wire services around the world. The pornographic parody of this image of the Aboriginal Other is not as far removed from Barbeau's sexualized representation of the Nisga'a woman performing the potlatch dance in *Saving the Sagas* as one might think. Bill Nichols argues persuasively that the pornographic and ethnographic film share some common terrain, in that both focus on producing a knowable body: 'Pornography and ethnography dwell on the body as a socially significant site. They extract, respectively, pleasure and knowledge from that site while at the same time demystifying and familiarizing it. Through the body the domestication of the Other occurs' (Nichols 1991: 215). The image from *Quebec Sexy Girls 2* attempts to define the Aboriginal Other as sexually available for the pleasure and knowledge of a white phallocentric Canada allegorized in the soldier. A similar legislating of signification is palpable under the scientific pretence of Barbeau's film, which ultimately seeks to define Aboriginal woman as sexually available for the white male explorer and by extension, given the film's circulation as part of a museum exhibit, white male Canada. Importantly, as Nichols makes clear, 'both pornography and ethnography promise something they cannot deliver: the ultimate pleasure of knowing the Other' (225). Both genres produce the *fantasy* of knowing the Other, a fantasy that spectators all too frequently misrecognize for reality.

Documents such as Obomsawin's film provide a valuable site of resistance to internal colonialism and the racist discourse of the colonial stereotype that perpetuates it. Although the Kanehsatake band council now holds title to some 160 formerly disputed properties and has the right to enact bylaws governing its territories, the public discourse on Aboriginal issues in this country is still debased by some whites who introject and project denigrating stereotypes of First Nations people.[32] These stereotypes have become so naturalized within some sectors of invader-settler culture that a Canadian Alliance candidate from Saskatchewan running in the 2000 federal election told a group of Aboriginal people, 'you can't scalp me because I haven't got much hair on top of my head' (quoted in Greenaway and Boswell 2000, A11). That a statement such as this can be made in the twenty-first century is ample evidence of Canadian society's need for more decolonizing Aboriginal self-representations that return the gaze to confront the white spectator with the vision of internal colonialism from the perspective of the colonized.

Charley Squash Goes to Town

Obomsawin contributes her vocal talents to the soundtrack of a much earlier and more light-hearted attempt at decolonization through filmic self-representation, Métis film-maker and writer Duke Redbird's *Charley Squash Goes to Town* (1969). Based on his Native comic strip character, Charley Squash, the film was produced by the NFB's Challenge for Change Programme and depicts the title character negotiating the contradictions of a colonized subjectivity that is interpellated by colonial stereotypes and the doubled command of Fuss's Imperial Subject: 'be like me, don't be like me' (1995, 146). The film follows Charley from childhood on the Squash Valley reserve to a job in the 'outside' white world where he is told by whites that he is not 'Indian' enough, and later that he is too 'Indian'. Charley's voice-over narration of his childhood by Isaac Beaulieu signals to the viewer the destabilization of colonial stereotypes Redbird's film will perform by invoking the colonial descriptor of Aboriginal difference, the savage.

Structuring images of himself in a loincloth and feathers playing, dancing, hunting and fishing, Charley's voice-over describes his childhood: 'When I was a youngster on the reserve, I was a happy little savage . . . I was the kind of little Indian boy everybody reads about in the books.' The onscreen image of Charley as a paint-and-feather Indian seems to be taken from 'the books', white books about, after Francis, imaginary Indians. When he gets to town he is expected to reflect back this exotic stereotype to the white Imperial Subjects who produce and desire it. As Charley explains, 'My friends at work didn't believe I was an Indian because I acted just like they did and I didn't even wear feathers.' Charley's similitude, his humanity, troubles the white Imperial Subject's understanding of a difference that is based on the construction of the Aboriginal Other as primitive savage. When he returns to the reserve that he left on a dogsled in a sports car, however, Charley's parents are angry because he 'looked and sounded just like a white man'. His white teacher and minister are angry because he hasn't joined a national Indian organization and does not praise the traditions of his people. This process of assimilation is signified in the establishing shot of the sequence depicting Charley's workplace; a tight close-up on a large portrait of his white employer pans down to focus on Charley sitting directly under the portrait in a business suit. Here, Charley is literally placed under the disciplining gaze of the Imperial Subject.

Responding to his parents', teacher's and minister's disappointment, Charley decides to study Native culture; however, he does not study the living culture of his reserve but a taxidermied Aboriginal culture re-assembled in white museums and re-presented in Hollywood films as a part of the historical past. Redbird's establishing shot for the sequence representing Charley's engagement with his culture places Charley in a museum in between a reconstructed dinosaur skeleton and a directional arrow indicating the location of the 'Indian' exhibit. Subsequent shots show Charley in an exhibition hall with a birch-bark teepee and canoes, in a library reading, and watching black-and-white Hollywood representations of cowboys and Indians on television. Charley's experience of his culture through the sign systems of white invader-settler culture that associate it with extinction in the sign of the dinosaur skeleton surprisingly awakens a sense of Native militancy within him.

When he returns to the office he says he 'was always pushing the Indian cause', something Redbird illustrates with shots of Charley getting arrested for protesting against the government, and of Charley at work surrounded by protest slogans reading 'THINK INDIAN', 'SEE RED', 'BE BRAVE'. This militant Native identity that challenges the authority of the Imperial Subject is antithetical to the politically impotent type of paint-and-feather Aboriginality his colleagues at work want to see reflected back, so they issue the command of mimicry, 'be more like me': 'My friends at work told me I should try to blend into the white society and stop protesting.' Following a heated altercation with his boss who is angry about newspaper photos of Charley protesting, he leaves, or is fired from his job. Charley's resistance to the colonizing gaze that would stereotype him is to commodify white stereotypes of Aboriginality and sell them back to their source. He hires a white man to sell war bonnets he makes to a white clientele, who, to paraphrase Keeshing-Tobias, do not recognize that it is their own image and reflection of the exotic 'Indian' they purchase (1990, 175). Shots of urban whites going about their daily routines in their exotic 'Indian' chic finery facilitate Redbird's return of the gaze by asking the white Western viewer to identify with a gaze that looks on the white subject with a demystifying and destabilizing irony. In a provocative reversal of what Fuss sees as colonialism's representational paradigm where 'the colonized are constrained to impersonate the image the colonizer offers them of themselves', Charley's commodification of the white colonial stereotype of the Aboriginal Other commands the colonizer to imitate his or her own fantasy of essential Aboriginal difference (Fuss 1995, 146).

Honey Moccasin

In contrast to Obomsawin and Redbird, Mohawk photographer and film-maker Shelley Niro's film *Honey Moccasin* (1998) constitutes oppositional looking or counter-cinema to white cinematic representations of the Aboriginal Other by, for the most part, refusing to look back, by refusing to acknowledge the white colonial gaze. In this way Niro's film creates spaces of agency for Native people where they can look beyond the white gaze to negotiate Aboriginal community. Niro describes the audience she envisions for the film she produced as part of *Reservation X: The Power of Place in Aboriginal Contemporary Art*, an exhibit at the Canadian Museum of Civilization:

The target audience for *Honey Moccasin* is First Nations, Natives and Indians. I want them to relate to the situations in this film without trying to find a way in. They're in as soon as the film starts. Most of the characters are Indians. There is only one non-native character, who makes a brief appearance. Conflicts and their resolutions come from the Native community. The entertainment, the social commentaries, the acts of wackiness all come from this fictional reserve.

(quoted in Smith 1998, 115)[33]

Billed by Paul Chaat Smith as the first independent Canadian feature film written by, directed by and starring Natives, *Honey Moccasin* focuses on a mystery unfolding on the fictional Grand Pine Reserve where powwow dance outfits and the materials for their construction are being stolen. Tantoo Cardinal, who reportedly wished for an opportunity, while on the set of *Black Robe*, to work on a film that represented the matriarchal aspects of Native culture, has her wish fulfilled in *Honey Moccasin*. Cardinal plays the title character Honey – storyteller, singer, owner of the popular Smokin' Moccasin Café, and amateur detective – who solves the mystery of the missing beads and feathers and thus helps to resolve the alienation of the cross-dressing Zachary John from his community and from his father.

The Smokin' Moccasin Café is a matriarchal space presided over by Honey where the community meet to be entertained and enlightened about their past as well as their present. When we first meet Honey she is onstage telling her patrons a chapter in community history, the story of her life that includes her birth, the loss of her parents in a car accident, growing up with her Aunt Mabel, her broken marriage and the birth of her daughter Mabel. Most of this is related through black-and-white flashbacks excepting her reference to Mabel who joins her onstage. During the flashback sequence representing Honey's birth, the film's only white character, a nurse, surfaces as an agent of assimilation who would change Honey's given middle name of Melon to Marilyn. The Smokin' Moccasin is the film's site for community, the performance venue that houses the powwow fashion show, Mabel's performance art and her film, and the reconciliation between Zachary and his father, between Zachary and his community. In Niro's words the Smokin' Moccasin 'becomes an extension of everyone's living room' (quoted in Smith 1998, 114).

As much as the film focuses on community issues to look beyond the white colonial gaze, part of what shapes the fabric of community on the Grand Pine Reserve is the collective experience of internal colonialism, something that is referenced in both the powwow fashion show and Mabel's performance of 'Fever'. Zachary John's theft of feathers and beads, although perpetrated by someone in the community (albeit an individual who has been away and is attempting to reintegrate), is reminiscent of white invader-settler society's appropriation of Native culture and provides Niro with an opportunity to demonstrate that, as Chaat Smith writes, 'being Indian takes more than feathers and beads' (Smith 1998, 111).[34] Aboriginal cultures are imaginative and resilient enough to survive the violence of forced assimilation and the campaign of geno-cide directed against them. *Honey Moccasin* posits a dynamic and resourceful Aboriginal cultural practice that renders visible techniques of *bricolage* that First Nations engage in to construct Aboriginal identity in the late twentieth century, strategies for survival that directors such as Morin (*Windigo*) and Barbeau (*Saving the Sagas*) are either ignorant of or elide. Johnny John and the elders of the Golden Oaks Club stage a fashion show with outfits made from alternative materials for the young people on the reserve who, according to Johnny John, are giving up too easily on their culture just because of the disappearance of feathers and beads. As Johnny John and the Golden Oaks see it, the reservation's youth are 'starting to wander from their teachings' and need to be shown 'how to use their brain and how to use all these other materials'. The 'new inventions' of the Golden Oaks modelled by the youth include powwow clothing made from canvas and wax, bottle caps, Fruit Loops cereal, suckers and candy, rubber tyre tubes and a broom bristle. The elders demonstrate how to construct Aboriginal alterity to the colonizer out of the colonizer's cultural materials. In Niro's words they 'find new ways to define what it means to be Indian' (quoted in Smith 1998, 111).

Following the fashion show, Mabel takes the stage to show her community 'what she does at film school'. A self-reflexive sign for Indigenous self-representation that inscribes First Nations cultural production into the diegetic world of the film, Mabel, like the elders, takes her raw materials from the domin-ant white culture and translates them in an Aboriginal art form, telling Aboriginal story. She appropriates the white pop song 'Fever' and sings it with her face pushed through a hole in a canvas teepee on to which images of human rights atrocities ranging from residential schools to Hiroshima are projected. Images of nuns holding Native babies (Figure 5.1) are narrativized by the song lyrics: 'Never know how much I love you / Never know how much I care / When you put your arms around me / I get a fever that's so hard to bear / You give me fever.' Images of Wounded Knee, US Indian relocations, and smallpox-infected Natives are flashed on the teepee as Mabel works her way through the song. Clearly, the kind of fever Mabel is singing about is the fever of death and disease. As Mabel sings, Niro cuts from close-ups of the performer to shots of the pro-jected images, the projector and shots of Mabel's audience (Figures 5.1–5.3). The projected images transform this piece of white popular culture into a site of Native resistance to colonialism; in Mabel's reworking of the song white desire for the Aboriginal Other produces a genocidal fever. The lyric 'Fever isn't such a new thing / Fever started long ago' is marked visually by an image of imperial dispossession, Cartier's claiming of Iroquois territory for France. Of course, the song's reference to Captain Smith and Pocahontas takes on new meaning in this context; instead of a celebration of love across cultural difference, the relation-ship between Smith and Pocahontas is re-visioned by Mabel as a nodal point in a genealogy of colonization, assimilation and genocide. Niro appropriates the

Figures 5.1–3 Honey Moccasin (1998).
Courtesy of Shelley Miro

images of the vanishing race discourse – diseased and dying Indians – and recontextualizes them. These images of the 'doomed primitive' are denaturalized as fallacious colonial discourse by Niro's incorporation of them in living, contemporary Aboriginal culture performed by a living Aboriginal artist for a living Aboriginal community. In Niro's world, the Western pop song is transformed from an acculturating discourse to a site of resistance and empowerment, in much the same way as she transforms the television. In Redbird's film the television is a sign of acculturation; it is the technology through which colonial stereotypes of the Native are circulated. Niro, however, aboriginalizes television, she translates it into a technology for Aboriginal self-representation, a decolonizing broadcast communications system called the Native Tongue that transmits local news and cultural events.

What Niro's fictive Native Tongue does on a local scale, the Aboriginal Peoples Television Network (APTN) hopes to do on a national scale. Launched in 1999, APTN provides a forum for the circulation of film, television and news programming by and for Native people. APTN's chairman Abraham Tagalik, an Inuk from Frobisher Bay, is optimistic that the network will trouble the stereotypes of Aboriginal peoples he grew up viewing as a child: 'It was cowboys and Indians – the John Wayne version. The natives were always the villains. They were criminals waiting to ambush people. That's carried over. It's not cool to be aboriginal. Our kids are not made to feel pride in their culture' (quoted in Clark 1999, 61). With the proliferation of Aboriginal self-representation and the development of a national network to circulate those self-representations, Marius Barbeau's 1931 assessment that 'at present the indications point convincingly to the extinction of the race' – something reflected in white films about Aboriginals in the 1990s – is proved categorically false (Barbeau 1931, 707).

6

MULTICULTURAL FIELDS OF VISION

> The European nation-state of Canada built itself around
> 'whiteness,' differentiating itself through 'whiteness' and creat-
> ing outsiders to the state, no matter their claims of birthright or
> other entitlement. Inclusion in or access to Canadian identity,
> nationality and citizenship (de facto) depended and depends on
> one's relationship to this 'whiteness.'
>
> Dionne Brand (1994, 173–4)

Film-maker and Governor-General-Award-winning writer Dionne Brand's thinking about Canadian nation as a racialized construct that structures whiteness as a
universal signifier for Canadian identity might strike some inside and outside
Canada as reactionary. Surely, they might argue, the Multicultural Act of 1988
makes diversity a foundational concept of Canadian identity? Brand's understanding of race and nation in the Canadian context is certainly supported by the
Othering of peoples of colour that we have seen the cinema of this nation produce in the chapters on early Canadian film, ethnographic film and films about
First Nations. One recurring image in these chapters is the different disposses-
sions of peoples of colour by white state apparatuses, reflected back to us by films
such as *Wonders of Canada, Saving the Sagas, Of Japanese Descent: An Interim
Report* and *Kanehsatake: 270 Years of Resistance.* First Nations and Japanese
Canadians are not the only groups to have their race used as a rationale for
dispossession. As Shelagh Mackenzie's documentary *Remember Africville* (1991)
makes painfully clear, the City of Halifax's decision to raze the African-Canadian
settlement of Africville in 1966 was informed by racism and greed, possibly more
than it was by a genuine concern for the living standards of the settlement's
inhabitants. Brand's comments are also echoed in *The Dark Side of the Nation,*
Himani Bannerji's thoughtful analysis of the work of multiculturalism in a Canadian state that, simultaneously, represents the nation as bicultural (French/
English) and multicultural. Whereas Bill C-93, the Multiculturalism Act, recognizes Canada's diversity, naming multiculturalism as 'a fundamental characteristic
of the Canadian heritage and identity', and reiterates the equality of all citizens
guaranteed by the Constitution in its preamble, in that same preamble it

re-inscribes the privilege of the two so-called founding nations by referencing the Official Languages Act. Bill C-93 emphasizes that the Official Languages Act 'neither abrogates nor derogates from any rights or privileges acquired or enjoyed with respect to any other language' (Government of Canada 1988). Ostensibly, the legislation recognizes that Canada's multicultural diversity eclipses the French and English binaries around which Canadian identity has been formulated historically; however, the embedding of the Official Languages Act within Bill C-93 troubles an understanding and implementation of multiculturalism in the context of a biculturalism that is signalled by official bilingualism.[1] Bannerji seizes on this moment of disjuncture as it translates into the practice of multiculturalism to argue:

> at the same moment that difference is ideologically evoked it is also neutralized, as though the issue of difference were the same as that of diversity of cultures and identities, rather than that of racism and colonial ethnocentrism – as though our different cultures were on a par or could negotiate with the two dominant ones!
>
> (Bannerji 2000, 96)

Clearly, the hierarchical mythology of two founding white European nations is re-inscribed in Canada's official multiculturalism. For Bannerji multiculturalism is itself 'a vehicle for racialization' in its establishment of an 'anglo-Canadian culture as the ethnic core culture while "tolerating" and hierarchically arranging others around it as "multiculture"' (78).[2] Bannerji's writing echoes Brand's in denaturalizing 'the ethics and aesthetics of "whiteness," with its colonial imperial/racist ranking criteria' that 'define and construct the "multi" culture of Canada's others' (78).

Brand and Bannerji are, by the terms of Charles Taylor's reading of Canadian multiculturalism, participating in what he calls, dismissively, the politics of rec-ognition (Taylor 1994, 62). Taylor's eurocentric resistance to a multiculturalism that would grant the kinds of recognition and equality Brand's and Bannerji's work demand, actually works to substantiate their contention that Canada, des-pite its multicultural posturing, continues to privilege whiteness as a universal signifier of belonging. Bannerji's critique of Taylor fleshes out what she sees as the eurocentric self-referentiality of his argument which, she argues, belies 'a particular socio-cultural location, considering some cultures to be "culture" while other, different cultures are components of multicultures' (Bannerji 2000, 134–5). Moreover, Brand's and Bannerji's reading of the conflicted identity pol-itics constituting Canada is confirmed in a 1993 Decima Research poll of 1,200 Canadians. As Brian Bergman reports, two-thirds of the sample group 'declared that one of the best things about Canada is its acceptance of all people from all races and ethnic backgrounds'; however, these same respondents confessed 'that they harbour negative views of some minorities' (Bergman 1993, 42). Racial intolerance was also reflected in another area of the poll where 72 per cent of the sample group stated that ethnic or racial groups should assimilate by adapting 'the Canadian value system rather than [maintaining] their differences'. Meanwhile, 41 per cent of those surveyed said that Canada's immigration policy allows in 'too many people of different races and cultures'. This poll, taken five years after the passage of Bill C-93 and twenty-two years after Trudeau introduced multiculturalism as policy, indicates the failure of multiculturalism as official policy or legislative act to perform anti-racist work.[3] And it is this all-important work of anti-racism that Bannerji sees being taken up not by 'official or elite multiculturalism', but by what she terms 'popular multiculturalism', a culture of resistance (Bannerji 2000, 5). The films that I am organizing under the rubric 'multicultural fields of vision' fall into this second category of 'popular multiculturalism' and constitute an oppositional or resistance cinema to the ethnographic white constructions of racialized subjects examined in Chapter 2.

Increasingly Canadian national cinematic culture is, after Bhabha, 'being produced from the perspective of disenfranchised minorities' (Bhabha 1994, 3). In a special issue of *Take One* devoted to non-white directors – 'Evidence: Race and Canadian Cinema' – film-maker Richard Fung writes about two important events he helped organize in the early 1990s, 'Shooting the System' and 'Race to the Screen'. 'Shooting the System' brought together 'emerging (and aspiring) film and videomakers of Aboriginal, African, Asian and Latin American backgrounds' for 'screenings, discussions about grant writing and the political issues of race and racism, especially related to the infrastructure of film and video production' (Fung 1994, 38). Fung's vision for 'Race to the Screen' was that it would 'help to develop a critical discourse around race and representation in Canada that would inform new work by non-white directors' (38). These two conferences indicate the developing community of film-makers engaged in the anti-racist work of resisting racialized mis-representations of a white cinematic apparatus through self-representation. These film-makers represent the dehumanizing violence of racialization; their work makes interventions into the hegemonic cinema of whiteness that has marked production in Canada historically to produce representations of their respective communities. While First Nations film-makers share some common ground with immigrant film-makers of colour – negotiating systemic racism – the fact of First Nations indigenous status and the violence of the state's attempted genocide of First Nations militates against including Native film-makers under the rubric of multiculturalism, which generally refers to immigrant groups.[4]

A chapter entitled 'Multicultural Fields of Vision' runs the risk of re-inscribing film-makers of colour as marginal, as in some ways 'less than' white film-makers. To echo Bannerji's argument, placing film-makers of colour in a separate chapter could simply model the ghettoizing work of official multiculturalism which arranges Other 'multi' cultures around a core culture. Clement Virgo makes a very important point in this context when he says that one of the reasons he avoids the 'black film-maker' label is because 'white artists can have a whole career telling stories about white people that are not culturally specific'. That is, white film-makers are called just film-makers without qualification, they and their films become naturalized as a cultural norm. On the other hand, he continues, the black label is, 'in pure form, also racist. It stems from a sense of privilege. It's assumed [when] you see a black film-maker, he has to be classified differently' (quoted in Schwartzberg 1994, S10). My intention is, however, not to ghettoize racial minority film-makers but to examine their work in a context where the differences of a racialization constructed and imposed upon their communities by the Canadian state may be fully engaged. This chapter will consider the oppositional cinema of Canadian film-makers of Asian, Indian and African-Caribbean heritage. Films under discussion here have not been selected because they are 'representative' of a particular community; 'representative' status is an illusory or indeterminate category at best. In the limited space available to me in a project of this scope, I have selected films exemplifying what Yasmin Jiwani calls a decolonization of the screen: 'an assertion of identity, of truth, of history of a particular people of their lives and their realities' (1996). Given the inevitable diversity within specific communities, not all members will agree on what constitutes the identity or truth of a people, as we shall see in Jiwani's troubling of Krishna's representation of the Indo-Canadian community in *Masala*.

Discussing the 'privileged regimes' of representation that facilitate the misrepresentation of Japanese Canadians, Roy Miki considers possible strategies for an oppositional representation, cautioning that 'the task of oppositional representation must not fall into the trap of simply reversing the binary structure' (1998, 183). Drawing on Rey Chow's conceptualization of a 'new ethnography' whereby previously ethnographized peoples take up 'the active task of ethnographizing their own cultures' (Chow 1995, 180) in a self-reflexive mode where the condition of being objectified informs cultural production, Miki argues for 'cultural forms in which the represented produce themselves through the co-ordinates that have set the historical contours of their identities' (Miki 1998, 183). This self-reflexive ethnographizing interrupts the dominant white discursive formations of Otherness, by in Miki's words 'inhabiting the dominant representations not as external frames of reference, but as internalized artifacts – artifacts that can be re-inscribed' (183). William Ging Wee Dere and Malcolm Guy, Mina Shum, Mieko Ouchi, Srinivas Krishna and Clement Virgo inhabit the dominant representations of their respective communities to explode dehumanizing racialized stereotypes and re-inscribe humanizing signs of difference in their place.

Moving the Mountain

Moving the Mountain (William Ging Wee Dere and Malcolm Guy 1993) represents the presented Chinese-Canadian community through the co-ordinates of the monstrous ethnographic laid down by films such as *Secrets of Chinatown* and other racist public discourses that, as we saw in Chapter 2, transformed the nation's Chinatowns into teratological spaces. In Dere's and Guy's film China-town is re-visioned and re-inscribed as a locus of family, culture, nourishment and belonging, while white colonial Canada occupies a teratological space. *Moving the Mountain* opens with Dere in the Chinese village of his ancestors and follows the immigrant route to Vancouver and eventually Montreal where Dere's father and grandfather settled and set up laundry businesses. The negotiation of a whiteness that constructs Chinese as an abject category subject to abuse and exclusion from the imagined community of Canadian nation shapes the narrative. The film is structured around interviews detailing the historical and continuing effects of racist Canadian legislation – the Head Tax and the Chinese Exclusion Act – on Chinese Canadians. Voice-over and testimonials in interviews articulate Chinese contributions to Canadian nation-building that challenge the Canadian state's representation of Chinese as aliens to the nation. Interview subjects also recount their experiences and responses to a virulent white racism. The interviews are punctuated by cuts to performance spaces in which contemporary Chinese-Canadian cultural producers perform acts of cultural resistance to racist stereotyping, thereby interrupting and denaturalizing racist discourse to name or define the nation space of Canada as systemically racist. All of this culminates in acts of political resistance with footage of Dere and one of his interview subjects, James Wing, participating in a demonstration march on Ottawa organized by the Campaign to Redress the Head Tax and the Chinese Exclusion Act.

The Head Tax and the Chinese Exclusion Act constitute the central co-ordinates through which the Canadian state Othered the Chinese in Canada. In contrast to European and American immigrants to Canada, no plans were made for the agricultural settlement of Chinese immigrants; they were envisioned as cheap labour, 'living machines', by the entrepreneurs who imported them (Avery and Neary 1977, 25). Not surprisingly, the defining of Chinese as cheap labour produced anxiety amongst local workers that eventually manifested itself in punitive immigration legislation.[5] Various Head Taxes imposed from 1885, at a rate of $50 a person, to 1903, at a rate of $500 a person, discouraged Chinese immigration to Canada, while the Chinese Exclusion Act of 1923 suspended Chinese immigration for twenty-three years, preventing wives and children from joining their husbands and fathers in Canada.[6] It is this violence to the Chinese family perpetrated by the Canadian state that Dere's film works to come to terms with, to redress, personally, socially and nationally. This state-sponsored violence to Chinese is visualized by Dere and Malcolm through the transition from footage of the Chinese countryside, shot from a train recreating the immigrant journey to Canada, to arrival on the shores of British Columbia. A cut is made from the tracking shot of Chinese landscape to a black screen upon which three successive intertitles are imposed, as train sound effects fill the soundtrack:

1885

CANADIAN PACIFIC RAILWAY
COMPLETED. CANADA IMPOSED
HEAD TAX ONLY ON
CHINESE IMMIGRANTS

1885–1923

DURING 38 YEARS,
81,000 CHINESE IMMIGRANTS
PAID $23 MILLION IN HEAD TAX
TO GET INTO CANADA.

1923–1947

FOR 24 YEARS
THE CHINESE EXCLUSION ACT
PREVENTED ALL *CHINESE*,
EVEN FAMILY MEMBERS,
FROM IMMIGRATING TO CANADA.

The black screen signifies the void into which Chinese are travelling, while the directors' decision to convey this historical documentation through text as opposed to voice-over conveys the textualization of Chinese in a national discourse that represents them as Other. Simultaneously, however, Dere's and Malcolm's re-presentation of this documentation evinces a self-reflexive ethnographizing moment that interrupts the original white nationalist co-ordinates that have set the contours of Chinese identity in Canada to re-inscribe Chinese as nation-builders whose labour was exploited to construct the master narrative of Canadian nation *par excellence*, the transcontinental railway. Moreover, Dere's and Malcolm's film inhabits the dominant form of representation – immigration legislation – to re-inscribe the white nation of Canada as one built on or profiting from a racism that coerced the transfer of $23 million from Chinese pockets to the nation's coffers. A subsequent Dere voice-over implies that the $23 million collected by the government from Chinese financed the railway for it was 'almost enough to cover the $25 million it gave the CPR'. Although Chinese immigrants might not have bankrolled the construction of the railway directly, their starvation wages undoubtedly rescued the project of the national railway from bankruptcy by saving the government an estimated $3–$5 million in labour costs.[7] *Moving the Mountain* further inhabits the dominant discourse by re-inscribing the experience of Dere's father and grandfather, and by extension all Head-Tax-paying Chinese immigrants in Canada, as 'a bittersweet journey that was uniquely Canadian', thereby re-visioning the experience of the alienated Other as central to an understanding of Canadian identity. What is uniquely Canadian here is the fraught history of race relations that is all too frequently written out of Canadian cinemas.

The representation of Dere's father in *Moving the Mountain* works to humanize and value the Chinese Canadian, creating an oppositional discourse to the dehumanizing abject constructions of Chinese in Canada as an undifferentiated monstrous mass that threatens whiteness circulating in public discourse and in films such as *Secrets of Chinatown*.[8] Dere's and Malcolm's camera eye inhabits the dehumanizing Head Tax certificate early in the film, translating the black and white photographic image it bears of Dere's grandfather into a humanizing full-colour family photograph through a dissolve. By the end of the film Dere's grandfather, once an alien to Canada, is written into Canadian nation through a close-up on another government document, the citizenship papers granted to him in 1951.

In contrast to the contention of *Secrets of Chinatown* that white Canadian subjects are under the surveillance of the Chinese eye and threatened with incarceration in filthy conditions, one of Dere's and Malcolm's interview subjects, James Wing, describes the 'sorrow' of his two weeks in the 'filthy' 'concentration camp' that served as the detention centre for new immigrants in Vancouver. Dere's images of Wing also inhabit and trouble the dominant white discourse on miscegenation anxiety reflected in legislation prohibiting white women from working with Chinese men and in the representation of Zenobia's white slavery relationship to the Black Robe in *Secrets of Chinatown*. Shots of Wing and his second wife, a white French-Canadian woman, in conversation with Dere (who remains off-camera) explode the racist question asked by Rande in *Secrets of Chinatown*: 'But why, I don't understand, you're a white girl, what are you doing in a place like this?' Wing's wife is clearly, unlike Zenobia, not under some kind of 'Oriental' spell, she is in love, and that love transcends racist constructions of Chinese. She tells Dere that her family accepted 'Jimmy' immediately; however, white anxieties about interracial relationships did manifest themselves when it came to her friends who, citing cultural differences, question how long the marriage will last.

The virulent racism against Chinese naturalized in *Secrets of Chinatown* and *Back to God's Country* is denaturalized in *Moving the Mountain* through interview segments in which people whom white racism objectified as abject and subhuman re-inscribe their humanity by relating their experiences of and responses to this vicious version of white nationalism. Owe Yee, a dignified, intelligent and kindly old man, humanizes the 'yellow man' stereotypes constructed in *Back to God's Country* and *Secrets of Chinatown* by articulating the pain and suffering racism caused himself and his contemporaries: 'Back then they really despised the Chinese. Sometimes the Chinese had rocks thrown at them. Landlords wouldn't let you rent. Chinese not welcome. Couldn't see a movie, saying Chinese are dirty.' Two Second World War Canadian Army veterans, Ken Lee and George Marr, relate how the name-calling of 'pig tail, rice eater, chink' that they resisted in school continued in the army. George had to slug it out with his Corporal to demonstrate the equality of white and Asian. Mr Lee and Mr Marr also reveal the ambivalence they felt about fighting for a country where they had no rights, until they were told those wrongs would be righted if Chinese-Canadian enlistment was forthcoming. Chinese-Canadian men like Ken Lee and George Marr risked their lives for Canada and for the inclusion of Chinese Canadians in the Canadian nation. As Marr comments, it's 'pretty hard to deny you full citizenship after guys have gone to war for you. We had offered our lives to our country.' Two years after the war, the Exclusion Act was repealed in 1947. In an interview sequence with the 'Gold Mountain widows', those women whom the Exclusion Act separated from their husbands until 1947, the full denigration and horror of white racism in Montreal in the late 1940s and early 1950s is revealed. 'Chinese wash shitty underwear for us, [the whites would] say', comments one member of the group. One woman tells Dere that the *Lau Fan* or whites yelled at Chinese women working in the laundries to 'bully them', while another adds, 'they bullied us to death', and still another says, 'They'd hit us if they felt like it. They just hated us.' This same group of women also offer their attempts at resistance: 'They'd call me Ching Ching, I'd call them Ching Ching right back. You'd yell at them but they wouldn't understand.' Following a testimonial from Dere's sisters on the racial epithets of 'chinee chinee, chinks' levelled at them after they arrived in 1950s Montreal, a cut is made to a performance space where these kinds of racial taunts are integrated into a self-ethnographizing performance by a Chinese-Canadian subject refusing complicity with the racialization uttered by the white racist. The performance re-inscribes the racial epithet as a hollow stereotype, revealing the ignorance of the racist. The space of performance is marked off from the documentary space of the film through *mise-en-scène*; the performer is shot against the black background of a recording studio, in front of a microphone.

Performer Charley Chin inhabits the co-ordinates of white racism to re-inscribe them as an anti-racist joke in a stand-up routine. Re-enacting questions that structure the Chinese as aliens to Canadian nation, Chin asks, in the voice of the white racist: 'Where are you *from?*' Answering his own question he replies, 'Toronto'. He restates the question with emphasis on 'from', signifying the white racist refusal to believe that Chinese are of the nation. Chin's most effective anti-racist joke short-circuits what Lloyd calls the 'visual structure of racism', refusing the racist or, in Lloyd's terms, 'the judging subject', a reflection of the projected 'underdevelopment' that would become an 'index of the judging subject's own superior stage of development' (1991, 74). Affecting a *faux*-toffee-nosed English accent, Chin inhabits the space of the white racists, asking 'why so many of our little Oriental friends seem to suffer from myopia?'. Chin responds in the voice of the Chinese-Canadian subject the white question attempts to racialize: 'We were straining our eyes about 2000 years ago, writing poetry and essays on philosophy by candle light about the same time your ancestors were resisting Roman attempts to introduce the practice of daily bathing and the Phoenician alphabet.' Other performances intercut with the documentary narrative include Sook-Yin Lee's ironizing inhabitation of Harold Weeks's racist song 'Chong (He Come From Hong Kong)' and Elvis Wong's rendition of 'Head Tax Blues'. Although I am differentiating between the main documentary footage of interviews, archival photographs and government documents, and what I am calling the performance spaces of the film, I would argue that these performance spaces also constitute documentary work. Here Dere and Malcolm record the voices of a living vibrant culture of resistance, that, as the lyrics to one of Chin's songs summarizes, are 'still here and going strong and getting tired of proving [they] belong'.

Double Happiness

Mina Shum's *Double Happiness* (1994), the first feature to be directed by a Chinese-Canadian woman, represents the more recent immigrant experience of a Canadian family who fled Mao's China. Shum's film relates a story of generational and cultural conflict between a Canadian-born daughter, Jade Li, and her father who emigrated from China. In what Kass Banning describes as a 'rewriting of the Oedipal drama in female terms', Jade must negotiate the doubled spaces of her father's Old World expectations and the New World cultural terrain, both of which play roles in forming her subjectivity (Banning 1999, 301). *Double Happiness* is a self-ethnographizing film that invites the audience to see Jade's family from her perspective; the entire film is shot from her point of view.

Shum's auto-referential aesthetic, her self-reflexive play with cinematic and televisual technologies of representation that have produced stereotypes of Chinese in North America, and constructed the dominant mythology of the white family as a norm in their failure to represent families of colour, is signalled to the viewer in the film's establishing shots.[9] In the film's first shot a clapper bearing the text – 'Jade Li monologue. Take 6. Director Shum. First Generation Film' – fills the screen, drawing our attention to the process of producing anti-racist cinematic culture. Subsequently, Jade looks directly into the lens and addresses the viewer:

> I said I would never make a big deal out of being Chinese . . . that kind of thing isn't exactly encouraged. But I wanted to tell you about my family – they're very Chinese if you know what I mean, but for the moment just forget that they're a Chinese family and just think of them as any old family, you know any old white family, although you could probably just turn on the TV set and see that. I grew up wondering why we could never be *The Brady Bunch.*

At this moment Jade initiates a process of self-ethnography. She re-presents the Chinese-Canadian family as like any other family, asking the viewer to see past racial and cultural difference to apprehend a very human story of family conflict, but, simultaneously she asserts her family's difference to a dominant white culture that would render her family invisible. *The Brady Bunch,* a popular American television series depicting the quintessential all-American, all-white family, constitutes a white marker for identification that disciplines the non-white viewer to identify with the white Other. As revealed by Jade, white productions such as *The Brady Bunch* can create a destructive double-consciousness – an internalization of the dominant white culture's values – that in turn produces a desire to be the white Other, to be assimilated.[10] However, the Brady's hermetically sealed facile world of white homogeneity is quickly dispatched by a cut from Jade to a wonderful sequence of shots of the extended family code-switching between Cantonese and English during dinner. The medium close-up shots are captured in pans from a camera positioned on the centre of the swivelling lazy Susan serving platter. Shum then cuts back to Jade, who reasserts her family's difference to rupture the American situation comedy's mythological white paradigm for the North American family: '*The Brady Bunch* never needed subtitles.' Shum deploys the co-ordinates of the white American sitcom only to demonstrate popular culture's erasure of difference, something that her own film will correct.

Elsewhere in the film Shum interrupts the signifying systems of a white popular culture that objectifies Chinese in North America as ethnographic stereotypes by inhabiting these co-ordinates of racialization in an ironizing performance that denaturalizes the stereotype and re-inscribes a Chinese-Canadian humanity. Shum represents the film industry as constraining Chinese to perform white essentialist versions of Chinese difference. At an audition for a small part as a waitress, Jade is asked to deliver her paltry two lines with an accent. Playing against type, Jade asks the director if he would like her to do a Parisian accent. Greeted with a blank stare and silence, Jade concedes to the desires of the white cinematic apparatus, lowers her eyes and performs white culture's version of her

Plate 21 Double Happiness (1994). © First Generation Films. 'Not the Brady Bunch'

essential difference, a subservient Asian woman who speaks broken English with an accent: 'Yes, a very good Chinese accent I can do for you.' By positioning Jade so that she inhabits the co-ordinates of racialized caricature that have structured Chinese-Canadian identity historically, Shum marks these co-ordinates as racist Orientalist fantasy, something produced by and for the white camera eye. Shum also subverts the popular culture stereotype of Chinese in North America as martial arts practitioners in Jade's camp performance of kung fu moves as she cleans the house while dancing and singing the 1970s pop classic 'Kung Fu Fighting'. Her laughter and exaggerated movements render the stereotype a bad joke, a sign incapable of referring back to any Chinese Canadians in the diegetic world of *Double Happiness.*

By This Parting

Alberta film-maker and actor Mieko Ouchi's experimental documentary *By This Parting* (1998) inhabits the co-ordinates of identity constructed by the Orders in Council that racialized and interned Japanese Canadians as enemy aliens to the state. Unlike the state-sponsored documentary *Of Japanese Descent: An Interim Report* where Japanese Canadians are appropriated as signifiers of the abject, threatening, unclean and silenced enemy alien by a white racist and nationalist propaganda discourse, Ouchi's film re-presents the experience of interned Japanese Canadians from their own perspective, in their own words and images. Ouchi provides a highly imaginative re-visioning of the internment experience through the intersection of different media – photographs, poetry, music and dance – to represent the story of an aunt, Mrs Chiba, who was interned at New Denver. Through voice-over, the poetry of New Denver Issei writer Chie Kamegaya, a contemporary of Mrs Chiba, narrates internment-era photographs of New Denver taken by Mrs Chiba. These photographs are cross-cut with images of Kita No Taiko (Edmonton's Japanese Drummers of the North) in performance at various locations in New Denver, and creative re-enactments of Mrs Chiba's life, all of which are structured by the four seasons (Figures 6.1–6.2). The film's press release describes the re-enactments as 'creative speculation about what [Mrs Chiba's] time was like' under internment in New Denver's TB Sanatorium.

Significantly, Ouchi's inhabitation of the historical co-ordinates that contoured the dominant culture's representation of Japanese-Canadian subjectivity is informed by the late twentieth-century present. Ouchi's film creates a memory collage that is both personal and national, emphasizing what she refers to in interview as 'the liquid relationship between past and present' that she realizes through the Taiko drummers and voice-over (Ouchi 1999). While shooting Anne Wheeler's film *The War Between Us* (1995) on location in New Denver, Ouchi says she became very much aware of the imbrications of past and present and the problematic of re-presenting the internment. Starring in the CBC movie of the week as Aya Kawashima, a young woman interned with her family at New

241

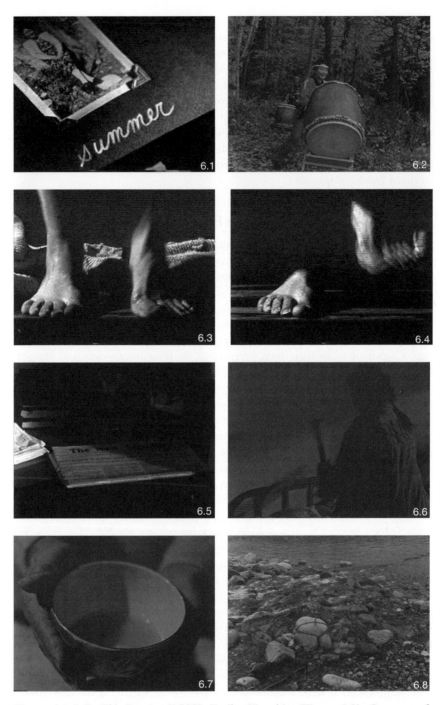

Figures 6.1–8 By This Parting (1998). Emiko Kinoshita (Figure 6.2). Courtesy of Mad Shadow Films Inc.

Denver, Ouchi found herself dressed in period costume speaking to Japanese-Canadian internment survivors living in New Denver. Before arriving on set Ouchi was worried about the representational work she was about to perform as an actor. 'My character was really the person that in some ways represented the emotional journey of Japanese Canadians, an iconic sort of character. I was suddenly asked to represent all these people that I didn't know and I didn't feel any connection to' (Ouchi 1999). Only later, when she was researching her first documentary, the autobiographical *Shepherd's Pie and Sushi* (1998), did she discover the New Denver photographs of her great-aunt and through them uncover the connection she has with interned Japanese Canadians. The Japanese Canadians she met on location for *The War Between Us* proved very welcoming because they saw in her performance a representation of their stories. Ouchi says, 'People would stop me on the street and pour out their heart to me – at restaurants, at stores, on the sidewalk.' Here, the production of Wheeler's film opens up an *unheimlich/heimlich* space for the return of long-repressed narratives of Japanese-Canadian alienation from the nation. It was also during the Anne Wheeler shoot at New Denver that Ouchi first encountered the haunted landscape of internment, something she would later translate into *By This Parting* through the presence of the Taiko drummers. 'There's a reverberation – you know I'm not superstitious, but when I was in New Denver, there was that feeling of spirits of ghosts, or of people's energy that had been there. There was a presence of people there and I tried to get that across.' For Ouchi, the drummers in *By This Parting* represent 'the emotional journey of the photos'. Articulating her vision of the film, Ouchi describes one sequence in which the drummers flee from the camera and disappear into the forest: 'It was hard for me in a way to describe to the drummers why I wanted them to run away into the woods, but to me it was about the ephemeral kind of spirit. Because you feel, you feel a sense of, it sounds sort of corny, but ghosts or spirits.' Not only are the drummers a sign of the past haunting the landscape of New Denver, the landscape of the nation's collective imagination, they are, simultaneously, a sign of the present revisiting the past. In Kita No Taiko Ouchi re-inscribes a living Japanese-Canadian culture that was not erased by internment or dispersal/exile, but survives to commemorate and mark a resistance to the racist work of the Orders in Council.

The acoustic signs of the film's voice-overs also create a dialogue between past and present, between the contemporary voice of Mieko Ouchi attempting to uncover and commemorate the past and the 1940s voice performing the poetry from Chie Kamegaya's 'Seasons in New Denver'. Through a dialogue of voices – Ouchi's and Kamegaya's – and images – Chiba's photographs, re-enactments, shots of the drummers and contemporary New Denver landscape – Ouchi re-inscribes the human suffering of Japanese Canadians elided by *Of Japanese Descent*. In marked contrast to the Canadian state's denial that the camps in BC are internment camps – the voice-over in *Of Japanese Descent* issues a corrective calling them re-location camps – *By This Parting* names the experience of New Denver through Kamegaya's poetry. 'How strange to be alone in such a place; in such a beautiful prison, surrounded by strangers who've become friends.' The drumming of Kita No Taiko and the performance of Tsuneko Kokobo as Mrs Chiba are instrumental in affecting the anger and frustration of the interned that are repressed by *Of Japanese Descent*, which depicts happy faces smiling back silently from TB wards, shops, cub pack and baseball game. As Ouchi says, the drumming provides an emotional supplement to the photographs. The photographs, black-and-white images of the mountains, the internment camp or of Mrs Chiba alone on the shores of New Denver or alone with the internment cabins in the background, are documents that cannot fully express the emotional life lurking underneath their flat monochrome surface.

The drumming, photographs, re-enactment and poetry come together most strikingly in the sequence of shots depicting Mrs Chiba's anger and frustration through dance. A close-up shot of Mrs Chiba's bare feet pummelling the floor of the sanatorium to the violent beat of the drummers is cross-cut with photos of the internment camp in winter and narrated by Kamegaya's poetry: 'icicles bar the north-side window / my house a cage' (Figures 6.3–6.4). This sequence is followed by a coda of shots where Kita No Taiko inhabit the roles of interned TB patients performing the rage and anger of internment, beating the walls of the sanatorium and their suitcases with copies of *The New Canadian* in time to a furious drumming soundtrack (Figures 6.5–6.6). *The New Canadian* newspaper, founded in 1938, was a Japanese-Canadian publication concerned primarily with race relations and the unconditional acceptance of Japanese Canadians in Canadian life. Published in English, it also provided a forum in which Japanese Canadians could make their thoughts known to the white majority.[11] The frustrated beating of this sign of anti-racist discourse initially signifies refusal on the part of white Canada to attend the sound of those it oppresses. However, the shots of the drummers as TB patients are soon cross-cut with images of a traditional Japanese tea ceremony that introduces a sense of peace suggesting that these signs of Japanese-Canadian resistance have registered with the state. When the preparation of the tea is complete, the cup turned round three times and its most pleasing side turned towards the camera and extended to the viewer (Figure 6.7), the frustration of the drummers ceases, and they collapse on the beds of the sanatorium. In a film that forges connections between past and present the offering of the cup signifies a connection to the viewer to a sad history of race relations that must not be repeated. Ouchi sees what comes before the tea ceremony as a humbling of the viewer, before she or he can receive the gift of hope for the future the ceremony represents (Ouchi 1999). On a personal level she is also trying to forge a connection with her aunt, Mrs Chiba, to whom the film is a tribute: 'It's me tying a ribbon around a rock saying this rock has a good spirit, you should take note of who this person was' (Ouchi 1999). Ouchi's words, of course, echo the voice-over that narrates the establishing swish pan shots of rocks in the New Denver landscape, one of which has a rope tied around it (Figure 6.8): 'They say in the Shinto religion that spirits exist in nature in the trees in the grass, and especially in the rocks. They tie ropes around rocks with good spirits to pay reverence to them to share them with others.' The internment experience of Mrs Chiba is the gift Ouchi shares with the viewer, a gift of pain, resistance, triumph and hope. With these images of Japanese-Canadian spirits existing in the rocks of New Denver and the images referenced earlier of the Taiko drummers animating the energy of interned Japanese-Canadian spirits, Ouchi re-inscribes Japanese-Canadian belonging to Canadian nation on the very site of its denial, the internment camp. Moreover, the act of re-inscribing Japanese-Canadian identity into the landscape does a semiotic violence to white nationalist mythology that would construct Canadian nation through the co-ordinates of its snowy white northern landscapes that make it part of the '"Aryan" family' of nations (Berger 1966, 7). Canadian imperialist George Parkin's racist contention that Canada's climate 'is certain . . . to secure for the Dominion and perpetuate there the vigour of the best northern races' is refused by Ouchi's film (quoted in Berger 1966, 7).

By This Parting re-inscribes Japanese-Canadian humanity and belonging to the nation by appropriating the documentary genre, something the state used to dehumanize and expel Japanese Canadians from the body of the nation in *Of Japanese Descent*. Ouchi's inhabitation of the foundational co-ordinates of Canadian cinema marks its limits and explodes Grierson's model of the 'public information' film as one of 'the most powerful forms of directive statesmanship' (quoted in Morris 1987b, 38) by eclipsing its confining and marginalizing codes. Expressing her anxiety about working with the documentary genre, Ouchi says of *By This Parting*:

> I think I was afraid about making my documentary about the internment because in some ways I had a different perspective from the very informational documentaries that came out about the internment because my film is not an informational documentary. It's an emotional, personal glimpse into what it feels like.
>
> (Ouchi 1999)

Unlike the Griersonian film of public information that is invested in interpellating white citizen subjects, Ouchi's film hails the viewer as an imaginative interpreter of documents. The spectator is structured to see through the subjective camera agency of an unknown Other, perhaps a relative, who leafs through Chiba's photographs, and stimulated by the possibilities they provoke begins imaginatively to piece together the emotional life of one interned Japanese-Canadian woman that would otherwise remain invisible.

Masala

The biting satire of Srinivas Krishna's *Masala* (1992) also targets the racism of the Canadian state, locating it in the Ministry of Multiculturalism and the Department of Historical Artifacts and National Heritage, both of which he represents as ISAs responsible for the preservation of white privilege. Krishna ascribes the term 'postcolonial' to *Masala* and locates it in a Canada that he describes as 'the homeland of the old colonial father' (Krishna 1992, 46). The signification of postcolonial and colonial in Krishna's comments and in his film engages both the inherent racism of empire-building and the residue of nineteenth-century British colonialism palpable in the late-twentieth-century white invader-settler culture that constitutes the dominant construction of national identity in contemporary Canada. A meditation on the meanings of home and belonging for a diasporic Indo-Canadian community, *Masala* is a structurally complex and very rich assemblage of ironized samplings from a diverse field of cultural texts including Bombay cinema, music video, Hollywood cinema, Canadian hockey and Canadian state apparatuses. Explaining his understanding of the word masala in relation to his work, Krishna reveals his vision for the play of cultural signifiers in his film:

> 'Masala' is a word which means a mixture of different spices. Making the film, I started with the word, not with the story. The film continuously revolves around this word because it's one of those words that is so rich. Masala is a mixture. All these different spices come together in Indian cooking, forming a flavour that wasn't there before; neither is it there in any one of the particular spices – one of the things that is greater than the sum of its parts. But it's a very tenuous unity. Mixture to me is about purity and impurity, authenticity and inauthenticity, truth of self, loss of self; particularly revolving around the idea of kitsch. Because things that are impure are often kitsch. Therefore, the other meaning of the word in the film refers to Bombay kitsch films.
>
> (Krishna 1994, 23)

This play of cultural signifiers is evidenced in a dense plot where a blue-skinned Lord Krishna right out of the *Mahabharata*-inspired Bollywood theological films competes for devotional space with the Minister of Multiculturalism and dons a Toronto Maple Leafs sweater to intercede on behalf of Harry Tikkoo in a narrative that asks: where is home for a diasporic Indo-Canadian community? Krishna, the director, began asking himself this question in the wake of the 1985 bombing of Air India Flight 182 en route from Toronto to New Delhi killing 329 passengers. Krishna, who knew people on the flight, sees the bombing 'as a momentous, horrible event' for the Indian diaspora and locates his film in the context of diasporic imaginings of the disaster by Salman Rushdie (*The Satanic Verses*) and Bharati Mukherjee ('The Management of Grief') (Krishna 1992, 43). For Krishna, the destruction of Flight 182 'began to mean . . . that there is no going home' (43). In Krishna's words, all of his characters 'are in the process of claiming a home, or rejecting a home' (43). The film's establishing shots depict the explosion of a flight making that return home, an explosion that kills the human character Krishna's brother and parents, marking the return home as an impossible journey. Krishna is haunted by his decision not to join his parents on the ill-fated journey home. The action of *Masala* is driven by Krishna's (the man's) negotiation of this trauma, his unsuccessful attempt to claim a Canadian home.

Released from jail five years after the tragedy and having completed a heroin detox programme, Krishna attempts to return to his extended family and the Hindu community of Toronto. In the course of this attempted re-integration he encounters various characters who are trying to construct home with varying degrees of success. After a nasty confrontation with white ex-girlfriend Lisa, Krishna surfaces at the opulent home of his bourgeois Uncle Lallu Bhai Solanki. Social-climbing sari merchants Lallu Bhai and his wife Bibi are hosting a party for the Minister of Multiculturalism to mark the upcoming opening of a Hindu temple funded by the ministry when Krishna's ringing of their doorbell inter-rupts the proceedings. Ironically, the minister is making a speech in which he metaphorizes Canada as 'a home large enough for all faiths, all communities and all individuals' when Krishna's arrival redirects the focus of those assembled and the camera to himself, an individual who cannot find a space in this multicultural structure. Krishna, a character whose childhood experiences of racism discipline him to reject his own community and culture in favour of full assimilation, is removed from the social terrain of Canada by white racist thugs, the same thugs who taunt his cousin Babu. Krishna, the director, troubles the truth claim of the pluralist discourse offered by the Minister, not only by interrupting it with the character Krishna's arrival but by the subsequent jump cut from a medium close-up shot of Krishna on the threshold of Lallu Bhai's home to a medium close-up on the face of a white racist thug harassing Babu, the same thug who will kill Krishna at the end of the film. In this series of shots Krishna (the director) juxta-poses the official representation of Canada as a nation embracing cultural and racial diversity to the racist response of whites who feel threatened by this destabilization of a white hierarchical social terrain and who project their frustrations on to the Other.

Formally, this cut from Lallu Bhai's home, where the platitudes of official multiculturalism are celebrated, to the home of his cousin Harry Tikkoo, where Babu is terrorized by racist attacks, also introduces the audience to contrasting significations of the home place for the Indian diaspora of Toronto. The Tikkoos' is a working-class home placed under threat of repossession by the bank. Despite his job working for the state as a Canada Post employee, Harry Tikkoo's pur-chase on a home place in Canada proves to be a tenuous one. The instability of the home as a sign of belonging affects Babu deeply, exacerbating the feelings of insecurity produced by the racist attacks he is forced to negotiate. Babu fantasizes about belonging through no-money-down real estate infomercials that he hopes will secure a home for his father, grandmother and sisters Rita and Sashi. Grandmother Tikkoo, on the other hand, attempts to secure the Tikkoo home in Canada through the intercession of Lord Krishna on her son's behalf. Communi-cating with Krishna through a videotape playing on her television screen,

Grandma articulates the alienation she and her family feel in Canada, and begs this avatar of Vishnu the Preserver for his help: 'Help us we are outsiders here. Make life the way it was before we came to this land of supply-side economics and no-money-down real estate.' The diasporic longing for the impossible return to the home place is manifest here in Grandma Tikkoo's virtual return home to India as it circulates in the diaspora through media texts.[12] Lord Krishna intervenes in the world of the diaspora by appropriating a Canadian stamp worth $5 million and sending it to Harry Tikkoo. Once in possession of the stamp, an object desired by the white nation, Harry is in a position of power and can secure a place of importance in the nation, but only through the agency of the Ministry of Multiculturalism and after withstanding threats from the Department of Historical Artifacts and National Heritage.

Krishna attempts to achieve a sense of belonging through the assimilating identification he makes with the white Hollywood James Dean masculinity of *Rebel Without a Cause* (Nicholas Ray 1955).[13] Krishna adapts the leather jacket and switchblade persona to protect himself in a world from which he is doubly alienated. Memories of his parents and uncle being subjected to racist attacks which they failed to repel leave him with disdain for his own culture. He views his parents and Harry Tikkoo as 'losers' because they were not 'tough' enough to fight back. When Lallu Bhai speaks to him in Hindi, he calls the language 'gibberish'. Speaking to his character Krishna's self-hatred and discomfort with Indianness, Srinivas Krishna explains:

> it comes in trying to take the *Rebel Without a Cause* kind of character and examine his alienation. In this case that's where it comes from. If you have enough racism directed against you, like it was here in the 70s, at some point you find yourself wavering between self-hatred and self-glorification.
>
> (Krishna 1992, 46)

Ironically, it is his identification with the tough white *Rebel Without a Cause* masculinity that figuratively and literally kills him. When the same white punks who have been harassing Babu, and who earlier screamed the racial epithet 'Paki' at Krishna and Babu from a passing car, accost Rita and Krishna on the street, it is the sign of the appropriated leather jacket that is used to racialize Krishna as a piece of shit. The leader of the three racist youths laughs at Krishna and confronts him with a racist joke: 'What do you call a Paki in a leather jacket? Full of shit.' Krishna, however, refuses to reflect back the subordinate Other image the joke demands. He rebels against racialization, denying the joker the sense of white racial superiority the joke is predicated upon. The white joker's failure to reduce the Indo-Canadian Other to a piece of shit short-circuits the visual structure of racism leaving him without an index of his superiority.[14] Devalued by his peers because he backed down to a 'Paki', the white joker's next step in performing his power over the Indo-Canadian Other is to remove the Other from the social terrain through murder; with the encouragement of his friends he stabs Krishna in the back. From the very first time he appears on Lulla Bhai's doorstep Krishna signifies as a disruptive figure of the *unheimlich*, a sign of what Srinivas Krishna says his film is about, 'the difficulty of living together' (Krishna 1994, 23). He is the return of the repressed, a spectral reminder of violent cultural irruptions in what the Minister of Multiculturalism contends is the diversity-embracing home of the Canadian nation. For Bibi his presence conjures up the deaths of her sister, brother-in-law and nephew who died in a terrorist attack she blames on Sikh separatists. Krishna is on Lallu Bhai's doorstep because Sikhs and Hindus have difficulty living together.[15] For the white punks, Krishna constitutes the *unheim-lich*, the unfamiliar, alien, literally non-*heimisch* or, translating from the German, non-native who ruptures the white racist mythology of the national home as a homogeneous white space.[16]

Official state multiculturalism is offered to both the Tikkoos and the Solankis as a route to a home in Canada, as a way of belonging to the nation. There are, however, rules for belonging, as the Minister of Multiculturalism explains to Sashi in the national space of his office, a large open room covered with Canadian flags. Responding to Sashi's questioning of the rules, the Minister reveals that 'with plain old human politics you may not always get justice, but at least you know how things work'. He proceeds to explain his understanding of multi-culturalism: 'You can come to Canada, set up an immigrant woman's collective, build your temples, have your processions, keep your identity' as long as you play by the rules. And this is the problem Harry Tikkoo raises. According to the minister, Harry angers white Canadians not because he has a $5 million stamp but because he refuses to play by the rules; in the words of the minister he refuses to 'compromise'; i.e. he will not simply do what the government demands. Harry's refusal to surrender his stamp to the Department of Historical Artifacts and National Heritage makes him a 'criminal' in the eyes of the Canadian state.

That Canada is 'a homeland of the old colonial father', as Srinivas Krishna puts it, is impressed upon the viewer not only through the white Minister for Multi-culturalism, but also by John MacDonald, the white agent from the federal gov-ernment's Department of Historical Artifacts and National Heritage who speaks with a crisp English accent when he arrives at the Tikkoo household to recover the stamp that Lord Krishna has brought into Harry's possession. Bearing the name of Canada's first Prime Minister, John MacDonald is a sign of entrenched white Anglo-Celtic power in Canada. The Government of Canada claims that the nineteenth-century stamp impressed with the image of a Canadian national icon, the beaver, is 'vital' to the preservation of Canada's national heritage. Clearly, the stamp is 'vital' to ensuring a very specific white Anglo-Celtic inheritance for the nation. The efforts to preserve this artefact of the white colonial nation disavow the diversity espoused by official multiculturalism, supporting the mythological white Canadian nation that haunts the Canadian social terrain in the acts of racist violence against Indo-Canadians represented in the film. Semiotically, the stamp is a signifier of the Dominion of Canada's white empire-building and becomes, for the government, the national Thing usurped by the Indo-Canadian Other. For as Slavoj Žižek argues, 'what is at stake in ethnic tensions is always the possession of the national Thing: the "other" wants to steal our enjoyment (by ruining our "way of life")' (Žižek 1992, 165). This appropriation of the national Thing, or what Žižek calls, after Freud, 'materialized enjoyment', is emphasized by Srinivas Krishna in Lord Krishna's 'theft' of the stamp from Canada Post while dressed as an iconic signifier of Canadian nation, the hockey player (Žižek 1992, 165). As we have seen in *Hot Ice*, hockey has, historically, been produced as the materialized enjoyment of the white nation; here it is purloined by the Other. In Krishna's film the stamp and hockey represent whiteness, specifically the phantasy of white nation as a materialized enjoyment that is troubled by the presence of the Other. The white male space of 'hockey talk' enjoyed by two postal employees is interrupted by the appearance of Lord Krishna and the aesthetic transformation of that formerly white phantasy space to an Indo-Canadian phantasy space as this is signalled to the viewer through *mise-en-scène* and soundtrack. This sequence of shots begins, significantly, in a Canada Post 'Dead Letters' delivery truck; Krishna represents the 1867 epistle of white privilege that Harry receives as a 'dead letter'. Two white male postal workers are listening to a radio broadcast lamenting that hockey 'ain't what it used to be' when *faux*-Bollywood music begins to fade in to the soundtrack displacing the broadcast. The camera then cuts to a behind-the-shoulder shot of the two men to reveal Lord Krishna, surrounded by dry ice, back-lit, swathed in blue light, wielding a hockey stick and sporting a Toronto Maple Leafs jersey. The slapshot he takes goes hurtling towards the windscreen of the truck, causing the driver to lose control, and the 'dead' letters, including the nineteenth-century missive of white Canadian nation that will eventually find its way to Tikkoo, to go flying out the back door of the truck. Tikkoo's appropriation of the stamp temporarily gives him something official multiculturalism does not, meaningful recognition. As he explains to his daughter, 'A plane load of people gets blown up and nobody seems to care. I get beaten up in the street and nobody seems to care. I hold this stamp in my hand and everybody cares.'

The co-existence of the Ministry of Multiculturalism and the Department of Historical Artifacts and National Heritage in *Masala* represents the kinds of contradictions that Himani Bannerji and Smaro Kamboureli locate in the Multicultural Act, the gesture towards cultural pluralism on the one hand, and the enshrining of 'founding' white nations on the other, that marks an inequitable Canadian social space. When Tikkoo refuses to hand over the stamp, John MacDonald informs him of the lengths to which the Canadian state will go to recover that nation's white inheritance: 'Prepare, the Canadian government will take action swiftly and ruthlessly.' The nation's official policy of multiculturalism as stated by the Minister to Sashi does not address the inequities of representation in positions of power faced by peoples of colour nor does it contribute to anti-racist work. In the world of *Masala*, official multiculturalism aids and abets the agenda of the Department of Historical Artifacts and National Heritage by

containing cultural differences through the spectacle of multicultural processions, foods and temples. Commenting on the practice of multiculturalism in
Canada, Srinivas Krishna says, 'Today, there's deep-rooted doubt about the
intentions behind the policies as they seem to become a way for politicians to
dole out money to ethnic groups, giving them the feeling they can preserve some
of their cultural identity. But that's really all – it's a way of buying votes' (Krishna
1994, 22). Bannerji is equally suspicious of the work performed by official
multiculturalism:

> Other than administering 'difference' differentially, among the 'minor-
> ity communities' multiculturalism bares the political processes of
> co-optation or interpellation. The 'naming' of a political subject in an
> ideological context amounts to the creation of a political agent interpel-
> lating or extending an ideological net around her/him, which confers
> agency only within a certain discursive-political framework.
>
> (Bannerji 2000, 116)

Ultimately, Tikoo's act of resistance is co-opted by the Ministry of Multiculturalism in a deal brokered by Sashi whereby he donates the stamp to the National
Museum of Philately and in exchange becomes the museum's honorary curator.
Tikkoo, however, is still held at a distance from the nation; he remains an 'honorary' member of a national body. This is the kind of multicultural move that
Bannerji reads as an interpellative function of the state's ideological apparatus
where 'administrative and ideological categories create *objects* out of the people
they impact upon and produce mainstream agencies in their name. In this way a
little niche is created within the state for those who are otherwise undesirable,
unassimilable and deeply different' (Bannerji 2000, 117).

The racially motivated murder of the unassimilable Krishna is overshadowed by
the multicultural celebration that marks the opening of the National Museum of
Philately, a scene that is cut to immediately following Krishna's death. The opening of the museum is presided over by the Minister of Multiculturalism, a white
official empowered in the name of the Other, a man to whom all those assembled
defer. Harry is quick to ingratiate himself with the Minister, and Grandmother
Tikkoo's devotions are no longer to Krishna but to the Minister, whom she
anoints and garlands with a traditional *mala*.[17] The 'political processes of coopta-
tion' are also visible in Anil Solanki's new role as the president of the youth wing
of the Minister's political party and Lallu Bhai's promise to make his son the next
Minister of Multiculturalism. As the discursive structure of the film indicates
through Krishna's death and the judging white gaze of the Minister of Multiculturalism through whose subjective camera agency we view the last shots of the
film, official multiculturalism does not interrupt the visual structure of racism.
The film suggests that, as Slavoj Žižek has argued,

multiculturalism is a disavowed, inverted self-referential form of 'racism

with a distance' – it 'respects' the Other's identity, conceiving the Other
as a self-enclosed 'authentic' community towards which he, the multiculturalist, maintains a distance rendered possible by his privileged position. Multiculturalism is a racism that renders its own position devoid of
all positive content (the multiculturalist is not a direct racist, he doesn't
oppose to the Other the *particular* values of his own culture), but none-
theless retains this position as the *privileged empty point of universality*
from which one is able to appreciate (and depreciate) properly other
particular cultures – the multiculturalist respect for the Other's
specificity is the very form of asserting one's own superiority.

(Žižek 1997, 44)

The racism that killed Krishna is not referenced in the official opening of the
National Museum of Philately either by the Minister or by Harry; multicultural
content is instead reduced to Grandma Tikkoo's preparation of what Harry
describes as 'a multicultural culinary treat'. In the film's final shots, the viewer is
structured by subjective camera to occupy Žižek's '*privileged empty point of universality*' to enter the subjectivity of Lloyd's 'Subject that *judges*' when she or he
observes the Other's performance of difference, Grandma's food preparation,
through the eyes of the Minister (Lloyd 1991, 75).

Srinivas Krishna's indictment of official multiculturalism as a racializing structure that co-opts and contains difference, *Masala* also performs the anti-racist
work of returning the white racist gaze. White viewers are forced to identify with
the gaze of the Indo-Canadian camera eye that reads the film's co-ordinates of
whiteness as the violent death-dealing racism of white punks or the condescending 'racism with a distance' offered by the Minister of Multiculturalism. Part of
Srinivas Krishna's anti-racist aesthetic is a re-inscription of the already presented
Indo-Canadian Other through the racializing co-ordinates of 'Paki' that have
stood in for Indo-Canadian historically. The character Krishna's rejection of this
racist appellation – his response to the racist white youths and his correction of
his girlfriend's assertion that he is a 'Paki', coupled with Srinivas Krishna's own
ethnographizing of his community, interrupts and denaturalizes white stereotypes of Indo-Canadian subjectivity. *Masala* re-inscribes flawed, and very human,
characters in the place of the abject 'Pakis' constructed by a white racism that
equates Otherness with excrement.

Srinivas Krishna's self-ethnographizing of the Indo-Canadian community has,
however, been received by some members of the Indian diaspora in Canada as an
internalized racism commodifying Indo-Canadianness for the vicious pleasure of
a white racist audience. The most polemical response to the film comes from
Yasmin Jiwani, who would almost certainly take issue with my application of her
earlier cited definition for decolonizing the screen to *Masala*. Jiwani's review of
the film appeared in the South Asian magazine *Rungh* and includes her descriptions of a heated exchange that took place between South Asian audience members offended by *Masala* and the film-maker after a Vancouver screening. Jiwani's

problems with *Masala* centre on the film's representation of sexuality and women. For her 'the sexual scenes in the film appeared to unveil parts of the community's code of relations, revealing the contradictions between community notions of *izzat* and actual social practices' (Jiwani 1992, 12). Jiwani is, no doubt, referring to the veiled Saraswati's sexual relations with Anil, something Krishna represents not as a reality but as a masturbatory fantasy of the boorish Anil. Failing to recognize this important distinction, Jiwani continues, articulating her fears that these representations are disclosed to 'a racist society that is quick to seize any representation that favours its interpretation of people of colour and their cultural traditions. There is no context provided in Krishna's egotistical and self-centred universe' (12). Furthermore, Jiwani's critique alleges that Krishna creates a skewed, utopian landscape that fails, outside of Krishna's murder, to represent unequal power relations in Canada (12). Clearly, her reading does not account for the unequal power relations *Masala* constructs between Indo-Canadians and the subordinating white Ministry of Multiculturalism or the Department of Historical Artifacts and National Heritage. Jiwani's interpretation of the film is undermined by the prescriptive inflection of her critique and her apparent refusal to differentiate between Krishna the director/writer and Krishna the character. Comparing Srinivas Krishna's representation of Indo-Canadians to Rudyard Kipling's colonial representation of Indians, Jiwani confuses the character Krishna's self-loathing and rejection of his Indianness with the interior life of his creator:

> There is no change in Krishna's world. The South Asian community has remained the same except in the form of Srinivas Krishna. His forays into the dominant society, into street life, somehow make him the only change agent around. His leather jacket is his sign of 'being with it,' and his sexual exploits qualify him not only as a hero but also as the modern renegade who seeks to dissolve a part of himself that he hates – his own Indianness.
>
> (12)

Before accusing Srinivas Krishna of '[trashing] his culture in a public arena which has no sympathy for the South-Asian reality', Jiwani argues that *Masala*, 'as a voice from an otherwise silent minority . . . acquires the burden of representation', that is, it has certain responsibilities to the South-Asian community that she feels it fails to live up to. From Jiwani's perspective, *Masala* does not humanize the Indo-Canadian community by interrupting the racist white discourse of 'Paki', but instead 'reduces' the South Asian community in Canada to 'a monolith, our differences become merely inflections in the great mix of symbols, customs and traditions; a mere fragment in the tiered mosaic that is Canada; we are one dimensional again' (13).

In an interview with Cameron Bailey, Krishna discusses the same angry Indo-Canadian responses to the film's Vancouver screening that Jiwani documents in

her review. He engages those hostile responses and discusses what he characterizes as the 'unfair expectations' placed upon his film.

> This film becomes something of a film that all Indians invest their
> expectations in, because it's one of the first ones made here. So I have to
> be some kind of representative, which is unfair. I understand why it's
> expected, but it's a really difficult position to negotiate. I didn't make
> the film to please Indians, and I didn't make it to displease Indians
> either.
>
> (1992, 42)

Asked whom he made the film for, Krishna at first says he is unsure, but then
replies that he made the film 'for certain ideas', and that in a way *Masala* will
invent its audience (42). In fairness to Jiwani's sense of one dimensionality,
Krishna does admit that he is self-consciously playing with stereotypes in *Masala*:
'The whole film deals with stereotypes, and those stereotypes are the way we
would like to stereotype ourselves, the way others stereotype, and the way we can
assume stereotypes to maneuver in society . . . Part of what the film does is imply
the complicity of the viewer in stereotyping' (42). The film is populated by stock
characters, as Krishna puts it, 'in the way that you would find stock characters in
Restoration comedies' (43). Certainly, the Minister of Multiculturalism, John
MacDonald and the white thugs are representative 'types' of an alienating whiteness encountered by Indo-Canadians. Similarly, Lallu Bhai Solanki and his
cousin Harry represent two 'types' of immigrant experiences and the character
Krishna is the quintessential first-generation Canadian 'type' caught between two
worlds neither one of which embraces him. Srinivas Krishna, however, is hoping
to make spectators aware of their own complicity in stereotyping (Krishna 1992,
42). For example, the sex scene between Saraswati and Anil that so offended
Jiwani and others represents Anil's stereotyping of women as sexual objects, it is
not Srinivas Krishna's stereotyping of South Asian women. The bedroom scene
between Saraswati and Anil is clearly marked off from the rest of the narrative as a
fantasy space through a *mise-en-scène* of red satin sheets, and dozens of candles,
set decoration that Krishna describes as 'Playboy goes to India'. Anil is awakened
from his reverie by a ringing telephone that prompts a cut from the bedroom
scene to Anil shaking off the fantasy and answering the phone. None the less,
Srinivas Krishna reports that he has been inundated by charges that in this scene
he is 'degrading women' or that he's 'a misogynist' (Krishna 1992, 42). Through
the self-referential presentations of stereotypes Srinivas Krishna is trying to reveal
a slippage between the stereotype and the person burdened with it. 'What I'm
trying to do is say that things aren't what they appear to be, people aren't the
stereotypes they appear to be' (42).

A second review of *Masala* by Sanjay Khanna published in *Rungh* alongside
Jiwani's provides a dissenting perspective that finds Krishna's film to be relevant
to the Indo-Canadian community: 'I think that *Masala* relates in some way to

each of us, as individuals, cutting our own deals, choosing how we want to live, create, destroy and present our stories.' Khanna concludes his review with some instructive insights on the reception of films by Indo-Canadian directors:

> If there have been complaints about the film, part of the reason is that it is one of the first of Canadian origin . . . to receive a wide audience. It is not the film of a single community: such a film would nearly be impossible to develop and write because Indians in Canada come from multifarious backgrounds. This is why I doubt the claim that it is the filmmaker's responsibility to take on the role of pleasing everyone 'Indian' in Canada when India itself is divided, fractured, and erupting in violence.
>
> (Khanna 1992, 16)

Rude

As Helen Lee points out, Black or African-Canadian directors, not unlike Native film-makers, were constrained to document, not fictionalize, their experiences by funding structures and programmes such as the NFB's Studio D and New Initiatives in Film privileging documentary production above features (Lee 1994, 8). Documentary, however, proved to be an important genre for visualizing the long-elided history of the Black presence in Canada and African-Canadian experiences of systemic racism. While white Canadians like to think Blacks have been treated more equitably in Canada than they have in the United States, there was slavery in colonial Canada, and racially segregated schools continued to be a Canadian reality into the 1960s.[18] The psychic and physical violence of racism negotiated by African-Canadians is documented in films such as *Home Feeling: Struggle for a Community* (Jennifer Hodge de Silva 1983), *Older, Stronger, Wiser* (Dionne Brand and Claire Prieto 1989), *Sisters in the Struggle* (Dionne Brand and Ginny Stikeman 1991), *Remember Africville* (Shelagh Mackenzie 1991) and *Speak It from the Heart of Black Nova Scotia* (Sylvia Hamilton 1992). These films and others begin to fill the lacuna left in the visual fabric of the national cinema by the aborted 1944 Crawley/NFB co-production *Negroes*. The more recent NFB productions cited above also supplement the deceptively 'benign' images of smiling African Canadians teaching school, learning the history of white invasion and settlement, practising medicine and playing the piano left to us in the raw footage of *Negroes* preserved in the National Archives. Films such as *Older, Stronger, Wiser* and *Remember Africville* name the racist and segregated cultural context in which *Negroes* would have been produced, factors which remain present, but unarticulated beneath the surfaces of *Negroes'* surviving images. However, it was not until 1995 that *Rude*, the first Canadian 35-mm dramatic feature written, directed and produced by a Black team, was released.

Clement Virgo's film represents a Black Canadian community, what he refers to in a press kit interview as 'transported Africans', in a highly aestheticized urban Canadian environment, and it is the concept of Blackness in Canada that I want to clarify before moving forward with a reading of Black community in *Rude* (Virgo 1995). As George Elliott Clark, Cecil Foster and David Sealy are quick to register, Blackness in Canada is not homogeneous, but contoured by a multiplicity of determiners such as class, history, gender, sexuality and cultural heritage.[19] The diversity of Canadian Blackness becomes clear in even a cursory glance at patterns of immigration, from the slaves and freedmen who immigrated to Nova Scotia and Ontario from the United States at the time of the Revolution and during the Civil War, to the African Americans who immigrated to Saskatchewan and Alberta from Oklahoma in 1909, or postwar immigrants from the Caribbean and more recent arrivals from the African continent. However, as Cecil Foster writes of the construction of diverse groups into a Black community in Canada,

> we are *blacked* out in a common community. And if the dominant culture agrees that the black community – a people that sold itself into colonialism – is a community, then a community we become. That is how we are forced to relate to the wider society, as a community, even if members are from different backgrounds and circumstances.
>
> (Foster 1996, 25)

This process of diverse identities shifting into a collective Black Canadian identity is usefully concepetualized and located in the context of cinematic representation by Stuart Hall in his thinking around the production of cultural identity in Third Cinema:

> Perhaps, instead of thinking of identity as an already accomplished historical fact, which the new cinematic discourses then represent, we should think, instead, of identity as a 'production', which is never complete, always in process, and always constituted within, not outside, representation.
>
> (1989, 68)

Virgo's production of Canadian Blackness is very much tied to the Caribbean-Canadian community in Toronto, specifically the Jamaican community from which the film borrows some of its music and Rastafarian iconography. Trying to find a genre for a film about Black characters that would trigger production money, Virgo soon found himself negotiating Hollywood's representation of inner-city life for African Americans, the ''hood' genre:

> I knew that to get this film made in Canada, it would have to have elements that were easily recognizable, elements that people who invest hundreds of thousands of dollars would recognize as commercial elements. That meant the 'hood, guns, a little bit of drugs. I consciously drew on those things, but I knew I didn't want to add to the slew of urban

'hood movies, I knew I couldn't imitate *Menace II Society* or *Boyz N the Hood*; I don't know anything about that world.

(Virgo 1995)

Not unlike the white Anglophone and Francophone directors we looked at in Chapter 4, Virgo must translate a Hollywood genre into a Canadian context. The difference in repetition Neale defines as genre is located in Virgo's desire to 'depict Black people who are struggling with more than drugs and guns – but also with loneliness, their sexuality, loss of love – situations and circumstances that all people experience' (quoted in Conquering Lion Productions Press Kit). According to the film's press kit, Virgo 'wanted to take the urban 'hood movie worn bare by too many exploitative efforts and open it up to new possibilities' (Conquering Lion Productions Press Kit). Virgo's appropriation of a Hollywood model for the representation of African-American experience is a compelling example of George Elliott Clarke's conceptualization of Canada as 'an American space that warps Americanité'. Clarke writes, 'remarkably, an African-Canadian sensibility may be articulated at the very point where it seems to vanish: at the moment when African-American texts seem to possess African-Canadian ones' (1998, 28). Virgo warps Americanité in his imagining of an African-Canadian 'hood: 'I created my own 'hood where a lion could roam, where mystical aboriginal spirits could dance among urban, transported Africans' (Virgo 1995).[20]

Structurally and aesthetically, *Rude* articulates its difference from the Hollywood 'hood film by taking three separate story lines and mediating them through pirate radio DJ Rude, a trickster figure whose image and voice haunt the visual and aural spaces of the film's three separate narratives. Rude's rich raps often narrate the emotional lives of the community including the film's three principal characters – recent ex-con and former drug-dealer Luke, the emotionally distraught Maxine who ponders an abortion after her breakup with André, and Jordan, the young boxer coming to terms with his emerging homosexuality. Rude's image dissolves in and out of shots in which these characters appear, and is frequently intercut with these characters. Adding to the surreal and abstract visual landscape of the film are Virgo's use of front-screen photography and Rude's projected shape-shifting self, the Conquering Lion of Judah, that appears wandering throughout the community and in shots with the three principals. Set on a Toronto housing project over Easter weekend, *Rude* tracks the destruction, redemption and resurrection of these three lives.

Rude herself is the fragmented, criminalized body of the community that is made whole, and resurrected over the Easter weekend. For Virgo, Rude is the 'collective consciousness', the 'voice of the community' (quoted in Conquering Lion Productions Press Kit). For the majority of her time on camera Rude is revealed to the viewer in dimly lit close-up shots which fragment her into pieces, a face, lips, head and torso, her eyes hidden by dark glasses. It is only on Easter Sunday that we see her full face in the frame: unobstructed by glasses, resurrected

257

and fully visible, she looks directly into the lens in a daylight shot. As an allegorical figuration of Black community, it is not surprising that she is criminalized by the police officer who calls promising to shut down her Black voice and imprison her. As is the case in many American urban centres, the Metropolitan Toronto police force, aided and abetted by mass media representations, has associated Blackness with criminality.[21] In a 1991 interview with Peter Jackson, Metropolitan Toronto Police Association President Art Lymer claims, 'We do not have a racist police force,' but then goes on to talk about 'Black Crime':

> some of the people that have come over here from Jamaica . . . are prone to violence, they are very violent. They have very little respect, you know, for life . . . It's the infiltration of drugs and the one main drug is crack and the people that were pushing that in the communities, 98 per cent of them were Blacks. And of the Blacks, I think about 90 per cent of them were from Jamaica.
>
> (quoted in Jackson 1993, 189)

As Jackson notes, Lymer's remarks are based on questionable evidence, as the Police Services Board 'forbids the collection of crime statistics by "race"' (189). In Virgo's film the intolerable racist oppression of Blacks in Toronto is played out on two fronts, Rude's subversive broadcast of African-Canadian experience and the manipulation and racialization of Luke and his brother Reece by the white American drug lord, Yankee.

The film's establishing shots position Rude and community in opposition to a white racist Canadian state. Virgo cuts from a medium close-up shot of Rude's alter ego, the Conquering Lion of Judah, to a medium shot of Rude speaking into the microphone on her revolving DJ console:

> I come to you via the last neighbourhood in the world, pirate radio. The signal stretches from the land of the Zulu-Zulu nation all the way to the land of the Mohawk nation. And for the next two nights we'll steal Babylon's airwaves and let them reevaluate their immigration policy. The trip is about you bringing the verbal intercourse and I'll bring the noise. So cock the hammer, sharpen your spears, throw stones, the *coup d'état* has begun.

Rude's invocation of the colonial contest constructs the white Canadian state as an invader-settler culture whose immigration policies continue a colonial practice of privileging white immigration above Black immigration. Later in the film when the police officer threatens to shut down her transmission of Black diasporic experience in Canada she reminds this agent of the white state that it was white colonial desire that established Blackness as Canadianness: 'Too late officer. You brought many Zulus to the land of the Mohawk. We are here to stay. See you.' Historically, it was white invader-settler culture that brought Blacks as

Plate 22 Rude (1995). © Conquering Lion Productions. DJ Rude (Sharon M. Lewis)

slaves to North America and contemporaneously Blacks in Canada are exploited as a cheap labour pool earning far less than whites.[22] Rude's re-naming of Canadian nation as Babylon, and her re-inscription of the Mohawk and Zulu Nations, indicts white Canada's complicity with British imperialism and draws a parallel between two subordinate groups whose access to power has been limited by white colonialism. She reminds her listeners that Canada has a long history of racializing and oppressing those it structures as Others to the nation. In this her first transmission of the film narrative, Rude also invokes Rastafarianism as an oppositional discourse of empowerment in her reading of the white Canadian state as Babylon. Considered a location of exile, a Patois dictionary defines Babylon as a 'corrupt society, government and institutions, as an oppressive force; the police as agents of' (Steffens 2000).[23] For Joseph Owens 'Babylon is, in sum, the whole complex of institutions which conspire to keep the black man enslaved in the western world and which attempt to subjugate coloured peoples throughout the world' (Owens 1976, 70).[24] Rude invites her listeners to vent their anger at the state through 'verbal intercourse', call-ins to the show that she hopes will work toward overthrowing what she sees as a racist regime. Through Rude and the Luke–Reece narrative Virgo represents whiteness as interpellating Blackness along the lines of an abject criminal subjectivity that produces self-destructive tendencies within Black subjects.

Rude's expression of Blackness through her theft of the state's airwaves defines her as a criminal to Officer Milliard, a stereotype she is willing to reflect back to him ironically as an act of resistance. Inflecting the white stereotype of 'criminal nigger' that Milliard imposes upon her with the empowering and trans-formational properties of Rastafari, Rude resists the white state's attempts to silence her truth, telling her listeners: 'Boys and Girls Babylon seeks my where-abouts. Officer Milliard, my description is simple. I am the Conquering Lion of Judah. Go on, take a look out your window, you might see me. I am the nigger with the gun in her hand.' The irony here is located in the doubled space Rude claims. She identifies herself to Milliard as the Conquering Lion of Judah, Ras Tafari, the deliverer of her community from the forces of Babylon, but knows that through the visual structure of racism all he will see if he looks out his window is 'the nigger with the gun in her hand'. Unlike some of her listeners, Rude is very much aware of the self-destructive dangers of what W.E.B. Du Bois has called double-consciousness, an insidious process whereby the dominant culture disciplines raced Others to see themselves through its racializing eyes. Writing about the African-American experience in 1903, Du Bois describes double-consciousness as 'a peculiar sensation . . . this sense of always looking at one's self through the eyes of others, of measuring one's soul by the tape of a world that looks on in amused contempt and pity' (1903, 16–17). Through this process Black subjects can come to see themselves as the gun-toting criminal 'nigger' stereotype. And it is the destruction of this stereotype that Rude calls for in her Destruction Rap: 'when I get high I like to destroy shit. Kick my kids in the head and *then go out and kill somebody that looks like me.*' Rude's call for self-destruction confuses one of her callers who asks, 'we niggers are going to des-troy ourselves tonight is that what you are saying?' Rude's response 'hm-mmm' affirms not the physical destruction of self but the psychic deconstruction of the internalized white stereotype of 'nigger'.[25]

What I am calling Rude's 'Destruction Rap' must also be read in the context of Luke's move to destroy the criminal 'nigger' stereotype in the scene immediately preceding Rude's call for destruction, and Reece's double-consciousness that allows the stereotype to destroy him. Luke refuses Yankee's offer to return to the world of drug dealing, throwing the drug money Yankee had given him earlier as a signing bonus on to the pool table and proclaiming: 'You're looking for a nigger. I'm not a dealer.' Reece, however, allows himself to be defined by Yan-kee, a character Virgo associates with the ugly underbelly of a criminal white imperialism through *mis-en-scène*. The cantered shots of Yankee's headquarters mark it off from the rest of the film as a locus of criminality and reveal a space adorned with the artefacts of a stolen African culture, masks and tribal shields from Zimbabwe. Yankee is a collector of things African including Luke and Reece, whom he regards as his possessions, things he can discard, in the case of Reece, but also things that he will not let go of without a fight, in the case of Luke. When Yankee hails Reece as 'an ugly fucking chimp' and tells him 'When a white man thinks of a nigger he thinks of you, when a white chick thinks about getting raped and murdered, you're the dick-grabbing nigger that she sees . . . You're a haircut posing as a Black man', Reece is unable to destroy the stereo-type; conversely he lets it destroy him. After internalizing Yankee's hateful constructions of Blackness, Reece attempts to rape his sister-in-law Jessica and then gets high on crack. Confronting him in the local stairwell-shooting gallery, Luke asks his brother, 'when do we become men?' In the discursive structure of the film narrative a malignant whiteness signified in Yankee inhibits the development of Black male subjectivity. In the context of Virgo's film, Black criminality has a white source, Yankee. Babylon or the Canadian state is also the locus of a criminalizing of Blackness in Officer Milliard's defining of Rude's voice as illegal. However, Rude's broadcast begins to destabilize white stereotypes of Blackness, she provides a public forum for a multiplicity of Blacknesses to speak for themselves.[26] The reconstruction of African-Canadian identities is effected in *Rude* through Black cultural forms such as the reggae and gospel music of the soundtrack, the orality of the narratives shared by Rude and her callers and Rastafarianism. Rude peppers her broadcast with references to sightings of His Majesty, the Conquering Lion of Judah, Ras Tafari, the Messiah who will deliver her community from Babylon. At one point she addresses her listeners as 'sufferers' and tells them there are sightings of 'our Majesty. He's out there, go on look for him in those unexpected secret places.' At another point she claims she is the Conquering Lion of Judah, 'the nigger with the gun in her hand'. The only 'nigger' with a gun in her hand is not a 'nigger' at all; Jessica, Luke's lover, is a Black woman who has infiltrated Babylon, she is a Metro Toronto cop, who delivers Luke and her son from the criminalizing clutches of Yankee, by shooting him dead. The Conquering Lion of Judah is indeed found in unexpected secret places. Jessica's gunshots are read by Rude as trumpets of Jah: 'Our majesty has forgiven us and our sins are washed away. We just heard trumpets disguised as gunshots signaling us home. So, all aboard the mother ship for those who want a chance at rebirth.' Rude's final message is an SOS for the African-Canadian diaspora, a voice-over that narrates a shot of a First Nations dancer performing in front of the Toronto skyline at dawn, and a shot of the Conquering Lion of Judah standing in front of the mural where Jessica liberated her family from Yankee: 'I'm sending out an SOS to the boys and girls that were taken from the mainland and brought to the land of the Mohawk and Ojibway. Home of the Braves. I'm sending out an SOS. If you are in reach of my voice give me a call. You know the number.'

Virgo's self-ethnographizing re-presentation of Black subjectivity takes the racializing co-ordinates of the criminalizing 'nigger with a gun' stereotype and through them re-inscribes a dignified Black humanity that will destroy the 'nigger' stereotype at its white source. Virgo, after Kaplan, returns the racializing gaze of a white society by structuring the vision of his spectators to identify whiteness with agents of repression, Officer Milliard, and, in the case of Yankee, criminality and repression. Jessica represents a potential route to forging a new sense of Black belonging to Canadian nation through the Blackening of white power structures.

The anti-racist work that I am arguing is effected through representation in the films discussed above, what Bannerji calls a popular multiculturalism, is, in part, financed by the political economy of official multiculturalism. *Moving the Mountain* was produced with the participation of Multiculturalism and Citizenship Canada, as were *Double Happiness* and *By This Parting*, while *Rude* was produced with the participation of Studio D's New Initiatives in Film programme. *Masala*, the one film that directly interrogates official multiculturalism, is the only film discussed that was not produced with the assistance of some government agency that facilitates multicultural policy. More recent programmes aimed at facilitating the work of film-makers of colour are the NFB's Ontario-based Reel Diversity Competition 2001 and its Documentary West unit's Diversity in Action Programme 2000–2001. According to its document, *Diversity in Action: A Cultural Diversity Initiative for Filmmakers of Colour 2000/2001*, 'Documentary West of the NFB is committed to increasing documentary and animation production by and about communities which are presently under-represented by the NFB' (National Film Board 2000). In spite of its contradictory logic – multiculturalism in a bicultural framework – official multiculturalism is contributing to a culture of resistance through the support it provides to minoritarian cultural projects. However, Bannerji's suggestion that the Canadian state has a long way to go before it becomes a liberal democracy is substantiated in the oppositional cinema of both First Nations and film-makers of colour.

7

SCREENING GENDER AND SEXUALITY

SCREENING GENDER

> Myth then, as a form of speech or discourse, represents the major means
> in which women have been used in cinema: myth transmits and trans-
> forms the ideology of sexism and renders it invisible – when it is made
> visible it evaporates – and therefore natural.
>
> Claire Johnston ([1973] 1999, 32)

This book has worked to denaturalize the stereotyping of women in Canadian
cinema and render visible the disempowering ideology of sexism at work in films
such as *The Wheatfields of Canada* (1908), *Clan Donald: A British Farm Colony*
(1925), *Back to God's Country* (1919) and *Drylanders* (1963) where the myth of
white woman as the inert womb through which white patriarchal nation is produced becomes 'natural'. We also troubled the woman-as-whore stereotype as it
is represented in *Back to God's Country* and *Saving the Sagas* in the racist spectacle of female Aboriginality. Through the characters of Dolores in *Back to God's
Country* and Xenobia in *Secrets of Chinatown* we saw how a phallocentric lens
translates woman into an object of desire, reduces her to a plot device that initiates the 'real' story, the quest of the male hero. We have been reading counter-
discursively to locate the male power structures producing and circulating these
fantasy projections of woman. In Chapter 4 we saw how women film-makers
begin to interrupt these mythologies in what I have read as Joyce Wieland's
problematic and conflicted gendering of Canada as a colonized female in *Patriotism, Part One* (1964) and *Reason Over Passion* (1967–9), and in Sandy Wilson's
privileging of a female Canadian experience over a male American one in *My
American Cousin* (1985).

How They Saw Us: Careers and Cradles

Although we have engaged cinematic constructions of femininity and masculinity
in our considerations of the cinema of invasion and settlement, ethnographic
cinema, and genre texts, I want to revisit the terrain of gender in this chapter to
read counter-cinema. One of the early, important moves towards a women's

counter-cinema in Canada was the re-contextualization of the national cinema's objectification of woman, a re-presentation of the evidence of the patriarchal camera eye through Studio D's 1977 re-release of old NFB titles in the *How They Saw Us: The Women's Archival Film Study Package* series. The eight films in this series were also re-titled with the series title *How They Saw Us* prefacing the original title to mark and denaturalize the phallocentric field of vision that created the original text. For example the 1947 *Canada Carries On* NFB film *Careers and Cradles* becomes *How They Saw Us: Careers and Cradles* in its 1977 reincarnation. Studio D director Ann Pearson and producers Kathleen Shannon and Yuki Yoshida inscribe the new context in which *Careers and Cradles* is to be read on two intertitles prefacing the film's original intertitle: 'This film has been re-released for its historic interest. The image it projects of women reflects the particular social demands and expectations of Canadian society at the time it was produced.' The second intertitle serves as an interpretative mechanism that manufactures a new feminist meaning inside a patriarchal text:

> CAREERS AND CRADLES. Made in 1947, this transitional film uses the celebration of token women of achievement as a way of justifying marriage as a career. It points forward to the 1950s emphasis on femininity and consumerism.

Although the language I have used above and the intervention that Pearson, Shannon and Yoshida make in a male bourgeois field of vision both echo Claire Johnston's conceptualization of women's cinema as counter-cinema, Johnston may be uncomfortable with including this kind of intervention under the rubric of counter-cinema, as her argument concerns work where women are the makers of the filmic text, not necessarily the re-makers. Dismissing as 'idealist mystification' notions that '"truth" can be captured by the camera or that conditions of a film's production (e.g. a film made collectively by women) can *of itself* reflect the conditions of its production', Johnston argues 'new meaning has to *be manufactured* within the text of the film' ([1973] 1999, 36). Although the work that Pearson, Shannon and Yoshida do to manufacture new meaning is performed, literally, *outside* of the original text, it attempts to hail or recruit spectators as subjects who will read what follows *inside* the text through a lens cognizant of the dominant sexist ideology that originally produced *Careers and Cradles*. However, the grafting of the subversive feminist intertitles on to a patriarchal narrative does begin to effect the break between ideology and text that Johnston calls for: 'Any revolutionary strategy must challenge the depiction of reality; it is not enough to discuss the oppression of women within the text of the film; the language of the cinema/the depiction of reality must also be interrogated, so that the break between ideology and text is effected' ([1973] 1999, 37). The 1977 interpretative intertitles alert the spectator to the ideological content of the film they are about to view: the celebration of token women of achievement as a way of interpellating female subjects who will embrace marriage as a 'career'. The

1947 introductory intertitle references a time when women were conducting a revolution and simultaneously contains protofeminist dissent by banishing it to the mists of history: 'Let's go back to the days when the hand that rocks the cradle was shaking the world.' This invitation to the viewer reveals the interpellative function of the film in its echoing of the title *Careers and Cradles*, placing woman's rocking of the cradle in the present active tense and woman as a world shaker in the past. Significantly, the intertitle is illustrated by a stylized line drawing depicting a male figure pursuing a female figure, anticipating the desiring gaze through which woman is objectified in the proceeding footage. From this intertitle a cut is made to a sequence of shots representing suffragette activism narrated by a male voice-over. Structuring a freeze-frame shot of a suffragette being carted off to jail by two police officers that dissolves into an image of a 'modern' postwar woman, the male narrator says: 'Women were fed up being the inferior sex. Today the campaigns of the suffragettes belong to history. There has been a revolutionary change in the status of women. In most parts of the Western World women can vote, own property, and practise any profession within their capabilities.' A disjuncture develops between this voice-over claiming that women have attained equality and the images of the 'modern' postwar woman which indicate an inequity in representation in her construction as, in Mulvey's term, 'object to be looked at'. Synchronous with the words 'revolutionary change', a series of shots is initiated representing woman as sexualized male fantasy. A medium close-up shot of the 'new woman' pulling a compact out of her purse cuts to a long shot of her straightening the seam in her stockings before cutting to two men observing her with lascivious smiles on their faces. From the medium close-up shot of the active desiring male gaze we cut to its specular object of desire, a close-up shot of the new woman fixing her makeup and hair in her compact mirror so that she might reflect back the image the dominant patriarchal culture desires (Figures 7.1–7.2).

These shots unfold as the male voice-over tells us about the advances woman has made in this brave new world of gender equality. Continuing with his narrative, the voice informs us that 'The most important gain was the self-respect and assurance that came with political equality. They now feel they're on an equal footing with the opposite sex. Man for his part is still adjusting himself to the idea.' This voice-over narrates a sequence of shots depicting the new woman riding the bus, standing above a seated male, demonstrating the equality of the sexes, that is he does not offer the 'weaker sex' his seat. However, the images synchronous with 'equal footing with the opposite sex' rupture any myth of equality the film narrative hopes to communicate. A cut to a close-up shot of the feet of the seated male and the standing female reveals a sight-gag, the literal unequal footing of the two sexes, the man in brogues, the woman in high-heeled shoes displaying her calf and ankle to the camera. Although we cut back to the indifferent look on the man's face, 'adjusting himself to the idea' of equality, the final image of the 'new woman' is one that fragments her body, the fetishizing shot of her feet in high heels. The eleven-minute documentary moves forward from here offering the viewer examples of successful women who enjoy careers in medicine, politics, astronomy, mechanical engineering, criminology, agriculture, journalism, literature and the arts, photography and publishing. However, woman's trajectory in *Careers and Cradles* mirrors that of Dolores in the earlier *Back to God's Country* by the former's construction of woman's lives outside the home as aberrations, and its containing of woman firmly in the domestic sphere in the closing shots of the film.

Narrating shots of a bride and groom leaving a church, the male voice-over asks and answers: 'And what of marriage as a full-time career? It's more popular than ever. For every eight women who married in grandmother's day, twelve choose marriage today.' Subsequent voice-over and images represent the modern woman as desiring consumer products, such as irons, pressure cookers, garbage disposal units: 'She wants them all.' Finally, the voice-over and the shots it narrates conflict again in the film's closing shots. Narrating a series of dissolving images depicting women in various career roles ending with the earlier shot of the 'new woman' checking her makeup and hair in a compact, the male voice-over assures the viewer that woman will never abandon domesticity. 'Although she will never abandon her role as wife and mother, she looks forward to a greater share in the world of today and tomorrow. A world which can be an adventure in happiness.' Potentially liberating images of a woman dressed in flying leathers and a plane ascending skyward towards the 'adventure in happiness' are abrogated by a cut back to the tarmac and the same woman grounded in male notions of female adventures in happiness, watching as the plane departs without her.

Although *Careers and Cradles* (1947) is an example *par excellence* of the figuration of femininity that Griselda Pollock sees patriarchal culture writing on to female bodies 'which are then disciplined to perform historically, culturally and socially specific regimes of sexual difference' (Pollock 1994, 7), *How They Saw Us: Careers and Cradles* (1977) creates new meaning 'by disrupting the fabric of male bourgeois cinema within the text of the film' through its inscription of

Figures 7.1–2 How They Saw Us: Careers and Cradles (1977). © National Film Board of Canada, 2001. All rights reserved

oppositional intertitles (Johnston [1973] 1999, 37). The interventions of Pearson, Shannon and Yoshida underscore the inequities of the national cinema's representation of women as signifiers in a man's discourse, where women are the narrated. Mary Ann Doane provides an eloquent description of this phallocentric optic where women constitute the looked at, acted upon, narrated, enigmatic problem to be solved: 'the cinema, the theatre of pictures, a writing in images of the woman but not *for* her. For she is the problem' ([1982] 1999, 132).

They Called Us 'Les Filles du Roy'

Québécoise film-maker Anne Claire Poirier, however, engages in a more active and sustained interruption of the dominant male-scripted mythologies of women in *They Called Us 'Les Filles du Roy'* (1974) and *Mourir à tue-tête* (1979), cinema *for* women that figures sexist ideology as the problem. With *They Called Us 'Les Filles du Roy'*, Poirier re-inscribes the female labour that helped to build and continues to maintain Québec nation through the conceit of letters addressed to absent men across a range of time beginning with invasion and settlement and continuing up to the early 1970s present of the film's production. In marked contrast to *Careers and Cradles*, this impressionistic documentary of women's lives is narrated by a female voice-over, thereby troubling the historical male monopoly on this transcendental, authoritative form of cinematic representation; Poirier evicts the 'symbolic father' from the cinematic space of enunciation.[1] Not unlike Joyce Wieland's gendering of Canadian nation, however, Poirier's gendering of Québec as a colonized white woman produces a problematic signification inserting whiteness as a universal signifier for Québec nation and absolving women of any complicity in the colonial project. Poirier acknowledges the colonization of First Nations by the snowshoed footfalls of an Aboriginal woman on the soundtrack that eventually materialize as a visual image who walks into a winter landscape shot, and by voice-over narration disavowing woman's role in colonization:

> But we weren't alone . . . though we acted as if we were; but we weren't. They're only savages you told me. We have every right . . . You had taken over their lands . . . You took everything, the caribou, the snow geese, the seals, the lakes, the mountains, the forests, and you took the women who were there. It was through the womb that we came to know each other the Indian woman and I. We fashioned new blood ties. I am proud when I discover her features in the faces of my children. It is a good and proper thing. I understand her even better now that I am a wife living in a conquered land, a colonized nation.

By unloading the moral responsibility of the colonial legacy on Québécois men, Poirier refuses what Anne McClintock argues were white women's 'ambiguously complicit' roles 'both as colonizers and colonized, privileged and restricted, acted upon and acting' (1995, 6). Despite white women's subordination to white men, they held a 'borrowed' power over colonized men and women as missionaries, teachers, nurses etc. Eliding this 'borrowed power', Poirier's voice of female Québec aligns itself with the colonized space occupied by First Nations women. This move to elide women's complicity in colonization, however, is undone by the very claims the voice-over makes about the white woman's essential role in the construction of Québec, a project coterminous with the colonization of First Nations. The female voice-over speaks of woman's role in inventing the new country and of raising children and making them into a nation. The entire film narrative attempts to recover the valuable but often undocumented work *les Québécoises* contributed to nation-building. Although Poirier makes First Nations woman visible, she is quickly dispatched, left behind in the film's representation of the historical world. The film presents a *pur laine* vision of Québec woman as *Québécoise* woman. After our fleeting glimpse of First Nations woman, no racial or ethnic minority women are presented as having contributed to the history of the Québec society. In the visual syntax of the film, *les Québécoises* displace First Nations women as figures in the Québec landscape. The same snow-covered and treed landscape in which we view the Native woman becomes the location for an interesting combination of shots and voice-over where *les Québécoises* lay claim to the land. A cut from one medium close-up shot of a white woman in the snowy landscape to another medium close-up shot of a different white woman in the same landscape is followed by a dissolve to a crane shot of five women cloaked in black, face down in the snow, arms spread as if embracing the ground. These shots are narrated by the following voice-over: 'Today we are called Marie, José, Suzanne, Hélène, Nicole, Monique. We are all descendants of the same race. We number a hundred, a hundred thousand. We are *les Québécoises*. Countless acts of faith, hope and love and many vows we had to take to God and to this our land.'

Continuing our discussion of *They Called Us 'Les Filles du Roy'* as part of a women's counter-cinema disrupting 'the fabric of male bourgeois cinema', let's return, briefly, to Poirier's transgressive use of female voice-over. In her concluding remarks on women's cinema as counter-cinema Johnston argues that 'ideas derived from the entertainment film should inform the political film, and political ideas should inform the entertainment cinema: a two way process' ([1973] 1979, 40). Poirier's adaptation of voice-over materializes this proposed aesthetic by, after Kaja Silverman, 'dis-embodying' the female voice contrary to the conventions of mainstream cinema where Silverman writes:

> for the most part woman's speech is synchronized with her image, and even when it is transmitted as a voice-off the divorce is only temporary: the body connected to the female voice is understood to be in the next room, just out of frame, at the other end of a telephone line. In short, it is always fully recoverable.
>
> (1984, 135)

There is no recoverable body to attach to Poirier's female voice-over. Continuing her discussion of the female voice in cinema, Silverman notes:

> the female voice almost never functions as a voice-over, and when it does it enjoys comparable status to the male voice-over in film noir – i.e., it is autobiographical, evoking in a reminiscent fashion the diegesis which constitutes the film's 'present,' a diegesis within which the speaker figures centrally.
>
> (136)

A political film documenting the lives of Québécoise women, *They Called Us 'Les Filles du Roy'* imports the female autobiographical voice-over of reminiscence from the entertainment film to constitute the film's present; however this generic 'difference in repetition' does not provide synchronicity between voice and body. Here the voice speaks for a multiplicity of female bodies that move across the screen. In this way the body of the speaking female subject resists recovery, resists reducibility to spectacle.

Poirier's female voice-over interrogates phallocentric representations of women, producing a counter-discourse interrupting these male mythologies of female subjectivity. One of the first myths that Poirier takes on is the monstrous feminine construction of *La Courriveau*, the woman convicted by an English court in 1763 of murdering her husband. Narratives circulated for years afterward of the flesh-eating *Courriveau*, sentenced to be hanged in chains until death, who continued to kill men from beyond the grave if they dared to pass the site of her execution.[2] As the camera tracks through a forested area at dusk alighting upon the crude empty metal approximation of human form that was *La Courriveau*'s death cage hanging from a tree, the female voice-over narrates (Figure 7.3):

> She was only thirty years old, *La Courriveau*. Do you remember how we used to frighten each other with tales of how she attacked men even after her death or so the legend goes? The Devil's creature. The witch. The Damned One. But do you know what really happened? Do you know that her trial was conducted in a language that neither she nor her witnesses could understand?

The metal cage becomes a visual sign of the image prison women are consigned to under a regime of phallocentric representation. From the shot of La Courriveau's death cage, criminalizing marker of the castrating woman, Poirier cuts to a contemporary shot of a prison for 'the Courriveau women of today' and then back to the hanging metal spectacle for woman while the female voice-over articulates woman's inequality under the law. Explaining the significance of the Courriveau case, the female voice-over tells us,

Figure 7.3 They Called Us 'Les Filles du Roy' (1974). © National Film Board of Canada, 2001. All rights reserved

It is the image of a criminal as shaped by legend. But of a female criminal and that's a lot more serious than a male criminal. Like a woman who's drunk. But it goes even deeper than that. What is a crime for us is not a crime for you. Prostitutes go to prison, but not the men who pay to use them. You claim that abortion is a criminal offence, but when you're with the boys you brag about all the women you've had. Do you ever stop to think about this?

Here the addressee of the female voice-over, the male subject, is confronted with the hypocrisy and inequity of a phallocentric representation of woman that criminalizes female subjectivity.

Poirier's film also creates a space for women's voices to articulate women's relationship to each other and the social order in a sequence where a group of young and old women sit around a table looking at photographs of their mothers and grandmothers. They are attempting to recover lives that have been lost to them through a patriarchal social order. Poirier cuts back and forth between photographs of the mothers and grandmothers and the women looking at the photographs, telling what they know of the women in the frozen black-and-white images. One of the women speaks of the social pressure that made men 'the reference points' creating a situation in which 'we don't really know our mothers'. Another offers, 'I think we're discovering nowadays the true relationship with one's mother. But society likes to make us forget that. We forgot their names just as they were obliged to give them up.'

Subsequent to the sequence of women discussing their relationships to each other and the world, relationships which have, for too long, been mediated by men, Poirier introduces an extended, poignant, beautifully shot and elegantly edited sequence foregrounding the labour of women's hands that is integral to the creation of the world. Shots of women working in the home, crocheting, cooking, cleaning, doing laundry, nurturing children and caressing their partners eventually yield to images of women working in menial jobs outside the home. Women are depicted in a range of activities from the manufacturing of clothing, to data entry and clerical work as well as bartending, and cleaning. One woman is

270

depicted cleaning the male preserve of the boardroom; no women are represented as occupying positions of authority. These shots of labouring women's bodies culminate in the image of the stripper or waitress serving or performing in a bar under the male gaze. Documentary shots of waitresses serving beer to men and taking turns dancing topless on the bar's stage are narrated by the film's female voice-over to interrupt and provide a response to a voyeuristic looking that would structure woman as sexualized spectacle. Speaking from the subject position of the stripper, the woman on display, the voice-over addresses the spectating male, interrogating and denaturalizing his phantasy of woman as silent, subordinate object: 'You only come to me when you are looking for a broad. Otherwise you wouldn't even be sure you were a man.' With this sentence the female voice-over confronts the male spectator with the knowledge that his masculinity is a construct predicated on a phantasy of woman as sexually available. Continuing to speak from the perspective of the exploited woman on display, the voice-over articulates the failure of the objectifying male gaze to see her, to see woman: 'I've been a call-girl, I've been a stripper. I dance almost naked and yet you still don't see me.' The objectifying and phallocentric male gaze sees only the phantasy it projects on to the female body, a phantasy that Poirier deconstructs through a symbolic and literal unveiling of the female body. Poirier fades to black from a freeze frame of the stripper and then fades in to a medium long shot of a female figure swathed in bandages, turning slowly on a dais as the bandages are unwound by another woman. The camera dollies in slowly until the woman's head is held in close-up, where it is revealed when the last length of bandage is pulled away. The camera then pulls back to first a medium, and then a long shot of the naked woman as the lighting is brought up to reveal the de-phantasized female body that the voice-over figuratively demythologizes in an attempt to disrupt the projection of male phantasy and render woman's body visible:

It is true they have always spoken ill of me. I've symbolized lust, sin, the devil, temptation. How many layers must be peeled off to discover that deep down my body has remained intact? And yet it's been exploited and humiliated in so many ways, for publicity, for scandal, and for profit. It's time we took back our own bodies and learned how to live in them, because only then will they regain their real beauty. Let's have our very own striptease, one that won't hurt for once. This might shock you or embarrass you, but look at me just the same. Because I am strong, courageous and of comely appearance. I am still a *Fille du Roy*. You call me Valérie. One day they dreamed up a Valérie. A home-grown Valérie, one of us. It was our first real skin-flick. At last, the uncensored body of *la Québécoise*. As if all those old lies were about to be unmasked. But there is no Valérie, except perhaps inside your own head.[3]

Mourir à tue-tête (*A Scream from Silence*)

Seven years later Anglophone film-maker Bonnie Klein indicts a pornography industry that exploits female bodies to reflect back the male phantasy of the sexually available woman on display in *Not a Love Story*.[4] Five years after the release of *They Called Us 'Les Filles Du Roy'* Poirier makes her best-known film about the violent materialization of male phantasy of woman as object on to the female body through rape, *Mourir à tue-tête* (*A Scream from Silence*) (1979). Poirier's film may be read as an answer to Johnston's call for the aestheticization of woman's interventions into the phallocentric field of vision; *Mourir à tue-tête* self-reflexively foregrounds and interrogates the cinematic conventions used to represent reality, in this case the reality of rape from a woman's perspective. Poirier's camera cuts from a harrowing rape sequence where the viewer sees from the subjective camera perspective of the raped to a dimly lit editing suite where two women are in the process of assembling the rape scene we have just been subjected to. As Joan Nicks's deft and insightful reading of this transition suggests, Poirier enacts a shift of power from the male rapist to the female director and editor:

> They stop the rapist's voice and control with the flick of a switch. Their technical control will determine the aesthetics and ideology of representing rape in and as film . . . In the editing room, women's work involves structuring and repositioning spectatorship through an interrogation of image-making processes. Here lies Poirier's inscription of feminist creativity and analytical control that takes the subversive text and informed spectatorship as the norm.
>
> (1999, 234)

The casting of the same actor in the roles of the rapist and the male director in the film's prologue suggests that cinema itself is the target of Poirier's re-visioning eye. Nicks offers the possibility of reading the rapist's attacks on the woman as 'attacks on Poirier's feminist camera, and simultaneously, as her diffusion of Hollywood's voyeuristic pleasure and the shot-reverse shot system' (235). Moreover, Nicks argues that the vision of Poirier's rapist is shot through with cinema's common coding of the female: 'from his perspective, the woman is mere surface, for his manipulation and framing' (237). Registering Johnston's call for an interventionist women's counter-cinema that manufactures new meaning *within* the text of the film, Poirier's repeated return to the two women in the editing room in *Mourir à tue-tête*, as Nicks argues, 'codifies a space that women artists must occupy to redirect film discourse' (232).

Our Marilyn

Brenda Longfellow redirects film discourse in her experimental documentary *Our Marilyn* (1987) through self-reflexive moves that aestheticize what Bill Nichols reads as her refusal of 'forms of visual pleasure grounded in a masculinist scopophilia criticized by Laura Mulvey' (Nichols 1991, 260). Longfellow repositions film discourse to locate, analyse and trouble the cinematic production of woman by reworking phallocentrically produced film images of Canadian marathon swimmer Marilyn Bell and Marilyn Monroe through voice-over, editing, optical printing and re-enactment to privilege the process of becoming and defer any fixing of gender identity. In an article considering *Our Marilyn* in the context of postmodernism and the discourse of the body, Longfellow reveals how psychoanalysis has informed her understanding of subjectivity as interminable process:

> The point insisted upon by psychoanalysis, however, is that the process of suturing the subject into meaning or gender is never complete, finite or without slippage. The process of the subject is not the once-and-for-all surrender to abyssal pleasures, the nihilist dreams of the postmodern, but a continual productivity, a continual process of oscillation between punctual meaning and its loss, between identity and its subversion.
>
> (1990, 182)

This oscillation is signified in *Our Marilyn* through voice-over in the developing and shifting identifications one of the film's female voices makes with, first, her namesake, Marilyn Bell, and then Marilyn Monroe. Narrating a close-up shot of a newspaper photograph of Marilyn Bell that fades into a close-up shot of Marilyn Monroe, the female voice reveals:

> You know, there were always two pictures on my wall. One of you and one of her, the other Marilyn, the one I wasn't named after, their Marilyn. Somehow these two images kept merging in my mind. Your body against the flag . . . hers against the red satin sheet of a Playboy centrefold. Growing up between your bodies, I could never decide what was the difference.

This offscreen voice dissolves into and out of others, the voice of her mother – a woman who went into labour during Marilyn Bell's swim across Lake Ontario – and the voice of Marilyn Bell. The voice-overs are, to use Silverman's term, disembodied, rupturing synchronicity between body and voice and any attempt to recover a totalized, discrete female identity. Discussing her intercutting of newsreel footage of Monroe entertaining troops in Korea with newsreel footage and re-enactments of Bell's swim, Longfellow raises the challenge facing feminist film theory and practice: 'How to image the female body differently within a tradition of representation in which the body image of woman has served as the ground of the most intense pleasure and anxiety within film' (1990, 185). She responds to this challenge with her film's 'radical rupture between voice and body' where 'the heterogeneity of the voices and commentary, always retrospective in relation to the visual immediacy of the swimmer's body, suspends the latter in a refusal of referentiality on the side of the "as yet not spoken," as that which is exterior to the symbolic contract' (1999, 185). This strategy enables the production of a body that is always becoming or in Longfellow's words 'a body struggling into vision' (185). Through this representation of female bodies and identities in flux, Longfellow proposes 'to interrogate the possibility of an other, of a figuration of voice, body and desire beyond the inherent limitations of hegemonic categories' (185–6). This interrogation is initiated by Longfellow's juxtaposition of Monroe and Bell both, as she puts it, 'enjoined in a spectacle of femininity, though from different sides, both upholding the contradictory parts of a unitary whole – the classical opposition of virgin/whore' (186). Longfellow re-writes these phallocentrically produced archival phantasy bodies with the optical printer to locate moments of aporia where patriarchal mythologies of woman begin to fall apart under the burden of representation, moments that reveal woman as more than inert cipher. Writing about her reworking of these images, Longfellow explains how the intensity of the optical printer rendered 'an invisible excess to the masquerade of femininity' visible:

> In two instances in the film the newsreel footage slows down, prolonging a gesture which reveals an undoing, a fraying at the seams of these ancient images of virgin/whore. One presents a coy complicitous Bell, her young virginal head draped in a towel which bizzarely [sic] ressembles [sic] a nun's cowl, who turns and stares into the camera. The other shows a transvestite Monroe, clad in a military uniform, who turns to offer a complicitous wink at the camera in an instance of delicious conspiracy.
>
> (186)

For Longfellow (186) this return of the gaze marks a moment when the voyeur is 'voyeurized', a term she borrows from Chris Marker. As described by Longfellow, the process of voyeurizing involves the interruption of a voyeuristic pleasure taken in the control over an 'oblivious object' that is here usurped by the 'willful "knowingness"' registered in the gaze returned from the screen. And it is in this 'playful acknowledgement of the game' of gendered looking relations uncovered by the optical printer that Longfellow believes resistance to patriarchal inscriptions on the female body resides (186–7). Of course the third body of the film, the body of re-enactment that Longfellow creates to re-present the arduous and interminable swim across Lake Ontario, provides an other space of resistance to male-scripted notions of a discrete, identifiable, fixable, knowable female identity and body. Through transfers between Super 8 footage, to 16-mm black-

and-white Longfellow also re-writes this body 'through the optical printer – its image, bleached, inscribed on different stocks, printed again and again, bearing the physical traces of authorship – of a body figuring a body: and the traces of its transformation where the body dissolves into abstraction, into carnal sensation and motion' (185).

Counter-cinema and the entertainment film: *Bye Bye Blues* and *I've Heard the Mermaids Singing*

To explore woman's cinema as counter-cinema we have looked at overtly political films of the experimental cinema. However, entertainment films such as Anne Wheeler's *Bye Bye Blues* (1989) and Patricia Rozema's *I've Heard the Mermaids Singing* (1988) – Canadian variations on the Woman's Film – provide a different but equally important site for reading women's cinema as counter-cinema. Unlike Poirier's and Longfellow's experimental avant-garde films which are widely known and respected within the academy, Wheeler's and Rozema's genre films have had a wider circulation in general release and through video distribution and television. These films are examples of, after Johnston, entertainment cinema informed by political ideas. Although it does not offer the radical formal interventions into bourgeois male cinema made by Poirier and Longfellow, *Bye Bye Blues* recovers an element of Canadian women's history not represented in any other Canadian feature film, the challenges and temporary opportunities presented to Canadian women by the Second World War. Charting the trajectory of a young military wife, Daisy Cooper, from the privilege of British Raj India through her separation from her husband during the war and her return to her father's house on the Canadian prairie, *Bye Bye Blues* focuses on Daisy's efforts as a single mother to negotiate a patriarchal symbolic order socially and economically. Upon her return Daisy finds herself living under the Law of the Father without an income while her husband languishes in a Japanese POW camp. Desperate for employment, Daisy asks for and is given, grudgingly, an opportunity to play piano in a local all-male band. Eventually she becomes the band's vocalist, a move that brings them greater popularity. Her father forbids her to play in the band, defining her as 'a mother and a wife' and telling her, 'while you're in my house you'll do as you're told'. Now earning her own money, Daisy and her children move into a rented home. Daisy's empowerment is, however, attained through her sexual difference, she is the female singer with the band, the female spectacle used to entice soldiers into the dance halls. Just as the band is about to break nationally, Daisy's husband returns from a Japanese POW camp, ending her affair with one of the musicians and re-establishing the domestic imperative that ends her career. Structurally, the film might be read as mirroring woman's trajectory in *Back to God's Country* where woman is permitted, temporarily, to circumvent the oppressive social structures of patriarchy that script her as wife and mother until the patriarchal social order is restored and she is unceremoniously pushed back into the domestic sphere. However, unlike *Back to God's*

Country and *Careers and Cradles*, *Bye Bye Blues* does not represent this entry into domesticity as an 'adventure in happiness', but as a lamentable loss. The final shots of *Bye Bye Blues* are not of the happy reconstituted family, rather they are composed of a reaction shot in which a tearful Daisy, standing alone, turns away from her husband's reunion with his sister and mother to watch her dreams disappear. Wheeler cuts away from a medium shot of Daisy to a subjective camera long shot revealing the band's bus, sign of Daisy's career and love affair, disappearing into the prairie landscape as Daisy sings 'Bye Bye Blues' on the soundtrack. Although very much removed from the aesthetic practices of Poirier and Longfellow, the documentary realism of Wheeler's film allows her to use conventional narrative to demonstrate the extent to which it entraps women.[5]

In contrast to Wheeler in *Bye Bye Blues*, the self-reflexive aesthetic practices of Patricia Rozema in *I've Heard the Mermaids Singing* reflect 1980s concerns with foregrounding the process of cinematic production. Rozema cuts back and forth between the narrative of the diegetic past and the main character and narratorial agent Polly's videotaped talking-head confession in the diegetic present that contextualizes and comments upon her relationship with the Curator and the Curator's lover, Mary Joseph, unfolding in the diegetic past. A temporary secretary in an art gallery, Polly is a frustrated artist and photographer whose rich phantasy life interrupts the main narrative in the form of black-and-white sequences where she scales Toronto office towers or flies through the air like a Canadian superhero. Polly inadvertently becomes a video artist when she steals the security camera from the gallery, a move that places her in control of the cinematic apparatus; as Robert Cagle observes, the film begins when she turns on the camera and ends when she turns it off (1999, 187). In terms of women's cinema as counter-cinema, Polly is a sign for woman as author of her own text. *I've Heard the Mermaids Singing* subverts classical cinema by structuring a narrative around one woman's phantasy life and refusing the Hollywood convention of compulsory heterosexuality that provides closure and gender fixity by pairing men and women off by the end of the film narrative.[6] If women's counter-cinema is, in part, predicated on the representation of women's phantasy lives and the working through of desire as Johnston suggests, then Rozema's film is certainly an important text in a transgressive Canadian women's cinema (Johnston [1973] 1999, 39–40).[7] In Rozema's film the traditionally male role of voyeur is feminized, assumed by a woman; Polly reads the world through the viewfinder of her camera. The libidinal economy phantasized by Polly, however, disrupts the desiring male gaze and replaces it with a female–female desire. After watching the Curator and Mary Joseph embrace on the security monitor, Polly confesses that she has fallen in love with the Curator, as an eroticized pan shot from Polly's perspective apprehends the Curator's body from toe to head. In a subsequent phantasy vision, an unusually erudite Polly tells the Curator: 'I believe that gender is irrelevant in matters of the heart, desire follows the heart' and then proceeds to quote Freud on polymorphous perversity, a state Polly recommends everyone should cultivate. In sharp contrast to the closing shots of *Back to God's*

Plate 23 I've Heard the Mermaids Singing (1988). Courtesy of Vos Productions Ltd

Plate 24 I've Heard the Mermaids Singing (1988). Courtesy of Vos Productions Ltd

Country and *Bye Bye Blues* where the patriarchal dream of marriage contains women's phantasies, the final shots of *I've Heard the Mermaids Singing* depict the opening of a space for women where Polly shares her phantasy life with the Curator and Mary Joseph.

At this juncture I would like to turn to David Cronenberg's *Dead Ringers* (1988) to read contemporary male phantasies of woman, and as a bridge to a discussion of the imbrications of gender and sexuality in John Greyson's *Making of Monsters* (1991) and *Zero Patience* (1993) and Aerlyn Weissman's and Lynn Fernie's *Forbidden Love: The Unashamed Stories of Lesbian Lives*. There is probably more scholarly and journalistic work published on Cronenberg than on any other Canadian film-maker, much of it engaging his representation of woman, with some critics applauding what they interpret as his ironizing of male phantasy and critique of misogyny and others condemning his work as misogynist male phantasy. I propose to locate *Dead Ringers* in this debate as a way of reading the construction of masculinity in the film through male myths of woman.

Dead Ringers

Dead Ringers (1988) charts the decline of two brilliant gynaecologists, the narcissistic twins Beverly and Elliot Mantle, who live and work together, sharing all things, including patients and lovers. Their almost incestuous intimacy is interrupted, temporarily, by Claire Niveau, a woman with a triple cervix who comes to their practice as a patient and becomes first Beverly's and then Elliot's lover. Exploiting their identical twin status, the Mantles take turns sleeping with and examining Claire in the guise of Beverly before she realizes the deception. When she becomes aware of the way they are sharing her and of their shared living arrangements Claire tells the twins she thinks their relationship is sick. Ultimately, however, she agrees to enter into a relationship with Bev and it is this relationship which triggers the twins' anxieties about castration and separation, something that, as Barbara Creed argues, is made very clear in Beverly's nightmare (1990, 126). Beverly dreams that he and Elliot are twins conjoined at the stomach, and that Claire tries to separate them by gnawing through what Creed describes as the 'long phallic piece of flesh' that binds them (126). Bev's falling in love with Claire brings about a short-lived separation from his brother. To deal with his conflicted feelings for both Claire and his twin, Bev begins taking drugs, a situation that spirals out of control, and leads to his rejection of Claire for Elliot. As the narrative unfolds, the audience witnesses several punishing gynaecological procedures and examinations that cause women embarrassment, fear and pain. The female body has provided a screen on to which the Mantle twins have projected their fantasies of women since childhood. In the film's prologue, pre-pubescent Mantles perform intra-ovular surgery on a plastic anatomy model. As he descends into madness Beverly has a set of grotesque gynaecological instruments resembling tools of torture manufactured for working on what he increasingly perceives as the mutant reproductive systems of women. Creed argues that Beverly displaces his fear of separation on to the body of woman, 'it is woman's body (not his own) which he imagines is literally castrated, mutant, monstrous' (140). At the height of his madness Bev uses the specially built gynaecological instruments to 'operate' on Elly in a frantic effort to cut the cord he imagines joining them, killing him before he collapses and dies on top of his brother.

Feminist critic Amy Taubin reads *Dead Ringers* as 'a dismantling of a patriarchal profession' but cautions that some will mistake Cronenberg's 'critique of misogyny for the thing itself' (1988, 68). Responding to Taubin's and other positive readings of the film, Florence Jacobowitz and Richard Lippe rail against 'the willingness on the part of politically conscious writers to endorse the most offensive misogynist product to emerge in quite a while' (1989, 65). Feminist critics Mary Pharr and Lynda Haas echo the positions of Taubin and Jacobowitz and Lippe in their dialogue on four Cronenberg films, *Videodrome*, *The Fly*, *Dead Ringers* and *Naked Lunch*: 'One of us saw Cronenberg as a misogynist, the other as someone sensitive to feminist perspectives, and we ended with both adopting a middle of the road attitude toward his work' (Pharr and Haas 1996, 29). Barbara Creed flags what she reads as Cronenberg's conflicted signification in *Dead Ringers*:

> a major problem confronting the spectator is that although, at one level, *Dead Ringers* appears to be presenting a devastating critique of the sado-masochistic potential inherent in the relationship between female patient and gynaecologist, at another level the film also plays to the sadistic desires of the spectator who might derive pleasure from watching pain inflicted on women's genital organs.
>
> (1990, 129)

Pharr and Haas begin their conversation with a quotation from Cronenberg in which this alleged producer of misogynist texts self-identifies as a feminist:

> I am a feminist in the sense that I agree that because of the structure that we are talking about – whether Christian medieval morality, and that's where it came from, or more basic things, like the man–woman split of responsibility for childbearing and all that – however it came about I do believe that Western culture is relatively misogynistic and certainly gives women a very second-rate role in society . . . And that we should say, 'we don't like this anymore, it's not necessary anymore, so let's change it.' To that extent, I'm a feminist. And I think that's the greatest extent you can be a feminist.
>
> (quoted in Pharr and Haas 1996, 29)

Women, however, often play secondary roles in Cronenberg's films and rarely do they play protagonists. For the most part women and their bodies, and this is certainly the case with Claire in *Dead Ringers*, are constructed as problems for Cronenberg's male protagonists to solve. In this respect the film's constructions of femininity are most productively read as signs of masculinity, formations of male phantasy. Claire's phantastic body, her triple cervix, is, as Creed notes, an image that is 'unrepresentable – except in fantasy'; it is a physiological impossibility (1990, 126). Knowledge of her tripartite womb translates her into an object of desire for the twins (135). Creed argues that Cronenberg creates a disturbing relationship between gynaecological practice and sexual desire in the scene where the masochistic Claire is tied to a bed with surgical clamps and tubing while Beverly has sex with her (135). Jacobowitz and Lippe read the same scene as a 'voyeuristic male fantasy in which Claire is complicit' (1989, 66). Developing this line of thinking further, they argue that Claire's construction as a masochistic nymphomaniac who can never become pregnant 'enhances her image as a male sexual fantasy' (66).

On the other side of that sexual phantasy, however, is a deep-rooted fear of woman and her reproductive system as symbolized in Beverly's dream which figures Claire as what Creed calls 'the monstrous mother of symbolic castration' (137). For Creed, the twins' association of separation anxiety with castration anxiety produces a phallic panic, a male hysteria, hence their need to 'uncover and control the mysteries of the womb' in their professional roles as gynaecologists (133). As Creed and Jacobowitz and Lippe argue, this male hysteria manifests itself through gynaecological violence to the female body (Creed 1990, 141; Jacobowitz and Lippe 1989, 67). For example, Bev rationalizes a patient's painful response to his violent insertion of the Mantle Retractor by telling Elliot that there is nothing wrong with the instrument designed by the twins, on the contrary, he says, 'it's the body. The woman's body was all wrong.' Where Creed reads phallic panic pointing to the impossible nature of the narcissistic fantasy motivating the Mantles' violent responses to women, Jacobowitz and Lippe see 'the inability of the twins to accept fully the extent of their love and commitment to one another' (Creed 1990, 50; Jacobowitz and Lippe 1989, 67). Not dissimilarly to Jeremy Irons, who plays the twins and 'found their attraction fundamentally homosexual, but Platonic' (quoted in Rodley 1992, 146), Jacobowitz and Lippe read a denial or fear of same-sex incest desire as producing the twins' fear of woman, of Claire (Jacobowitz and Lippe 1989, 67). For it is Claire who suggests to Bev that the twins' relationship may be homosexual when she discovers their living arrangements and that they have been sharing her sexually: 'You live together. Do you sleep in the same bed?' Furthermore, she suggests to Bev that he can't 'get it up unless [his] brother is watching'. In Jacobowitz's and Lippe's reading of the film this refusal to acknowledge their mutual desire for each other kills the twins. From this perspective, the Mantles' phallic masculinity, manifest in their misogynist fantasies of monstrous, mutant women, is activated by a fear of their own possible homosexuality. Such a reading reveals how homosexual desire is regulated in *Dead Ringers* through the twin oppressions of misogyny and homophobia.[8]

SCREENING SEXUALITY

> Homophobia is an equation
> It increases with our pride
> Calculate the ebb and flow dear, it
> Increases when we hide.
> John Greyson, *The Making
> of Monsters* (1991)

The Making of Monsters

In John Greyson's musical *The Making of Monsters* (1991) homophobia regulates homosociality. The male bonding of the teenage hockey players who murder their high-school librarian in a vicious gay-bashing is predicated on the performance of an aggressive heterosexual masculinity that actively constructs homosexual masculinity as an abject body to be excised from the social terrain. Based on a 1985 case where five teenage boys kicked a gay man to death in a Toronto park, *The Making of Monsters* disrupts notions that anti-gay violence is 'normal' by denaturalizing the production of a ruling phallic masculinity legitimated through sport and advertising discourses. Such discourses contribute to an oppression that, as R. W. Connell argues, 'positions homosexual masculinities at the bottom of a gender hierarchy among men':

> Gayness, in patriarchal ideology, is the repository of whatever is symbolically expelled from hegemonic masculinity, the items ranging from fastidious taste in home decoration to receptive anal pleasure. Hence, from the point of view of hegemonic masculinity, gayness is easily assimilated to femininity. And hence – in the view of some gay theorists – the ferocity of homophobic attacks.
>
> (Connell 1995, 78)

In a sequence of shots in which he cuts from black-and-white hockey footage to the testimony of character witnesses at the boys' trial, to black-and-white footage of a television beer commercial and back to testimony of the boys' normalcy, Greyson establishes a correlation between the production of a hegemonic heterosexual masculinity and the televisual signs of hockey and beer advertising. The male-on-male violence of hockey viewing, a rite of Canadian masculinity, is interrupted by the breweries sponsoring *Hockey Night in Canada* with commercials saturated with the signs of macho masculinity and compulsory heterosexuality. Greyson represents the beer commercial as a montage of hyper-masculine images – motorcycle men, jocks and cowboys – that eventually cut to blonde, pneumatic women. Ironically, these same male images are appropriated and queered by gay culture to signify as icons of gay masculinity. However, in the compulsory heterosexuality organizing male sport and the beer commercial, the presence of the blonde women regulates homosociality, repressing male–male desire. In the

Plate 25 The Making of Monsters (1991). 'High Sticking.' Reproduced by kind permission of John Greyson

discursive structure Greyson creates through editing, these images form the dominant ideology of compulsory heterosexuality that hails or recruits male subjects
for membership in the 'norm'. The cross-cutting of court-room testimony that
links hockey and the beer commercial correlate normalcy with hockey, beer
drinking, heterosexuality and ultimately homophobic attacks. Bare-chested
fathers and coaches wearing goalie masks, ciphers of the ruling masculinity, test-
ify to the normalcy of the teenage killers and, by extension, their savage homophobic attack:

He might yell faggot at another player but it didn't mean anything.

They were normal teenage boys. Any queer who goes there knows it's dangerous. Somehow this guy must have provoked them.

They were normal teenage boys. It was the peer pressure and the beer.

This testimony, which Greyson said he based on the testimony provided by 'an inordinate number of hockey coaches' at the trial of the boys involved in the 1985 killing, evidences a naturalizing of heterosexual male violence against gays and suggests that the innocent victim of the attack 'asked for it' (Greyson 1998).

The possible irruption of homosexuality in a homosocial context is dispatched through an attack on the homosexual subject. As the female voice-over of Greyson's film notes, there is 'a good chance statistically that one of the five boys who killed Maguire is gay'. This situation is echoed in Virgo's *Rude* where the homosocial world of male sport, in this case boxing, produces male subjects who are disciplined to perform their heterosexual masculinity through anti-gay violence. Jordan, a boxer coming to terms with his homosexuality, is pressured by his peers to demonstrate his 'normalcy' by participating in the beating of a gay man who cruises a local park. Greyson unveils the homosexual tensions in the homosociality of hockey in a choreographed musical sequence where young men clad in nothing but sox, jocks and goalie masks engage in the contact sport of 'high sticking'. *The Making of Monsters* closes with another musical number that refuses victimization, advocating the 'bashing' of the ideological sources of patriarchal homophobia:

> Bash back baby the street is ours
> Bash the schools
> Bash the churches
> Bash the courts
> Bash the liberal fools

The opening and closing lyrics of Greyson's film advocate an activist intervention into homophobia by making homosexuality visible, by refusing to be a victim of the homophobia that closets and kills.[9]

Tom Waugh writes of what I might call the fear of a Queer Canon, the invisibility of gay texts in the canon of Canadian cinema, what he refers to as 'the official canon or family of canons that has currency in our syllabi and on our postage stamps' (1999, 18).[10] As a corrective, Waugh offers a Queer Canon and a Canon Queered. Waugh's Queer Canon includes *A Chairy Tale* (Claude Jutra 1957), *Winter Kept Us Warm* (David Secter 1965), *Outrageous* (Richard Benner 1977), *Chinese Characters* (Richard Fung 1986), *The Making of Monsters* (John Greyson 1991), *Zero Patience* (John Greyson 1993) and *The Hanging Garden* (Thom Fitzgerald 1997). In an effort to locate sexual dissidence in supposedly 'straight' films, Waugh sets about queering such titles as *The Ernie Game* (Don Owen 1967), *The Bay Boy* (Daniel Petrie 1984), *The Silent Partner* (Daryl Duke 1978) and *Hard Core Logo* (Bruce McDonald 1996). The exclusion of queerness from the construction of a national cinema and a national culture is something I want to address through a reading of Greyson's *Zero Patience* as a cinematic performance of Queer Canadian Nation.

Cinema and fictive sexuality in the nation state: *Zero Patience*

The exclusion of a dominant group's others in social or cultural formations helps to create what Etienne Balibar describes as a 'fictive ethnicity', that is the fictive ethnicity of the fabricated 'community instituted by the nation state' (Balibar 1991, 96). The heterosexist Canadian state's exclusion of gay and lesbian others (its failure to recognize same-sex marriages, same-sex benefits, the historical criminalization of same-sex acts, and disqualification of gays and lesbians in the military) constructs a fictive sexuality of the community instituted by the nation state: the heterosexual Canadian nation, a fiction John Greyson exposes in his queer representation of nation, *Zero Patience* (1993).[11] The dominant cinematic signification of Canada is white and heteronormative. Griersonian state-sponsored documentaries such as *Peoples of Canada* (1947) and *Welcome Neighbour* (1949) – both of the National Film Board's *Canada Carries On* series – present a straight resource-rich Canada peopled by white heterosexual couples and their children who exhibit labour and wares for the camera to induce foreign investment. Despite their potential for queer readings, the plots of camp Hollywood representations of Canada like the homosocial worlds of mounties and lumberjacks found in films such as the 1954 musical *Rose Marie* directed by Mervyn Leroy, are driven by a binary heterosexual pairing, and encoded with gender fixity. As documented by Pierre Berton, these filmic versions of Canada displaced indigenous imaginings of nation and became, through the American monopoly on global film distribution, hegemonic cinematic signs for Canadian nation.[12] Greyson's *Zero Patience* considers another case of misrepresentation, the American print and electronic media's transformation of an HIV-infected French Canadian, Gaetan Dugas, into a promiscuous gay serial killer, Patient Zero. It was claimed that Zero infected the North American continent with the AIDS virus. On the level of a national allegory, this mythical imagining was very convenient; a French-speaking foreigner infects America the good, the heartland of morality. Some Canadian media outlets such as *Maclean's*[13] resisted the pathological monster caricature found in the *New York Post* and *New York Times*, and on all three American television networks.[14] These American media representations of Dugas were pulled from Randy Shilts's book *And the Band Played On*.[15] The work was later produced as a film (Roger Spottiswoode 1993), despite evidence from Dugas's doctors refuting Shilts's Patient Zero vision, and documenting Dugas's contribution to determining the sexually transmitted nature of the syndrome.[16] As part of its oppositional approach to the Shilts's version of Dugas, *Zero Patience* traces the role of ideology in the cultural construction of homosexuality and AIDS.

Ideology and the cultural construction of homosexuality and AIDS

Greyson's work is informed by an awareness of what Louis Althusser calls ideological state apparatuses (ISAs). *The Making of Monsters* interrogates the dominant heteronormative ideology of a popular culture and education system that interpellates homophobic subjects who murder their homosexual teacher. Greyson contextualizes his film with an introductory intertitle suggesting the Toronto Board of Education's complicity in perpetuating homophobia: '[T]o this day, only gym teachers are mandated by Toronto's Board of Education to teach Sex Education and no curriculum addresses homophobia or gay issues.' If we accept that ideology is in part the 'discourse that invests a nation or society with meaning', the education system and cinema, along with other ISAs such as the church and family, structure or interpellate subjects as heterosexual members of the national community (Hayward 1996b, 181). In Althusser's language the student in the classroom and the spectator in the cinema are 'hailed' or recruited as heterosexual, structured as straight by a ruling ideology that constructs homosexuality as an abject category excluded from belonging to the national community.[17] Hollywood's construction of homosexuality as a monstrous and effeminate pathology is well documented by Richard Dyer, Diana Fuss, Vito Russo and Parker Tyler.[18] As Dyer comments, this stereotyping defines homosexuality 'in terms that inevitably fall short of the "ideal" of heterosexuality (that is, taken to be the norm of being human)' and passes this definition off as 'necessary and natural' (Dyer 1984, 31). This normalizing of heterosexuality prompts the mother of the murdered teacher in Greyson's *The Making of Monsters* to comment that 'it's normal to kill homosexuals' in a homophobic society. The queer cinema of John Greyson is a militant, interventionist system of representation that subverts the cultural assumptions formed by a ruling heterosexist ideology, the second stage in what Lee Edelman theorizes as homographesis:

> homographesis would name a doubled operation: one serving the ideological purposes of a conservative social order intent on codifying identities in its labour of disciplinary inscription, and the other resistant to that categorization, intent on *de*-scribing the identities that order has so oppressively *in*-scribed.
>
> (Edelman 1994, 10)

As Jean-Pierre Oudart has theorized, to deconstruct a system of representation 'it is necessary that this system be situated within the historical framework of its production' (Oudart 1990, 203). Greyson locates the deconstructive narrative of

Zero Patience in the matrices of the Hollywood musical, horror and the documentary genres, contextualizing these heteronormative forms within a genealogy of foundational texts in homophobia as represented in the film by the historical character of nineteenth-century explorer and anthropologist Sir Richard Francis Burton, who quotes from his own Victorian (homo)sexology on the sotadic zones, and from Freud.

Re-presenting the queer subject: ideology, difference, genre

Greyson's appropriation of the cinematic apparatus and its genres that deny homosexuals subject-formation dismantles the spectacle of the gay other constructed by a white, male, heteronormative and homophobic camera eye. The Hollywood musical, horror and documentary genres are freighted with ideologies placed under de-scription in *Zero Patience*. The Hollywood musical hails or recruits spectators to take part in an American dream of courtship, marriage and consumer culture. The plot usually concerns the white heterosexual couple – Fred Astaire and Ginger Rogers or Judy Garland and Mickey Rooney – who perform the rituals of the imagined American community: the attraction of boy–girl opposites, their union in marriage and their success as measured by their buying power in a consumer culture.[19] These couples are a logical extension of the disciplining marker for Victorian sexuality cited by Foucault: 'The legitimate and procreative couple laid down the law. The couple imposed itself as model, enforced the norm, safeguarded the truth, and reserved the right to speak' (1990, 3).

The musical is a utopic vision[20] of American nation endeavouring to give the viewer the sensation of what Jane Feuer suggests it would 'feel like to be free' (Feuer 1982, 84). This national allegory also interpellated the Canadian audience that the US motion picture industry considers a major component of its domestic market. This idealized community however excludes not only racial others, as Ella Shohat and Robert Stam have observed, but also sexual others, lesbians and gay men, whom it attempts to imprison in a straight paradigm that lays down the law of heterosexuality as a narrative route to freedom (Shohat and Stam 1994, 223). Owing to its exclusionary nature, but also to the pronounced and self-reflexive theatricality of the genre, the Hollywood musical has long been subject to transgressive, queer readings (think of the resonance of *The Wizard of Oz* (Victor Fleming 1939), and iconic figures such as Judy Garland and Carmen Miranda in gay cultures).

Jack Babuscio sees the musical along with the horror film as genres 'saturated with camp', and it is the concept of camp in the musical that interests me here (1984, 44). Babuscio suggests gay audiences identify with the notion of life as theatre, something foregrounded in musicals, the playing of roles: passing for straight, or refusing to play out the heterosexual role scripted for us by society (45): 'Camp, by focusing on the outward appearances of roles, implies that roles, and in particular, sex roles, are superficial – a matter of style' (44). Greyson develops this transgressive reading strategy into an inscriptive practice. He hijacks and questions a mainstream cultural form that expels homosexuality and translates women's bodies into a voyeuristic choreographed, commodity exchange, to produce a work that represents people of colour, celebrates male-to-male sex and valorises the male body as an object of desire. *Zero Patience* borrows heavily from the set pieces of Hollywood musicals as choreographed by Busby Berkely, to create an intertextual dialogue, part parody, part homage, where the routines of *Zero Patience* refer back to and interrogate their heterosexist sources in Hollywood musicals like *Footlight Parade* (Lloyd Bacon 1933).[21] The structures of the Hollywood musical are relocated in a field of irony here to enable the singing and dancing performances of queer nation. You'll not find many singing arseholes or naked male chorus lines in the Hollywood musical; however, you will find camp performances of male-to-male love – for example Scotty and Frank's cheek-to-cheek rehearsal of 'I've Got a Feeling It's Love' in *Footlight Parade* – and this is why I would argue that Greyson's intertextual dialogue is, partly, homage. Greyson's musical, however, travels beyond homage to hail or recruit queer subjects to take part in activist politics directed against multinational pharmaceutical corporations and their commercial exploitation of the AIDS epidemic.

Zero Patience blurs genre boundaries; the ghost story (present in Zero's return from limbo), the horror genre and the documentary are all at play in this narrative. I am primarily concerned here with the musical, documentary and horror genres. The problematic truth claim of documentary film is present in Greyson's metacinematic technique. Codes and conventions of the documentary genre are inserted into the film's narrative, as signalled by the female voice-over narration of Burton's history and twentieth-century activities, and Burton's own work as a documentarist in his film on Zero. The Hollywood musical and the documentary are generic markers of American and Canadian national cinemas, and their intersection here underlines their failure to signify queer nation in their conventional configurations. The Griersonian tradition of the NFB has been the dominant sign for Canadian cinema internationally. Grierson's colonial film policy for Canada enshrined the documentary as *the* Canadian film form, encouraging Canadians who wanted to make feature films to go to the United States, and effectively obstructing the development of a Canadian feature-film industry in the postwar years.[22] As I have already argued, the Hollywood musical constitutes a dream vision of American nation, and as such is very much a part of cultural imperialism, selling American ideology, and consumer goods to a global market. Greyson travels to Hollywood, metaphorically, to make a feature illustrating the documentary's shortcomings in a way that Grierson could never have anticipated; with Canadian and UK funding Greyson deploys the Hollywood musical against itself to tell a queer Canadian story that an American pseudo-documentary work – *And the Band Played On* – misrepresents.[23] As Robert L. Cagle comments, 'Dugas became lost in the processes of signification, as the real person behind the constructed persona was put under erasure. After the publication of Shilts's book, no one was interested in an airline host from Quebec, but the man who brought AIDS to North America was big news' (1995, 73). The discursive construction of Dugas as Zero by documentary forms is communicated to the viewer of Greyson's film in its opening shots: the still, digitized, black-and-white image of Zero, intercut with the classroom shots of the boy reading from Burton's translation of *Arabian Nights*. Credits are superimposed on these shots of Zero, mimicking the media's projection of what Cagle calls a 'vampiric spectre' on to Dugas (71). The black-and-white, digitized quality of the image draws attention to its artifice, and its inability to signify, its failure to refer back to a referent existing in material reality. The signifier Patient Zero does not refer back to Gaetan Dugas, but only to itself as a media-generated, and 'documentary', aberration.

This opening sequence brings Burton, Zero and the documentary forms together, framing the film ideologically. The *mise-en-scène* of the classroom structures our reception of what is to follow. The classroom is located in an ideological state education apparatus that attempts to discipline people's thinking in prescribed, state-sanctioned ways, a space in which Burton's translation of *Arabian Nights*, with its infamous and pejorative 'documentary' essay on homosexual practices, is consumed by young minds. An imperial text, Burton's 'Terminal Essay', shaped and, in the context of the genealogy of homophobic texts drawn by Greyson's narrative, continues to shape cultural imaginings of homosexuality as perversion, vice, illness. So, we as spectators then are going to be taught a lesson, cultural prejudices against homosexuals are going to be undone or examined in another type of classroom, the cinema, where prejudice can be taught or undone.

The horror and documentary genres intersect in Burton's work as a documentary taxidermist. Burton is a maker of monsters. As a taxidermist he manipulates and fixes dead tissue to perform his Hall of Contagion narrative, a narrative in which he has secured a starring role for Zero. Burton's production of homosexuals as monsters is based on empiricism, an approach that shares with essentialist conceptualizations of the documentary film the naive notion that the documentarist is simply recording an unmediated reality. However, as Michael Renov has observed, in documentary film-making 'Always issues of selection intrude (which angle, take, camera stock will best serve); results are indeed *mediated*, the result of multiple interventions that *come between* the cinematic sign (what we see on the screen) and its referent (what existed in the world)' (1993b, 26). In a manner similar to the way he arranges and fixes the tissue of the unfortunate animals whose stories he presumes to tell, Burton creates a taxidermied Zero through the editing process: the cutting of celluloid tissue. The 'documentary' film produced by Burton picks up on the Shilts-fuelled phantasy of Dugas as a vampire. Burton edits his film to produce a meaning unavailable in the raw footage: Zero was a homosexual monster. Courtesy of Burton's cuts and splices, Zero's mother is represented as declaring 'Zero was the devil, bringing his boyfriends home, flaunting his lifestyle under our noses'; an inversion of what

Plate 26 Zero Patience (1993). Seeing and listening to Miss HIV. Reproduced by kind permission of John Greyson

the camera recorded. This monster-making continues Greyson's parodic dialogue with Hollywood, specifically the horror genre which with regularity produces images of homosexuals as serial killers: Norman Bates in *Psycho* (Alfred Hitchcock 1960), the killer in *Dressed to Kill* (Brian De Palma 1980) and more recently Buffalo Bill in *Silence of the Lambs* (Jonathan Demme 1991). Ironically, although Burton is the only character who can see Zero, he cannot look at Zero through his distorting camera lens; Zero's failure to register in Burton's viewfinder signifies the documentary medium's failure to represent Dugas.

Greyson's narrative is fraught with a tension between visibility and invisibility, sight and blindness: the vision of Zero's former lover George is deteriorating owing to retinitis, and the public is blinded by the media's dominant inscription of Dugas as the monster Zero. Zero, however, liberates himself from the vampiric monster construct by refusing to identify with this media image and listening to his HIV-infected bloodstream. Looking through a microscope at a slide of his blood, Zero, Burton and the viewer observe a water-ballet – reminiscent of Berkely's 'Waterfall' routine in *Footlight Parade*, and of Esther Williams's films – in which a personified Miss HIV announces that Zero did not bring AIDS to North America. At the end of this number Miss HIV splashes Zero with his own blood, causing the liquid to travel up the lens of the microscope and wash over his eyes and face. At this moment Zero becomes visible on Burton's video camera. With Burton's help Zero displaces the Hall of Contagion Zero Patient image of himself, by diving into the image and literally short-circuiting the electronic media that generate it. Greyson's film has 'zero patience' for a media that inscribes people living with AIDS and homosexuals as criminal and therefore, in Edelman's terms, de-scribes such inscriptions.

Foundational homophobia: the documentary evidence undone

At this point, it is necessary to return to Oudart's notion that a system of representation, in this case patriarchal homophobia, be situated within the historical framework of its production. Greyson contextualizes his deconstruction of homophobia through not only the co-ordinates of Hollywood genres but also imperial Victorian sexology. Historically, Burton's empirical, colonizing gaze constructed African and Indian colonial others and homosexuals as objects. An architect of Western homophobia, Burton's whiteness, his presumed heterosexuality, and his 'scientific' authority position him as one who controls the image of the racial and sexual other. *Zero Patience* continues, and then subverts this trajectory. Greyson's Burton spies on men in a gay bath-house from a position of privilege; the camera is hidden in his groin under a towel, but only briefly before he is exposed literally and figuratively. The proximity of the camera lens to his genitals signals Burton's conflicted sexuality, and suggests that he is seeing with his penis. As much as Burton contends that his work is motivated by scientific interests, the position of the camera lens belies his fetishizing of the men in the baths as objects of desire, a male-to-male form of active scopophilia where a bipolarized male spectator self-identified as straight, passing for gay, engages in projecting his repressed homosexual desire on to the gay 'performers' in the shower scene from a position of power; he represents them as dysfunctional animals through his lens.[24] Burton's camera eye initially constructs the homosexual subject as living in a predatory sexual jungle, framing the gay man as a pathology, characterized by what he terms 'self-destructive behaviour'. Burton hypothesizes: 'Denial seems to be a major component of the homosexual's dysfunctional psyche.' The historical Burton also recorded homosexual practice in a similar manner, basing his documentation on a voyeuristic expedition to a Karachi brothel on behalf of the British Empire.[25] Pointing to Burton's detailed account of 'pederasty, transvestism, [and] troilistic fellatio, etc.' (McLynn 1990, 42), Burton biographer Frank McLynn makes the inference that Burton himself was a participant in these activities (52). Moreover, Thomas Wright's biography reveals Burton's fantasy of being buggered as punishment for breaking into a harem (quoted in McLynn 1990, 52). Not only do these narratives foreground Burton's conflicted sexuality, they also underline his penchant for passing – a bipolarized man, passing for a straight-identified man, passing for a gay Muslim.

In Greyson's filmic world Burton undergoes a transformation. Early in the

Plate 27 Zero Patience (1993). 'When you pop a boner in the shower / Don't blush, be proud, display!' Reproduced by kind permission of John Greyson

narrative, the viewer is asked to identify with Burton's straight looking; we view the world through his camera. Burton provides us with jaundiced agency to Zero and his world; however, we are positioned very differently by the end of the film. We can see the beginnings of this queer interpellation of Burton in the shower sequence where his camera is read as an erection and his homophobic gaze is returned as a cruising gaze by the gay men who attempt to teach him the performance aspects of bath-house etiquette: 'When you pop a boner in the shower / Don't blush, Be proud, Display!'[26] The interpellation process is continued during his encounter with the ACT UP activists in the musical number 'Control' where he is denied subjectivity, and placed in the object position of the homosexual AIDS patient who is denied control over his body. Subjected to probing and prodding of the medical system, he is dragooned into medical experimentation to profit pharmaceutical companies. Burton's voyeurism, his obsessive measuring and looking, constitute signs of latent homosexuality later made manifest in his sexual experience with Zero. It seems that the tyrannically empirical Burton *can* learn something from experience. Here empiricism, the experimental-observationist 'science' upon which all of Burton's work is based, is used to undermine Burton's and other Victorian categories of heterosexual and homosexual. Burton's sexual identification is heterosexual white male; however, the film subverts this identity. The female voice-over narrating our introduction

291

to Burton at the beginning of the film suggests that his swashbuckling hyper-masculine persona might be an attempt to compensate for his sexless marriage and obsessive penis measuring (McLynn 1990, 219). As viewers we come to see Burton's straight-identification of himself as a misrecognition. Increasingly, Burton begins to identify with the subjects of his inquiries, Patient Zero and homosexuality, a process that leads to his lovemaking with Zero in the Hall of Contagion. Within the film Burton is as much a sign for heterosexist ideology and homophobia as he is a character; his recognition of himself as other, his physical and ideological embrace of homosexuality, provides the film with a wonderful aporia where the rhetorical lies of homophobia are made legible, are de-scribed. Whereas classical Hollywood narratives interpellate spectators as white, male and straight, this film interpellates or hails the spectator as queer.

One of the more memorable scenes in *Zero Patience* has to be the singing butt puppet duet in which Zero and Burton consider cultural constructions of homosexuality, and trace a genealogy of homophobic and misogynist texts. Part of the work that Greyson's film attempts is a refiguration of the anus – represented historically as a location of violence, excrement, criminality and death – as a positive site of pleasure.[27] This scene interrogates the symbolic overdetermination of the anus and the phallus in Freudian and Lacanian psychoanalysis. 'The law of the father doesn't recognize the hole', we are told. The hole in this context is a sign for passive vaginal or anal reception of the penis. Hole here is a sign for lack. Internalization of patriarchal cultural codes creates a hierarchical masculinity that feminizes passive male anal receptivity and associates it with lack, thereby denying gay men, and women, subject-formation.[28] This thinking contends that in order to hold power – to be a subject – one must have mastery of the penis, and not be subject to that mastery, not have one's hole dominated. 'The phallus is the ruler,' as Burton sings, 'it's the cock who's in control.' In Greyson's lyrics the listener can detect a palpable slippage between the physical penis and the conceptual phallus which underlines the conscious selection of the penis as a model for the symbolic formation of male power, the phallus.[29] The song also deconstructs the hetero-constructed pathology of homosexuality – the anus as a grave – popularized in Freudian readings of homosexual practice as the fulfilment of a death wish[30] and 1980s media reports which Leo Bersani argues associated anal sex with AIDS and self-annihilation.[31] Greyson's *Zero Patience* undoes the binaries of hole and phallus. As the song says:

> An asshole's just an asshole, skip the analytic crit
> The meanings are straightforward
>
> Cocks go in and out comes shit
>
> If the asshole's not so special
> Then the phallus can't be either
> Patriarchy would crumble if we started getting wiser[32]

This lyric does violence to hierarchical power differentials defined by binaries: male/female, phallus/hole, straight/queer.

Zero Patience de-scribes oppressive in-scriptions of homosexuality by appropriating hegemonic systems of representation, and refutes the expulsion of gayness from the Canadian nation by making the formerly invisible Dugas visible, and the formerly illegible Queer Nation legible. Greyson's success here is due, in part, to his ability to uncover processes of identification and misrecognition – between Burton and Zero, between Zero and his media-constructed image, and between spectator and screen. Successful genre coding of both the Hollywood musical and horror films is dependent on spectator expectations of gender fixity and heteronormativity as these have been received from previous exposure to genre texts. However, as Stephen Neale posits, and as Greyson's film demonstrates most effectively, genre is 'difference *in* repetition' (1980, 50). Neale argues that a genre text is not static, that it takes the normative codes of a genre and 're-works them, extends them, or transforms them altogether' (1990, 58). This is precisely the type of work attempted by Greyson's film. *Zero Patience* plays on audience expectations for generic identification – for example, the trajectory of the white heterosexual couple – by queering them and creating new co-ordinates for identification with a gay couple, in the love story of a sexually conflicted, immortal Victorian sexologist and a gay ghost. Diana Fuss's conceptualization of identification provides an illuminating frame of reference through which we can view identification processes in *Zero Patience*:

> In perhaps its simplest formation, identification is the detour through the other that defines a self. This detour through the other follows no predetermined developmental path, nor does it travel outside history and culture. Identification names the entry of history and culture into the subject, a subject must bear the traces of each and every encounter with the external world. Identification is from the beginning, a question of relation, of self to other, subject to object, inside to outside.
>
> (Fuss 1995, 2–3)

The history and culture represented in *Zero Patience* will leave their indelible traces on all who encounter it.

Forbidden Love: The Unashamed Stories of Lesbian Lives

The repression and articulation of Canadian lesbian history and culture are documented in *Forbidden Love: The Unashamed Stories of Lesbian Lives* (Fernie, Weissman 1992). Not unlike Greyson's deconstruction of a homophobic system of representation, Aeryn Weissman and Lynne Fernie deconstruct a lesbophobic system of representation by locating this system in, after Oudart, 'the historical framework of its production'. The film's colour-leached establishing shots locate spectators in what they soon discover is a 1950s lesbian pulp novel depicting the forced separation of two female lovers, Beth and Laura, at a country railway station under the controlling gaze of Beth's husband Neil. The names Laura and Beth invoke two central characters from lesbian pulp novelist Ann Banon's *Beebo Brinker* novels, *Odd Girl Out* (1957), *I Am a Woman* (1959), *Woman in the Shadows* (1959), *Journey to a Woman* (1960) and *Beebo Brinker* (1962), a correspondence that is confirmed later by an onscreen interview with Banon. After refusing to join Laura in the city, Beth runs back into the arms of Neil. Fernie and Weissman then cut to Laura in medium close-up waving goodbye, before pulling back to a long shot. At this point, full colour bleeds into the shot before the image dissolves into a garish pulp cover version of Laura with the full title of the film appearing lettered on to the image. This melodramatic pulp, along with lurid newspaper headlines, constituted the dominant cultural representation of lesbian lives in the 1950s. Lesbian desire was structured as forbidden love that ended tragically when, according to the dictates of the genre, compulsory heterosexuality or death intervened. In the case of the newspaper narratives, lesbian desire was interrupted by the surveillance of a heterosexist state that raided lesbian bars and arrested their patrons as deviants. Ironically, as Weissman's and Fernie's film reveals through interviews with women who frequented lesbian bars in 1950s and 1960s Vancouver and Toronto, the pulp novels, despite their formulaic punishment of lesbian lovers, became important objects of identification for lesbians of the period, as they were, by and large, the only accessible representations of female same-sex relationships. Diane Hamer, in her discussion of the significant role Banon's novels played in lesbian identification, argues that 'Banon's novels did not merely reflect the reality of being a lesbian as she knew it in the 1950s, but also helped to produce one' (Hamer 1990, 51).[33]

The narrative of Beth and Laura is interrupted by a series of interviews with nine women who were part of the bar scene in the 1950s and 1960s and by shots of newspaper headlines about raids on lesbian bars. As the film unfolds, the pulp narrative of Laura and Beth is re-written or in Edelman's terms de-scribed. Laura is not punished for her same-sex desires, but rewarded when she begins an affair with a woman in the city. The lesbian viewer is also rewarded by the directors' representation of what was 'unrepresentable' in the visual culture of the 1950s, lesbian sexuality in the lovemaking of Laura and Mitch, the girlfriend she finds in the city.[34]

The documentary talking-head interviews with the nine women also work to de-scribe the conservative social order's pathologizing of lesbian subjectivities through documentary 'evidence' of criminality or perversion circulated in newspaper articles. These resilient and generous women share with the viewer their experiences of carving out successful lives for themselves under the gaze of a state surveillance prohibiting lesbian sociality. Through interview and stock footage of lesbian bars and police raids, Weissman and Fernie represent the type of surveillance of gay and lesbian desire Greyson writes about: 'surveillance strives to produce a picture of lesbians and gay men as pathological, deviant, dangerous and diseased' (Greyson 1993, 391). A tracking shot across various newspaper articles with headlines reading, 'POLICE NAB NUDE "QUEERS"!', 'Cops Burst In On Mass Homo Carnival of Lust', 'The Sick Life' is narrated by one of the interview subjects, Lois M. Stuart:

> It was well known that the Toronto police got their kicks from picking up women. Taking them out to Cherry Beach, some of them were raped, some of them were badly beaten up and they just left them there. I guess they got away with it because the women were gay and who cared about gay women? Gay women couldn't complain, there was nobody to complain to. If you went to court you didn't exist.

This combination of voice-over and image – where the criminalized and patholo-gized of the image speaks her experience – troubles state-sanctioned homophobic discourse, unveiling the pathological and criminal natures of a corrupt legal system that persecutes and prosecutes same-sex desires.

NOTES

INTRODUCTION

1 See Cheryl Binning, 'Film Past and Future: Preserving Canada's Heritage', *Take One* Spring (2001): 31–2.
2 See ibid., 32, and 'AV Preservation Makes 2001 Selects', *Playback*, 5 March 2001, 15.

1 IMMIGRATION AND EMPIRE-BUILDING

1 This term is Diana Brydon's reversal of 'settler-invader'. Brydon's reversal stresses that 'the narrative of settlement in itself occludes and denies the prior fact of invasion' (Brydon 1995, 16–17).
2 'British' is a particularly unstable signifier that, depending on the addressee, may be received as a referent for England, Scotland and Wales, or for the geographical and cultural space of England. For a discussion of the variant usages of 'British' see Robert Crawford, *Devolving English Literature* (Oxford: Clarendon, 1992): 45–110.
3 This gendered representation develops the well-worn trope in imperial discourse of figuring Canadian territory as a passive female body awaiting to be acted upon by the male invader-settler. See my discussion of this gendered iconography in 'Canada and Scotland: Conceptualizing "Postcolonial" Spaces', *Essays on Canadian Writing* 56 (1995): 135–61 (144–5).
4 Richard Dyer suggests that following Christianity and race, imperialism is the third element of whiteness. 'The white spirit', Dyer argues, 'organises white flesh and in turn non-white flesh and other material matters: it has *enterprise* . . . Imperialism displays both the character of enterprise in the white person, and its exhilarating expansive relationship to the environment' (Dyer 1997, 15).
5 Quotations of film narrative are transcribed from intertitles.
6 Raymond Williams remarks upon the difficulty, given its urban connotations, of ascribing the term 'bourgeois' to 'non-urban capitalists (e.g. agrarian capitalist employers)' even though 'the social relations they institute are clearly bourgeois in the developed C19 sense' (Williams 1976, 48). John is a part of a newly developing property-holding agricultural bourgeoisie in Western Canada, who exploit the project of colonization to ascend from non-propertied working class to join the landholding capitalist classes.
7 'National' might be considered a problematic descriptor for late-nineteenth- and early-twentieth-century Canada by those who confuse Nation-State with national community. I am deploying 'nation' and 'national' to mark, after Benedict

Anderson, the 'imagined community' that is projected by a collectivity before the Nation-State is legislated into existence. Canadian nationalism existed long before the formation of a Canadian Nation-State; Canada First, the country's earliest nationalist group, was founded in 1868, and articulated an autonomous Canadian nationality within an imperial federation with Britain. The specific 'birth' date of the Canadian Nation-State is a specious argument at best; Confederation (1867), the Balfour Report (1926), the Statute of Westminster (1931), the Citizenship Act (1946) and the Constitution Act (1982) all play pivotal roles toward establishing a Canadian Nation-State.

8 As the first feature produced by the NFB, every effort was made to ensure excellent distribution of *Drylanders*. The NFB estimated that more than a million cinema-goers would view the film in its first year of release (National Film Board 1964, 22). As a teaching package the film was viewed by at least as many Canadian students.

9 See David Hawkes for a summary of Althusser's theory of ideological state apparatuses (Hawkes 1986, 121–4).

10 Louis Althusser discusses the concepts of hailing or recruitment by the ruling ideology in his influential essay 'Ideology and Ideological State Apparatuses (Notes towards an Investigation)'. See Althusser (1971, 162–5).

11 For a discussion of 'interspecies communication' in the film see Armatage (1991, 42–4).

12 For a brief history of the film's production, distribution and box office gross see Turner (1992, 54–6).

13 See Turner (1987) and Armatage (1991).

14 For more on the phallus and identification see Stephen Heath's interpretations of Freud in the context of culture and film: Heath 1992, 52.

15 In Curwood's novel, the bully is a stage Irishman. Within the film narrative, however, the character's French-Canadian ethnicity is signified through costuming, the habitant-like sash he wears around his waist.

16 In the epigraph to her thoughtful analysis of the relationship between soap and empire Anne McClintock quotes a Unilever company advertising slogan: 'Soap is Civilization.' See McClintock (1995, 207–31).

17 Nell takes credit for suggesting the split-screen sequence in *Back to God's Country*. See Shipman (1987, 78).

18 Since its publication, Mulvey's theory of visual pleasure has been subject to much debate about its focus on what Mulvey calls, in her own revisiting of her 'Visual Pleasure and Narrative Cinema' essay, the 'masculinization' of the spectator position (Mulvey 1989c, 29). The question Mulvey asks in 'Afterthoughts on Visual Pleasure and Narrative Cinema' is the question that many of her critics ask: 'What about the women in the audience?' (1989c, 29). In his essay 'The Difficulty of Difference', D. N. Rodowick, while praising Mulvey's work on visual pleasure and narrative cinema, interrogates how Freudian binaries limit Mulvey's theory. 'When Mulvey defines the look according to its objective and subjective, as well as active and passive relations, it is a look made for the male subject. Consequently, the only place for the female subject in her scenario is as an object defined in the receiving end of the glance or the unrealized possibility of a counter-cinema' (Rodowick 1991, 16). Aware of how Mulvey's Freudian context can potentially re-inscribe the binaries of active male/passive female, I am using Mulvey here to read the patriarchal status quo of 1919 as it is represented in *Back to God's Country*, an application of Mulvey that B. Ruby Rich valorizes in a 1978 conversation with Michelle Citron, Julia Lesage, Judith Mayne, Anna Marie Taylor and the editors of *New German Critique* (Citron *et al.* 1999, 116). In the same conversation Anna

Marie Taylor speaks to the perception that Mulvey's analysis is constrained by its Oedipal framework. 'If it's not the truth about human social organization, it's the primary model by which the psychoanalytic institutions of the prevailing social organization itself explained the workings of the family and the law of the father carried to the entire social structure as patriarchal order. Freudian analysis can therefore be instrumental for understanding and therefore changing the representations of women as they're deeply established and repeated everywhere in culture' (Citron *et al.* 1999, 118).

19 See Turner (1987).

20 In this part of his discussion of sexual difference and ways of seeing Heath is paraphrasing Jacques Lacan. Later in the essay he quotes Freud on the relationship between the eye and the phallus: 'the substitutive relation between the eye and the male organ . . . is seen to exist in dreams and myths and phantasies'. As quoted in Heath 1992, 77. See also Sigmund Freud, 'The Uncanny', *Standard Edition*, vol. XVII, 231.

21 For a discussion of feminist counter-discourses to the keyhole shot in cinema see Mayne (1984, 49–66).

2 WHO IS ETHNOGRAPHIABLE?

1 The film's importance to producing citizen subjects becomes clear in the history of its circulation. *Hot Ice* was exhibited in educational institutions across the country – Ontario Department of Education, Toronto, Ontario; Department of Education, Charlottetown, Prince Edward Island; Ontario Agricultural College, Guelph, Ontario; Moose Jaw Film Council, Department of Education, Vancouver, British Columbia; London Public Library, London, Ontario; University of Manitoba, Winnipeg, Manitoba; University of British Columbia, Vancouver, British Columbia; Department of Education, Halifax, Nova Scotia; Regina Public Library, Saskatchewan – until it was withdrawn from circulation in 1964.

2 See Ferguson (2000, 8).

3 I am grateful to Patty Milligan for making me aware of the archival photographs at the Glenbow Museum in Calgary, Alberta.

4 For a discussion of 'North' as a racist signifier for Canada see Berger (1966).

5 Bird's intertitles refer to Ukrainians variously as Galicians and Ruthenians; Galicia and Ruthenia represent two regions of Ukraine.

6 Founded in 1908, Lord Baden-Powell's Scouting movement has been perceived as a symbolic system creating and preserving ideal national and imperial histories through the training of boys in citizenship. The subtitle of Baden-Powell's manual, *Scouting for Boys*, is 'A Handbook for Good Citizenship'. For analysis of the nationalist and imperialist aspects of Scouting see MacDonald (1993).

7 See Balibar's discussion of the relation between religion and national ideology. 'Incontestably, national ideology involves ideal signifiers (first and foremost the very name of the nation or "fatherland") on to which may be transferred the sense of the sacred and the affects of love, respect, sacrifice and fear which have cemented religious communities' (1991, 95).

8 For a discussion of nationalism and gender see McClintock, 'No Longer in a Future Heaven: Nationalism, Gender and Race' (1995, 352–89).

9 The British Privy Council reversed this decision in 1929.

10 See McLaren (1990, 9). The CCF (1932–61) was the socialist forerunner of Canada's New Democratic Party.

11 Marilyn Barber notes the difficulties in attributing specific views to Woodsworth as Arthur Ford wrote the section on Ruthenians; however, she does suggest that

Woodsworth's willingness to acknowledge general authorship of the book indicates that he shared Ford's views. See Barber's introduction to Woodsworth (1972, x).

12 As early as 1938 John Murray Gibbon represents Ukrainians as a component in what he conceptualizes as the mosaic of Canadian nation (1938, 282–307). However, Gibbon's mosaic exploits ethnic difference as commodity. An amateur folklorist and a publicist for the CPR, Gibbon staged folk festivals across the Canadian West during the 1920s to attract passengers to CPR trains and guests to the company's hotels (Francis 1997, 82). In Gibbon's paradigm ethnic difference becomes an entertainment spectacle consumed by Anglo-Canadian and Anglo-American tourists.

13 I do not mean to conflate the complex and disparate individual relationships Paul Kane and Emily Carr had with different Native cultures, but to emphasize that both artists idealized their Aboriginal subjects and that their success was predicated on the continued, no matter how lamented, disappearance of First Nations in Canada. For a thoughtful discussion of Kane's and Carr's work in the context of the 'vanishing race' discourse see Francis (1997, 16–43).

14 For a discussion of *Nass River Indians* (1927) and its relationship to the two films cut from it, *Saving the Sagas* (1928) and *Fish and Medicine Men* (1928), see Jessup's insightful essay (1999). Appendix 3 to Jessup's essay provides a reconstructed shot list for *Nass River Indians* (82).

15 See Francis (1997, 184).

16 Jessup's reconstruction of *Nass River Indians*, from a negative of the film, as well as a knowledge of *Saving the Sagas*, and *Fish and Medicine Men* indicates that this intertitle refers back to shots of young Nisga'a women working at a salmon cannery, shots not included when *Saving the Sagas* was cut from the original *Nass River Indians*. See Jessup (1999, 64).

17 Eric Cheyfitz, in a penetrating analysis of translation and colonization, writes: 'from its beginnings the imperialist mission is, in short, one of translation: the translation of the "other" into the terms of the empire, the prime term of which is "barbarian," or one of its variations such as "savage," which, ironically, but not without its precise politics also alienates the other from the empire' (1991, 112).

18 See Jessup (1999, 68–9).

19 See Jessup (1999, 66, 68).

20 See Kay J. Anderson's account of legislative regulation of Chinatown's limits in Vancouver (1994, 231–3).

21 See the letter that Anderson quotes from in which a white citizen voices her irrational anxieties about Chinese incursions into what she deems is the white cultural space of Vancouver (1994, 238).

22 Critical reception of the film confuses the location of Chinatown. Colin Browne's account of the film locates the setting as Victoria's Chinatown where much of the location shooting for the picture took place (1979, 260), while Peter Morris names Vancouver's Chinatown as the film's setting (1978, 191). As Morton's novel is set in Vancouver, and the film's establishing shot shows a map of the west coast with only Vancouver and Seattle labelled, I agree with Morris that Vancouver is the setting.

23 See Morris's reference to *Secrets of Chinatown* in the context of his informative discussion of the 'quota quickie' (1978, 191).

24 For more on Bishop and the history of Commonwealth Productions and Central Films see Morris (1978, 188–95).

25 After completion of the CPR, white anxiety over the Chinese presence in British Columbia resulted in the imposition of head taxes restricting, and eventually suspending, Chinese immigration to Canada after 1923 with the Exclusion Act

(Anderson 1991, 56–63, 139–41). Chinese in Canada were denied the franchise (53) and subject to discriminatory labour legislation (52).

26 One of the better-known Fu Manchu films, MGM's *The Mask of Fu Manchu*, starring Boris Karloff, was released in 1932. For a discussion of the representation of Chinese in the Fu Manchu novels of Sax Rohmer and in Hollywood films see Eugene Franklin Wong, *On Visual Media: Asians in the American Motion Picture's Racism* (New York: Arno Press, 1978): 95–102.

27 See Gary Y. Okihiro's discussion of Charles H. Pearson's influential idea of the yellow peril. Pearson predicted that peoples of colour 'marshalled and led by the Asians . . . would challenge white rule and spread and expand beyond the tropical band into the temperate, more desirable zones, and thereby threaten the very heart of the white homeland' (1994, 129–30).

28 For more on white anxieties around miscegenation see Young (1995, 101–3).

29 For a discussion of white patriarchal legislation 'sparing' the white women from the Chinese man, see Anderson (1991, 158–64).

30 See Dyer on the matter of whiteness and representations of the white Christian male as the idealized form of humanity (1997, 27–30).

31 As I did in my discussion of *Saving the Sagas*, I am adapting Mulvey's work on the sexual imbalance in looking relations to read a racial imbalance in looking relations. See Mulvey (1989b, 20).

32 Mulvey associates visual unpleasure with the threat of castration in her discussion of the female figure's lack as 'something that the look continually circles around but disavows' (1989b, 21).

33 See Dyer (1997, 28). Frantz Fanon makes a similar argument for the white colonist's projection of sexuality on the African: 'Projecting his own desires onto the Negro, the white man behaves "as if" the Negro really had them' (1967, 165).

34 See Julia Ching on the secrecy surrounding Taoism (1993, 85).

35 Dyer summarizes the work of Toni Morrison, Edward Said and others as suggesting that white discourse 'reduces the non-white subject to a function of the white subject' (1997, 13).

36 For a discussion of these events see Adachi (1991, 199–277).

37 The term 'Japanese Canadian' marks a racialized subject and is the administrative term the government developed to replace 'person of Japanese race', the term which appeared in the Orders in Council disenfranchising and interning Canadians of Japanese ancestry. However, as Roy Miki writes, the state's new term 'inscribed the racialized "Japanese" as the subordinating limit of "Canadian"'. None the less, Japanese Canadian was the term preferred by those whom it was used to designate. See Miki (1998, 194).

3 PRODUCING A NATIONAL CINEMA

1 For a brief history of the CGMPB see Backhouse (1974).

2 See Cowan (1930, 10).

3 On Grierson's recommendations see D. B. Jones, *Movies and Memoranda: An Interpretative History of the National Film Board of Canada* (Ottawa: Canadian Film Institute, 1981): 21.

4 Peter Morris cautions that there is evidence to suggest that NFB audience claims during Grierson's tenure at the board were exaggerated (Morris 1986, 27).

5 *Peoples of Canada* (1947) is a revised version of *This Is Our Canada* (1945).

6 Although the first Indo-Pakistani immigrants had arrived in British Columbia in 1903, by 1910 Indian immigration to Canada was restricted by an Order in Council requiring continuous passage from India to Canada when no shipping lines

provided such passage. The *Komagata Maru* incident of 1914 exemplifies Canada's racially exclusionary immigration practices. The *Komagata Maru*, a Japanese freighter carrying mostly Sikh immigrants, was detained for two months in Vancouver in 1914 under the continuous passage policy. During detainment passengers were not permitted to leave the confines of the ship. On 23 July the ship was towed out of the harbour by port authorities. While confined to the ship one passenger died and several suffered from serious malnutrition. Ultimately, the *Komagata Maru* and its passengers were refused entry into the country and upon their arrival back in India twenty-six would-be immigrants to Canada died in skirmishes with Indian authorities. See Fleras and Elliott (1996, 75–6).

7 See Winks (1997, 303).

8 The Orangeman's Parade is a triumphalist procession commemorating the Protestant victory of William of Orange over the Irish Catholic community in the Battle of the Boyne in 1690.

9 The NFB archive in Montreal holds no production notes on *Negroes*, and a conversation with William O'Farrell Sr, a Crawley employee in the 1940s, failed to shed any light on the film's aborted production. After viewing the cutting copy of *Negroes* NFB director and producer Jerry Krepakevich suggested that the unknown director hadn't shot enough useful footage to cobble together a film.

10 One interesting NFB film of this period, *Welcome Neighbour* (Leslie McFarlane 1949), encourages all Canadians, and especially Canadians in the service industries, to embrace American tourism.

11 The National Archives of Canada restored Dominion Productions' 1946 melodrama *Bush Pilot* with financial support from TMN-MOVIEPIX in 1997.

12 For a detailed discussion of *cinéma direct* see Euvard and Véronneau (1980, 77–93).

13 Euvard and Véronneau question whether or not *Pour la suite du monde* constitutes Cinéma direct. Although Perrault uses real people, not actors, Euvard and Véronneau argue that they are rehearsed and that the event of the Beluga whale hunt is not a spontaneous one, but a re-enactment of a disappeared traditional practice for the camera (1980, 82–3).

14 For a detailed reading of *Québec–USA* see Chapter 4.

15 For a discussion of commercial cinema during this period see Pierre Pageaut, 'A Survey of the Commercial Cinema' in Handling and Véronneau (1980).

16 For a discussion of the formation of and work by the Interdepartmental Committee on the Possible Development of Feature Film Production in Canada, see Dorland (1998, 92–110).

17 See Telefilm Canada's website: http://www.telefilm.gc.ca/en/org/hist.htm (accessed 10 November 1999).

18 Ibid.

19 See Telefilm Canada's website: http://www.telefilm.gc.ca/en/affint/coprod.htm (accessed 10 November 1999).

20 Ibid.

21 Ibid.

22 Ibid.

23 Ibid.

24 Both Wheeler and Burns made their comments as a part of the Robarts Centre for Canadian Studies' *Triumph of Canadian Cinema 2000–2001* series forum, 'Can I Make the Films I Want to Make in Canada Today?', 12 September 2000, Toronto. I am grateful to Seth Feldman, Robarts Chair, who co-ordinated the *Triumph of Canadian Cinema* series and made a tape of this conversation available to me.

25 See Canadian Press, 'Film Fund Could Hit $100M', *The Edmonton Journal*, 15 September 1999: C3.

26 See Wyndham Wise, 'Take One's Annual Survey of Canadian Features Released in the GTA', *Take One* Spring (2001): 48. Wise's survey of screen time in the Greater Toronto Area found that 34 Canadian features played on 568 screens.
27 See Johnson (1996).

4 NARRATING NATIONS/MA(R)KING DIFFERENCES

1 The National Policy's tariff structure was designed to encourage US manufacturing firms to invest in production locations in Canada, as opposed to exporting manufactured goods into the country. See Phillips (1979).
2 See Colleen Fuller, 'Fade to Black: Culture Under Free Trade', *Canadian Forum*, August 1991: 5–10, and Roy MacSkimming, 'Publishing in a Blockbuster Culture', *Canadian Forum*, March 1991: 18–20.
3 See Fredric Jameson's discussion of a US-led multinational capitalism that constitutes a 'global, yet American, postmodern culture' (Jameson 1993, 5).
4 See also 'The Quebec Act' in Hilda Neatby, ed., *The Quebec Act: Protest and Policy* (Scarborough, ON: Prentice-Hall, 1972): 49.
5 For a history of language legislation in Canada from the eighteenth century into the 1990s and more detail on the Official Languages Act see Wilfrid Denis, 'Language Policy in Canada', in Peter S. Li, ed., *Race and Ethnic Relations in Canada* (Toronto: Oxford University Press, 2nd ed., 1999): 178–216.
6 The most significant of these negotiations was the Meech Lake Accord (1987), a constitutional amendment proposed by the Mulroney government which, among other things, would have recognized Québec as a distinct society. The accord was defeated when it failed to get unanimous ratification by the provinces in 1990. On the constitutional process see Michael Burgess 'Meech Lake: The Process of Constitutional Reform in Canada, 1987–1990', *British Journal of Canadian Studies* 5.2 (1990): 275–96. See also M. D. Beheils, ed., *The Meech Lake Primer: Conflicting Views of the 1987 Constitutional Accord* (Ottawa: University of Ottawa Press, 1989).
7 Although 60 per cent of Quebeckers rejected Sovereignty Association in 1980, 49.6 per cent voted in favour of it in 1995.
8 Her interests in representing nationalism cinematically eventually led her to shoot *Pierre Vallières* (1972), a 'mouthscape' that focused on the lips of the radical Québécois nationalist reciting three essays. Wieland refers to the film as a mouthscape in her document *Pierre Vallières: Notes from the Filmmaker*. Joyce Wieland clippings file, Canadian Filmmakers Distribution Centre.
9 See Parpart (1999, 257).
10 See my discussion of this Atwood poem in Chapter 3, p. 87.
11 See Anne McClintock's discussion of male nationalisms' exploitation of women's bodies to define 'the limits of national difference and power between men' (1995: 354).
12 Like her 'mother', the male-authored Britannia, Canada possesses hermaphrodite powers and can be transformed from 'Daughter of the Empire' or the Miss Canada figure of late-nineteenth-century and early-twentieth-century political cartoons into a white phallic entity that colonizes the territory of the continent's First Peoples. This phallic potential is manifest in Canadian history in immigration poetry figuring Canada as a woman inviting male British colonists to conquer her. In Canadian film history, titles such as Freer's *Harnessing the Virgin Prairie* draw on the patriarchal sign systems of empire- and nation-building to metaphorize territories as empty, the subordinate bodies of virgin women which, as McClintock

puts it, passively await 'the thrusting male insemination of history, language and reason' (1995, 30).

13 Despite the ideological work of displacing First Nations performed, unwittingly (?), by her gendering of the nation as a white female victim of imperialism, Wieland did engage the politics of relations between invader-settler and Native in other works. Her 1973 Isaacs exhibition was structured around the Cree and the flooding of their lands by the James Bay Hydro project. See Gunda Lambton, *Stealing the Show: Seven Women Artists in Canadian Public Art* (Montreal and Kingston: McGill-Queen's University Press, 1994): 91.

14 See Brenda Longfellow, 'Gender, Landscape, and Colonial Allegories in *The Far Shore*, *Loyalties*, and *Mouvements du désir*', in *Gendering the Nation: Canadian Women's Cinema* (Toronto: Toronto University Press, 1999): 165–82 (167).

15 See Metz (1975: 18).

16 Jim Leach discusses a similar dynamic where he sees Canadian films inflecting American genres to tell Canadian stories. See his consideration of genre in the films of David Cronenberg, Québec cinema and what he tentatively calls post-Canadian cinema in 'North of Pittsburgh: Genre and National Cinema from a Canadian Perspective', in Barry K. Grant, ed., *Film Genre Reader II* (Austin: University of Texas Press, 1995): 474–93.

17 See Elsaesser (1992, 512–35).

18 O'Regan's concept of indigenization is drawn from semiotician Yuri Lotman's theory of culture as a 'semiosphere', where all national cultures pass through five stages that transform them from receiving cultures to transmitting cultures. See O'Regan (1996, 214) and Lotman, *Universe of the Mind: A Semiotic Theory of Culture* (Bloomington and Indianapolis: Indiana University Press, 1990): 146–7.

19 See Sigmund Freud, 'The Uncanny', in *The Penguin Freud Library Volume 14. Art and Literature*: 339–76.

20 In a discussion of melodrama and ideological analysis, Christine Gledhill raises the issue of 'the degree to which the melodramatic text works both on an "imaginary" level, internal to fictional production, and on a realist level, which refers to the world outside the text' (Gledhill 1987, 37).

21 Quoted dialogue is taken from the English subtitles of the NFB film.

22 In developing his argument that Antoine is representative of an old and corrupt social order, Heinz Weinmann makes an interesting correlation between the bourgeois shop owner Antoine and the symbol of social hierarchy in old Québec, the segnieur as he is represented in Phillipe Joseph Aubert de Gaspé's 1863 novel *Les anciens Canadiens*. See Weinmann (1990, 71).

23 Quoting Jutra, Jim Leach notes the director's awareness of the signifying power of Québec's asbestos country as one of the first sites of the ' "political agitation and labour unrest" that set the stage for the Quiet Revolution' (Leach 1999, 137).

24 According to Freud *das heimlich* and *das unheimliche* are inextricably linked: 'for this uncanny is in reality nothing new or alien, but something which is familiar and old-established in the mind and which has become alienated from it only through the process of repression' ('The Uncanny' (note 19), 363–4). Jutra's denaturalizing of inequitable social relations illuminates a knowledge of a Québec repressed by social structures.

25 Pallister sees the film as a sociological study in poverty (1992, 252).

26 Translations of dialogue are taken from the film's English subtitles.

27 While Manon has access to the novel in her paperback copy of *Wuthering Heights*, it is not a display of class status like the hardcover copy of the book she takes from Viau-Vachon's library.

28 Quoted dialogue is taken from the film's English subtitles.

29 Paul, Pierre's father, relates an anecdote to Hitchcock in which Duplessis explains to Pierre's grandfather the reason why he always wears an old broken-down hat: 'This is what the French Canadian wants to be and this is the French Canadian.'

30 According to Mulvey, 'ideological contradiction is the overt mainspring and specific content of melodrama' (1989d, 75).

31 While theories of spectator identification have argued that the spectator is constructed by the meanings of the text (Baudry 1986), more recent work recognizes that the subject can resist or collude with the dominant ideology of a text to construct meaning. See Hayward (1996, 332 and 182).

32 See Schiller. For Herbert Schiller cultural imperialism is the sum of processes by which a society is brought into the modern world system and how its dominating stratum is attracted, pressured, forced and sometimes bribed into shaping social institutions to correspond to, or even promote, the values and structures of the dominating system (1976, 32).

33 Promotional material on the back of the Warner Brothers' video box for *I Confess* reads: 'Partially filmed in Quebec on location highlighting that city's Old World traditions'.

34 The English actress Kristin Scott Thomas is the exception here, playing the peripheral role of Hitchcock's secretary.

35 Brendan Kelly's (1994) review in *Variety* notes Lepage's 'numerous tips of the hat to famed Hitchcock scenes'.

36 I am drawing on Linda Hutcheon's theorizing of parody in which she cites Laurent Jenny on 'the role of self-consciously revolutionary texts . . . to rework those discourses whose weight has become too tyrannical' (Hutcheon 1985, 72).

37 See Lyotard on postmodernism as directing scepticism towards totalizing systems or metanarratives (Lyotard 1984, xxiv).

38 Parpart quotes Kenneth McRoberts who argues that under Canadian federalism a region, in this case Québec, may occupy the spaces of core and periphery simultaneously (McRoberts 1979, 299).

39 Regarding foreign and Central Canadian investment, Parpart's meticulously researched essay cites David Black's informative research on the economics of coal on Cape Breton. See Black (1980, 13).

40 See Urquhart (1999, 17) and Parpart (1999b, 65).

41 For a discussion of the imbrications of internal colonialism, capitalist production and the construction of a castrated masculinity in *Margaret's Museum* see Parpart (1999b).

42 'Because it reproduces the family and within it the displaced sense of alienation, the melodrama makes visible, in the form of familial tensions, the exploitation and oppression differingly experienced by members of the family [at the hands of the labour process].' See Hayward on the displacement of alienated labour into the domestic sphere under her entry for melodrama (1996, 203).

43 See Kleinhans (1978, 41–2) and Mulvey (1989b, 39). See also Hayward (1996, 203).

44 For discussions of the Highland emigration and the clearances, see T. C. Smout, *A History of the Scottish People 1560–1830* [1969] (London: Fontana Collins 1972): 311–37.

45 On internal colonialism within Britain see Daniel Hechter, *Internal Colonialism: The Celtic Fringe in British National Development 1536–1966* (London: Routledge, 1975).

46 Ironically, the location shooting for the scenes set in the mine was done in one of the world's largest miner's museums, the Scottish Mining Museum at

Newton Grange, Scotland, where miners made redundant by the collapse of the coal industry conduct tours of the pits.

47 See Gledhill (1985a: 77).

48 On commodity fetishism see Karl Marx, *Capital* 1.4.

49 David Lynch's *Blue Velvet* (1986) is a US film that plays with melodrama to interrogate the tensions between appearances and reality extending from the Eisenhower dream to a 1980s vision of drugs and violent crime in an American middle-class 'neighbourhood'.

50 See Thomas Elsaesser's seminal essay (1992, 524) and Mulvey (1989d, 74).

51 See my discussion of Atwood's poem 'Backdrop Addresses Cowboy' in Chapter 3, p. 87.

52 For more on Hollywood's stereotypical representation of Canada see Berton (1975). On Hollywood's construction of Canada in *Rose Marie* (Mervyn LeRoy 1954) see my essay (Gittings 1998).

53 I am indebted to Robyn Fowler for making me aware of this reference.

54 As Wilson reveals in interview, the concept of *My American Cousin* developed, in part, out of 16-mm home movies shot by her father that she edited into a film she called *Growing Up in Paradise* (1977). See Cole and Dale (1993, 253).

55 The success of *My American Cousin* in the American and Canadian markets prompted Wilson to take Sandy down south for a visit with Butch in the sequel *American Boyfriends* (1989), an ill-fated journey that did not live up to the artistic or commerical success of the original.

56 Geoff Pevere reads Jackie Bangs as a 'pistol-packing American outlaw figure' which she is and is not. See Pevere (1992b: 37). Blaine Allan comes closer to the mark in his observation that her identity 'remains deliberately ambiguous, and in flux'. See Allan (1993, 77).

57 Ramsay quotes Dane Lanken, who suggests that *Goin' Down the Road* is the first made-in-Canada movie to get a positive response at home and abroad. *Back to God's Country*, shot in Canada (exteriors) and California (interiors), was highly successful at the domestic box office, in the US market and in Europe. See Turner (1992). Also quoted by Ramsay is Jim Beebe, who sees *Goin' Down the Road* as 'the first real English-Canadian movie'. See Ramsay (1993, 33).

58 Atwood articulates her understanding of Canadian cultural products as victims of a US and formerly British imperialism (1972). For a discussion of the shortcomings of Atwood's thesis see Davey (1984).

59 See Black (1980).

60 A more striking use of the western genre as an ideological tool of US imperialism is the 'cultural diplomacy' engaged in by *Green Berets* (Ray Kellog, John Wayne 1968). Although it is set in Vietnam, its star and co-director, John Wayne, an icon of the Hollywood western, and the film's jingoistic plot invoke the narrative of US expansion present in the western, hailing or recruiting spectators to support US military intervention in Vietnam.

61 See Gledhill on gender and sexuality in the western (1985b, 69).

62 In Connell's testimonial of his own gender formation by Hollywood we have an excellent illustration of Teresa de Lauretis's understanding of cinema as a social technology that produces gender. De Lauretis adapts Michel Foucault's thinking about the technology of sex to conceptualize a technology of gender. See De Lauretis, 'Technologies of Gender' (1987, 2).

63 See De Lauretis, 'Technologies of Gender'.

64 See Schatz (1981, 54–7) Horrocks (1995, 68–70).

65 The film's credits acknowledge Killiam Shows as the source of these stagecoach scenes. According to Blaine Allan's research on Borsos, the director obtained stock

footage from Killiam Shows' agent John Rogers entitled 'Stagecoach scenes' and 'Stagecoach robbery, bandits, posse'. I am grateful to Blaine Allan for sharing his research notes on this footage with me.

66 Although Bill Miner is reported to have travelled to Europe after his escape from prison in British Columbia, the historical record does not reference Kate Flynn. Unlike the happy ending of *The Grey Fox*, which sees Miner living in Europe with his lover, the historical Bill Miner was recaptured by American authorities and died in a Georgia prison in 1913 after a failed escape. See Frank W. Anderson, *Bill Miner . . . Stagecoach and Train Robber* (Surrey, BC: Heritage House Publishing, 1982): 53.

67 For a brief history of Bill Miner and his exploits in Canada see Frank W. Anderson.

68 See Chapter 3 on the tax-shelter film.

69 Although there is not a lot of hard evidence that the British tamperd with the 1948 referendum, rumours of interference in the democratic process persist. See Gwynne Dyer's assessment of the possible subversion of democracy in Newfoundland in 1948, 'Newf Truth', *Globe and Mail*, 27 March 1999, natl ed.: D1–D2.

70 See Nichols (1991, 59) on the reflexive mode of documentary representation.

71 Althusser differentiates between ISAs which function by ideology and RSAs which function predominantly by violent repression, but also by ideology. See Althusser (1971, 138).

72 The entire text of the FLQ manifesto is available in Spry's film but also appears in a very useful reference text alongside other documents pertinent to the October Crisis. See Saywell (1971, 46–51).

73 In addition to Rosenthal's interview with Spry concerning the production of *Action*, see Gary Evans's discussion of the film (1991, 189–90).

74 The NFB was not the only ISA of the federal government that was resistant to Spry's work on the film. The CBC refused to give him videotape of the FLQ Manifesto being read on air. Eventually, an illicit half-inch tape was unearthed surreptitiously and transferred to film. See Spry (1980, 251). For six months the CBC refused to broadcast *Action*, claiming that there wasn't an audience for it. Media pressure on the CBC to air the film was successful and might have contributed to the record public affairs audience of close to five million people who tuned into the national broadcast of the film in French and English. See Spry (1980, 254–5).

75 On the ethics and power differentials at stake in the documentary interview see Nichols (1991, 47).

76 For a discussion of the Patriote Rebellions see Fernand Ouellet, 'The Rebellions of 1837/8', in J. M. Bumstead, ed., *Interpreting Canada's Past. Volume One. Pre-Confederation*, 2nd ed. (Toronto.: Oxford University Press, 1993, 412–36).

77 I am indebted to David Annandale for his assistance in translating this text from the film.

78 I am quoting from the document entitled 'Foreword' in the press kit for *Octobre*.

79 See Pelletier's *The October Crisis* (Toronto: McClelland and Stewart, 1971). Trans. Joyce Marshall.

80 See Vallières's *The Assassination of Pierre Laporte: Behind the October '70 Scenario* (Toronto: James Lorimer and Company, 1977). Trans. Ralph Wells. See also Francis Simard, *Pour en finir avec octobre / Talking It Out: The October Crisis from Inside* (Montreal: Guernica, 1987). Trans. David Homel. Some of the accusations made by many critics of Trudeau's deployment of the War Measures Act were vindicated recently with the declassification of British documents. In a November 1970 meeting with his British counterpart, External Affairs Minister Mitchell Sharp confided that during the October Crisis the Trudeau government had 'no

evidence of an extensive and co-ordinated FLQ conspiracy' (quoted in Wallace 2001, A1).

81 Vallières's book (note 80) also follows this logic, arguing that Pierre Laporte was sacrificed by Bourassa and Trudeau 'for reasons of state' (84).

82 On Trudeau and the White Paper see Dickason (1997, 363–5).

5 VISUALIZING FIRST NATIONS

1 See Ward Churchill's discussion of Indian stereotypes in Hollywood film (1992, 231–41). See also Jacquelyn Kilpatrick's genealogy of Indian stereotypes from the dime novel to the wild west show (1999, 1–15).

2 See John L. Tobias (1983, 40–1).

3 See Olive Patricia Dickason on the Indian Act (1997, 259).

4 As Cheryl Suzack notes in her entry on First Nations and Women, First Nations is a term distinct from Métis and Inuit that 'does not replace individual, culturally-specific tribal names' (Suzack forthcoming).

5 Most North American reviews of *Black Robe* compared it favourably to Costner's film. See Scott (1991); Gilmor (1991). See also Ward Churchill's essay in which he summarizes and takes issue with the glowing reviews *Black Robe* received for its sensitivity and accurate representation of Native cultures from the *Globe and Mail*, the *New Yorker* and the *New York Times* (1992b).

6 Twice nominated for an Academy Award, Beresford had directed major Hollywood films such as *Tender Mercies* (1983) and *Driving Miss Daisy* (1989) before he worked on *Black Robe*.

7 In her discussion of the white appropriation of Native stories, Lenore Keeshing-Tobias asks if some whites consider Native stories to be natural resources like water and trees 'just waiting for the hand of the white man's civilization to make them useful? Something else to sell to the Americans?' See Keeshing-Tobias (1990).

8 I am paraphrasing Rony's comments on the work of Edward Sherriff Curtis here. Rony writes that Curtis never intended his cinematic mythology of the Indian to include 'the complex ways the Native Americans have negotiated the presence of whites in the Americas' (1996, 91).

9 Drew Hayden Taylor refers to *Clearcut* as 'an awful movie' because of what he sees as the film's representation of the Native as sadistic torturer. See 'Indian Movies Speak with Forked Tongue', *Toronto Star*, 10 March 1995, D2.

10 Deborah Root suggests that 'Peter, the white liberal lawyer, *produces* Arthur out of his own anger, guilt and frustration, and out of what he had read in books about Native violence and anger' (1993, 47).

11 Toronto's Sunrise Films acted as the film's Canadian producer.

12 The casting of Parillaud and Lee could well be one of the exigencies of international co-productions, ensuring bankable stars to attract audiences in a variety of markets. Ward says that he once thought he would 'use an actual Inuit' for the role of Avik and looked as far afield as Greenland and Alaska but eventually was looking in New York and Los Angeles where he found Lee. See Henry Sheehan, 'Search all over the "Map" Turns up a Charismatic Avik', *Ottawa Citizen*, 14 May 1993, E1. Perhaps he should have looked more closely in the Canadian Arctic, where Inuit film-maker Zacharias Kunuk casts Inuit in his productions. See Jane George, 'TV from the True True North', *Edmonton Journal*, 25 February 1997, B6.

13 See Terry Lusty's review 'Dance Me Outside Maintains Stereotypes', *Windspeaker*, April 1995, 18.

14 See the NFB document *Aboriginal Filmmaking Program and Training Initiatives for Aboriginal Peoples in Filmmaking*, August 1977, 7.

15 Ibid., 4.

16 Ibid., 6.

17 See the website for *Atanarjuat*: http://atanarjuat.com/. *Atanarjuat* was awarded the Camera d'Or at Cannes 2001.

18 For a history of Mohawk claims to territory at Kanehsatake see Geoffrey York and Loreen Pindera, *People of the Pines: The Warriors and the Legacy of Oka* (Toronto: Little Brown and Company, 1991): 82–113.

19 See Donna Goodleaf's account of the raid on the Pines (1995, 56).

20 From the footage remaining after the final cut of *Kanehsatake*, Obomsawin produced three more NFB films, *My Name is Kahentiiosta* (1995), *Spudwrench – Kahnawake Man* (1997), and *Rocks at Whisky Trench* (2000).

21 For a study of the Canadian newspaper industry's mostly negative representation of the Mohawks during events at Oka see Warren H. Skea, 'The Canadian Newspaper Industry's Portrayal of the Oka Crisis', *Native Studies Review* 9.1 (1993–4): 15–31.

22 In fairness to the journalists working at Oka, it must be noted that, as Obomsawin's film documents, the Canadian army did its best to ensure that reporters could not do their job by cutting phone lines and supplies and attempting to seize journalists' audio and video tapes. Commenting on the army's interference with the freedom of the press, *Globe and Mail* reporter Geoffrey York tells Obomsawin's camera: 'I think the thing that's the most unbelievable is that in a country like Canada, we're allowing the army to tell us what can be published in our newspapers and what can be put on our nightly news.' For more on the army's management of the media at Oka see Sandy Greer, 'Mohawks and the Media: Alanis Obomsawin's *Kanehsatake: 270 Years of Resistance*', *Take One*, Winter 1994, 18–21.

23 In a nationally televised statement Mulroney also referred to the Mohawks behind the barricades as a 'band of terrorists' and 'warrior-led' negotiators. See Terrance Wills, 'Mulroney Supports Use of Army, Urges Mohawks to Yield', *The Gazette*, [Montreal] 29 August 1990, A4.

24 Joe Deom, a negotiator for the warriors, testified under oath that he met a representative of NPR Inc. who told him that his firm had been engaged by the federal and provincial governments to 'propagandize'. Deom learned from other public relations firms that NPR Inc.'s 'expertise is in discrediting and misrepresenting the facts' (quoted in Goodleaf, 1995, 68).

25 For more on the co-optation of the media during the Oka Crisis see Greer 1994 (note 22): 20.

26 Obomsawin's cameras record the warrior's own strategies for returning the surveillant, colonizing gaze of the Canadian army that would define Aboriginality. To prevent the army's gaze from penetrating their positions the warriors used two large mirrors to reflect back the state's lights and lenses and eventually erected a tarpaulin to block the view of the army.

27 Donna Goodleaf relates two horrifying racially motivated attacks on Mohawk women by whites in Chateauguay. In one incident a white mob chased a teenaged Mohawk girl through a shopping mall until the police intervened, in another a woman was hit by a car door and beaten severely by a white woman and her boyfriend. On the racism and violence exhibited by Chateauguay residents see Goodleaf (1995, 60–5).

28 Obomsawin's *Rocks at Whisky Trench* (2000) deals specifically with the stoning of Mohawk vehicles.

29 The Warrior Society at Kanehsatake and Kahnewake represents the interests of the traditional Longhouse peoples, sometimes in opposition to the band councils

whose power is derived from the Indian Act. Alfred describes the Longhouse as 'a parallel system of government' (1995, 132). For a history of the tensions between the Longhouse and the band council at Kahnewake see Gerald R. Alfred, *Heeding the Voices of Our Ancestors: Kahnawake Mohawk Politics and the Rise of Native Nationalism* (Don Mills, ON: Oxford University Press, 1995): 129–48.

30 The circulation of racist stereotypes of First Nations women was in evidence at Oka when Obomsawin was berated as a 'squaw' and had other racist insults hurled at her by Canadian soldiers while she went about her work near the barricades (York and Pindera 1991, 375).

31 See 'We Stand on Guard', *Edmonton Journal*, 19 November 1995, A2.

32 See 'Kanesatake [*sic*] Narrowly Ratifies Self-governance' .

33 I would like to thank Rob Appleford for drawing this article to my attention.

34 On the white appropriation of Native culture see Francis (1997, 184–5).

6 MULTICULTURAL FIELDS OF VISION

1 My rehearsal of this argument is indebted to Smaro Kamboureli's incisive and cogent analysis of the contradictions located in Bill C-93's intertexts. See Kamboureli, 'The Technology of Ethnicity: Canadian Multiculturalism and the Language of Law', in David Bennett, ed., *Multicultural States: Rethinking Difference and Identity* (New York and London: Routledge, 1998: 208–22).

2 As Bannerji notes, English language, culture and ethnicity stand outside the marginalizing framework of multiculturalism: 'English language and Canadian culture then cannot fall within the ministry of multiculturalism's purview, but rather within that of the ministry of education, while racism makes sure that the possession of this language as a mother tongue does not make a non white person non ethnic.' See Bannerji (2000: 113).

3 A more recent poll conducted by *Maclean's* magazine and Global Television published similar findings: 71 per cent of those polled agreed with the statement 'Canada should . . . insist that immigrants adopt Canadian values', while 33 per cent agreed that Canada should increase the number of immigrants to the country each year and 49 per cent disagreed with this increase. See Robert Sheppard, 'We Are Canadian', *Maclean's*, 25 December 2000/1 January 2001: 26–32 (32).

4 The 'Interpretation' section of the Multiculturalism Act excludes Aboriginal people from the legislation. See Kamboureli and the inherent contradictions of Bill C-93 evinced through this exclusion and the universalizing language of the legislation. Kamboureli (note 1): 216–17.

5 Workers' anxiety about Chinese immigration produced such anti-Chinese lobby groups as the Working Men's Protective Association, Knights of Labour and the Asiatic Exclusion League. See Donald Avery and Peter Neary, 'Laurier, Borden and a White British Columbia', *Journal of Canadian Studies* 12.4 (1977): 25.

6 For a discussion of anti-Asian sentiment in British Columbia from the mid-nineteenth century to 1907 see ibid., 24–34.

7 See Pierre Berton, *The Last Spike* (Toronto: McClelland and Stewart, 1971): 206, 204.

8 See '*Secrets of Chinatown*: the monstrous ethnographic' in Chapter 2 and an excerpt from the 1902 Report of the Royal Commission on Chinese and Japanese Immigration quoted by Kay J. Anderson (1991, 223) and by me on p. 55.

9 For a survey of the representation of race in Canadian and American film and television see Alan Smith, 'Seeing Things: Race, Image, and National Identity in Canadian and American Movies and Television', *American Review of Canadian Studies* 26.3 (1996): 367–90.

10 I am referring here to W. E. B. Du Bois's concept of double-consciousness whereby the dominant culture disciplines raced Others to see themselves through its racializing eyes. Writing about the African-American experience in 1903, Du Bois describes double-consciousness as 'a peculiar sensation . . . this sense of always looking at one's self through the eyes of others, of measuring one's soul by the tape of a world that looks on in amused contempt and pity'. See Du Bois [1903] (1961, 16–17). While Jade grows out of her desire to become *The Brady Bunch*, Clement Virgo's character Reese is condemned to see himself through a racializing white gaze.

11 See Adachi [1976] (1991, 159–60).

12 See Vijay Mishra's comments on 'the idea of a homeland that is always present visibly and aurally (through video cassettes, films, tapes and CDs)' in his essay 'The Diasporic Imaginary', *Textual Practice* 10.3 (1996): 434. Ironically, Grandma Tikkoo's 'return' to India through the films of Bollywood might take on a new wrinkle, given recent developments in Bollywood location shooting. Since 1995 Canada has been a preferred location for Bollywood producers, with approximately twelve films shooting here every year to exploit such visuals as Roy Thompson Hall, the Parliament buildings, Niagara Falls and the Rocky Mountains. Apparently, the diversity of architectural styles and Canadian landscapes attracts Indian directors who are in search of the exotic and romantic. See Sarah Elton, 'Hooray for Bollywood', *National Post*, 27 January 2001, natl. ed., B6.

13 Srinivas Krishna tells Cameron Bailey that he started writing what he thought 'would be a very simple genre picture, some kind of *Rebel Without a Cause*, alienated youth thing'. See Krishna (1992, 45).

14 I am borrowing again from Lloyd's incisive conceptualization of race and representation. See Lloyd (1991, 74).

15 During the writing and production of *Masala* the press and law-enforcement authorities suspected that Sikh terrorists blew up Air India Flight 182 to avenge Indira Gandhi's 1984 attack on the Golden Temple and to draw attention to the plight of Sikh separatists fighting for the establishment of a Sikh homeland, Khalistan, in India's Punjab state. In late October 2000 the RCMP charged two Vancouver Sikhs with 331 counts of murder (this figure includes the two baggage handlers who died when a second bomb exploded at Tokyo's Narita airport).

16 See the James Strachey translation of '*heimisch*' as 'native' in Freud (1990, 341).

17 The garlanding may also be read as a postcolonial mimicry of colonial practice on the Indian subcontinent where colonial administrators were garlanded with the *mala*, a practice that extends to members of the contemporary Indian bureaucracy. This reading would complement Krishna's location of his film in 'the land of the colonial father'. I am grateful to Mridula Nath Chakraborty for suggesting this interpretation of the scene.

18 On slavery in Canada, see Winks (1997, 1–113). On segregated schools see Winks (385–6).

19 See Clarke (1998); Foster (1996); David Sealy, 'Canadianizing Blackness: Resisting the Political', in Rinaldo Walcott, ed., *Rude: Contemporary Black Canadian Cultural Criticism* (Toronto: Insomniac Press, 2000): 87–108.

20 Rinaldo Walcott's reading of the film refuses this interpretation, asserting 'the inability to work with the imagined realities of blackness in Canada are clearly not broached by the filmmaker(sic)' (1997): 57. While Walcott points to what he reads as Virgo's failure to problematize the place of home, dismissing Rude's rap invoking the Mohawk and Zulu Nations as 'never explored in any sustained manner', his argument is not, to me, a cogent one. The place of home, I will argue, is problem-

atized in terms of structures of belonging that shape Rude's broadcasts, and the police response to them.

21 For a discussion of the policing of Blackness in Toronto and media representations of Black youth in Toronto as criminals see Jackson (1993, 181–200).

22 Quoting a 1992 study for Multiculturalism and Citizenship Canada of the occupations of Blacks in the Greater Toronto Area, a region that comprises more than 75 per cent of the Canadian Black population, Cecil Foster reports that 'the largest job classifications for Blacks are in clerical (21 per cent), manufacturing (16 per cent) and services (13 per cent)'. According to the same study 83 per cent of Blacks living in the area have an annual income of $25,000 or less. See Foster (1996, 24).

23 I am indebted to Peter Harcourt for this reference. See his essay 'Faces Changing Colour Changing Canon: Shifting Cultural Foci Within Contemporary Canadian Cinema', *cineACTION* 45, February (1998): 9.

24 Many thanks to Stephen Slemon for making me aware of Joseph Owens's book.

25 Paul Chafe's insightful reading of DJ Rude's 'Destruction Rap' in a graduate research paper shares much with my own, independently arrived-at interpretation of this scene.

26 Rude receives calls from people within the Black community who take issue with her broadcast, people who speak their difference to Rude's representation of a Black community. For example, one caller takes exception to Rude's references to sightings of the Conquering Lion of Judah, her defining of a Black community through Jamaican co-ordinates: 'Like what are these people talking about? Are they nuts? I mean are we living in a goddamn zoo or what? Only a bunch of ganja-smoking fucked-up Jamaicans would come up with that shit. There is no lion in the goddamned projects, okay.' Another, homophobic, caller complains about Rude's frank talk about sexuality, providing her with an opportunity to delineate the elision of homosexuality in the Black community: 'Haven't you heard nigger, we got no fags, lesbians, dykes, queers, homosexuals in the Black Community.'

7 SCREENING GENDER AND SEXUALITY

1 Kaja Silverman, in her discussion of the female voice in cinema, says of the male voice-over: 'the capacity of the male subject to be cinematically represented in this disembodied form aligns him with transcendence, authoritative knowledge, potency and the law – in short, with the symbolic father' (Silverman 1984, 134).

2 For one example of a Courriveau narrative see Charles G. D. Roberts's translation of nineteenth-century Québécois writer Phillipe Aubert de Gaspé's 'La Courriveau' in Alberto Manguel, ed., *The Oxford Book of Canadian Ghost Stories* (Toronto: Oxford University Press, 1990): 1–10.

3 *Valérie* (Denis Héroux 1969) was the first in what became a lucrative series of soft porn films from Québec that *Variety* dubbed 'maple syrup porno'. See Magder (1993, 135–6).

4 Klein's documentary takes a pro-porn Montreal stripper, Linda Lee Tracey, and the viewer on a tour of porn stores, peep shows, porno films and a *Hustler* magazine photo shoot in which Linda Lee poses for and is humiliated by porn photographer Suze Randall. Linda's experiences on the tour change her mind about the porn industry, and she comes to see herself as the exploited woman on display when she is positioned before the lens of *Hustler* by Randall. B. Ruby Rich has written a provocative critique of this film in which she criticizes it as simplistic: 'Conversion cinema in action'. See B. Ruby Rich, 'Anti-porn: Soft Issue, Hard World', in Kay Armatage, Kass Banning, Brenda Longfellow and Janine

Marchessault, eds, *Gendering the Nation: Canadian Women's Cinema* (Toronto: University of Toronto Press, 1999): 62–75 (64). Rich argues that 'this anti-porn film is an acceptable replacement for porn itself' where 'the gaze of horror substitutes for the glaze of satiation' (65). Rich asks whether 'this alleged look of horror is not perhaps a more sophisticated form of voyeurism' (65).

5 My thanks to Cecily Devereux for helping me work through this idea.

6 For a discussion of lesbian subjectivity and compulsory heterosexuality see Adrien Rich's influential essay 'Compulsory Heterosexuality and Lesbian Existence', *Signs: Journal of Women in Culture and Society* 5 (1980): 631–60.

7 For a dissenting view see Marlon Harrison, 'Mermaids: Singing Off Key', *cineAction!* 16 (1989): 25–30. Harrison resists readings of *Mermaids* which position it as a feminist film, arguing that the three female characters figure as stereotypes in a narrative that is offensive to women and lesbians. The substantiation of this argument, however, is not compelling. Harrison asserts that Mary Joseph and the Curator will be read 'traditionally' as whores by the audience and interprets their costuming in leather as 'reinforcing yet another symbol of the bad girl' (29). An alternative reading of leather's signification in this context is as a marker for the superficial pretensions of the Queen Street art scene in the 1980s, a way of mocking the Curator, whom the film reveals as a fraud lacking any real vision. Harrison's claim that Polly never comes clean about her sexuality fails to account for her declaration of love for the Curator and her fantasy where she advocates Freud's polymorphous perversity to the Curator. Harrison's reading of Polly's voyeurism as a surrogate for the male gaze elides potential readings of her as a surrogate for Patricia Rozema, the film's director, without offering any evidence that she 'looks' phallocentrically. Finally, Harrison's suggestion that Polly's image is 'trite and offensive to women' because of her mimicking of the Curator and her incompetence as a secretary seems, to me, to miss the point entirely. Yes, Polly is an impressionable, naive eccentric woman who is 'organizationally impaired'; however, Polly, although she labels herself an 'unsuccessful career woman', is the only successful human being in the film. Unlike the Curator, she doesn't play at being an artist, she actively pursues her photography 'hobby'. She is the only character in the film who is honest with herself and others and she is revealed, in the end, to be an artist. Of the three women Polly possesses the only genuine imagination, the artistic vision that Mary Joseph and the Curator recognize in the final shots of the film.

8 See Eve Kosofsky Sedgwick on the maintenance of homosociality in her introduction to *Between Men: English Literature and Male Homosocial Desire* (New York: Columbia University Press, 1985): 1–20.

9 Greyson's film ends on a disturbing note signalling to the viewer the need for more activist work in a social unlearning of homophobia. One of Greyson's actors was gay-bashed in a public park in October 1990. The Matthew Sheppard case in the United States served to remind people that there is still a lot of work to be done in this area. In a 1998 article entitled 'Queer Fear' Eleanor Brown, the managing editor of Canada's gay and lesbian newspaper, *Xtra*, details the alarming rate of violence against gays and lesbians in Canada. A Vancouver police spokesperson, Sergeant Rick McKenna, says of the city's gay and lesbian community: 'Without a doubt it's the most highly victimized group in Vancouver' (D3). Brown suggests that this may be due to the establishment of a bashing-information phone line and the possibility that police relations with the gay and lesbian community are on a better footing than they might be with 'for example, the city's aboriginals' (D3). See Brown, 'Queer Fear', *The Globe and Mail*, 24 October 1998, D1 and D3.

10 Waugh's reference to postage stamps invokes scenes from ten films that appeared

on stamps introduced by Canada Post to commemorate the centenary of cinema in Canada in 1996. The ten films – *Arrival of a Train at Lyon Perrrache Station, France, Back to God's Country, Hen Hop!, Pour la suite du monde, Goin' Down the Road, Mon oncle Antoine, The Apprenticeship of Duddy Kravitz, Les ordres, Les bons débarras, The Grey Fox* – were selected, in the case of the first four, to represent pioneering efforts, and, in the case of the last six, through surveys of rankings made by the Toronto International Film Festival Group in 1983 and 1994. The limited-edition stamps were sold with a booklet that contained a list of what it called 'Canada's Ten Best' culled from the surveys of the Toronto International Film Festival Group: *Mon oncle Antoine, Jésus de Montréal, Goin' Down the Road, Le déclin de l'empire américain, Les bons débarras, Les ordres, The Apprenticeship of Duddy Kravitz, The Grey Fox, I've Heard the Mermaids Singing, The Adjuster.*

11 Until 1969, homosexuality was illegal under Canada's criminal code and punishable by a maximum sentence of fourteen years in prison. For a chronology of the lesbian and gay liberation movement's efforts to roll back prejudicial legislation in Canada see MacLeod (1996).

12 See Berton (1975).

13 See Steacy and Van Dusen (1987).

14 For a discussion of media representations of Gaetan Dugas see Douglas Crimp, 'How to Have Promiscuity in an Epidemic', *AIDS: Cultural Analysis/Cultural Activism*, ed. Douglas Crimp, *October* 43, Winter (1987): 237–71 (241–6). In the same issue of *October* Leo Bersani comments on the *60 Minutes* reporting that constructed Dugas's sexual habits as 'murderously naughty' (202). See Bersani, 'Is the Rectum a Grave?' (197–222). See also David Ehrenstein, 'More than Zero', *Film Comment* 29.6 (November/December 1993): 84–6 (85).

15 Randy Shilts, *And the Band Played On: Politics, People and the AIDS Epidemic* (New York: St Martin's Press, 1987).

16 For a detailed analysis of the distortions of Shilts's work see Douglas Crimp, 'How to Have Promiscuity in an Epidemic' (note 14).

17 Althusser discusses the importance of education, communications and film as ideological state apparatuses (1971, 128, 146, 148).

18 See Dyer (1984); Diana Fuss, 'Oral Incorporations:*The Silence of the Lambs*', in Fuss (1995, 83–105); Vito Russo, *The Celluloid Closet: Homosexuality in the Movies*, rev. ed. ([1981] New York: Harper and Row, 1985); Parker Tyler, *Screening the Sexes: Homosexuality in the Movies* (New York: Rhinehart and Winston, 1972).

19 See Hayward's entry for musical, *Key Concepts in Cinema Studies* (London and New York: Routledge, 1996): 234–47.

20 See Richard Dyer, 'Entertainment and Utopia', in Dyer (1992, 17–34).

21 I am grateful to Kim Beach for suggesting the possibility of reading homage in Greyson's intertextual dialogue.

22 See Grierson ([1944] 1988, 51–67) (58–9).

23 The budget for *Zero Patience* was raised from Telefilm Canada, the Ontario Film Development Corporation, Channel 4 Television UK, Cineplex Odeon Films, the Ontario Arts Council, the Canada Council and the Canadian Film Centre.

24 I am adapting Laura Mulvey's conceptualization of scopophilia from her influential essay 'Visual Pleasure and Narrative Cinema', *The Sexual Subject: A Screen Reader in Sexuality* (London and New York: Routledge, 1992), 111–24. Mulvey suggests that men cannot be subject to this gaze: 'According to the principles of the ruling ideology and the psychical structures that back it up, the male figure cannot bear the burden of sexual objectification. Man is reluctant to gaze at his exhibitionist like' (117). Although the existence of a homogeneous homosexual or

heterosexual gaze stretches credulity, this scene in Greyson's film, and the success with male audiences of films foregrounding highly eroticized male bodies (the *Terminator*, *Rocky*, and *Rambo* series) bring Mulvey's theory of male-to-male looking into question. Drawing on Paul Willemen's responses to Mulvey, Stephen Neale argues that 'Mulvey doesn't allow sufficient room for the fact that in patriarchy the direct object of the scopophilic desire can also be male. If scopophilic pleasure relates primarily to the observation of one's sexual like (as Freud suggests), then the two looks distinguished by Mulvey (i.e. the look at the object of desire and the look at one's sexual like) are in fact varieties of one single mechanism: the repression of homosexuality.' See Neale (1980, 56–7) and Paul Willeman, 'Voyeurism, the Look and Dwoskin', *Afterimage* 6 (1976): 43.

25 See McLynn (1990, 41–2).

26 Quoted from the press kit for *Zero Patience*. This reading of the shower sequence developed out of a conversation with Garrett Epp, whom I would like to thank for reading an earlier version of this section.

27 For commentary on representations of the anus see Leo Bersani 'Is the Rectum a Grave?' (note 14); Lee Edelman, 'Seeing Things: Representation, the Scene of Surveillance, and the Spectacle of Gay Male Sex' in Diana Fuss, ed., *Inside/Out: Lesbian Theories, Gay Theories* (New York and London: Routledge, 1991): 93–116.

28 On patriarchal masculinity and gayness see Connell, (1995, 78).

29 See Richard Dyer's comments on the relationship between penis and phallus in 'Don't Look Now: The Male Pin-up' in *The Sexual Subject: A Screen Reader in Sexuality* (London and New York: Routledge, 1992): 265–76 (274).

30 Although Freud believed that the notion of sexual development implied a norm, his concept of a universal bisexuality was, as Jeffrey Weeks notes, more enlightened than some of the American work on male homosexuality published in the 1960s and 1970s. See Weeks's entry on homosexuality in Elizabeth Wright, ed., *Feminism and Psychoanalysis: A Critical Dictionary* (New York and London: Routledge, 1992).

31 See Bersani, 'Is the Rectum a Grave?' (note 14), 202–3, 222.

32 Quoted from the press kit for *Zero Patience*.

33 Although Hamer's re-evaluation of Banon's novels locates them in the controversy of butch/femme stereotyping and the pathologizing of lesbian subjectivity, she argues that Banon's work makes a positive intervention in 1950s definitions of lesbianism. Amy Villarejo, however, is wary of embracing these novels in the ways that she understands Fernie and Weissman's film to be doing. She cautions that 'to recirculate these novels as affirmative celebrations of lesbian identity is . . . to reduce the complexity of social relations to the register of sexuality, to read them, in effect, as realist representations of lesbian lives rather than fantasy worlds' ('Forbidden Love: Pulp as Lesbian History', in Ellis Hanson, ed., *Out Takes: Essays on Queer Theory and Film* (Durham and London: Duke University Press, 1999): 316–45).

34 In her reading of the film Jean Bruce suggests that 'the happy ending of the pulp romance in the film can be seen as a means to reconstruct the aesthetics of melodrama for lesbian political revision'. See Bruce, 'Querying/Queering the nation', in Kay Armatage, Kass Banning, Brenda Longfellow and Janine Marchessault, eds, *Gendering the Nation: Canadian Women's Cinema* (Toronto: University of Toronto Press, 1999): 274–90 (285).

BIBLIOGRAPHY

Adachi, Ken. *The Enemy That Never Was: A History of the Japanese Canadians.* Toronto [1976]: McClelland and Stewart, 1991.

Alfred, Taiaiake. *Peace, Power, Righteousness: An Indigenous Manifesto.* Don Mills, ON: Oxford University Press, 1999.

Alioff, Maurice. 'The Outsider: Pierre Falardeau.' *Take One* Fall (1994): 8–13.

Allan, Blaine. 'Canada's Sweethearts, or Our American Cousins.' *Canadian Journal of Film Studies* 2.2–3 (1993): 67–80.

Althusser, Louis. 'Ideology and Ideological State Apparatuses (Notes towards an Investigation).' In Ben Brewster, trans., *Lenin and Philosophy and Other Essays.* London: NLB, 1971: 123–73.

Anderson, Elizabeth. *Pirating Feminisms: The Production of Post-war National Identity.* Dissertation AAT 9702776, Minneapolis: University of Minnesota, 1996.

——. 'Studio D's Imagined Community: From Development (1974) to Realignment (1986–1990).' In Kay Armatage *et al.* eds, *Gendering the Nation: Canadian Women's Cinema.* Toronto: University of Toronto Press, 1999: 41–61.

Anderson, Kay J. *Vancouver's Chinatown. Racial Discourse in Canada, 1875–1980.* Kingston and Montreal: McGill-Queen's University Press, 1991.

——. 'The Idea of Chinatown: The Power of Place and Institutional Practice in the Making of a Racial Category.' In Gerald Tulchinsky, ed., *Immigration in Canada: Historical Perspectives.* Toronto: Copp Clark Longman Ltd, 1994: 223–46.

Armatage, Kay. 'Dog and Woman Together at Last: Animals in the Films of Nell Shipman.' *Cineaction* 24/25 (1991): 42–4.

Arroyo, José. 'Bordwell Considered: Cognitivism, Colonialism and Canadian Culture.' *CineAction* 28 (1992): 74–88.

Association coopérative de productions audio-visuelle. *Octobre.* Press Kit 1994. Film file held at the Toronto Film Reference Library.

Atwood, Margaret. *Survival: A Thematic Guide to Canadian Literature.* Toronto: Anansi, 1972.

——. 'Backdrop Addresses Cowboy.' In *Poems 1965–1975.* London [1968]: Virago, 1991: 70–1.

——. *Surfacing.* Toronto: McClelland & Stewart, 1992.

Avery, Donald and Peter Neary. 'Laurier, Borden and a White British Columbia.' *Journal of Canadian Studies* 12.4 (1977).

Babuscio, Jack. 'Camp and the Gay Sensibility.' In Richard Dyer, ed., *Gays and Film*. New York: Zoetrope, 1984: 40–57.

Backhouse, Charles F. *Canadian Government Motion Picture Bureau 1917–1941*. Ottawa: Canadian Film Institute, 1974.

Balibar, Etienne. 'The Nation Form: History and Ideology.' In Etienne Balibar and Immanuel Wallerstein, eds, *Race, Nation, Class: Ambiguous Identities*. London and New York: Verso, 1991: 86–106. Trans. Chris Turner.

Bannerji, Himani. *On the Dark Side of the Nation: Essays on Multiculturalism, Nationalism and Gender*. Toronto: Canadian Scholars Press, 2000.

Banning, Kass. 'Playing in the Light: Canadianizing Race and Nation.' In Kay Armatage, Kass Banning, Brenda Longfellow and Janine Marchessault, eds, *Gendering the Nation: Canadian Women's Cinema*. Toronto: University of Toronto Press, 1999: 291–310.

Barbeau, Marius. 'Our Indians – Their Disappearance.' *Queen's Quarterly* 38 (1931): 691–707.

Baudry, Jean-Louis. 'Ideological Effects of the Basic Cinematic Apparatus.' In *Narrative, Apparatus, Ideology*. New York: Columbia University Press, 1986: 286–98.

Beaucage, Marjorie. 'Films About Indigenous Peoples.' *Fuse* Winter (1992): 27–9.

Berger, Carl. 'The True North Strong and Free.' In Peter Russell, ed., *Nationalism in Canada*. Toronto: McGraw-Hill Company of Canada, 1966.

Bergman, Brian. 'A Nation of Polite Bigots?' *Maclean's*, 27 December 1993: 42–3.

Berton, Pierre. *Hollywood's Canada: The Americanization of Our National Image*. Toronto: McClelland & Stewart, 1975.

Bhabha, Homi K. 'The Other Question . . .' *Screen* 24.6 (1983): 18–36.

——. 'Introduction.' In Homi Bhabha, ed., *Nation and Narration*. London and New York: 1990: 1–7.

——. *The Location of Culture*. London and New York: Routledge, 1994.

Black, David. 'The Cape Breton Coal Industry: The Rise and Fall of the British Steel Corporation.' In Don McGillivary and Brian Tennyson, eds, *Cape Breton Historical Essays*. Sydney, NS: College of Cape Breton Press, 1980: 110–29.

Blonsky, Marshall. 'Introduction. The Agony of Semiotics: Reassessing the Discipline.' In Marshall Blonsky, ed., *On Signs*. Baltimore: Johns Hopkins University Press, 1985: xiii–li.

Bracken, Christopher. *The Potlatch Papers: A Colonial Case History*. Chicago: University of Chicago Press, 1997.

Brand, Dionne. 'Notes for Writing thru Race.' In *Bread Out of Stone: Recollections Sex Recognitions Race Dreaming Politics*. Toronto: Coach House Press, 1994: 173–83.

Brault, Michel. 'Interview with Michel Brault.' *Cinetracts* 10, Spring (1980): 37–48.

Brooks, Peter. *The Melodramatic Imagination: Balzac, Henry James, Melodrama and the Mode of Excess*. New Haven: Yale University Press, 1976.

Browne, Colin. *Motion Picture Production in British Columbia, 1898–1940: A Brief Historical Background and Catalogue*. Victoria, BC: British Columbia Provincial Museum, 1979.

Brydon, Diana. 'Introduction: Reading Postcoloniality, Reading Canada.' *Essays on Canadian Writing* 56 (1995): 1–19.

Butler, Judith. *Gender Trouble: Feminism and the Subversion of Identity*. London and New York: Routledge, 1990.

Byford, Chris. '*Highway 61* Revisted.' *CineACTION* 45 (1998): 11–17.

Cagle, Robert L. ' "Tell the story of my life . . .": The Making of Meaning, "Monsters," and Music in John Greyson's *Zero Patience*.' *The Velvet Light Trap* 35, Spring (1995): 69–81.

——. 'A Minority on Someone Else's Continent: Identity, Difference and the Media in the Films of Patricia Rozema.' In Kay Armatage, ed., *Gendering the Nation: Canadian Women's Cinema*. Toronto: University of Toronto Press, 1999: 183–96.

Canadian Police Association, 'We Oppose Terrorism.' 12 September 1990.

Canadian Press, 'Film about FLQ "Scandalous," Senator Says.' *Globe and Mail*, 22 February 1993: C1.

Carter, Sarah. 'Two Acres and A Cow: "Peasant" Farming for the Indians in the Northwest, 1889–1897.' In J. R. Miller, ed., *Sweet Promises: A Reader on Indian–White Relations in Canada*. Toronto: University of Toronto Press, 1991: 353–77.

Cheyfitz, Eric. *The Poetics of Imperialism: Translation and Colonization from The Tempest to Tarzan*. New York and Oxford: Oxford University Press, 1991.

Ching, Julia. *Chinese Religions*. Basingstoke: Macmillan, 1993.

Chow, Rey. *Writing Diaspora: Tactics of Intervention in Contemporary Cultural Studies*. Bloomington: Indiana University Press, 1993.

Churchill, Ward. *Fantasies of the Master Race: Literature, Cinema and the Colonization of American Indians*. Monroe, Maine: Common Courage Press, 1992a.

——. 'And They Did it Like Dogs in the Dirt . . .' *Z Magazine* December (1992b): 20–4.

Cinémaginaire Inc., Enigma Film Ltd., Cinéa. *Le confessionnal* Press Kit. Film file held at the Toronto Film Reference Library.

Cinexus Productions, *Windigo*. Press Kit. Film file held at the Toronto Film Reference Library.

Citron, Michelle *et al.* 'Women and Film: A Discussion of Feminist Aesthetics.' [1978] In Sue Thornham, ed., *Feminist Film Theory*. New York: New York University Press, 1999: 114–21.

Clandfield, David. *Canadian Film*. Toronto: Oxford University Press, 1986.

Clark, Andrew. 'An Electronic Meeting Place.' *MacLean's*, 6 September 1999: 60–1.

Clarke, George Elliott. 'Contesting a Model Blackness: A Meditation on African-Canadian African Americanism, or The Structures of African Canadianité.' *Essays on Canadian Writing* 63 (1998): 1–55.

Cohan, Steven and Ina Rae Hark. 'Introduction.' In Cohan and Hark, eds, *The Road Movie Book*. London and New York: Routledge, 1997: 1–14.

Cole, Janis and Holly Dale, eds. *Calling the Shots: Profiles of Women Filmmakers*. Kingston, ON: Quarry Press, 1993.

Conlogue, Ray. 'For Michel Brault, the Era Is Over.' *Globe and Mail*, 19 November 1999, natl ed.: R3.

Connell, R. W. *Masculinities*. London: Polity Press, 1995.

Conquering Lion Productions Inc. *Rude*. Press Kit. Film file held at the Toronto Film Reference Library.

Cook, Pam, ed. *The Cinema Book*. London: BFI, 1985.

Cornwell, Regina. 'True Patriot Love: The Films of Joyce Wieland.' In Seth Feldman and Joyce Nelson, eds, *Canadian Film Reader*, Toronto: Peter Martin Associates Ltd, 1977: 285–9.

Corrigan, Timothy. *A Cinema Without Walls: Movies and Culture After Vietnam*. New Brunswick, NJ: Rutgers University Press, 1991.

Cowan, James A. 'Is There a Chance for Empire Films?' *MacLean's Magazine*, 15 October 1930: 10, 82–4.

Creed, Barbara. 'Phallic Panic: Male Hysteria and *Dead Ringers*.' *Screen* 31.2, Summer (1990): 125–46.

Crofts, Stephen. 'Reconceptualizing National Cinema/s.' *Quarterly Review of Film & Video* 14.3 (1993): 49–67.

Davey, Frank. '*Survival*: The Victim Theme.' In *Margaret Atwood: A Feminist Poetics*. Vancouver: Talon Books, 1984, 153–61.

De Lauretis, Teresa. *Alice Doesn't: Feminism, Semiotics, Cinema*. Bloomington: Indiana University Press, 1984.

——. 'Rethinking Women's Cinema: Aesthetics and Feminist Theory.' In Patricia Erens, ed., *Issues in Feminist Film Criticism*. Bloomington: Indiana University Press, 1988: 288–308.

Dick, Ronald. 'Regionalization of a Federal Cultural Institution: The Experience of the National Film Board of Canada 1965–1979.' In Gene Walz, ed., *Flashback: People and Institutions in Canadian Film History*. Montréal: Mediatexte Publications, 1986: 107–33.

Dickason, Olive Patricia. *Canada's First Nations: A History of the Founding Peoples from Earliest Times*. Don Mills: Oxford University Press, 1997.

Doane, Mary Ann. 'Film and the Masquerade: Theorizing the Female Spectator.' In Sue Thornham, ed., *Feminist Film Theory*. New York: New York University Press, 1999: 131–45.

Dorland, Michael. *So Close to the State/s: The Emergence of Canadian Feature Film Policy*. Toronto: University of Toronto Press, 1998.

Du Bois, W. E. B. *The Souls of Black Folk* [1903]. Greenwich, CT: Fawcett Publications, 1961.

Dumont, Marilyn. 'Black Robe: A Jesuit World Review.' *Windspeaker*, 25 October 1991: 13.

Dyer, Richard. 'Stereotyping.' In Richard Dyer, ed., *Gays and Film*. New York: Zoetrope, 1984: 27–39.

——. *Only Entertainment*. London and New York: Routledge, 1992.

——. *White*. London and New York: Routledge, 1997.

Eagleton, Terry. *Ideology: An Introduction*. London: Verso, 1991.

Eamon, Greg. 'Farmers, Phantoms and Princes: The Canadian Pacific Railway and Filmmaking from 1899 to 1919.' *Cinémas* 6, Fall (1995): 9–32.

Edelman, Lee. 'Literature/Theory/Gay Theory.' In *Homographesis: Essays in Gay Literary and Cultural Theory*. New York and London: Routledge, 1994: 3–23.

Elder, Bruce. 'Claude Jutra's *Mon oncle Antoine*.' In Seth Feldman and Joyce Nelson, eds, *Canadian Film Reader*. Toronto [1973]: Peter Martin Associates Ltd, 1977: 194–9.

Ellis, David in collaboration with Julia Johnston. *Split Screen: Home Entertainment and the New Technologies*. Toronto: Friends of Canadian Broadcasting, 1992.

Elsaesser, Thomas. 'Tales of Sound and Fury: Observations on the Family Melodrama.' In Gerald Mast, Marshall Cohen and Leo Braudy, eds, *Film Theory and Criticism: Introductory Readings*. [1974] New York: Oxford University Press, 1992: 512–35.

Euvard, Michel and Pierre Véronneau. 'Direct Cinema.' In Piers Handling and Pierre

Véronneau, eds, *Self Portrait: Essays on the Canadian and Quebec Cinemas*. Ottawa: Canadian Film Institute, 1980: 77–93.

Evanchuck, P. M. 'An Interview with Don Sheib.' *Motion* March–April (1973): 10–14.

Evans, Gary. *John Grierson and the National Film Board: The Politics of Wartime Propaganda*. Toronto: University of Toronto Press, 1984.

——. *In the National Interest: A Chronicle of the National Film Board of Canada from 1949–1989*. Toronto: University of Toronto Press, 1991.

Fanon, Frantz. *Black Skin White Masks*. New York: Grove Press, 1967.

Ferguson, Sue. 'Hockey's Blacked-Out History.' *Maclean's*, 22 May 2000: 8.

Feuer, Jane. *The Hollywood Musical*. Bloomington: Indiana University Press, 1982.

Fleras, Augie and Jean Leonard Elliott. *Unequal Relations: An Introduction to Race, Ethnic and Aboriginal Dynamics in Canada*. 2nd ed. Scarborough, ON: Prentice Hall Canada, 1996.

Foster, Cecil. *A Place Called Heaven: The Meaning of Being Black in Canada*. Toronto: HarperCollins, 1996.

Fothergill, Robert. 'Coward, Bully or Clown: The Dream-life of a Younger Brother.' In Seth Freldman and Joyce Nelson, ed., *Canadian Film Reader*. Toronto: Peter Martin Associates, 1977: 234–50.

Foucault, Michel. *The History of Sexuality, Volume 1, An Introduction*. Harmondsworth: [1976] Penguin, 1990. Trans. Robert Hurley.

Francis, Daniel. *The Imaginary Indian: The Image of the Indian in Canadian Culture*. [1992] Vancouver: Arsenal Pulp Press, 1997.

——. *National Dreams: Myth, History and Canadian Memory*. Vancouver: Arsenal Pulp Press, 1998.

Francis, R. D., Richard Jones and Donald B. Smith. *Origins: Canadian History to Confederation*. 2nd ed. Toronto: Holt, Rinehart and Winston of Canada, 1992a.

——. *Destinies: Canadian History Since Confederation*. 2nd ed. Toronto: Holt, Rinehart and Winston of Canada, 1992b.

Freud, Sigmund. 'The Uncanny.' In Albert Dickson, ed., *The Penguin Freud Library Volume 14. Art and Literature. Jensen's Gradiva, Leonardo Da Vinci and Other Works*. Harmondsworth [1919]: Penguin, 1990: 339–76.

Fung, Richard. 'Conference Calls: Race as Special Event.' *Take One*, Summer (1994): 38–9.

Fuss, Diana. *Identification Papers*. London and New York: Routledge, 1995.

Gallagher, Tag. 'Shoot-out at the Genre Corral: Problems in the "Evolution" of the Western.' In Barry Keith Grant, ed., *Film Genre Reader*. Austin: University of Texas Press, 1986: 202–16.

Garrity, Henry. 'True Lies: Autobiography, Fiction and Politics in Jean-Claude Lauzon's *Léolo*.' *Québec Studies* 20, Spring/Summer (1995): 80–5.

Gasher, Mike. 'Notes on the TV-Film Dialectic and the Promise of Convergence.' *Point of View* 30, Fall (1996): 23–6.

George, Jane. 'TV from the True North: Inuit Can't Get Enough of a TV Series about Seal Feasts, Caribou Hunts and Igloo Life.' *Edmonton Journal*, 25 February 1997: B6.

Gibbon, John Murray. *Canadian Mosaic: The Making of a Northern Nation*. Toronto: McClelland & Stewart, 1938.

Gilmor, Don. 'Going Native.' *Saturday Night*, September 1991: 36–9.

Gittings, Chris. 'Imaging Canada: The Singing Mountie and Other Commodifica-
tions of Nation.' *Canadian Journal of Communications* 23.4 (1998): 507–22;
Australian Canadian Studies 16.2 (1998): 83–97.

Gledhill, Christine. 'Melodrama.' In Pam Cook, ed., *The Cinema Book*. London: BFI,
1985a.

——. 'The Western.' In Pam Cook, ed., *The Cinema Book*. London: BFI, 1985b.

——. 'The Melodramatic Field: An Investigation.' In Christine Gledhill, ed., *Home is
Where the Heart Is: Studies in Melodrama and the Woman's Film*. London: British
Film Institute, 1987: 5–39.

Goodleaf, Donna. *Entering the War Zone: A Mohawk Perspective on Resisting
Invasions*. Penticton: Theytus Books, 1995.

Government of Canada. 'Canadian Multiculturalism Act.' (1988) Online, Internet, 7
December 2000. Available FTP: http://www.pch.gc.ca/multi/html/act.html.

Greenaway, Norma and Randy Boswell. 'Alliance Accused of Racism, Again.'
Edmonton Journal, 22 November 2000: A11.

Greer, Sandy. 'Mohawks and the Media: Alanis Obomsawin's Kanehsatake: 270 Years
of Resistance.' *Take One* Winter (1994): 18–21.

Greyson, John. 'Security Blankets: Sex, Video and the Police.' In Martha Grever, John
Greyson and Pratibha Parmar, eds, *Queer Looks: Perspectives on Gay and Lesbian
Film and Video*. Toronto: Between the Lines, 1993: 383–94.

——. Personal Interview. June 1998.

Grierson, John. 'A Film Policy for Canada.' [1944] Reprinted in Douglas Fetherling,
ed., *Documents in Canadian Film*. Peterborough, ON and Lewiston, NY:
Broadview Press, 1988: 51–81.

——. *Grierson on Documentary*, ed. Forsyth Hardy. [1946] London: Faber, 1966.

Gruneau, Richard and David Whitson. *Hockey Night in Canada: Sport, Identity and
Cultural Politics*. Toronto: Garamond Press, 1993.

Hall, Stuart. 'Cultural Identity and Cinematic Representation.' *Framework* 36
(1989): 68–81.

Hamer, Diane. ' "I Am a Woman." Ann Banon and the Writing of Lesbian Identity in
the 1950s.' In Mark Lilly, ed., *Lesbian and Gay Writing: An Anthology of Critical
Essays*. Philadelphia: Temple University Press, 1990: 47–75.

Handling, Piers. 'Canada's Ten Best.' *Take One* Fall (1994): 21–3.

Harris, Christopher. 'Grab Back Control of TV and Film, Group Urges.' *Globe and
Mail* [Toronto], 19 April 1991: C1.

Hawkes, David. *Ideology*. London and New York: Routledge, 1986.

Hayward, Susan. 'Ideology.' In *Key Concepts in Cinema Studies*. London and New
York: Routledge, 1996a.

——. 'Melodrama.' In *Key Concepts in Cinema Studies*. London and New York:
Routledge, 1996b.

——. 'Framing National Cinemas.' In Mette Hjort and Scott Mackenzie, eds,
Cinema and Nation. London and New York: Routledge, 2000: 88–102.

Heath, Stephen. 'Difference.' In Screen, ed., *The Sexual Subject: A* Screen *Reader in
Sexuality*. London and New York: Routledge, 1992: 47–105.

hooks, bell. 'The Oppositional Gaze. Black Female Spectators.' *Black Looks: Race and
Representation*. Toronto: Between the Lines, 1992a: 115–31.

——. 'Representations of Whiteness in the Black Imagination.' In *Black Looks: Race
and Representation*. Toronto: Between the Lines, 1992b: 165–78.

Horrocks, Roger. *Male Myths and Icons: Masculinity in Popular Culture*. London: Macmillan, 1995.

Hoskins, Colin, Stuart McFadyen and Adam Finn. *Global Television and Film: An Introduction to the Economics of the Business*. Oxford and New York: Oxford University Press, 1997.

Hutcheon, Linda. *A Theory of Parody: Teachings of Twentieth-century Art Forms*. London and New York: Methuen, 1985.

——. *Splitting Images: Contemporary Canadian Ironies*. Toronto: Oxford University Press, 1989.

Jackson, Peter. 'Policing Difference: "Race" and Crime in Metropolitan Toronto.' In Peter Jackson and Jan Penrose, eds, *Constructions of Race, Place and Nation*. London: UCL Press, 1993: 181–200.

Jacobowitz, Florence and Richard Lippe. '*Dead Ringers*: The Joke's On Us.' *cineAction!* Spring (1989): 64–8.

Jameson, Fredric. *The Political Unconscious. Narrative as a Socially Symbolic Act*. [1981] London and New York: University Paperback/Routledge, 1986.

——. *Postmodernism, or, The Cultural Logic of Late Capitalism*. [1991] Durham, NC: Duke University Press, 1993.

Jessup, Lynda. 'Tin Cans and Machinery: *Saving the Sagas* and Other Stuff.' *Visual Anthropology* 12 (1999): 49–86.

Jiwani, Yasmin. '*Masala* Take One: The Audience That Didn't Count.' *Rungh* 1.3 (1992): 10–13.

——, interview subject. 'Decolonizing the Screen.' Dir. Loretta Todd. In the series *Through the Lens: An Alternative Look at Filmmaking*. The Western Moving Picture Company. Videocassette, 1996.

Johnson, Brian D. 'Black Beauty: A Movie Takes Off Like a House on Fire.' *Maclean's*, 30 September 1991: 68.

——. 'A Place in the Sun: Robert Lantos and Alliance are Basking in the Big Time.' *Maclean's*, 3 June 1996: 52–4.

Johnston, Claire. 'Women's Cinema as Counter-cinema.' [1973] In Sue Thornham, ed., *Feminist Film Theory*. New York: New York University Press, 1999: 31–40.

Jones, D. B. *Movies and Memoranda: An Interpretive History of the National Film Board of Canada*. Ottawa: Canadian Film Institute, 1981.

'Kanesatake [*sic*] Narrowly Ratifies Self-governance.' *Edmonton Journal*, 16 October 2000: A5.

Kaplan, E. Ann. *Looking for the Other: Feminism, Film and the Imperial Gaze*. London and New York: Routledge, 1997.

Keeshing-Tobias, Lenore. 'The Magic of Others.' In Libby Scheier, Sara Sheard and Eleanor Wachtel, eds, *Language in Her Eye: Views on Writing and Gender by Canadian Women Writing in English*. Toronto: Coach House, 1990: 173–7.

Kelley, Theresa M. *Reinventing Allegory*. Cambridge: Cambridge University Press, 1997.

Kelly, Brendan. Rev. of *Windigo*. *Variety* 26 September–2 October 1994: 62.

——. ' "The Confessional" ("Le confessionnal")' *Variety*, 22.8 May 1995: 94.

Khanna, Sanjay. '*Masala* Take Two: Cutting Your Own Deals.' *Rungh* 1.3 (1992): 14–16.

Kilpatrick, Jacquelyn. *Celluloid Indians: Native Americans and Film*. Lincoln and London: University of Nebraska Press, 1999.

Kirkland, Bruce. 'Digging Fencepost.' *The Toronto Sun*, 9 March 1995: 59.

Kleinhans, Chuck. 'Notes on Melodrama and the Family Under Capitalism.' *Film Reader* 3 (1978): 40–7.

Knelman, Martin. *This Is Where We Came In: The Career and Character of Canadian Film*. Toronto: McClelland & Stewart, 1977.

Kostash, Myrna. *All of Baba's Children*. Edmonton: Hurtig Publishers, 1977.

Krishna, Srinivas. 'What the Story Is: An Interview with Srinivas Krishna.' Interview with Cameron Bailey. *CineACTION* 28, Spring (1992): 38–47.

——. 'Where Is this Place Called Home?' Interview with Roy Grundman. *Cinemaya* 23, Spring (1994): 22–7.

Leach, James. 'Second Images: Reflections on the Canadian Cinema(s) in the Seventies.' In Seth Feldman, ed., *Take Two*. Toronto: Irwin Publishing, 1984: 100–10.

——. *Claude Jutra: Filmmaker*. Montreal: McGill-Queen's University Press, 1999.

Lee, Helen. 'Coming Attractions: A Brief History of Canada's Nether-cinema.' *Take One* 5, Summer (1994): 4–11.

Leong, Ian, Mike Sell and Kelly Thomas. 'Mad Love, Mobile Homes, and Dysfunctional Dicks.' In Steven Cohan and Ina Rae Hark, eds, *The Road Movie Book*. London and New York: Routledge, 1997: 70–89.

Lloyd, David. 'Race Under Representation.' *Oxford Literary Review* 13.1–2 (1991): 62–94.

Longfellow, Brenda. 'Postmodernism and the Discourse of the Body.' *Canadian Journal of Political and Social Theory/Revue canadienne de théorie politique et sociale* 14.1–3 (1990): 179–89.

Lusty, Terry. '*Dance Me Outside* Maintains Stereotypes.' *Windspeaker* April 1995: 18.

Lyotard, Jean-François. *The Postmodern Condition: A Report on Knowledge*. Minneapolis: University of Minnesota Press, 1984. Trans. Geoff Bennington and Brian Massumi .

——. *The Postmodern Explained: Correspondence 1982–1985*. Minneapolis: University of Minnesota Press, 1992. Translation ed. Julian Pefanis and Morgan Thomas.

McClintock, Anne. *Imperial Leather: Race, Gender and Sexuality in the Colonial Contest*. London and New York: Routledge, 1995.

MacDonald, Robert H. *Sons of the Empire: The Frontier and the Boy Scout Movement, 1890–1918*. Toronto: University of Toronto Press, 1993.

McGovern, Celeste. 'From Noble Savage to Urban Hipster.' *Alberta Report* 22.15 (1995): 44–5.

McLaren, Angus. *Our Own Master Race: Eugenics in Canada, 1885–1945*. Toronto: McClelland & Stewart, 1990.

MacLeod, Donald W. *Lesbian and Gay Liberation in Canada: A Selected Annotated Chronology, 1964–1975*. Toronto: ECW Press/Homewood Books, 1996.

McLynn, Frank. *Burton: Snow Upon the Desert*. London: John Murray, 1990.

McRoberts, Kenneth. 'Internal Colonialism: The Case of Quebec.' *Ethnic and Racial Studies* 2.3 July (1979): 293–318.

Magder, Ted. *Canada's Hollywood: The Canadian State and Feature Films*. Toronto: University of Toronto Press, 1993.

Manning, Erin. 'The Haunted Home: Colour Spectrums in Robert Lepage's "Le confessionnal".' *Canadian Journal of Film Studies* 7.2, Fall (1998): 49–65.

Mayne, Judith. 'The Woman at the Keyhole: Women's Cinema and Feminist Criticism.' In M. A. Doanne, P. Mellencamp, and L. Williams, eds, *Revision: Essays in Feminist Film Criticism*. Los Angeles: The American Film Institute Monograph Series/University Publications of America, 1984: 49–66.

Metz, Christian. 'The Imaginary Signifier.' *Screen* 16.2, Summer (1975): 14–76.

Miki, Roy. 'Unclassified Subjects: Question Marking "Japanese Canadian" Identity.' In *Broken Entries: Race, Subjectivity, Writing*. Toronto: Mercury Press, 1998: 181–204.

Morris, Peter. *Embattled Shadows: A History of Canadian Cinema 1895–1939*. Montreal and Kingston: McGill-Queens University Press, 1978.

——. 'The First Six Decades.' In Piers Handling and Pierre Véronneau, eds, *Self Portrait: Essays on the Canadian and Quebec Cinemas*. Ottawa: Canadian Film Institute, 1980: 1–10.

——. 'Backwards to the Future: John Grierson's Film Policy for Canada.' In Gene Walz, ed., *Flashback: People and Institutions in Canadian Film History*. Montreal: Mediatexte, 1986.

——. 'The Taming of the Few: Nell Shipman in the Context of Her Times.' In *The Silent Screen and My Talking Heart: An Autobiography*. Boise, ID: Hemingway Western Studies Series, Boise State University, 1987a: 211–20.

——. 'Re-thinking Grierson: The Ideology of John Grierson.' *Dialogue: Canadian and Quebec Cinema* 3 (1987b): 21–56.

——. 'In Our Own Eyes: The Canonizing of Canadian Film.' *Canadian Journal of Film Studies* 3.1 (1994): 27–44.

Mosse, George L. *Nationalism and Sexuality: Middle-class Morality and Sexual Norms in Modern Europe*. Madison, WI: University of Wisconsin Press, 1985.

Mulvey, Laura. 'Notes on Sirk and Melodrama.' In *Visual and Other Pleasures*. Bloomington and Indianapolis: Indiana University Press, 1989a: 39–62.

——. 'Visual Pleasure and Narrative Cinema.' In *Visual and Other Pleasures*. Bloomington and Indianapolis: Indiana University Press, 1989b: 14–26.

——. 'Afterthoughts on "Visual Pleasure and Narrative Cinema" inspired by King Vidor's *Duel in the Sun* (1946).' In *Visual and Other Pleasures*. Bloomington and Indianapolis: Indiana University Press, 1989c: 29–38.

——. 'Melodrama Inside and Outside the Home.' In *Visual and Other Pleasures*. Bloomington and Indianapolis: Indiana University Press, 1989d: 63–77.

——. 'Some Thoughts of Fetishism in the Context of Contemporary Culture.' *October* 65 (1993): 3–20.

Nash, Jay Robert and Stanley Ralph Ross. *The Motion Picture Guide*, vol. 5. Chicago: Cinebooks, 1987.

National Film Board of Canada. *National Film Board Annual Report 1963–64*. Montreal: National Film Board of Canada, 1964a.

——. *A Teacher's Guide to* Drylanders. Montreal: National Film Board of Canada, 1964b.

——. *Diversity in Action: A Cultural Diversity Initiative for Filmmakers of Colour 2000/2001*. Vancouver: Pacific Centre NFB, 2001.

Neale, Stephen. *Genre*. London: British Film Institute, 1980.

——. 'Questions of Genre.' *Screen* 31.1, Spring (1990): 45–66.

Newman, Peter C. 'Will Canada Survive a Post-national World?' *Maclean's*, 12 June 1995: 40.

——. 'The Year of Living Dangerously.' *Maclean's*, 20 December 1999: 51–6.

Nichols, Bill. *Representing Reality: Issues and Concepts in Documentary.* Bloomington and Indianapolis: Indiana University Press, 1991.

——. *Blurred Boundaries: Questions of Meaning in Contemporary Culture.* Bloomington: Indiana University Press, 1994.

Nicks, Joan. 'Aesthetic Memory in Anne Claire Poirier's Cinema.' In Kay Armatage *et al.*, eds, *Gendering the Nation: Canadian Women's Cinema.* Toronto: University of Toronto Press, 1999: 225–45.

Okihiro, Gary Y. *Margins and Mainstreams: Asians in American History and Culture.* Seattle and London: University of Washington Press, 1994.

O'Regan, Tom. *Australian National Cinema.* London and New York: Routledge, 1996.

Ouchi, Mieko. Personal Interview. 4 June 1999.

Oudart, Jean-Pierre. 'Notes for a Theory of Representation.' In *Cahiers du Cinéma 1969–1972: The Politics of Representation*, ed. Nick Browne. Trans. Annwyl Williams, Cambridge, MA: Harvard University Press, 1990: 203–12. Originally published as 'Notes pour une théorie de la répresentation', *Cahiers du Cinéma* 229 and 230 (May–June and July 1971).

Owens, Joseph. Dread: *The Rastafarians of Jamaica.* Kingston, Jamaica: Sangster Book Store, 1976.

Pallister, Janis L. *The Cinéma of Québec: Masters in Their Own House.* London: Associated University Presses, 1995.

Parpart, Lee. 'Feminist Re-mappings of the Passive Male Body.' In Kay Armatage *et al.*, eds, *Gendering the Nation: Canadian Women's Cinema.* Toronto: University of Toronto Press, 1999a : 253–73.

——. 'Pit(iful) Male Bodies: Colonial Masculinity, Class and Folk Innocence in Margaret's Museum.' *Canadian Journal of Film Studies* 8.1 Spring (1999b): 63–86.

Pendakur, Manjunath. *Canadian Dreams and American Control: The Political Economy of the Canadian Film Industry.* Detroit: Wayne State University Press, 1990.

Pevere, Geoff. 'Family Ties: Québécois Film-maker Jean-Claude Lauzon Already Knows Canada Is a Dysfunctional Family.' *Canadian Forum* December (1992a): 23–4.

——. 'On the Brink.' *CineAction* 28 (1992b): 34–7.

——. 'Dances with Natives.' *Globe and Mail*, 10 March 1995: C2.

Pharr, Mary and Lynda Haas. 'Somatic Ideas: Cronenberg and the Feminine.' *Post Script* 15.2 (1996): 29–39.

Phillips, Paul. 'The National Policy Revisited.' *Journal of Canadian Studies* 14 (1979): 3–14.

Pieterse, Jan Nederveen. 'Image and Power.' In Raymond Corbey and Joep Leerssen, eds, *Alterity, Identity, Image: Selves and Others in Society and Scholarship.* Amsterdam: Rodopi, 1991.

Pollack, Griselda. 'Feminism/Foucault – Surveillance/Sexuality.' In Norman Bryson, Michael Ann Holly and Keith Moxey, eds, *Visual Culture: Images and Interpretations.* Hanover and London: Wesleyan University Press, 1994: 1–41.

Ramsay, Christine. 'Canadian Narrative Cinema from the Margins: "The Nation" and Masculinity in *Goin' Down the Road.*' *Canadian Journal of Film Studies* 2.2–3 (1993): 27–49.

Randoja, Ingrid. 'Ransen Rising.' *Take One* Fall (1995): 28–31.

Renov, Michael. 'Introduction: The Truth About Non-fiction.' In Michael Renov, ed., *Theorizing Documentary*. London and New York: Routledge, 1993a: 1–11.

———. 'Towards a Poetics of Documentary.' In Michael Renov, ed., *Theorizing Documentary*. London and New York: Routledge, 1993b: 12–36.

Rodley, Chris. *Cronenberg on Cronenberg*. London: Faber and Faber, 1992.

Rodowick, D. N. 'The Difficulty of Difference.' In *The Difficulty of Difference: Psychoanalysis, Sexual Difference and Film Theory*. London and New York: Routledge, 1991: 1–17.

Rony, Fatimah Tobing. *The Third Eye: Race, Cinema, and Ethnographic Spectacle*. Durham and London, Duke University Press, 1996.

Root, Deborah. 'The Anxious Liberal: Natives and Non-Natives in Recent Movies.' *cineACTION* 32, Fall (1993): 43–9.

Rose, Jacqueline. *Sexuality in the Field of Vision*. London and New York: Verso, 1986.

Rosen, Philip. 'Document and Documentary: On the Persistence of Historical Concepts.' In Michael Renov, ed. *Theorizing Documentary*. London and New York: Routledge, 1993: 58–89.

———. 'Nation and Anti-nation: Concepts of National Cinema in the "New" Media Era.' *Diaspora* 5.3 (1996): 375–402.

Rozon, René. 'Michel Brault's *Les Ordres*.' *Take One* 4.9, Jan.–Feb. (1974): 34.

Said, Edward W. *Orientalism*. [1978] London: Vintage, 1979.

———. *Culture and Imperialism*. [1993] London: Vintage, 1994.

Saywell, John. *Quebec 70: A Documentary Narrative*. Toronto: University of Toronto Press, 1971.

Schatz, Thomas. 'The Western.' In *Hollywood Genres: Formulas, Filmmaking and the Hollywood System*. New York: Random House, 1981: 45–80.

Schiller, Herbert I. *Communications and Cultural Domination*. White Plains, NY: International Arts and Science Press, 1976.

Schwartzberg, Shlomo. ' "Film-makers of Colour" Resist Being Pigeon-holed.' *The Financial Post*, 13 August 1994: S10.

Scott, Jay. 'A Hideous Period of History Wrapped in a Frosty, Ebony Shroud.' *Globe and Mail* [Toronto] 5 September 1991: C1 and C3.

Shehid, Gamal Abdel. 'Writing Hockey Through Race: Rethinking Black Hockey in Canada.' In Rinaldo Walcott, ed., *Rude: Contemporary Black Canadian Cultural Criticism*. Toronto: Insomniac Press, 2000: 69–86.

Shipman, Nell. *The Silent Screen and My Talking Heart: An Autobiography*. Boise, ID: Hemingway Western Studies Series, Boise State University, 1987.

Shohat, Ella and Robert Stam. *Unthinking Eurocentrism: Multiculturalism and the Media*. New York and London: Routledge, 1994.

Silverman, Kaja. 'Dis-Embodying the Female Voice.' In Mary Ann Doane, Patricia Mellencamp and Linda Williams, eds., *Revision: Essays in Feminist Film Criticism*. Los Angeles: The American Film Institute/University Publications of America, 1984: 131–49.

Smith, Paul. 'The Will to Allegory in Postmodernism.' *Dalhousie Review* 62.1 (1982): 105–22.

Smith, Paul Chaat. 'Shelley Niro: Honey Moccasin. Home Alone.' In Gerald McMaster, ed., *Reservation X*. Fredericton, NB: Goose Lane Editions, and Hull, Québec: Canadian Museum of Civilization, 1998: 109–19.

Soukup, Katarina. E-mail to the author. 15 November 2000.

Spry, Robin. 'Action: The October Crisis of 1970.' Interview with Alan Rosenthal. In Alan Rosenthal, ed., *The Documentary Conscience: A Casebook in Film Making*. Berkeley and Los Angeles: University of California Press, 1980: 245–57.

Steacy, Anne and Lisa Van Dusen. ' "Patient Zero" and the AIDS Virus.' *Maclean's*, 19 October 1987: 53.

Steffens, Roger. 'Babylon', *Patois Glossary*. Online, Internet, 30 December 2000. Available FTP http://www.hermosarecords.com/marley/patois.html.

Stoney, George. 'You are on Indian Land.' Interview with Alan Rosenthal. In Alan Rosenthal, ed., *The Documentary Conscience: A Casebook in Film Making*. Berkeley and Los Angeles: University of California Press, 1980: 346–56.

Suzack, Cheryl. 'First Nations and Women.' In Lorraine Code, ed., *Routledge Encyclopedia of Feminist Theories*. London and New York: Routledge. Forthcoming.

Taubin, Amy. 'Body Double.' *The Village Voice*, 27 September 1988: 68.

Taylor, Charles. 'The Politics of Recognition.' In Amy Gutman, ed., *Multiculturalism: Examining the Politics of Recognition*. Princeton, NJ: Princeton University Press, 1994: 25–73.

Thomas, Bob. 'Natives Pan Portrait of Ancestors.' *Vancouver Sun*, 21 December 1991: H5.

Tobias, John L. 'Protection, Civilization, Assimilation: An Outline History of Canada's Indian Policy.' In Ian A. L. Getty and Antoine S. Lussier, eds, *As Long as the Sun Shines and the Water Flows: A Reader in Canadian Native Studies*. Vancouver: University of British Columbia Press, 1983.

Todorov, Tzvetan. *The Conquest of America: The Question of the Other*. New York: Harper and Row, 1984. Trans. Richard Howard.

Turner, D. J. *Canada's Recovery and Restoration of Back to God's Country*. Boise, ID: Canadian Studies Program, Boise State University, 1987.

——. 'Ernest Shipman: Some Notes,' *Griffithiana* XV.44/45 September (1992): 54–6.

Turner, Graeme. *National Fictions: Literature, Film and the Construction of Australian Narrative*. Sydney: Allen and Unwin, 1986.

——. *Making It National: Nationalism and Australian Popular Culture*. Sydney: Allen and Unwin, 1994.

Urquhart, Peter. 'The Glace Bay Miners' Museum/Margaret's Museum: Adaptation and Resistance.' *Cineaction* 49 (1999): 12–18.

Vallières, Pierre. *Nègres blancs d'Amérique: Autobiographie précoce d'un 'terroriste' québécois*. [1968] Montréal: Éditions Parti Pris, 1969.

Van Alphen, Ernst. 'The Other Within.' In Raymond Corbey and Joep Leerssen, eds, *Alterity, Identity, Image. Selves and Others in Society and Scholarship*. Amsterdam-Atlanta, GA: Rodopi, 1991: 3–16.

Virgo, Clement. Interview with Clement Virgo. Conquering Lion Productions Inc. *Rude*. Press Kit, 1995. Film file held at the Toronto Film Reference Library.

Walcott, Rinaldo. 'The Politics of Third Cinema in Canada.' Reading the Narrative of Clement Virgo's *Rude*. In *Black Like Who?* Toronto: Insomniac Press, 1997: 53–69.

Wallace, Bruce. 'The Real Story Behind the 1970 October Crisis.' *Edmonton Journal*, 6 January 2001: A1, A3.

Wallerstein, Immanuel. 'The Construction of Peoplehood: Racism, Nationalism,

Ethnicity.' In Etienne Balibar and Immanuel Wallerstein, eds, *Race, Nation, Class: Ambiguous Identities*, London and New York: Verso, 1991: 71–85. Trans. Chris Turner.

'Warning on Canadian Native Health.' *Edmonton Journal*, 27 November 1999: A9.

Waugh, Tom. 'Cinemas, Nations, Masculinities: The Martin Walsh Memorial Lecture (1998).' *Canadian Journal of Film Studies* 1.8, Spring (1998): 8.44.

'We Stand on Guard.' *Edmonton Journal*, 19 November 1995: A2.

Weinmann, Heinz. *Cinéma del'Imaginaire Québecois de* La petite Aurore à Jésus de Montréal. Montréal: l'Hexagone, 1990.

White, Hayden. 'Historical Pluralism.' *Critical Inquiry* Spring (1986): 480–93.

Wilkin, Dwane. 'Telefilm Canada Stiff-arms Igloolik's Movie-makers.' *Nunatsiaq News*, 29 May 1998: 9.

Williams, Raymond. *Key Words: A Vocabulary of Culture and Society*. London: Fontana, 1976.

Winks, Robin W. *The Blacks in Canada: A History*. 2nd ed. Montreal and Kingston: McGill-Queen's University Press, 1997.

Wise, Wyndham. 'Canadian Cinema from Boom to Bust: The Tax-shelter Years.' *Take One* 22, Winter (1999): 18–24.

Wood, Christopher. 'The Vanishing Border.' *Maclean's*, 20 December 1999: 20–3.

Woodsworth, James S. *Strangers Within Our Gates or Coming Canadians*. [1909] Toronto: University of Toronto Press, 1972.

Yamaguchi, Joanne. 'Who is the American Cousin? Canadian Cinema, Cultural Freedom and Sandy Wilson's American Cousin.' *CineAction* 16, Spring (1986): 70–2.

York, Geoffrey and Loreen Pindera. *People of the Pines: The Warriors and the Legacy of Oka*. Toronto: Little, Brown and Co., 1991.

Young, Robert. *Colonial Desire: Hybridity in Theory, Culture and Race*. London and New York: Routledge, 1995.

Žižek, Slavoj. *Looking Awry. An Introduction to Jacques Lacan through Popular Culture*. [1991] Cambridge, MA: MIT Press, 1992.

—— 'Introduction.' In *Mapping Ideology*. London and New York: Verso, 1994.

——. 'Multiculturalism, or, the Cultural Logic of Multinational Capitalism.' *New Left Review* 225 (1997): 28–51.

SELECT FILMOGRAPHY

I have provided information below so that readers might obtain some of the films that I have discussed at length.

Alliance Atlantis (within Canada)
http://www.allianceatlantisvideo.com/en/now-available-to-own.asp
Black Robe
Dance Me Outside
Highway 61
Le Confessional
Rude
Zero Patience

Canadian Filmmakers Distribution Centre
Email: cfmdc@interlog.com
Honey Moccasin
Patriotism, Part One
Reason over Passion

***Gerda* Film Production Inc**
Email: brendal@yorku.ca
Our Marilyn

Mad Shadow Films
Email: palourde@freenet.edmonton.ab.ca
By this Parting

National Film Board of Canada
Within Canada
Tel: 1 800 267 7710
Fax: 1 514 283 7564

In the USA
Tel: 212 629 8890
Fax: 212 575 2382
Email: newyork@nfb.ca

In the UK
Tel: 020 7258 6480
Email: london@nfb.ca

On the Web
http://www.nfb.ca/homevideo
Action: The October Crisis of 1970
Back-breaking Leaf, The
Charlie Squash Goes to Town
Drylanders
Forbidden Love: The Unashamed Stories of Lesbian Love
How They Saw Us: Careers and Cradles
Incident at Restigouche
Just Watch Me: Trudeau and the 70s Generation
Kanehsatake: 270 Years of Resistance
Minoru: Memory of Exile
Mon oncle Antoine
Of Japanese Descent: An Interim Report
Peoples of Canada
Québec-USA ou l'invasion pacifique
Reaction: Portrait of a Society in Crisis
Remember Africville
Road to Saddle River
You Are on Indian Land

National Archives of Canada
Toll free: 1-866-578-7777 (Canada and USA)
Reference Services: 613-992-3884
              Fax: 613-995-6274
Consult the following web site for audio visual materials:
http://www.archives.ca/02/020206/02020602_e.html
An Unselfish Love IDCISN 17955
Back to God's Country IDCISN 178893
Clan Donald: A British Farm Colony IDCISN 211317
Education of the New Canadian, The IDCISN 12247
Hot Ice: The Anatomy of Hockey. Canada's National Game
    IDCISN 210800
Nation Building in Saskatchewan: The Ukrainians
    IDCISN 140375

Negroes IDCISN 82936
Saving the Sagas IDCISN 195745
Secrets of Chinatown IDCISN 24503

INDEX

Note: page numbers of illustrations are italicised.

LIBRARY
ST. LOUIS COMMUNITY COLLEGE
AT FLORISSANT VALLEY